C000057434

ISRAEL AND THE DAUGHTERS OF THE SHOAH

ISRAEL AND THE DAUGHTERS OF THE SHOAH

Reoccupying the Territories of Silence

RONIT LENTIN

Berghahn Books
New York • Oxford

First published in 2000 by

Berghahn Books
www.BerghahnBooks.com

© 2000 Ronit Lentin

All rights reserved.
No part of this publication may be reproduced in any form
or by any means without the written permission
of Berghahn Books.

Library of Congress Cataloging-in-Publication Data

Lentin, Ronit
  Israel and the daughters of the Shoah : reoccupying the territories of
  silence / Ronit Lenitn.
      p. cm.
  Includes bibliographical references (p.) and index
  ISBN 1-57181-774-3 — ISBN 1-57181-775-1 (alk. paper)
      1. Holocaust, Jewish (1939-1945)—Personal narratives—History and
  criticism. 2. Holocaust, Jewish (1939-1945)—Influence. 3. Children of
  Holocaust survivors—Israel—Interviews. 4. Women—Israel—
  Interviews. 5. Holocaust, Jewish (1939-1945)—Social aspects—Israel. I.
  title.

D804.195 .L46 2000
940.53'18—dc21

                                                     00-060886

British Library Cataloguing in Publication Data
A catalogue record for this book is available
from the British Library.

Printed in the United States on acid-free paper.

ISBN 1-57181-774-3 hardback
ISBN 1-57181-775-1 paperback

The women pass by near us. They are shouting. They shout and we do not hear anything. This cold, dry air should be conducive in an ordinary human environment. They shout in our direction without a sound reaching us. Their mouths shout, their arms stretched out toward us shout, everything about them is shouting. Each body is a shout. All of them torches flaming with cries of terror, cries that have assumed female bodies. Each one is a materialized cry, a howl–unheard.

Charlotte Delbo, *Auschwitz and After*

Who would say   that I have   mourned
enough?

Irena Klepfisz, *A Few Words in the Mother Tongue*

Contents

Acknowledgements

Many people have helped me in the process of telling the story that was, among many other things, my life. It could not have been written without the collaboration and friendship of the narrators, Orna Ben Dor, Naomi Ben Natan, Rivka Keren, Batia Gur, Tania Hadar, Karmit Gai, Lea Aini, Savyon Liebrecht, and in particular, Nava Semel, who has accompanied the project since its inception. Their stories, poems, and films inspired me to begin this work, and helped me to persevere. Special thanks to Dr Barbara Bradby of the Department of Sociology, Trinity College Dublin, who midwived the doctoral dissertation which forms the basis for this book rigourously, yet kindly, and who has become a close friend in the process. Thanks to the Departmental Research Fund and to Trinity Foundation for their financial support.

Many people in Israel assisted me. Zvi Dror of kibbutz *Lochamei Hagetaot* kindly shared his experiences of collecting testimonies. Professor Dan Bar On of Ben Gurion University illuminated a dark corner in relation to my 'split subjectivity'. Dina Wardi, Dr Yitzhak Mendelsohn, and Billie Laniado shared their experiences with me, as did Helen Epstein, whose book was the first of its kind.

Liz Stanley's work on auto/biography was a crucial methodological inspiration. Reading Ruth Linden's *Making Stories, Making Selves* was a turning point. Liz and Ruth have been extremely supportive and have become my friends. Joan Ringelheim's work on Shoah and gender was another turning point. She kindly shared her work with me, which I in turn share with my students. Their influence is evident in this book.

As ever, deepest love and thanks to Louis, Alana, and Miki who were always supportive, loving and encouraging. Alana gave me invaluable editorial support in the final stages of writing. Thanks too to my cousin Lior Shieber. Finally, to my dear mother Lia, who has been sending me Shoah-related books for more years than I care to remember. Her stories about 'there' and her love and strength have inspired me and kept me going throughout my life and work.

PROLOGUE

IF I FORGET THEE ...

1

Only when the bus chugs up the hill, the evening light, across the dusty bus window, beyond the layers of recycled air-conditioned air, touching and not touching my warm cheek, do I become homesick. Homesick at home, only at home, in the Jerusalem of my youth.

Absurd? Every time I leave, the craving stops. The craving for the home I left twenty-seven years ago for the land from which one emigrates, to which so few immigrate.

I was one of those few. In a file marked 'personal papers' I have a carbon copy of my post-nuptial naturalisation papers, together with one Eva MacAonghusa, another post-nuptial blow-in.

In my parents' home, a book, in Hebrew, by one Efraim Schwartzman, dark green cover – what else? – *The Irish War of Independence*. Black and white photographs of the founding fathers (plus one Constance Markievicz) of the Irish state, the state I was not to know would one day be home.

> Think of it: *heym* and *home* the meaning
> the same   of course   exactly
> but the shift   in vowel   was the ocean
> in which I drowned

> (Klepfisz, 1990c: 228).

2

The evening light. Nothing like it in the world.

Despite the fact that the Jerusalem of my youth has long become the domain of the ultra-orthodox, the domain of the extreme rightwing. Despite the furious building, covering every hilltop with apartment blocks, despite the fact that every inch of 'nature' has been reclaimed.

In the spring, the desert air blows into town, bringing with it memories of mountains. Nothing like it in the world.

Walking the streets which have changed since I was living here, yet retain the fervour of youth. 1967: postwar revolution in the air, painting slogans against the occupation on the walls, conspiring in smoky rooms to overturn (our) Jewish homeland. Now it all sounds so passé, almost banal. Yet not much remains of our wet dreams of home to Palestinians, and home to Jews, in a (secular democratic) together which has soured, like a carton of old milk.

3

On the way to the Palestinian National Authority, many homes were demolished. Homes of parents whose children, yes, children, were soldiers and were killed defending the indefensible. Parents whose grief never ends.

Homes of parents whose children, yes, children, threw stones and rebelled among the olivegroves on the hills of the West Bank.

Homes blown up in retaliation against parents whose children.

Women left screaming on the rubble that was once home, television cameras picking up their grief-stricken faces. And then moving onto the next story, next trouble spot. But the rubble remains. And olive trees are uprooted and replanted in the (Jewish) settlement on the next hilltop.

All in the name of home. National home. Homeland.

Homeland in Hebrew – *moledet* – from the same root as *laledet* – giving birth.

Mother-land. The violent homebirth of nation-states.

4

Jerusalem was later. My childhood passed on Mount Carmel, where Lia, my mother, still lives. Lia, my significant (m)other.

Plucked from their affluent home in northern Romania, Lia and her parents left on the last week it was possible to do so. All their belongings in one hamper, and foreign currency stuck in Grand-mother's silk stockings.

Lia's birthplace, Vatra Dornei, a spa town in the Carpathians, along quiet streams. Another home. I journeyed there, to research a book, my life. Their house on a street called after the family name. Wealthy Jews, bankers, sawmill owners. Long gone from a town where only a handful of Jews remain. Their house, called Villa Lia, to celebrate Mother's birth, now home to four or five Romanian families.

Leaving Vatra Dornei feels like leaving home, like death. There are demons there which inhabited my soul, stealthily, refusing to be exorcised.

Mother cannot understand the pull. When she left, she left that world behind. She has no other home, is never homesick, because she never leaves home, has never left home since that time, in the middle of that war.

I, her eldest child, re-enacted the diasporic experience, voluntarily migrating from my violent mother-land, my violent national home.

Home-leave. Layers upon layers of home-leaves.

5

Dia-spora.

I was a member of 'the (Israeli) first generation to redemption', coached to despise those 'dia-spora Jews', for having allegedly gone passively to their death during the Shoah, 'like lambs to the slaughter'. Israel was the place where Jews would be proud again, would take up arms to fight their 'enemies', would never again 'go to their death like lambs to the slaughter'.

I was also a member of a family of Shoah survivors. An act of nam-ing I was only able to engage in while researching this book.

Up until then, I 'knew and did not know' at the same time. But I did not acknowledge I had a stake in that big slaughter.

Lia's family, those who did not get away on that fateful week, were deported to Transnistria, a camp in Northern Romania. Her grandfa-ther, her favourite uncle, another uncle, a cousin – a little girl – all died, lost in the snow, sent on a labour detail, starved to death. The others arrived, broken, ill, in the uncomprehending Israel of the 1950s.

Their new home. Where I and my generation refused to hear their stories, constructing instead our own stories of armed struggles for independence.

Now I know. Not only that in constructing itself as a 'new Jewish entity' did Israel construct itself as masculine thereby 'feminising' dia-spora Jewry and the Shoah.

But also that hero and non-hero, Israeli and Jew - we are all the same. All (wo)men together.

In re-enacting the dia-sporic experience, in re-exiling myself from my mother-land, I am a Jew again. The epitome of strangerhood, homeless in my adopted Irish home.

6

The evening light of Jerusalem. Nothing like it in the world.

Not even the orange sky over Connemara. Or the caramelised watery reflection over the Ha'penny Bridge.

Nothing like it in the world. Home is the late-night intimacies one can only have in one's (m)other-tongue. Jerusalem – the only place in the world where I can breathe freely.

> Night.   Jerusalem.   *Yerushalayim.*
> Jerusalem.   If I forget thee
> Oh Jerusalem   Jerusalem
> Hebron
> Ramallah Nablus Qattana   if I
> forget thee oh Jerusalem
> Oh Hebron   may I forget
> my own past   my pain
> the depth of my sorrows.
>
>   (Klepfisz, 1990b: 240).

I do not forget.

Not only because, as Klepfisz vows, forgetting the injustices of the present obliterates the depth of past sorrows.

Nor because, by adding a Jewish past to my 'new Hebrew' Israeli past, I still have not found home in the dia-spora of my own making. Or because in the Ireland of my dia-sporic adult choice I'll forever be a (m)otherless-'other', whose memories play a different tune.

But, perhaps, because you can only be homesick at home. In that tragic, magic, Jerusalem evening light.

CHAPTER 1

INTRODUCTION: THE TERRITORIES OF SILENCE

Introduction

The destruction of a third of Europe's Jews by Nazism is unquestionably the worst catastrophe in the history of contemporary Judaism and a formative event in the history of Zionism and the state of Israel. Understandably therefore, the Shoah, written about, analysed and given various political interpretations, is a shaping public discourse in the history of the state of Israel. As one of the pre-state Israeli generation, the Shoah and its public commemoration played a central role in my own formation. My preoccupation with Shoah victimhood stood in sharp contrast to dominant discourses which, resulting from the construction of a stereotypical 'new Hebrew' active subjectivity, taught me and my generation to reject diaspora Jewry and its alleged passivity in the face of catastrophe.

This book is a culmination of years of preoccupation with the meaning of the Shoah for me, an Israeli woman, some of whose family were victims, but whose close relatives fled the fire by emigrating 'in time' to the promise of Zion. It is a culmination of my need to break the silence about the Shoah in a society which constructed itself as the Israeli antithesis to the diaspora Jew, and to excavate a 'truth' from underneath the mountain of Zionist nation-building myths and silences. These myths and silences not only had deep implications for the formation of my generation, but also a profound impact on the Israeli-Palestinian conflict. This book is a personal act of reckoning, and of mourning the loss of life that was the Shoah, and the inability, or unwillingness, to mourn that very loss by an Israeli society absorbed in acts of survival.

There is a close link between Israeli-Zionist discursive representations and Israel's sociopolitical reality. Zionist political leaders, many
of whom were also intellectuals and writers, not only played a role in
making history, they also wrote history, thus influencing how history
was perceived and remembered. Their interpretations of the history
they made became general 'truths' and accepted myths (Zertal,
1996a: 15). Similarly, Israeli cultural and literary discourses, due to
the central societal role played by poets and novelists, have always
been instrumental in shaping both the perceptions of reality and reality itself (Gover, 1996: 28–9). There are few cultures where the word
'state' replaces so readily the word 'country'. Indeed, Laor argues, a
large proportion of Israeli terms and images have been dictated from
above: 'people were brought here and settled and given names and
identification numbers, and a past and, of course, a future' (Laor,
1995: 10). In this volume I aim to make visible the contradiction
between Zionist myths of the Shoah as a catastrophe which happened
not to 'us' Israelis, but to a diaspora Jewish 'other', and the post-Shoah
Israeli reality which discursively employed the Shoah to justify the
occupation of Palestinian lands and people, and its excesses. These
myths of the supposed passivity, weakness, pathology, and non-virility
of that Jewish 'other' contradicted the reality that the survivors,
despite their suffering and despite being stigmatised in Israeli society,
proved to be as active, strong, psychologically sound and 'virile' as the
next Israeli. They also contradicted the fact that no Israeli fitted the
simplistic heroic mould which Zionism constructed.

Field research for this book was conducted between 1992 and
1996, the four years of the Rabin-Peres government which ended after
the assassination of Prime Minister Yitzhak Rabin in November 1995,
with the election, in May 1996, of the right-wing government of
Binyamin Netanyahu. Netanyahu was replaced, in May 1999, by
Ehud Barak, leader of the One Israel Party (formerly the Labour party),
seen as the successor of Rabin's political way.

Informed by a reflexive feminist auto/biographical research
methodology, *Israel and the Daughters of the Shoah* centres on the personal narratives of nine Israeli writers and film-makers who are
daughters of Shoah survivors. In their life and work, these women
have excavated the meanings of being daughters of survivors in Israeli
society. The narratives were elicited through open-ended in-depth
interviews in autumn 1992, a short time after Rabin acceded to power.
For the narrators, it was a time of transformation and hope, personal
and political: they, and I, were hopeful about the possibility of a shift in
the employment of Shoah discourses to justify the excesses of the
Israeli occupation, although I did not share their optimism about the
peace process itself.[1]

The research process had a profound transformatory effect on me in naming myself, for the first time, a daughter of a family of survivors. Similarly, their 'research' processes (which resulted in their books, poems, and films) had a transformatory effect on the narrators. In offering the nine narrators a forum to break the silences of their Israeli Shoah daughterhood, I seek to bridge the 'memory gap' (Grunfeld, 1995) between the traumatic legacy of the Shoah and the discourses available to represent it. 'Stories', or personal narratives, are the only means at our disposal to close the gap between ontology[2] and representation.

As well as their own transformation, I argue that the narrators' works were instrumental in assisting in the shift in Israeli attitudes to the Shoah and its meanings. In making our 'stories' we not only make our selves (Linden, 1993), we also 'make' and help to shape societal discourses and perceptions by breaking the silences about un-named traumatic experiences such as the Shoah.

Before discussing the three main 'territories of silence' which this book aims to re-occupy, I will address four semantic-thematic issues: the use of the term 'Shoah'; a tentative definition of Israeli Shoah survivors and their children; the centrality of the terms 'territories' and 'occupation' of the sub-title in the Israeli context; and finally, the centrality of silence to the 'story' of Israel and the Shoah.

Firstly, I use the Hebrew word 'Shoah' meaning catastrophe, cataclysm, disaster, to describe the annihilation of a third of the Jewish people by the Nazis before and during the Second World War, rather than the English language term 'Holocaust'. Naming the catastrophe and the metaphorical process of that naming have profound political meanings, particularly in the Israeli context (as will be discussed in chapter 4). The Jewish lexicon had already contained a set of precedents and terms by which to understand the catastrophe and the appropriate ritual days of mourning by which to commemorate all past and present disasters. The term *khurban* (destruction in Hebrew), denoting the destruction of the first and second temples, suggested itself to Jewish writers to describe the unfolding massacre of Europe's Jews. However, *khurban*, with its attendant religious connotations, did not appeal to the Zionist leadership in Palestine. The term 'Shoah' was deliberately sought by Zionism to allow for new, Erez Israeli,[3] rather than Jewish-diasporic meanings.

Although I oppose the appropriation and 'Zionisation' of the Shoah by political Zionism, which discursively rejected the alleged passivity of Europe's Jews, I prefer the term 'Shoah' to the term 'Holocaust'. 'Holocaust' derives from the Greek *holocauston*, meaning 'whole burnt', referring in Septuagint to sacrifice by fire as distinct from the Hebrew term for sacrificial offering, *olah*. Many Jews, aware of the Christian notion of a Jewish calvary and sacrifice, reject the term (Young, 1990: 87).[4]

Secondly, the word 'survivor' is problematic because, as Lagerwey reminds us (1998: 18), some say that no one really survived the Shoah. Indeed, in Hebrew the word is 'nitzolim' – 'those who were saved' – echoing Fania Fenelon's (1981: 117) description of people who were physically alive after liberation as having 'come out with their lives'. In the debate as to who is an Israeli Shoah survivor, some say that only those who lived under the Nazi occupation or were subject to the 'Final Solution' are entitled to call themselves Shoah survivors. About 100,000 people who were children during the Shoah live in Israel today, most are aged between 50 and 65 (Porian, 1996: B6). In the *Shoah Encyclopaedia* (Gutman, 1990) there is no definition under 'survivors'. Legally and historically, it is possible to define as 'Shoah survivor' a person who lived under Nazi rule during the Second World War and who was subject to the policy of the 'Final Solution' and remained alive. Bar On (1994) problematises this definition and broadens it to allow for self-definition.

Self-definition, however, is fraught with hierarchies and contradictions. Some survivors of rescue operations such as the Kästner train,[5] for instance, found it hard to relate to what happened to them, because it was not considered 'real' suffering in comparison to the suffering of camp or ghetto survivors. According to Bar On (1994: 27), objective and subjective definitions of survivorship relate to one's self-legitimisation and to the legitimisation of one's close group regarding one's experiences during the Shoah. Survivors sometimes tend to self-grade themselves and create hierarchies between those who were deported to concentration camps and who have a tattooed number on their forearms, those who lived in ghettos and were not deported to concentration or extermination camps, those coming from 'mixed' Christian-Jewish families, and those who had emigrated to Palestine prior to the War, but whose families were exterminated. There is also a hierarchy between members of resistance organisations and members of the Jewish police, or the *Judenräte*, the Jewish councils.

Rather than enter into the debate over the classification of 'real' and 'less real' Shoah survivors, I prefer to allow for self-definition in the definition of 'Israeli Shoah survivors'. 'Survivor' is a socially constructed identity, yet the term tends to reify Jews' experience under Nazi occupation. Survivors construct their diverse identities as survivors, yet they share both commonalties and differences, which need to be explored empirically (Linden, 1993: 87–8).

Equally complex is the definition of Israeli 'children of Shoah survivors', termed both in the literature and popularly 'the second-generation'. This is a contested term, since some (e.g., Ravnitsky, 1986; Hazan, 1987) believe either that children of survivors have no characteristics distinguishing them from other Israelis, or that they do not have the same entitlements as do their survivor-parents (Dror, 1992). Despite the temptations of 'certain postmodernisms' (Linden, 1996: 11) to include all Jews born after the Shoah in the broad definition of 'children of survivors', a 'reality' specific to Israelis whose parents did experience the Shoah, diverse, problematic and complex as it may be, does indeed exist. Self-definition is again a central criterion and in some cases, self-definition as a child of survivors is an act of 'naming' and of 'making the self' as we 'make our stories'.

Thirdly, the terms 'territories' and 'occupation' of the subtitle are, I argue, central to any study of contemporary Israel, impossible in isolation from the Israeli-Palestinian conflict. The conflict, despite its profound effect on Israeli social formation, has historically been neglected and marginalised in Israeli sociology, blinded by the hegemonic conception of the conflict, part of the Israeli political consensus, in which sociology has played a central role (Ehrlich, 1993: 253, 259). The 1977 elections, which broke the thirty-year political hegemony of socialist Zionism (in the shape of the Labour-Mapai party) and brought Menachem Begin's right-wing Likud party to power, signalled a shift in the sociological discourse from identification with the establishment to a more autonomous position. But only in recent years has Israeli sociology taken up a critical position vis-à-vis Israeli society (Ram, 1993b: 17).

One strand in the critical Israeli sociology of the 1980s and 1990s, along with élite theory, Marxism, pluralism, and feminism, is the analysis of Israeli society as a settler-colonial society. Because this was the most critical perspective towards Zionism, Israel's fundamental ethos, it has been kept out of the Israeli sociological agenda until relatively recently. Prior to becoming an academic perspective, the colonisatory perspective had been theorised by Israeli-Jewish marginal radical political groupings, such as Matspen (Schnall, 1979; Wigoder and Wigoder, 1999), to which I belonged in the late 1960s. The controversy provoked by the 1967 war and the ensuing occupation of Palestinian territories allowed this perspective to be gradually incorporated into the Israeli sociological discourse (Ram, 1993b: 29).

According to the colonisatory perspective, the major force in shaping Israeli society was the process of colonising an already inhabited land. This perspective views Israel being a settler-colonial society as the decisive factor in Israeli social formation (Kimmerling, 1983; Shafir, 1989; Ram, 1993; Abdo and Yuval-Davis, 1995).

Post-colonial theories have rarely been employed to theorise the position of Jews, rather than Palestinians in settler-colonial analyses of Zionism. But, as Boyarin argues (1997a: 279), Herzlian Zionism as well as being seen as the solution to the 'Jewish question', was based on European Jews giving up their 'primitive' distinctiveness, showing 'manly' virtues and becoming as 'civilised' as their Aryan neighbours (as argued below in chapter 6). Zionism can thus be seen as both a de-colonisation process (Jews freeing themselves from the Euro-Aryan yoke) and a re-colonisation process (in relation to the land of Israel and the indigenous Palestinians). However, this call on post-coloniality does not sit comfortably with theories of diaspora: we must ask, in relation to the negation of the Jewish diaspora implied in narratives of the newly constructed Israeli nation, where does homeland begin and diaspora end.

Following Nandy's reading of colonisation as the feminisation of the colonised (1983), occupation and territories, as well as masculinity and militarism, are as central to Israeli social formation as they are to the link between statehood and gender. Simona Sharoni (1992) argues that the Israeli-Palestinian conflict has had a deep impact on women's lives and on the social construction of gender relations in Israel. The social construction of manhood in Israel has its roots in a particular historical context, especially in relation to the Shoah and the creation of the Jewish State. I concur with Sharoni's argument that the state of Israel can be seen as 'a reassertion of masculinity, justified by the need to end a history of weakness and suffering by creating an image of an Israeli man who is exceedingly masculine, pragmatic, protective, assertive and emotionally tough' (Sharoni, 1992: 457). Resulting from the ongoing occupation, Zionist ideology has made 'national security' a top priority, offering Israeli men a privileged status and legitimising national, ethnic and gender inequalities. Linking occupation and gender relations, Sharoni argues that 'in a context where every man is a soldier, every woman becomes an occupied territory' (ibid.: 459).

Finally, silence, and silencing, are central to my argument. In order to consolidate the Israeli Zionist narrative, silences had to be constructed. Survivors were tutored in self-silencing during the Shoah, which was an event which 'had no witness', because the Nazis did all they could to wipe out not only the Jews, but also their memory. They were also silenced by pre-state and early state Zionist narratives that privileged heroic myths constructed around the partisans and around Erez Israeli youth. There is a link between silencing the survivors and silencing the truth about the dispossession of the Palestinians. Laor (1995: 115–70) argues that the silence about the dispossession of the Palestinians and the atrocities involved during and after the 1948 war, initiated by Israel's first Prime Minister David Ben Gurion, became the silence of the state, academia, and the media. 'Ben Gurion believed in silence because he believed in the power of words to be remembered, to be studied, to become "truth". Therefore he did not speak about the expulsions' (Laor, 1995: 125).

This silence, which shaped the childhood of my generation, and the fictions of the Palestinians leaving their homes and their lands of their own free will, must be linked to silencing the survivors. Indeed, traumatic events are often dealt with by banishing them from consciousness: survivors of trauma, political or personal, often silence themselves and are silenced by society. This has been typical of Shoah survivors, many of whom remained silent for several decades. According to Funkenstein (1993: 22), the memory of Shoah survivors is fragmented. Although many camp survivors wanted to remember, they had been robbed of their identity by the Nazis. The Israeli writer Aharon Appelfeld, who survived as a lone child in the ghetto and the forest, writes this about the delicate balance between language and silence:

> Speaking is hard for me, not surprisingly: during the war people did not speak. Every disaster states again: what is there to say, there is nothing to say. Anyone who was in the ghetto, in the camps and in the forests is familiar with this silence, bodily ... Only after the war did the words return. People began asking and wondering, and people who were not there asked for explanations ... (But) words cannot deal with large catastrophes: they are poor, wretched vehicles, which soon become false ... We often surround big catastrophes with words in order to defend ourselves. My first written words were sort of desperate attempts to find the silence which surrounded me during the war and to return me to myself. With my blind senses I understood that within this silence rests my soul. (Appelfeld, 1999: 95–6)

Israel and the Daughters of the Shoah is primarily concerned with re-occupying the territories of silence. The following section lists three conceptual silences which I attempt to re-occupy metaphorically in this book: the silence about the Shoah in sociology (including Israeli sociology); the silence about the link between gender and the Shoah; and the silence about social scientists' auto/biographical involvement in their research process.

The territories of silence

Sociology and the Shoah

The ongoing debate as to the possibility of speech, or discourse, about the Shoah was inspired by Adorno's famous claim that 'after Auschwitz it is no longer possible to write poems' (1949) and fuelled by survivors such as Elie Wiesel, who insisted that only survivors were entitled to speak about the Shoah (Wiesel, 1984). On the one side of the debate are those who argue that the best response to the Shoah is silence (Steiner, 1969: 165). Studying the Shoah includes the temptation to succumb to a Foucauldian 'archaeology of silence' (Foucault, 1967: xi). We must ask, however, whether such archaeology of silence is in itself not an order, an organised language, a project, a syntax, a work (Derrida, 1978: 25–6). I side with those (e.g., Celan, 1968; Langer, 1975), who argue, as Adorno himself did later (1962), that surrendering to silence would be a surrender to cynicism and by implication, to the very forces that created Auschwitz in the first place. An archaeology of silence is not sufficient, nor is it ultimately possible, despite the understandable tendency to regard the Shoah as 'unspeakable' and respond to it with silence.

The Shoah must indeed be excavated, studied, compared, analysed and footnoted. The first silence I wish to re-occupy therefore is the silence about the Shoah itself within sociology. Zygmunt Bauman argues for incorporating the Shoah into sociological inquiry, since it 'has more to say about the state of sociology than sociology in its present shape is able to add to our knowledge of the Holocaust' (Bauman, 1989: 3). Bauman examines some of the few sociological studies of the Shoah (e.g., Fein, 1979; Tec, 1986) to chart two approaches through which the significance of the Shoah has been marginalised by sociology. One approach presents the Shoah as something which happened exclusively to the Jews; this makes the Shoah unique, uncharacteristic and sociologically inconsequential. This approach presents the Shoah as a consequence of European antisemitism[6] (or, as Goldhagen [1995] argues more specifically, German antisemitism), and thus as a one-off episode which does not add to our understanding of modern society's normal state. The other approach presents the Shoah as a primeval and culturally extinguishable 'natural' predisposition of the human species, pre-social and immune to cultural manipulation and as such, of no sociological interest.

Against these two approaches, Bauman argues that the Shoah was 'born and executed in our modern rational society, at the high stage of our civilisation and at the peak of human cultural achievement' (Bauman, 1989: x). It is therefore relevant to the main themes of sociological inquiry, as 'an outcome of a unique encounter between factors by themselves quite ordinary and common'. Every 'ingredient' of the Shoah – rationality, technology, bureaucracy and state violence – was 'normal', in the sense of being fully in line with everything we know about our civilisation.

The machinery of destruction, Bauman quotes Shoah historian Raul Hilberg as saying, 'was structurally no different from organised German society as a whole... (it) *was* the organised community in one of its special roles' (Hilberg, 1983: 994). Arguing for using, amongst others, Weberian diagnoses of the tendencies of modern society, Bauman takes sociology to task for not applying sociological analyses to the study of the Shoah.

Since Bauman wrote his book, there have been other orchestrated genocides, for example in Bosnia and Rwanda, to the study of which may be applied the criteria he applies to the study of the Shoah. Bauman's central argument is that if such genocide could happen on such a massive scale in Nazi Germany, at the heart of European civilisation, then it can happen anywhere where 'instrumental rationality, and its modern, bureaucratic form of institutionalisation, which had made the Holocaust-style solutions not only possible, but eminently "reasonable" is the ruling spirit' (Bauman, 1989: 18).

Bauman calls for a substantial revision of the orthodox sociology of morality and argues that the assumption that society is essentially a humanising, moralising device and that immoral conduct can be explained only as the malfunctioning of 'normal' society, has been disproved. Immorality is socially constructed and society may make immoral conduct more, rather than less, plausible. The social production of distance and the technology of segregation and separation which promote indifference to the plight of the Other, as successfully produced by Nazism, are societal achievements in the management of morality. Bauman concludes with another quote from Hilberg:

> Remember, again, that the basic question was whether a western nation, a civilised nation, could be capable of such a thing. And then, soon after 1945, we see the query turned around totally as one begins to ask: 'Is there any western nation that is incapable of it?' ... In 1941 the Holocaust was not expected and that is the very reason for our subsequent anxieties. We no longer dare to exclude the unimaginable. (Hilberg, 1980: 98–9)

The American-Jewish sociologist Ruth Linden, in a book subtitled *Feminist Reflections on the Holocaust* (Linden, 1993), also bemoans the sociological silence about the Shoah, and proposes a change of terminology to 'a phenomenology of surviving' as the central concern of a sociology of the Shoah. Unlike that of Bauman, her sociology of the Shoah would be 'empirically based and sensitive to problems of constructing and interpreting personal and historical narratives'. It would explore broad theoretical issues, such as 'how human agency is exercised under genocide'. Sociologists, she suggests, could collect and analyse survivors' testimonies, and clarify problems of 'knowing' and complicity by analysing personal narratives of perpetrators and bystanders. A sociology of the Shoah must reconcile the pre-determined annihilation of the Jews with the Jews' refusal to die as individuals and as an ancient culture. The Jews must be viewed as interacting, knowing subjects, reasoning their way from one day to the next (Linden, 1993: 85–6).

The state of Israel (alongside other Jewish self-appointed spokespersons, who denounced attempts to dissolve the uniquely Jewish character of the Shoah in the misery of an indistinct 'humanity') rejected all attempts to draw universal, rather than national, lessons from the Shoah. It employed the Shoah as an instrument of political legitimacy and has resisted attempts to compare the Shoah to contemporary genocides. At the same time, the young Israeli state constructed itself in opposition to the passivity implied in the discourse of Jewish victims allegedly 'going to their death like lambs to the slaughter'. It met Shoah survivors upon their return from the Nazi hell with silence, and an inability, or unwillingness, to listen to their horrific experiences.

Survivors' experiences and the experiences of their children have, by and large, not been addressed by Israeli sociology. The few sociological studies that have been published (e.g., Boldo, 1983; Yuchtman-Ya'ar and Menachem, 1989; but with the exception of Kemp and Herzog, 1999, who analyse testimonies by women who were incarcerated in Ravensbrük) do not analyse survivor or 'second-generation' testimonies. Sociology is conspicuously absent from Israeli studies of the relationship between Israel and the Shoah by comparison with historical studies (e.g., Segev, 1991; Zuckermann, 1993; Yablonka, 1994; Hacohen, 1994),[7] and psychological studies (see Wardi, 1990, for a comprehensive survey).

The Shoah, and Israeli discourses about the Shoah, as well as survivors' accounts, are undoubtedly socially constructed, and must therefore be available for sociological scrutiny. In employing personal narratives of daughters of survivors compelled and able to articulate the transmission of their parents' Shoah experiences in the face of societal silencing and stigma, I aim to add to the breaking of that particular silence. In so doing, I aim to provide a sociological forum for speaking about the Shoah and about children of Shoah survivors in the Israeli context, and to position an auto/biographical sociological examination of 'second-generation' narratives in the context of Israeli discourses of state and nation construction.

Shoah and gender

Bauman does not bring gender into the equation. Linden's analysis, on the other hand, is 'feminist' in the self-definition sense (see Reinharz, 1992), but also in the insistence that 'self' and 'other' are inseparably fused in a dialectic of situated knowing (Linden, 1993: 147; Haraway, 1988: 592–3). The second territory of silence the book aims to re-occupy is therefore the silence about the link between Shoah and gender. According to Hilberg, 'the final solution was intended ... to ensure the annihilation of all Jews. Yet the road to annihilation was marked by events that specifically affected men as men and women as women'

(Hilberg, 1992: 126). Although it has been argued that 'the greatest atrocities at Auschwitz were committed against Jewish women and children' (Ainsztein, 1974: 788–9), and that 'the concentration camp is an ultimate expression of the extreme masculinity and misogyny that undergirded Nazi ideology' (Goldenberg, 1990: 163), gender-specific Shoah research began only in the late 1970s and is still strongly resisted by those who claim that raising questions about women trivialises the Shoah.

The American historian and philosopher Joan Ringelheim who pioneered gender-specific Shoah research, argues (1992: 19–23) that regarding the Shoah as uniquely Jewish creates a division between Jewish experiences and those of Roma and Sinti, the disabled, Communists, Socialists, homosexuals, Jehovah's Witnesses, Poles, Russians, POWs and other 'asocials', whose Shoah experiences remain silenced and unnamed (and often, because of different traditions of literacy, unwritten and unpublished). This approach, which differentiates between Jews and 'others', arises from the need to prevent the denial of the Jewish tragedy, as practised by neo-Nazi and extreme Muslim anti-Zionist groups and backed up by some historians (*Antisemitism World Report*, 1995: xviii-xix; see also Lipstadt, 1993).[8] This leads to framing the Shoah as a metaphysical evil, removing it beyond human history, speech or rationality.

Another approach to the study of the Shoah sees no difference between experiences of Jews, viewing the 'Jewish experience' as a univocal monolith. Just as the exclusivity-uniqueness approach ignores the complexities of non-Jewish experiences, the univocal approach ignores the complexities of Jewish experiences. No two Jews experienced the Shoah in the same way, and what happened to the Jews cannot be reduced to a 'single sharp image of victimisation' of the concentration camp. The Nazis intended to kill all Jews, but the end, or 'extermination', does not describe the process.

Shoah studies, mostly conducted by male historians,[9] do not take into account the experiences and perceptions of women during the Shoah. These experiences tend to be neutralised into a so-called 'human' perspective, which, on examination, turns out to be masculine. But women were killed not only as Jews, but also on account of their 'biological destiny', as the producers of the next 'racially inferior' Jewish generation. According to Ringelheim:

> A study of women and the Shoah calls into question some of the claims about the uniqueness of the Holocaust and the sameness of the Jewish experience, and thus even the ways in which the Holocaust is remembered. But there are deeper effects and more difficult tasks: to enlarge our understanding of the event by reclaiming the hidden experiences of women. Even if we assume that women and men suffered equally at the

hands of the Nazis, we find that, in one way or another, to one degree or another, they experienced their circumstances as women and men, and as Jews. (Ringelheim, 1992: 21)

Ofer and Weitzman (1998) also argue that questions about gender lead to a richer understanding of the Shoah. More specifically, they focus on four structural sources of gender differences during the Shoah: the culturally defined gender roles of Jewish men and women before the War, which endowed the two sexes with different skills, knowledge and expertise; the Jews' 'anticipatory reactions' to what they believed the Nazis were going to do to Jewish men (but not to Jewish women and children); the differences in the nature and degree of harassment, work requirements, arrests and regulations that the Nazis imposed on Jewish men and women, even though they were all destined for death; and the different reactions of Jewish men and women in the ghettos, in hiding, in the forests and in the camps. Though not arguing that women's experiences were totally different from those of men, since both women and men were targeted because of Nazi constructions of their 'race' rather than their genders, Ofer and Weitzman claim that just like other differences between Shoah victims (countries of origin, age, class), gender must be attended to so that we attempt to make sense of the enormity of the destruction (Ofer and Weitzman, 1998: 1–18).

At the early stages of her research Ringelheim recorded women's experiences during the Shoah, arguing that gender-defined conditions and traditional responses against women made them vulnerable. They were vulnerable to sexual abuse, rape and murder, the necessity of killing their own and other women's babies, forced abortions and sterilisation, and other forms of sexual exploitation (by Nazis but also by Jewish men) in the ghettos, in the camps and in hiding.

There are no gender-specific extermination figures, but Ringelheim's detailed analysis of deportation figures and displaced persons statistics suggests that women probably make up more than half of the dead. The figures also suggest that, because they were less 'useful' to the Nazis as workers, fewer women than men were spared from immediate gassing; and that fewer women than men survived the extermination camps (Hilberg, 1992; Ringelheim, 1993).

Ringelheim found that according to claims by survivors, women's survival resources included forming alternative 'families' which became networks for maintenance that might have been related to survival rates, in that they were able to transform their habits of raising children or their experience of nurturing into the care of non-biological families (Ringelheim, 1985, 1993). In 1985, however, reflecting on her earlier research, she took herself to task for adopting a 'cultural feminism' stance (Alcoff, 1988), thus opting for a cosy 'happy ending' through accounts of female friendships and survival. Cultural feminism shares with liberalism a belief in individual solutions and in humanism and addresses a universal 'woman' while privileging some women over others, a tendency criticised effectively by majority world feminists in relation to western feminism (e.g., Mohanty et al., 1991; Ahmed, 1982). A cultural feminist stance, which tends to valorise oppression, damages not only our politics, but also our research, according to Ringelheim.

Ringelheim argues that the 'archaeological' perspective on women's culture must be re-examined. Indeed, excavating an 'archaeology of silence' is not sufficient without contextualising women's Shoah experiences within Nazi ideological racism and sexism. Furthermore, privileging women's bonding as a strategy of survival, and valuing, in line with feminist theorists such as Chodorow (1978) and Gilligan (1982), relationship over autonomy and caring over justice, perpetuate the dichotomy of female nurturing and attachment versus male autonomy and individuation (Goldenberg, 1990: 152). Praising some victims for their coping skills (or blaming them for their lack of such skills) also presents a danger, according to Ofer and Weitzman (1998: 15), of shifting the blame away from the Nazis on to the survivors themselves. Judith Baumel, however, disagrees with Ringelheim's view that stressing women's communal coping strategies valorises oppression, and argues that women's survival strategies must be studied as different (rather than better or worse) than men's in order to realise the depth of communal bond in crisis, and the importance of its gender dimension as a conceptual tool (Baumel, 1999b: 329–47). Similarly, Lagerwey (1998), who analyses published Auschwitz stories by men and women, found evidence 'of women's unique experiences, of sexuality, friendship and parenting, their mutual concern and assistance to each other, their emotional capacity, their unselfish and sacrificial sharing and great flexibility – in sum, a moral superiority that even the horrors of Auschwitz could not obliterate'. On the other hand, 'true to my expectations, I found that the stories written by men told of personal isolation, personal survival at any cost, ruthless competition, and pragmatic allegiances. Male survivors framed their narratives in order and coherence, and often de-emphasised emotions' (ibid.,: 75). However, re-reading the narratives, Lagerwey realised that 'the stories of Auschwitz are too complex to fit neatly into gender stereotypes' and that the narratives are 'not only gendered voices; there are nationalised voices, ethnic voices, ideological voices' (ibid.,: 104, 108). Ultimately, she writes about what she initially thought of as merely 'gendered' narratives, as 'narratives of chaos' (ibid.,: 127).

Another, deeper silence about gender and the Shoah is the silence about women's experiences of sexual exploitation during the Shoah (Ringelheim, 1997; Lentin, 1997; 1999a). Positing the 'split memory' between gender and the Shoah, Ringelheim argues that sex and all experiences connected with sex, rape, abortion, sexual abuse and pregnancy are intimate parts of women's lives and therefore never easy to talk about. Facing women survivors' sexual exploitation confronts us with our own sexual vulnerability as women. And for family members:

> the rape of mothers, grandmothers, sisters, friends, or lovers during the Holocaust is difficult to face. The further possibility that mothers or sisters or lovers 'voluntarily' used sex for food or protection is equally difficult to absorb ... but to dismiss situations that relate so specifically to women makes it impossible to begin to understand the victimisation of women. It may even make it impossible to really see Jewish women as victims, or visualise their victimisation. (Ringelheim, 1997: 25)

Ringelheim further takes herself to task for not being able to ask a survivor-interviewee what had happened when the survivor told her that she had been raped in Auschwitz, and argues that the incident reveals important things about 'how deeply [researchers] may not want to hear; and about the ways in which we avoid listening no matter how directly a survivor [male or female] may tell us what happened (e.g., cannibalism, hiding in a latrine, killing new-born babies). Sometimes we avoid because we are afraid; sometimes we avoid because we don't understand the importance of what is being said' (Ringelheim, 1997: 27).

Despite what seems to me a persuasive argument for the study of gender in relation to the Shoah, opposition to this line of work is alive and well. In 1992 Ringelheim wrote about the antagonism her early research aroused in renowned commentators such as Cynthia Ozick. In 1998, after the publication of Ofer and Weitzman's anthology, Gabriel Schoenfeld (1998a), writing in *Commentary* magazine, accused feminist scholars of the Shoah of spreading feminist 'propaganda' (Lipstadt, 1998: 12). Replying to articles by feminist scholars of the Shoah in *Lilith* magazine, Schoenfeld attacked Ringelheim, Linden, Ofer and Weitzman, and Lipstadt for revisionism and for 'the shameful things that feminist scholars have been writing about the Holocaust' (Schoenfeld, 1998b: 42).

The picture in Israel is not much different. Prominent Israeli Shoah historians (most notably Bauer, 1978; 1980; 1982; 1989; 1994a; Friedländer, 1978; 1982; 1988; 1992; Gutman, 1990, among others) do not consider gender. Only in the late 1990s did Israeli scholars (e.g., Dalia Ofer, in Ofer and Weitzman, 1998; Judith Tydor Baumel, 1999a; 1999b; Adriana Kemp and Hanna Herzog, 1999; and Esther Fuchs, 1999) begin to address the gendered aspects of the Shoah.

Israeli historiography has been enriched by several studies (as mentioned above) of the complex relations between Israelis and the Shoah. While Israelis, these studies argue, were reluctant to accept the alleged passivity of the victims, official Israeli discourses and ceremonies privileged the sporadic armed resistance acts over Shoah victimhood. Segev (1991), Yablonka (1994) and Hacohen (1994) document the ways in which Israelis stigmatised the survivors and discriminated against them. Zertal (1996a) charts the exploitation of the survivors to further the political objectives of the future Israeli state. Grodziusky (1998) documents the 'zionisation' of the Shoah as expressed by pre-state emissaries to the displaced persons camps. However, while Shapira (1992) and Zertal (1996a) refer, marginally, to the gender implications of the Shoah for the early staters, most other studies tend to be gender-blind.

Several studies (e.g., Hazelton, 1978; Sharoni, 1992; 1994; Shohat, 1991; Shadmi, 1992; Boyarin, 1997a; 1997b; 1997c; Gluzman, 1997) argue that Zionism, based on constructing a 'new Jew', who would differ from 'his' Jewish diaspora ancestors, gave men a newly constructed masculinity with which to re-formulate the diaspora Jewish subjectivity and re-invent it as 'Israeli', a construction of which they are extremely critical. However, as I am aware of no other study which links this with the silencing and stigmatisation of Shoah survivors in Israeli society, my aim is to make this link and break the silence about Shoah and gender in the Israeli context.

There also appear to be no gender-differentiated sociological studies of Israeli children of survivors (although there have been several psychological studies which incorporate a gender dimension, notably Marcus, 1986; and Wardi, 1990). I centred my research on personal narratives of daughters of Shoah survivors against the backcloth of Israeli society in order to break the silence about the link between Shoah and gender in the Israeli context. *Israel and the Daughters of the Shoah* is an auto/biographical undertaking in that I share with the narrators a gendered Israeli subjectivity, 'split' between belonging to a family of survivors on the one hand, and to the first Israeli-born generation, which was brought up to despise Shoah victims and survivors on the other.

Researchers' 'intellectual auto/biography'

This brings me to the third territory I wish to re-occupy: the silence, often implicit in sociology, about researchers' auto/biographical involvement with the material they study. There are some research projects, born, as Liz Stanley (1996) argues, out of 'necessity', which carry within them transformatory possibilities for the researcher. If indeed feminist researchers carry out particular research because of the resonance between the topic or approach and the personal context of the research, and if indeed our 'intellectual auto/biography' (Stanley and Wise, 1993) can explicate, beyond a simple narrative of life 'as it is lived', the processes by which understandings are reached, then the myth of the detached scientific observer must be done away with. Instead we have an 'experiencing because knowing subject', whose 'ontologically based reasoning provides the claims to knowledge' (Stanley, 1996: 47).

This volume is a testimony to this duality of experiencing and knowing, a duality, moreover, of a 'split' or double subjectivity. Because of my membership of the Israeli 'first generation to redemption', which was schooled to despise diaspora Jewry and, by extension, Shoah victims and survivors, it was only while researching this book that I was able to 'name' myself a member of a survivor family. During the course of researching and writing these two very conflicting subjectivities became intertwined. Positioning my 'auto/biographical I' (Stanley, 1992) at the ontological centre of the study, and basing my research on auto/biographical personal narratives of Israeli daughters of survivors, I argue for the centrality of women's lived experiences as a 'scientific resource' (Harding, 1987). The experience of my split subjectivity has been the 'necessary' epistemological and ontological focus informing my research.

Auto/biographical personal narratives, particularly narratives of trauma, because of their complex and often fragmented nature, rarely offer us possibilities of conventional sociological validation. Personal narratives cannot stand limited definitions of 'truth' that admit only one standard at a time for the perception and interpretation of a small segment of a complex reality. Instead, women's personal narratives offer the plural truths of experience, history and perceptions, amongst other things, of the construction of a gendered self-identity. Ultimately, women's personal narratives and the knowledge they impart are 'as true as our lives' (Personal Narratives Group, 1989: 262–3). However, if researchers are open to it, auto/biography offers endless performative, but also transformative possibilities, in terms of constructing the self, and often also of transforming society.

When I began working, I 'knew' several things about Israel and the Shoah, if 'knew' is the right word for something perceived instinctively but also experientially. I 'knew' that Shoah survivors were denigrated by Israelis in subtle and not so subtle ways. I also 'knew' that Israeli society was, and is, a masculine construction built, although women have always been active participants in society, on axioms of ongoing 'no-choice' military struggle, which, necessarily, privileges male soldiers who share in the dividends of military, political and social power to the detriment of women. My goal was to link the theorisation of

Israel as a masculine construction with the stigmatisation of Shoah survivors. My instinct was to work with Israeli daughters of survivors who were the first members of the 'second-generation' to put their experiences of being children of survivors in the public domain, in artistic form.

What I did not 'know' prior to beginning work on this book, was how deeply implicated I was in all this. My own parents were not, strictly speaking, Shoah survivors, but most members of their families were deported to Transnistria, a series of ghettos in Southern Ukraine, where some of them perished. When the narrators spoke of coming from 'silent families' where one 'knew and did not know' about the Shoah at the same time, I did not realise to what extent my own family was such a 'silent family'. My mother's insistence, until a very short time ago, that she had never needed to speak of her past life, a life she abandoned at the age of 19 to go to Palestine, was beginning to ring hollow. As I began working on the narratives, I realised, on the one hand, how much she *did* talk about her Romanian-Bukovinian past. On the other hand, and somewhat contradictorily, I realised just how silent my own parents had been about the Shoah despite having lost several members of their families. Because Mother and her family managed to escape on time, they never saw themselves as survivors – the mantle of Shoah survivors was not lightly assumed (as argued above).

As I was researching, the signs of that silence became more and more apparent. The whispered stories of Mother's relatives who congregated in Grandmother's sitting room, whispers hushed when we, the Israeli-born children, were about. The compulsive attitudes to food, feeding us too much, worrying when we did not eat enough. My parents' decision not to speak to us in German, their mother tongue, in which they talked to each other. The need to make constant contact, the fear of separation. As well as Grandmother's grunting and weeping in her sleep, never quite forgiving herself for having left her own mother behind when she journeyed to Palestine. The family trees I was obsessively drawing with Grandfather when I was a young child. And the shamed refusal to admit to my two Yiddish middle names, given after lost relatives, as Yiddish, the Jewish (Ashkenazi) 'mother tongue' (Lentin, 1996a) was erased in favour of Hebrew, our virile old-new language.

The realisation that I had always been engaged in 'researching' my split subjectivity – in my fiction writing (Lentin, 1976; 1978; 1989; 1996b), but also in my obsessive interest in all Shoah accounts from a very young age – meant that in the course of working on this book, it has become auto/biographical, in the sense of constructing my self and my life through my identification with the narrators' lived experiences.

But there was more. From the very early stages I felt compelled to turn inwards. Like Ruth Linden, upon her return from the American

Gathering of Holocaust Survivors, where she collected 200 life histories of survivors, I too kept feeling I was still 'in the field' long after I returned from field trips to Israel. Indeed, I had never left the field, because I *was* the field. This was a 'liminal time when my social boundaries – the membrane between me and the rest of the world – were fragile and fluid' (Linden, 1993: 4–5).

The narratives forced me to confront the dichotomous relations between my membership of the 'first generation' and Shoah survivors. At the same time they made me re-examine my membership of that 'first generation' which, having rejected European diaspora Judaism, has in recent years started to re-invent its Jewish roots and diaspora connections. One manifestation of this is the re-claiming by many Israeli children of European parents of their families' Jewish-European surnames, which they had been coerced in the Israeli Defence Forces (IDF) and other Israeli institutions, to Hebraicise.

The narratives brought to mind 'moments of being' (Woolf, 1978) from my own life. As a *Sabra*, exhorted to be a stronger Jewish child, I, like other Israeli-born children, was contemptuous towards relatives who had arrived from 'there' and who spoke with a 'diasporic' accent.[10]

During the research process, recalling my youthful contempt towards the survivors, I became conscious of another 'split'. I had a stake in a sense of belonging to a survivor family on the one hand, and in a profound Israeli guilt towards the survivors on the other. This duality is linked to what psychoanalyst Dinora Pines (1993) quotes Freud as describing as 'disavowal' or 'the blindness of the seeing eye in which one knows and does not know a thing at the same time' (Freud, 1925: 235). Writing about women survivors whom she saw in analysis, Pines confesses to her own 'survivor guilt': 'I have engaged not only in the rediscovery of my patients' Holocaust history and its impact on their lives, but also ... in the rediscovery of my own. Thus I too am deeply affected by the guilt of the survivor. The sense of psychic continuity that is important to us all was brutally broken in my patients' lives, but also to some degree in my own' (Pines, 1993: 223).

The study of narrative must struggle with the question of how much one needs to know about others to feel that one can understand something about them. Since 'life history subjects are... actively inscribed by means of narrative strategies' (Linden, 1993: 136), no matter how meaningful, researchers can never arrive at a 'complete' picture. Narrators are amply expert in organising and creating plots from disordered experiences, and narratives do not mirror a world 'out there', but are constructed, creatively authored, rhetorical and interpretative.

Auto/biography is a social construct comprising both social reality and the subjects' experiential world, which is why they raise the question of how to proceed from auto/biographical text to life itself (Rosenthal, 1993: 60). One clue to this dilemma is to consider life and story as part of the same fabric, in that life informs and is formed by stories. The meaning of life cannot be determined outside of the stories told about it; nor can the meaning of a story be determined without reference to human life as it is lived (Widdershoven, 1993: 2–20).

Liz Stanley (1993) provides another clue to the relation between the self (auto), life (bio) and text (graphy). Accounts of the past which constitute the major part of our lives, are structured by means of referential assumptions, but they do so because people are well aware that these are historiographical accounts, not history itself. The process of 'accounting' that auto/biographies constitute is an important means of making real and present what we all know is actually memory and past. Stanley stresses that 'all writing derives from, is the product of, helps to construct lives'. Experiential claims are not less, but certainly not more, problematic than other kinds of knowledge-claims, and both narrative and 'experience' are suitable grounds for analytic investigation (ibid.,: 206). Ultimately, she argues, 'whatever rhetorical means, the experiential basis of knowledge is denied or silenced, nonetheless all knowledge of the world is rooted in the knowledge-production processes, engaged in by inquiring and experiencing therefore knowing subjects' (ibid.,: 214).

One way of illuminating women's multiple realities is to elicit the narrative realities behind societal patterns. Personal narratives of Israeli daughters of Shoah survivors are one way of re-interpreting the dichotomy between 'masculine' Israel and the 'feminised' Shoah and of breaking the silence about the stigmatisation of the survivors in Israeli society. Starting from a feminist perspective of a woman (who is also a sociologist and a fiction writer) researching other women (who are fiction writers and film-makers) with whom she has much in common, my research strategy was dialogic. The resulting narratives are therefore the product of the interaction between the narrators and me, gendered situated subjects within the Israeli 'second-generation' ontology.

As an embodied, located subject, who is herself split between two Israeli subjectivities, that of an Israeli-born and that of a daughter of a Shoah-surviving family, I find myself thinking, and writing, in a multiplicity of voices – those of the sociologist, the writer, the Israeli, the Jewish woman, the exile, the daughter of a survivor family, the feminist, to name but a few. My narrators, some of them similarly 'split', also speak in multiple voices: we are all, in important ways, 'multiple personalities' (see Scott, 1997). The concerns with auto/biography, Stanley (1992) argues, teaches us that 'the self' is a fabrication. It is not a lie, but a highly complex truth, which relies on cultural conventions and depends on or derives from a particularly socially located viewpoint.

I chose to write about writers and film-makers since in my own fictional writing I have been engaged in 'researching' my Israeli split subjectivity just as the narrators have been 'researching' their ontology as Israeli daughters of Shoah survivors. The narrators' stories are 'stories-within-stories' and 'stories-about-stories', told to me by women who are themselves story-tellers, about their own lives and their parents' Shoah survival and post-Shoah Israeli stories, enabling them, and me, to 'make our lives' as we make our stories. Ultimately the narratives are not only a 'collection of stories', dependent on the researcher's location and identities as knower, but representations of a reality, problematic, partial, mediated, uncertain and ambiguous as it may be, which does indeed exist (Linden, 1996: 12).

'Breaking the conspiracy of silence'

Israel and the Daughters of the Shoah uses personal narratives and a feminist re-reading of Zionist/Israeli discourses to ask whether, in the context of the gendered construction of nation, we can speak about a 'masculinisation' of Israel and, conversely, a resultant 'feminisation' of the Shoah and Shoah survivors. The process began with my 'theory' of the gendered relationship between Israel and the Shoah. The next stage was to conduct qualitative open-ended interviews with nine Israeli daughters of Shoah survivors who are writers and film-makers. Their ensuing auto/biographical personal narratives largely confirmed my 'theory'. However, gender was not uppermost in their minds; they were more concerned with being daughters of Shoah survivors in Israeli society. Therefore, another methodological strategy was brought in. A critical feminist re-reading of Zionist and Israeli discourses, official and unofficial, confirmed, at a different discursive level, my theory of the masculinisation of Israel versus the feminisation of the Shoah and its survivors, and further contributed to breaking the silences surrounding the encounter between Israel and Shoah survivors.

Structurally, because it is data-driven, the book begins with a presentation of the narratives (chapters 2 and 3). I use two narrative presentation strategies: chapter 2 presents Nava Semel's narrative in its entirety. I have chosen Semel's narrative not as an 'ideal type' but rather as a 'key story' to the interpretation of the other stories. The trajectory it presents, from being a silenced child of Shoah survivors, stigmatised in the new state of Israel, and at the same time a member of the first Israeli generation, to being a writer who is re-interpreting the puzzle of her Shoah daughterhood, resonated most with my own trajectory.

I have chosen, with the narrators' full permission, not to mask their identities. Social scientists often define anonymity and confidentiality as ethical issues employed in order to protect research subjects and guide researchers' conduct. Anonymity often masks cultural constructions of privacy and power, and negotiating the terms of inscription with our narrators can introduce 'an unprecedented level of accountability into ethnographic writing' (Linden, 1993: 111). The narrators, all of whom are prominent writers or film-makers, gave me permission to use their names, and I have chosen to present the nine narratives, in chapter 3, as a combined text, thematically divided for meanings, rather than treat them as individual narratives, precisely because the narratives present a 'collective story' (Richardson, 1990), in that their accounts examine the construction of a female subjectivity through their interaction with Israeli society and Israeli historiography of the Shoah. In their work they challenge the cultural dichotomous stereotypes of Israelis versus Shoah survivors, and offer an alternative 'counter' narrative.

The main themes presented by the narratives are narrators' experiences of the silencing of Shoah experiences in their families and in Israeli society; their construction as gendered players in the Shoah commemoration trajectory, which stressed acts of resistance above passive victimhoood; the differences between the ways their mothers and their fathers communicated their Shoah experiences; the stigmatisation of their parents and their own stigmatisation in Israeli society; the narrators' own 'otherness' as writers or film-makers and the mixed critical reaction to their work; and the reasons why they chose to put their stories on Israel's cognitive map and thus 'break the conspiracy of silence'.

As narratives are meaning-making structures, they must be preserved, not fractured, by investigators, who 'must respect respondents' ways of constructing meaning and analyse how it is accomplished' (Riessman, 1993: 4–5). This is not as simple as it sounds, and ethnographers are often tempted to conflate narrators' words with their own interpretations, by either effacing their own subjectivities, or by concealing the circumstances of text production under a 'scientific' mantle. Employing a dialogic approach, I have opted to include 'verbatim materials ... sufficient to allow the reader some direct participation' (Myerhoff, 1980: 31). I have, however, 'heavily edited and selected, inevitably' those verbatim materials, assuming a stance of authority, although there is also dialogism at work, in that all parties involved – writer, reader and informant – participate in the text (Kaminsky, 1992: 7). Ethnography, undoubtedly a text, is also a fiction, to the extent of its production by a social scientist who is also a fiction writer, or as Stanley (1992) suggests, a 'fabrication'. Because the point of view of the researcher and the researched do not always coincide, I have used several text presentation styles: the narrators speaking in the first person, the text producer speaking in the third person about the narrators, and both speaking in the recorded conversation sections. I have translated the narrative text from the Hebrew, my (and most of the narrators') mother tongue, in which I prefer to 'speak of intimate things' (Spivak, 1992: 187). While unable to translate literally, I have attempted to retain the flavour of the Hebrew language, trying to retain the narrators' sentence structure wherever possible.

In the remainder of the volume I use a variety of other strategies to theorise silence and the dichotomous relation between the 'masculinisation' of Israel and the ensuing feminisation of the Shoah. In particular, I ground the masculinisation thesis in Zionist and early nation-building texts (e.g., Herzl, 1896; Nordau, 1955 [1909]; Bialik, 1960 [1902]; Ya'ari, 1947 [1918]; Lamdan, 1927) and seek 'theoretical' confirmation in theorists such as Goffman (1968) and Bauman (1991) as well as theorists of masculinity such as Boyarin (1997a; 1997b; 1997c), Gluzman (1997) and Mosse (1996). However, because the narratives are my main data, the themes I explore in chapters 4, 5 and 6 have been suggested to me by the narratives and are grounded in and inspired by the narratives.

Chapter 4 analyses the history of Shoah commemoration and 'memorisation' and links its various stages to my own auto/biography. The trajectory begins with contempt for the survivors for their alleged passivity and my own inability to listen to my relatives' stories as a child and young person. At the age of forty I travelled to Romania to research those very stories which ended up in my novel *Night Train to Mother* (Lentin, 1989, 1990), an account of the 'intimate memory' which the Israeli Shoah commemoration machinery did not privilege until quite recently.

Chapter 5 discusses the pathologisation of the survivors and of the 'second-generation' in the literature and in Israeli society and criticises the tendency to silence survivors' accounts as part of a uniformity self-imposed upon Israeli society which negated the diaspora and mobilised the Shoah to the Zionist cause.

Chapter 6 posits a theoretical construction of the feminisation and fem(m)inisation (with double m, after Boyarin 1997a; 1997b, in the sense of the *femme* in the femme-butch pair) of stigma in the relationship between Israel and the Shoah. Because the stigmatisation of the survivors, and of their children, was a central theme brought up by all the narrators, I draw on Goffman's theory of stigma as an instrument used by 'normal' society for social grading, defining itself in turn (Goffman, 1968), and on Bauman's argument that stigma is a convenient weapon in the defence against the unwelcome ambiguity of strangers, the 'ambivalent third' in the 'friends' versus 'enemies' binary opposition (Bauman, 1991). I argue that Israeli society, privileging militarism and discourses of 'national security', premised on a dominance-oriented masculine structure (Connell, 1994: 158), constructed itself as 'friend' in opposition to the Palestinian 'enemy'. Negating the Jewish exile, Israel stigmatised Shoah survivors, necessarily cast as ambivalent strangers who did not conform to the stereotypically active, fighting, masculine 'new Hebrew' norm, reintroducing instead 'old' Jewish values which threatened that new norm. The 'new Hebrew' hegemonic masculinity used nation-imagining discourses to silence and stigmatise Shoah survivors, thus contributing to its own dominance and to the survivors' subordinate position. The Zionist reconstruction of the 'new Hebrews' in opposition to diasporic Jewry also resulted, as argued by Ben Dor and Kaplanski (1988), Segev (1991), and Yablonka (1994), in discriminating against them when they first arrived.

The more complex argument of the fem(m)inisation of that stigma derives from the internalisation of the 'masculine' construction of the 'new Hebrews' and the 'emasculation' of diaspora Jews. In constructing what it means to be 'Israeli', Israeli society, anxious about its own fitness for a role of authority, assumed hegemonic masculine norms and adopted a stigmatising classification system of dominance and subordination. This system divided between the masculine 'normals', Israeli-born, or those who could 'pass' as Israeli-born, and the feminine stigmatised, newly arrived survivors (and, later, Jewish immigrants from Arab countries).[11] To illustrate this fem(m)inisation, I analyse the popular text 'My sister on the beach' by the *Palmach* pre-state army commander Yitzhak Sadeh (1945). A story of an encounter between a young female survivor and a group of pre-state soldiers, Sadeh's account signifies the new Hebrews' deep terror of diaspora Jewry. According to Zertal (1996a: 490–6), who employs Freud's *Unheimlich* thesis, the diaspora returned to haunt the Erez Israeli masculinity not because of its unfamiliarity, but as its repressed, unconscious, feminine 'other'.

Counter-narratives: auto/biography as an act of reckoning

Israel and the Daughters of the Shoah appears to be the first sociological attempt to link the 'masculinisation' of the 'new Hebrews' with diaspora-negation and the stigmatisation and feminisation of Shoah survivors. Working auto/biographically with personal narratives of daughters of Israeli Shoah survivors (and thus closing the 'memory gap' between ontology and representation), as well as re-reading Zionist discourses from a feminist perspective, I am better able to make sense of the history of contemporary Israel and its relationship with the Shoah, as discussed in chapter 6. If the construction of the mas-

culine 'new Hebrew' subjectivity discursively stigmatised the survivors
and feminised the Shoah, the writings of the narrators may indicate a
shift of emphasis towards greater complexity and inclusiveness in the
parameters of Israeli 'normality'. According to Bauman (1991)
ambivalence is the only option for modernity; narrator Karmit Gai
argues that the present stage is characterised by Israelis realising that
'otherness' is a universal Israeli condition 'because, after all, no one fitted the mould'.

It has taken Israel forty years to begin the act of reckoning its complex relationship with the Shoah, in relation not only to the huge loss,
but also to the uses made of the Shoah in nation-building and in justifying the ongoing conflict and occupation. Likewise, it has taken many
individual Shoah survivors forty years – a generation – to be able to
begin to speak of their experiences. The narrators began writing their
'daughters of survivors' accounts in the mid-1980s, forty years after
the end of the War. Their books and films are auto/biographical enter-
prises as much as this book is my own auto/biographical project. They
are also acts of reckoning which, like all auto/biograpical projects, re-
interpret the past, but in important ways, also envision the future.

Emphasising the constantly changing and contested nature of the
boundaries of the nation and its narratives, Homi Bhabha (1994)
posits counter-narratives, emerging from the nation's margins, from
cultural and national hybrids, which slot, albeit none too smoothly,
into the 'inter-national' space of the stranger, between 'enemies' and
'friends'. The accounts by Israeli children, and particularly daughters
of Shoah survivors, which present anti-heroic antagonists to the
heroic Zionist narration of nation, are such counter-narratives, as
argued in chapter 7. Despite the hurt, despite the stigmatisation and
the silencing, daughter-writers speak of their deep need to write, and
deal, even unconsciously, with the presence of the Shoah in their lives.
The creative works by children of survivors have been described by
narrators as 'breaking the conspiracy of silence'. Nava Semel borrows
Shoah imagery when she likens the compulsion to turn her mother's
experiences into stories to 'forced labour' (Semel, 1986: 44).

The real work of mourning the Shoah has not yet seriously begun
in Israeli society, despite the proliferation of public memorials, ceremonies and publications. I do not wish to argue, simplistically, that
only women are able to mourn the Shoah without drawing nationalist lessons from the annihilation of Europe's Jews. But I do argue that
through the auto/biographical accounts of my narrators' post-Shoah
experiences, I am able to sustain an argument on the gendered relationship between Israel and the Shoah. My own auto/biographical
project, of research and of writing fiction about the experience of
being a daughter of a family of Shoah survivors, has enabled me not

only to make my self while telling my story, but also to mourn, by engaging in the auto/biographical act of reckoning.

As Stanley (1993) puts it, the process of 'reckoning', or 'accounting', that auto/biographies constitute, is an important means of making real and present what we all know is memory and past. Perhaps the writing, by the narrators and by me, is the consequence of the shifting boundaries of silence about the Shoah, not the cause. However, I have little doubt that the narrators' works have been instrumental counter-narratives in re-occupying some territories of silence in relation to the legacy of the Shoah in Israeli society, and therefore in beginning the long process of reckoning and mourning.

Notes

1. Lea Aini has drawn my attention (personal communication, March 2000) that she has progressed away from the anger and despair of her 1992 interview with me. I am certain that other narrators have also moved on, as has Israeli society, although I believe my views as expressed in this volume are still valid, as I hope the narrators would broadly agree.
2. My use of the term 'ontology' in this book draws on Stanley and Wise, who define 'feminist ontology' as the theory of 'reality' or being, which rejects Cartesian binary ways of understanding the relationship between the body, the mind and emotions (Stanley and Wise, 1993: 194–5).
3. Erez Israel, literally 'the land of Israel', refers to the pre-state entity in Palestine, governed, between 1919 and 1948, by the British, under a special mandate.
4. I do not italicise the word Shoah, as I do other Hebrew words. When citing other works I have left the term 'Holocaust'.
5. Dr Rudolf Israel Kästner, the Hungarian Jewish leader, managed, through negotiations with the Nazis, to rescue 1,685 Jews who went on a train to Switzerland. This operation was the subject of a trial in 1954 (see chapter 4). For a discussion of Kästner's changing image as a testimony to the changing image of the Shoah, see Ofer, 1993 and Weitz, 1993.
6. I follow Helen Fein in using the term 'antisemitism' rather than 'anti-Semitism'. This, according to Fein, implies more than dropping the hyphen; it means taking antisemitism seriously as a thesis without an antithesis, for there is no 'Semitism' (Fein, 1987: ix)
7. There are also many historical studies of the relations between the pre-state Erez Israeli *Yishuv* leadership and the Shoah, e.g., Bet Zvi, 1977; Porat, 1986; Shapira, 1992; Eshkoli, 1994; Weitz, 1994; Zertal, 1996a,; Grodzinski, 1998.
8. Shoah denial plays a role in every organisation and periodical which is overtly or covertly antisemitic and is often used to mask antisemitism. While French and German laws against Shoah denial have some effect, deniers find other means. Thus Ernst Zundel in Canada, against whom legal means were employed to end his Shoah-denial activities, has turned Canada into a major centre for denial material. Using books, newsletters, videotapes, cable and public access television and the internet, his material appears in fifteen languages in forty countries. However, an American-Jewish Committee-funded survey in the US, Germany, Australia and Poland, found that denial has little impact on mainstream opinion and remains the preserve of hardened antisemites (*Antisemitism*

World Report, 1995: xix). For a comprehensive survey of Shoah denial see Lipstadt, 1993.

9. Some notable examples of studies written by male historians and making no gender connections are Arad et al., 1981; Bauer, 1982; Gilbert, 1985; Gutman, 1990; to name but a few. Lucy Dawidowicz's study (1975) also makes no gender links. However, there have been several studies of women in the Shoah, e.g., Rittner and Roth, 1993; Ofer and Weitzman, 1998; Lagerwey, 1998; Fuchs, 1999; Baumel, 1999a, 1999b.

10. The importance of the 'right', that is *Sabra* Hebrew accent, is developed in chapter 6. See also Almog, 1998.

11. Gluzman, 1997, discusses the parallel between women and Palestinians in early Zionist writings.

CHAPTER 2

'WRITING IS THE CLOSING OF CIRCLES'

Introduction

I met Nava Semel on 25 November, 1992 in the apartment she shares with her husband Noam Semel, director of the Tel Aviv Cameri Theatre, and their three children, Iyar and twins Eal-Eal and Nimdor. Semel was born in 1954 in Tel Aviv. Her father, Itzhak Artzi, a former Knesset member and deputy mayor of Tel Aviv, was born in Bukovina and is not a concentration camp survivor. Her mother, Margalit (Mimi) Artzi (nee Liquornik), also born in Bukovina, is a survivor of several concentration camps, including Auschwitz and Kleineshenau. The twins, born in the United States while Noam Semel served with the Israeli consulate in New York, have U.S. passports. 'This too is part of my being a daughter of survivors', Semel explained, 'at least when the helicopters come to rescue the survivors here, they would be saved'. Semel's brother, Shlomo Artzi, is a leading Israeli popular singer. Semel is small, short-haired, and very intense. Her use of the Hebrew language is very precise. She had obviously done a lot of thinking about being a daughter of Shoah survivors and has written both fiction and journalism on the subject.

Nava Semel describes her childhood as an 'ordinary Israeli childhood'. She served in the army as a news producer with *Galei Tsahal*, the army radio channel. She began writing when she had her first child. Her collection of short stories, the first 'second-generation' fiction collection published in Israel, *Kova Zekhukhit* ('A Hat of Glass') (1985), met with a wall of silence when it first appeared, but has since been written about extensively. The collection was re-issued in 1998 with an introduction by the literary critic Nurit Govrin. Several stories have been translated into English, German, Spanish, Turkish and French and translations appeared in Germany and Italy in 2000.

In all of the stories there is a 'child of' persona and they are all based on the various stages of learning about and coming to terms with her parents' survival, as Semel explains in the following narrative. Indeed, in all of her books, the reality is often viewed from a child's viewpoint.

Her one-woman play *Hayeled meAchorei Haeinayim (The Child Behind the Eyes)* (1987), a monologue of a mother of a Down's Syndrome child, had many showings in Israel and abroad and several radio broadcasts internationally. In 1996 it won the Austrian radio play of the year award. Her two novels for young people, *Gershona Shona (Becoming Gershona)* (1988/1990), and *Maurice Havivel Melamed Lauf (Flying Lessons)* (1991/1995)[1] deal with young people living among Shoah survivors in search of an Israeli identity. Both were translated into English. In 1996 *Flying Lessons* was selected in Germany as one of the thirty best books of the year. The novel *Rali Masa Matara ('Night Games')* (1993) is the story of a group of Israeli forty-something friends playing a treasure hunt on the 1987 Day of Independence, half a year before the *Intifada* broke out. The novel *Isha al Neyar ('Bride on Paper')* (1996) tells of life in a pre-state Israeli moshava (collective settlement) in the 1930s. Semel also translates plays, mostly on Shoah-related themes.

In 1996 Semel won the Prime Minister's Award, a twelve-month writing scholarship. In 1999 she collaborated with her father in writing his biography (Artzi and Semel, 1999), documenting the story of a young Zionist journeying from Europe to Israel, as well as writing the script for a documentary film on Transnistria, based on her journey to Southern Ukraine in 1998 (Simionovics, 1999). The film was screened by Israel Education Television in 1999.

After our initial meeting, which proved seminal to writing this book, Semel and I remained in close contact. I have chosen to present her entire narrative not as an 'ideal type', but because it seems to be the 'key story' to the interpretation of the other narratives. The narrative encompasses most of the elements highlighted by the other narrators and theorised in later chapters. These include breaking the silence surrounding the Shoah and Shoah survivors, the confrontation between the Jewish Shoah and Israel's 'new Hebrews', ceremonial memory versus intimate memory and the 'masculinised' Israeli 'normality' versus the stigmatisation of Shoah survivors. Moreover, perhaps because my parents, like her parents, came from Bukovina, the trajectory Semel's narrative presents, her 'thematic field', from the split subjectivity of being a silenced child of survivors, stigmatised in the new state of Israel, and a member of (our) first *Sabra* generation, to being a writer who is re-interpreting the puzzle of Shoah daughter-hood, resonates most with my own trajectory.

Semel has been central to my work, not in the sense of being a 'key informant', nor in the sense of being a 'co-author', but our collaboration raises important issues about voice and authorship. Like the other narrators, Semel has been engaged in 'researching' the meaning of being a daughter of Shoah survivors in Israeli society, and, like the other narrators, she is a 'woman of voice', who has broken the silence about the Shoah in her own family and in Israeli society by writing herself onto Israel's cognitive map. The feminist strategy of 'giving voice' to voiceless people might seem superfluous, if it were not for Semel's and the other narrators' recurring stories about silence. While this book is based on their narratives, 'it is the researcher who narrates, who "authors" the ethnography' (Stacey, 1991: 23). The question of authority and authorship is particularly thorny when researchers insist on a collaboration process with their informants, but ultimately produce the research text themselves, no matter how modified or influenced by the narrators. My work with Nava Semel and the other narrators was dialogic, yet the question of 'giving voice' remains open. Dialogue as a research strategy employs Myerhoff's notion (1992) of the 'third voice', born by the virtue of the collusion between researcher – a sociological narrator, embodied, situated and ultimately responsible for her own words, her own 'multiple selves' – and narrators.

Although (mostly in reply to my questioning) Semel does deal with the gender element of Israeli Shoah metaphors and commemoration, gender is not her prime concern. Her narrative does, however, serve to illustrate the extent to which both the Shoah and Israel are gendered constructs. Furthermore, Semel's viewpoint is continuously gendered: she refers to herself first as daughter, then as mother and wife. The stages of self-identification as the daughter of a Shoah survivor and the parallel process of writing her first collection of short stories, are closely linked with stereotypical gender roles. She first hears of her mother's experience in the kitchen, while her mother is ironing: mothers and daughters seem to communicate in a special way in kitchens. The second time is when she brings a boyfriend home, another gendered rite of passage. Semel describes them as 'guests' in her mother's living room, where refreshments are being served and the mother's Shoah experience is offered to her daughter, through the boyfriend. She first begins to write when she has a baby and is 'isolated', in a 'bubble' with her new baby, while her husband is busy with a new job. Her writing begins in parallel to the experience of young motherhood and continues in parallel with older, more experienced motherhood, when it is no longer 'in a bubble', but part of a routine which includes taking and collecting her young twins from kindergarten and later school, feeding them, worrying about her adolescent, and later soldier, son and so on. In imparting her narrative, Semel makes the construction of her gender identity transparent. Theorising it, she positions the masculine state vis-à-vis the individual self, although she seems to 'buy into' accepted discursive norms when she rejects my suggestion that fighting women models are essentially masculine models, offering instead a 'unisex' fighter-model.

Semel's narrative is clearly organised and channels to one central thematic field, which occupies the final part of the narrative, the trajectory from (a) what Semel describes as 'the position of the rejected', the embodiment of the offspring of the diaspora Jew, the survivor, the 'lamb to the slaughter'; to (b) learning 'to live in peace with what there is'. In other words, a trajectory from being a silenced child of survivors, living with the secret world of the 'code word Auschwitz', in an Israel which internalised, yet repressed, the memory of the Shoah, to an adult writer who is using her writing as the 'closing of circles'.

The process of using her writing as a means of coming to terms with her 'daughterhood' begins with writing compulsively, in order to confront the 'black hole', the 'code word', and to break the silence and close the circle. Only years after 'A Hat of Glass', can the daughter-writer write less densely, less compulsively, her writing more integrated into her daily life. The Shoah, however, keeps occupying centre stage even when the writer believes she has written it out of her system. But it is now more casually mentioned, seeping into the plots almost unnoticeably.

Parallel to the narrative about writing, is the narrative about self-discovery, a growth narrative beginning with the story of a girl with eating problems, who sees herself as a victim, and developing into the story of a woman, a mother, who learns to accept and 'live peacefully with what there is', using her writing as an indispensable aid in this growth process.

The narrative presented here is broken into five main sections. The sectioning was self-evident, since Semel ordered her narrative expertly, both chronologically and thematically. All I did was add sub-headings.

The first section, 'An ordinary Israeli childhood', is Semel's own presentation of her biography. It begins with an assumption of ordinariness, but what is described as 'an ordinary Israeli childhood' transpires to be 'normal' only in the sense of a counter-narrative to the hegemonic masculine Israeli 'normality' to be described in chapter 6. It is, in fact, the exact opposite of that 'normality' and demonstrates that no Israeli actually fitted the hegemonic mould. Very soon after the beginning of Semel's narrative, we are clearly into secrets, silences, 'black holes', 'code words'; everything that is not a 'born in Israel' normality, if such a thing exists.

The second section, 'Writing', deals with the parallel processes of 'writing stories' and 'making selves': the processes involve Semel's self-discovery and identification as a daughter of Shoah survivors through discovering her mother's Shoah survival 'stories', and at the same time making these stories her own by formally writing them as 'short stories'. This section demonstrates how the process of self-discovery is also the process of distillation and creation.

The third section, 'Ceremonial versus intimate memory', building on topics highlighted through the narrative-about-narratives (stories), deals with the juxtaposition of ceremonial versus intimate Shoah memory. Here too, the personal weaves in with the public, culminating in the account of the negative critical reception for 'A Hat of Glass' by an Israel which, in 1985, was not yet ready to confront the Shoah.

In the fourth section, 'The process of repression', which begins with an attempt to generalise from the previous section, Semel focuses on the intimate and personal, and discusses childhood secrets and their implications. Here, again, the painfully personal touches upon the core issues of the contradictions between the conceptual Israel and the conceptual Shoah.

The final section, 'Writing is the closing of circles', returns to the process of writing and completes the central argument that only through writing was Semel able to complete the trajectory and face the shame and guilt involved in being a daughter of survivors in contemporary Israel, and, using the bricks of her life, to close the circles.

The narrative is produced through the interaction between Semel and myself. Throughout the narrative she addresses me and asks me for confirmation: 'do you understand?' 'do you remember?' 'think of a home in the 1950s, 'it's part of what you called at the beginning of our conversation ... the Israeli historiography', 'do you know how it feels?' The direct reference to me is sharpest when Semel refers to a character in a book as coming from Gura Humora, my father's birthplace. Or when she speaks of her triumph in allowing her children not to eat when they do not feel like it, and throwing food out. We share the same psychic 'data bank' relating to memory and to food, and she does not have to elaborate in order for me to understand exactly what she is talking about; our identification is symbiotic.

Life stories are indeed not finished products ready to be 'served up' on demand, but evolve around a thematic topic, usually established by the interviewer, in a manner judged by the narrator to be of interest to the listener (Rosenthal, 1993: 65). Although I tried to keep the conversation as open-ended as possible, my theoretical focus, that of juxtaposing Israel and the Shoah as gendered, did influence the narratives. Throughout our conversation I commented on what Semel said in order to assist her in explicating or 'evaluating'. Narrators say in evaluation clauses ('the soul of the narrative') how they want to be understood (Labov, 1972; 1982; Riessman, 1993: 20). Semel's narrative is framed by my comments. I have cut the narrative according to Semel's requests; she saw the final version and approved. By leaving large sequences of the narrative undisturbed, I aim to allow Semel to speak for herself.

An ordinary Israeli childhood

'Good and well -educated children'

I was born in 1954, in Israel, in a *ma'abara* [transit camp] near Tel Aviv. My parents came from Bukovina, a region that was Austro-Hungary until World War I and then became Romania [...] Hebrew was spoken at home.[2] I am a second child, my brother was born five years before me. I had an ordinary Israeli childhood with all the usual stops, primary school, secondary school, a north Tel Aviv childhood, the struggle of a family for, let us say, economic independence, or for a reasonable economic ceiling where one could bring up a child. No special deprivation.

My father worked at what is called *askanut* [activism], or politics, he was a politician and then the boundaries changed. Through the years, he worked in the Jewish Agency, did a little press work, then party political work and finally, became a member of the Knesset and was deputy mayor of Tel Aviv for twenty years. A very large chunk of his life was devoted to dealing with issues of *Aliya* [Jewish immigration to Israel], and with new immigrants. In recent years he has been working at assisting Shoah survivors. He established a foundation, named after him, which assists elderly survivors with geriatric problems. He is also a member of an international claims conference for the refund of Jewish property.

My mother had a clerical job, I suppose, in the National Lottery. She never made a career for herself.

I wrote from the moment I remember myself. Even before I could write, I wrote stories in my head. I wanted to be a writer ... from the moment, I suppose, of my very beginning. The question was actualisation and publication. I dared come out with it only after my first son was born. Then I started to publish. Essentially, I think I could take responsibility for the writing only once I learned to take responsibility for a child.

This is a biography, I think, which is very typical of those born in the 1950s in Israel. With the regular stops. I forgot, of course, the army, in this case *Galei Tsahal* [the IDF radio station], which is also north Tel Aviv, good and well educated children. Good and well educated children, from 'a good home'.

There are many references here to a middle-class, urban ('north Tel Aviv' has connotations of the 'better' side of Tel Aviv) upbringing. The term 'good and well-educated children' denotes the Ashkenazi, urban, middle-class background I share with Semel (although I was born in Haifa). The fact that our parents come from the same place offered a common ground which necessitated minimal explanations. A lot of

Israeli history is enfolded in this biographical introduction: a middle-European origin; the early struggle of a newly arrived family; her father's pre-state and state political activism (in the liberal General Zionist Party, the Independent Liberal Party and and later in the Labour Party); the gender division between a publicly involved father and a private mother, who had a 'little job', not a career; schooling; army service. Semel does not mention her university education, but she does mention motherhood, which she later describes as a trigger to writing. The key word 'trigger' appears several times throughout the narrative, always spoken in English, or Anglicised Hebrew (*triggerim*). The narrative is strewn with images of weaponry, perhaps due to the consciousness of war and defence, which surrounded us as young Israelis, perhaps relating to the Shoah.

' I belong to the category of silent families'

NS

Essentially, I belong to the category of silent families. The basic fact was known, and I don't know how it was known, but it was the fact that my mother survived Auschwitz. Details, there was never any verbal, direct mention of the experience of the Shoah. It was a sort of knowledge, a basic knowledge, you can say. An infallible axiom at home ...

RL

What age were you when they spoke about it, I mean when they mentioned it for the first time?

NS

I don't remember that they mentioned it at all. I remember a real mention only on the day they caught Eichmann.[3] I remember what I call non-verbal transmission, the physical sight of my mother listening to the radio at six, at twilight, when Ben Gurion announced in the Knesset that Eichmann had been caught. And my mother standing by the radio and physically shaking. I remember myself pulling at her dress and asking who this man was and she said only the name, Eichmann, I don't remember anybody explaining to me who he was. Because the man who owned the grocery store, at the end of our street, Brandeis Street, was called Astman and I used to, they used to send me to buy half a loaf of bread, which I used to bite at on the way home. I was afraid for a very long time to go to the grocery store and buy bread, because I thought that the man who owned the grocery store was a criminal. By the way, this man and his wife were Shoah survivors.

This is one reference I remember. The second reference I remember, specifically, was when I brought home from the school library Katzetnik's *Bet Habubot* (House of Dolls) [1953].[4] I chose the book because of the title, I thought it was a children's book. And when I brought the book home, my mother saw it and, I can remember it to this day, it was wrapped, do you remember those brown paper wraps which they used to wrap library books in? And she didn't let me read the book. She closed it, she closed it with a bang, returned it to my satchel and said, tomorrow you are returning this book to school and you will not read it. And this is why I did not read Katzetnik until I was 26.

Apart from these references, there were, so to say, 'seeping' exchanges of information, or transmission of non-verbal information, through body language and through crises and catastrophes that always, in some way, were compared [...] And then there was the word 'Auschwitz'. The word 'Auschwitz', in my childhood, was identified with sleeping pills at night, with black clothes, with terror, and with something very terrifying, which I didn't want to know exactly.

'Heroic Shoah biography' versus 'lamb to the slaughter'

As for my father's biography, he brings what I call a 'heroic Shoah biography'. Because he was in the underground, he was a member of the 'Zionist Youth' and he was active during the Shoah. He forged passports, changed identities and later travelled to Transnistria, as part of the operation to save the orphans. He did relate directly to his past, heroically, of course.

I think that at a certain age, I am not quite clear when, a very clear identity was created for me, I think, after they started to show at school – television did not exist then – after they started to show visual pictures of what they called in the Israeli ethos 'lamb to the slaughter', the lines of naked people opposite the gas chambers. Clearly, very manipulatively, in my head, I added two and two and made the right connection and identified my mother with these people. And this created a far sharper and stronger block so as not to confront the subject, a block between me and the subject.

One of the most absurd things, in retrospect, is the fact that I participated, like all good girls from good homes, in the ritual ceremonies of *Yom HaShoah* at school. But I never, never imagined that I should have gone home, on that very day, and asked my mother directly, because she had been there. I mean there was a complete dissociation. I think that in this respect I am representative of a whole generation for whom there was a dissociation relating to the ritualism, which undoubtedly was also based on heroic rituals in these years of shaping the Israeli psyche. In those days *Yom HaShoah* was more the 'Heroism and Shoah day' than the other way round. And the Anielewicz[5] myths were fortified. And it was undoubtedly very hard for me to identify my mother with the Anielewicz myth. Because I think that I had already fixated the image of those going to their death 'like lambs to the slaughter'. And those people about whom this phrase 'lamb to the slaughter' was said were spoken of with a considerable measure of contempt, by contrast with that Anielewicz heroism.

RL
So at home you had both, the Shoah and the heroism?

NS
Yes. Although in relation to my father's heroism, it's hard to say he
actually took arms; but his heroism could be talked about, he was able
to relate to his past. My mother, on the other hand, had a black hole in
her biography. If she spoke about her childhood, she referred to it up to
the age of eighteen, and if she spoke about her adult life, she returned to
it at the age of twenty-three. That means that five years were missing,
but I never gave it a thought until I became an adult myself and understood that a part was missing in this chain.

Semel summarises the two main Israeli 'narratives' which co-exist to
this day in relation to the Shoah. On the one hand there is the story of the
Jewish victims who are seen as having gone to their deaths passively, and
who have therefore not been given pride of place in the mythologised
memory of the Shoah. On the other hand there is the story of 'heroic rituals'. Chapter 4 discusses the tensions between these two representations.
In relation to the heroic myths, Semel refers to Mordechai Anielewicz, the
leader of the Warsaw ghetto uprising, who has become the symbol of
armed resistance during the Shoah. She juxtaposes the 'Anielewicz myth'
with the victims and with her own self-image as a would-be victim.

Semel argues that although the heroic myths were constructed by
'the state', she is a 'representative of a whole generation for whom there
is a dissociation relating to the ritualism'. It seems to me that she is also
referring to another form of dissociation, that of a victim dissociating
herself from trauma. In her work with victims of sexual abuse, Annie
Rogers identifies two forms of oppression: cultural denials and lies, leading to repression, and physical and sexual abuse, leading to dissociation.
The cultural denials and lies relating to the Shoah may have led to a
process of repression, which Semel refers to later. According to Rogers,
memories that have been dissociated are recalled with greater difficulty
than memories that have been repressed, leaving gaps in narrative, frag-
ments of a memory sequence. Roger concludes from listening to sexually abused girls and women and from her own history of abuse that
'dissociation is a brilliantly creative solution to living through trauma
and coming to terms with traumatic memories' (Rogers, 1994: 6).

Semel's mother's voice, silenced until she was able to tell her daughter the story of the 'black hole in her biography', may represent such
dissociation. The voices of Rogers' interviewees are disruptive and full
of gaps, and require careful listening by a psychotherapist. Semel was
able to be a careful listener to her mother's life story, and she pieced
together bravely her mother's story in order to weave her own. She
knows, however, that her mother's story is fragmented and full of
gaps, as she says later: 'there were of course many patches ... to this
day I have unclear sections ... the chronicle I would write would be
partial, subjective, with unbridgeable gaps ... '.

This section of the narrative also exemplifies the gender break between fathers speaking and mothers remaining silent in relation to the Shoah. Chapter 3 refers to the differences between survivor fathers and survivor mothers in relation to this study's narrators.

Mother – 'Someone with a life, with an incredible drama'

RL
Was there ever a time when you asked her, at a later age?

NS
One day she volunteered to tell. It was the first time in my life that she volunteered to tell and there were two triggers. One was an event in my private life, and in her biography ... She chastised me gently and I burst out, saying she didn't know anything about real life ... She was ironing and she put down the iron, burning the garment and, shooting from the hip, she simply threw at me her whole biography, about which I knew nothing. And I simply stood, I remember my mouth, not being able to say one word, I was simply paralysed between my nose and my chin. I simply didn't know what to say. This was the first time it descended on me.

The second time was in the presence of a third party. In my last year at school I had a boyfriend, a soldier. And on *Yom HaShoah* he came home from the army, in uniform, and somehow she sat us both in the living room at home, like guests. It was very amazing, she served us coffee, and started speaking about having been in Auschwitz, in an extermination camp. She spoke to me through him. He, by the way, came from a family who were seven generations Israelis, people who had founded Israeli industry, so that he did not have so-called personal connection [to the Shoah]. And he listened very carefully and asked her questions tactfully, with interest. And I felt she was speaking to me, above his head. This was the first time she spoke directly about the Shoah.

When the other incident happened, at which I discovered she had a whole life about which I knew nothing in those five years. I remember I rang my brother, I couldn't stop myself. And I told him, at first as a curiosity, with wonderment that my mother had a life, that beyond the maternal, beyond what I call 'the banana and the sweater, hides someone with a life, with an incredible drama. My brother was incredulous for many years.

This is something which I have met as a result of writing 'A Hat of Glass' [Semel, 1985] and later when I collected reactions; many children of Shoah survivors told me that when they discovered the real story, their first reaction was disbelief. How could it have happened – you jumped from trains? *You* jumped? My mother told me, amongst other things, later, when things sort of came out, that she escaped at least twice from that notorious left side to which she had been sent by Mengele. She managed to escape to the right. It seemed so illogical. I do not doubt the truth of her story, and I know illogical things *did* happen. But it's hard to believe that my mother, whom I perceived as so passive, so conventional, was able to do such an active thing. This, by the way, was a question I eventually put to her, and I asked her how. How was it possible to do such a thing. And she claimed that logic doesn't work in such moments and that she doesn't have a clue as to why she did what she did. The dramatic events she detailed were her two escapes from the left side, and one jump from a moving train when she was transferred from one camp to another after Auschwitz.

Another action was after liberation, when she and another survivor entered German houses, in Zitau, the site of her last camp from which she was liberated by the Russians, looking for food, shoes and clothes, because they were liberated with only a shift and it was May and still quite cold, and her encounter with a Russian officer. And because she knew one word in Russian *Jidovka* [Jewess],[6] and because he was Jewish, he started talking to her in Yiddish, she was the first Jew he met after liberation. And he took her under his wing and returned her to her parents' house in a military train, within four days after liberation, her parents had already returned from Transnistria. She was liberated from East Germany, Transnistria had been liberated several months earlier ...

This action, travelling with a strange Red Army Soviet officer, on an arms train, he locked her in for four days telling her not to open the door to anyone but him, because all the other soldiers were potential rapists, soldiers who had been to Stalingrad and had not seen a woman. He locked her in and brought her food. She cannot even remember his name. All these active and dramatic stories ... It was difficult for me to equate these things with her present persona.

The over-protectiveness of Shoah survivor parents is documented in the psychological literature and many children of survivors speak about it. The 'banana and sweater' syndrome is, however, familiar to many Israeli children of Semel's and my generation. It is based on the stereotypical Israeli-Jewish mother who chases her child with a sweater (in case it gets cold) and a banana, which she must eat, to grow up and be strong (and become the antithesis of the stereotypical weak diaspora Jew). In the same token 'passive', 'conventional' survivor parents were constructed as weak and 'Jewish' – again in contrast to the 'new Hebrew' construct. Therefore any 'heroic' exploits, such as escaping the notorious concentration camp 'selections', or jumping from a moving train, were dissociated from their perceived image as anxious, worried parents.

Writing

Writing Mother's story – 'A Hat of Glass'

Semel describes three stages of becoming acquainted with her mother's story, which are also stages of self-identification as a daugh-

ter of survivors. Each stage gives birth to one or more short stories. The
first stage (and the first short story) was the discovery that her mother
had a 'story'. She first hears her mother's story in her late teens, but
the short story is written only after she has her first child, at the age of
twenty-five. The second stage is facilitated by declaring herself to Jane
Fonda, and the third, by an encounter with Shoah denial in Egypt.
This marks the initial stage of self-discovery and writing, after which
she confronted her mother, who agreed to tell her 'the full story',
resulting in the completion of the collection of stories.

Semel describes the process of writing as a journey of self-discovery
through several encounters which forced her to identify herself openly
as a daughter of survivors and exit the isolation resulting from having
grown up in a 'silent family'. This process of identification has all the
characteristics of 'coming out' ('I am a daughter of a Shoah survivor'),
and is also a process of 'naming', and of breaking the silence and the
isolation: making the self as we make our stories. Ironically, the
process was conducted in the complete isolation of her young motherhood: key words are 'isolated', 'bubble', 'me and the baby'. They return
later in the narrative when she contrasts her past isolation with her
present, more integrated process of working out Shoah materials in
her writing.

> My first book was a book of poetry, which dealt with a dialogue between
> a mother and her unborn child. It was written during my first preg-
> nancy and in the labour ward. It did not relate to anything, apart from
> a very basic thing, a parent-child dialogue. The second book, 'A Hat of
> Glass', I began to write at the age of twenty-five, when I had a baby of
> two or three months old. We moved to Haifa, I was completely isolated,
> isolated from the family, living in a bubble. Without a job. Until then I
> had several nine-to-five jobs. Now I had a partner who was sucked into
> a new job, running Haifa Theatre, and who was rarely at home. So it
> was me and the baby. I started to write short stories, and, after writing
> three skeletons of stories, I realised what I was writing.

The Kapo

> One of them was the story 'A Hat of Glass', which was based on some-
> thing my mother had told me. This was a story she had told me and
> my boyfriend in my last year in school, on that organised *Yom
> HaShoah*. This was a story about a concentration camp, it's the only
> story in the collection which takes place 'there', about the lesbian
> Kapo who saved other inmates, as told through her victim. This was
> the first story. The second story in the collection was 'A Journey to the
> Two Berlins' in which a person sits *Shiv'a*[7] in mourning for his
> mother, and suddenly discovers, after her death, her link to the Shoah
> and to Germany, to someone in Germany who had helped her, or
> saved her, or whatever.

Jane Fonda

The third story was about the journey with Jane Fonda. This, by the way, is authentic, because it actually happened. I really was, by chance, with Jane Fonda in a car and I think it was one of the triggers for the whole book. It happened a few months after we moved to Haifa. Fonda was a guest of the theatre and Noam and I accompanied her from Tel Aviv to Haifa in a Foreign Ministry limousine with a Foreign Ministry official. Fonda interrogated me all the way, she literally pushed me to the corner and for a whole hour asked me questions about the Shoah. She opened by saying that she had a friend in Los Angeles, who was a survivor of Dachau, who, for thirty years had repressed the whole thing, and who, now, when the children had left home, when everything was financially and socially wonderful, suddenly began having nightmares. She stopped sleeping and saw a psychologist and gradually the whole business of Dachau came out. The woman was amazed, because she claimed she hadn't thought of it for thirty years. All her life began to crumble. Fonda asked me if it was possible that people could repress a traumatic thing that happened so many years before. Here the second question was whether a trauma experienced by a parent is significant for a child.

This was a question I would have never asked myself had this wise American woman not pushed me in that car ride. And it was the first time I said, I can remember it physically, 'I am a daughter of a Shoah survivor'.

My identification with her, with my mother, was specific. This conversation made me very uncomfortable, very resistant, very mixed up. I was aggressive, I didn't know what to, I didn't quite understand why we couldn't pass the time speaking of something pleasant, such as films, for instance. By the way, Fonda had just been filming *Julia*, which must have been meaningful for her.

We got out of the car, the conversation came to an end and everything stopped. But the difficult feelings stayed with me for a very long time. When I wrote the story, I reconstructed the conversation. It is a very short story. The shortest in the collection. Only while writing, did I understand what she was talking about, from her own point of view. Because her own mother committed suicide, at home, when she was ten or twelve. The trauma was so strong that she was trying to check with me what was left with me from a parent's trauma and when do these people choose to commit suicide, how come they had the ability to survive, while her mother, who had not experienced the Shoah or anything else which 'justified' a suicide, did it at home, near her children. This must haunt her very much.

Why – these are the things you can never explain – why was I in the car with her, why was she in that particular mood, why did she locate me, of all people, in order to hit me with all these questions, she did not let me off the hook, she extricated the answers from me, she pulled the strings with such power, that for a long time after I left that car, I felt something was torn. Something very basic broke to pieces. This was the third story I wrote.

When I discovered what I had written, when I read the three stories together, I abandoned them immediately, because I understood very well what I had written. I understood that the three stories pulled me as if by magnet to that place, to that forbidden code word, to that forbidden code word 'Auschwitz'.

There is a break in the flow of the narrative here, I stopped it with a question relating to the meaning of the 'code word "Auschwitz"' in Israeli society in general. Semel supplied an evaluation of the alienation meted by Israeli society to the survivors, who all the same immersed themselves in the process of building their new land and rehabilitating their lives (key words and phrases are 'hostile', 'alien', 'no one listening', but also 'life urge', 'fast rehabilitation', 'sucked into the giant vacuum cleaner of building Israel', and 'momentum of doing'). However, my intervention does not keep her away from her own narrative for long. Immediately after contextualising her own narrative in the general explanation, she returns to the third encounter which facilitated her 'coming out'.

RL
Is this connected to the status of the Shoah in Israeli society in general, do you think?

NS
It is not unconnected. I always see the micro as not unconnected to the macro. In my opinion, the Israeli climate was, if not hostile, certainly alien and not aware of how to digest these people who arrived with traumas, and with a lot of guilt on the part of the *Yishuv* [pre-state Jewish settlement] in Erez Israel. Because, it transpires that some of the facts [about the Shoah] did reach [the *Yishuv*] and no one wanted to believe them. Plus the fact that the survivors themselves, because they felt – I am making a simplistic and very quick analysis – because they felt there was no one listening, they closed up and this suited their psychic state of surviving as a result of a life urge and fast rehabilitation. So they chose to deal with the practical aspects of life. I always think that what saved them from such a large collective trauma, which, by the way, they did not even clarify to themselves, was the fact that very quickly they were sucked into the giant vacuum cleaner of building Israel, into the momentum of doing, of practice, of livelihood, of bread, of moving from tents in a transit camp to an apartment in some apartment block and so on. And then they had to send the child to school and have him bring home good grades. Therefore their children saw them as the ultimate, absolute model of parenthood. What I call 'the banana and sweater'. Therefore the disbelief was even greater, because you could not have suspected that behind the parent who is chasing you with a banana and a sweater the whole day and the whole night, could hide such enormous dramas ...

It was almost impossible to link that parental model with a human model. My dialogue with my mother began when I decided she was a human being, not only my mother. And I was going to examine the biography of that human being.

I abandoned the stories for a very long period, almost ten months. But I didn't burn them, or throw them away. I stuck them in some drawer but the drawer had a metaphysical force. I literally battled against it, it had a presence ...

Egypt

Ten months later we went to Egypt. It was after the [1979] peace agreement with Egypt. Noam decided he wanted to produce an Egyptian play and he knew there was a novel by Naghib Mahfouz and he decided to ask him for an adaptation. He decided that as part of the peace process, we would go to Egypt to ask Mahfouz's permission. We went to Alexandria. We knew only in which coffee house Mahfouz used to sit. It was a gamble. We flew to Cairo with Sasson Somech, [8] and went to Alexandria. We found the coffee house and he was there. Sasson said to him 'I have two friends from Israel who would like to meet you' and Mahfouz said 'welcome, *tfadal*'. We entered the coffee house stunned. He welcomed us as if we were his long lost brothers. He signed a contract with Noam within an hour and then he began inviting other people to join us. We spent two days with him, most of the time in the coffee house, that was the intellectual centre during the summer months and many people came to meet the Israelis, it was the first time they met Israelis. It was a two-day non-stop banquet.

At some point a man sat beside me. He was presented to me as an Egyptian-born nuclear physicist, who was living in Heidelberg. At some stage he started talking about the first revisionist studies of the Shoah. This was 1980, remember. This was the time of that French PhD which denied the Shoah. And he said, look, people are writing studies saying that what happened to the Jews in Europe during the War, he did not use the word 'Holocaust', was not accurate. Certainly many people died, because in the camps, and he immediately said, like in Stalin's Gulags, hundreds of people were murdered, and hundreds died of hunger, typhus and dysentery and I have no doubt that at least three million Jews died during the war, just like three million Russians, and two million Hungarians, and God knows what. But I am telling you that there are people who claim, he did not say that this was his opinion, that this whole business of a systematic murder machine, and of crematoria, is, I cannot remember exactly his words, a Jewish exaggeration, or over-reaction.

It was summer. A very hot day. Alexandria is at least as hot as Tel Aviv. I wore a sleeveless dress and I did the following thing [she demonstrates pointing at her arm] and screamed: 'Don't tell me that Jews, that the story of the extermination is the invention of the sick brain of the Jews. I am a daughter of a Shoah survivor and my mother arrived from Auschwitz'. And only when there was complete silence in the coffee house did I realise I was screaming. And I stood like that, with my arm extended, and he apologised immediately. And Naghib Mahfouz was very angry that someone dared insult his guest, you know. And somehow the whole business was smoothed over.

And when we flew to Israel, some two nights later, I opened the
drawer and sat down to write. This was the final trigger. To write it.

When Semel speaks of 'writing it' she refers to her awareness that
she would have to write the collection, understanding where she was
going and what she was doing. More specifically, the Egypt incident
refers to 'The Woman of Fayum', a story about an Israeli antique
dealer who is a son of survivors, who completes his collection of
Roman portraits in an antique shop in Alexandria, where an Armen-
ian rival bidder casts doubts upon the Shoah by talking of the Armen-
ian genocide.

'Opening the code word "Auschwitz" ... someone was asking at last'

Semel's sense of responsibility to her mother is evident throughout
the narrative. In order for her to open the code word, she had to do it
with her mother's knowledge and at the same time protect her from
the implications of 'naming' that code word. The use of metaphors
such as 'hand grenade', 'weapon' and 'blackout' (associated in Israel
with times of war), indicate the sense of danger involved in transforming the mother's 'story' into the daughter's 'short story' – 'stories
within stories'. The word 'trigger' is used again, this time literally.
Daughter-writer has to open the code word in order to heal herself but
the process is ultimately healing for her mother too, releasing her from
her enforced silence: 'someone was asking at last'. The process of documenting the 'black hole' is conducted again in the gendered territory
of the kitchen. In the journey, the daughter-writer serves three functions: she is daughter, therapist and chronicler. And in chronicling her
mother's story, she is writing her own: 'making stories, making selves'.
The mother's story, like the stories of Rogers' clients, is full of gaps,
patches and 'don't knows' (Rogers, 1994).

> But the first action, the first conscious action, was to decide that with-
> out really opening that frightening code word, 'Auschwitz', I would not
> be able to write the book. First of all I had to do it with her knowledge.
> Again, in my childish subconscious, the same image returned, the
> image of the hand grenade. Because some of that secret pact of silence
> at home was created by the fact that the child feels that she has great
> responsibility. She was not to misuse her weapon. She has a grenade
> and she is holding on to the trigger. If you say the word 'Auschwitz',
> something bad would happen to your parent. She would collapse, she
> would cry, she would scream, she would again have a headache. My
> mother suffered migraines when I was a child. It was one of my worst
> memories. Locking herself up in her room, in the dark, drawing the
> shutters. It was linked in my mind with black out. Her mysterious
> headaches with which she would lock herself in for hours. I expected

such physical manifestations and I came to her with my legs trembling, with fear, to do what I had to do. And I said to her – we sat in the kitchen, which is not like being a guest at home – and I said to her, I had started to write something and it leads 'there'. And I would like you to know and I would like to know if you are prepared to co-operate with me, if you are prepared to open. And the thing that amazed me was the sense of relief on her face, as if someone was asking at last.

'We started a journey in time, documenting that black hole'

And we started a journey in time, in which I served three functions. I was her daughter, but I was a sort of psychologist, who made it easier for her to go back in time, and I was also her chronicler, a little Josephus Flavius, who was sitting in the kitchen, documenting that black hole. I returned her to age eighteen and attempted to walk with her step-by-step, chronologically, until the liberation day and what happened later. There were, of course, many patches, which, having repressed so much, she was no longer able to reconstruct. To this day I have unclear sections, hidden sections, resulting from her sinking memory. Her memory is clear in its main points, in the central traumas. In the decisive moments, as she said 'I don't know why I jumped out of that train window', she almost could not remember the action itself, or what she was thinking while doing it. On the other hand, she could remember what happened afterwards, very clearly. I mean there were different weights of memory, and I had to tell myself that in the framework of such deep repression, the chronicle I would write would be partial, subjective, with unbridgeable gaps, and that this was how it was going to stay.

'Her chronicle, my own chronicle'

Answering my question about the duality of purpose of chronicling her mother's story while constructing her own life, leads Semel to the story of another story ('But the Music does not Cover') and its significance both in her mother's and in her own life. This section ends with a 'literary criticism' evaluation summary, theorising the link with events in her mother's life that found their way into Semel's subconscious when she was writing.

RL
So at some stage you were writing her chronicle, or yours?

NS
Hers. I began with her chronicle. And at the same time I was writing the book. My own chronicle was being written during my own writing .... I think there were two levels here, which I juxtaposed. Or so it seems. If you remember the story 'But the Music does not Cover', I wrote it at home, during our conversations. There is a section in which Veronica, a young German woman, is summoned to the mother of the man (an

Israeli son of survivors) she is going to marry. Veronica is quite alarmed, she knocks at the door and the mother throws a packet into her lap saying, 'open it, it's yours'. When she opens it, it contains a purse and she is stunned, because of course it isn't hers. When I began describing the purse, when I lifted the pen off the paper. I realised I was describing a real purse. The story was fictional, but the purse, I could see it, I could touch it and I knew it existed. I didn't understand the connection, it was a description of a very strange purse.

Think of a home in the 1950s, with almost nothing. At home, in my miserable toy drawer, with the two and a half bits I had, there was something which looked like a sort of pouch, with strings, made of velvet, black velvet, and embroidered in pearls, with tapestry-style roses. Amazingly beautiful. Why should such an item be in a young girl's toy drawer? After all it was valuable, it was a very, very beautiful, mature artefact, an evening purse. I remember as a girl that one of my favourite pastimes was to pull the tapestry threads and unravel it and all the little beads would scatter around the house. And it made this noise, trr, trr, of the unravelling. It took me years to unravel all these roses, because they were embroidered very tightly, these pearls.

Suddenly I had a picture in my head of me doing it and my mother watching and saying nothing. I was unravelling this purse for years and only at the very end did I remember that at the age of twelve of thirteen I made it into an evening outfit for dolly Barbie. On my own. That was the end of its life. But in fact I ruined a very beautiful artefact and no one ever said a word.

It was night when I wrote the description of that purse. Suddenly it came up. I knew it was real. I could not restrain myself, I rang my mother and said to her, I want to ask you something. Did we have such a purse at home? What is this purse? I remember it clearly. And then she said to me: 'It is the only thing I took from "there"'.

Think of it. When she was roaming around with that Soviet officer and that second inmate, in German houses, to take clothes, and shoes. Because they found nothing in the abandoned houses, the officer escorted them with a rifle and would break into houses where people lived in Zitau, using the butt of his rifle, enter and, threatening them with his rifle, would say to them, 'give me shoes, give me food, give me sugar, flour, give to these women'. And these frightened Germans would open their wardrobes and pull stuff out. Or he would tell them to show him where the wardrobe was, and my mother and the second woman would take a coat, or a pair of shoes. She always remembers looking for shoes, she could never find shoes to fit her. One day she saw the purse and took it. It was not an item she needed, sort of. I suppose she felt guilty for taking it and – perhaps I am introducing symbolism where it does not exist, although I think it does – therefore she allowed me to unravel this thing for years, to ruin it, until it fell apart with my childhood things.

The amazing thing is that I had never known that this item came from 'there'. So how come that in my unconscious, the strangeness of the item was linked with her hidden biographical world? I mean, knowledge finds its very circuitous ways. It was really amazing. It was one of the events during the writing of the book when I understood that things are pulled out of me too, that what I call the collected non-verbal information gets out of the right drawers and connects to the right channels. All the time a puzzle is being put together here.

One of the researchers who did write about 'A Hat of Glass' in recent years said it was not accidental that the first story, 'A Hat of Glass', opens with an image of a puzzle, in which the unnamed heroine, if you remember, is walking in Tel Aviv and thinks she sees Clarissa. And then she says, 'the truth is pieces of ... '.[9]

I cannot remember when I wrote this section, whether it was during one of the re-writes, but it became the first paragraph of the book. The researcher also noted that I was breaking something which is structured as a novel into short stories, but which I am turning seemingly on purpose into short stories. In his opinion there is one hero throughout the book, wearing different faces, he is more or less the same age, more of less with the same biographical world, wandering from story to story, changing costumes. Therefore this process of fragmentation is not accidental and is rooted in the first paragraph of the first story. I admit I had not noticed it.

'Children of': 'looking into the mirror from different angles' (the next books)

Semel's narrators, in all her books, are children or young people, often children of survivors, like her, engaged in interrogating their contested Israeli identity. Through discussing her next books, Semel offers me another evaluation, this time of the issues involved in the reception of Shoah survivors in Israeli society. These are recurring themes in the interviews with the other narrators and in the literature. The issues which dominate *Becoming Gershona* (1988; 1990) and *Flying Lessons* (1991) are:

- dissociation (a daughter of survivors who does not know her parents are survivors, but senses her differentness and therefore mistakes the new immigrant boy from Poland, who has re-named himself Nimrod – a pre-Jewish Canaanite name – adopted by the 'new Hebrews' as one antithesis to the diaspora, for a 'true *sabra*');
- the acquisition of a new identity;
- the passing on of names of dead relatives and the reluctance to carry the name of a Shoah victim (a theme she returns to in section III in relation to her own biography);
- Israelis' refusal (or inability) to absorb the new immigrants and their lack of sensitivity towards the survivors;
- the process of repressing the memory of the Shoah and substituting it with a new Israeli identity;

– loss, the lack of memory and the enforced process of repression (which she develops in the next section).

– *Rali* (1993), however, marks Semel's (and Israel's?) passage to a new era in which the Shoah becomes part of contemporary life, rather than merely a traumatised memory.

RL
My impression is that apart from Clarissa, all the stories, including *Gershona* and *Flying Lessons*, are about daughters, 'children of' ...

NS
Hadara[10] is not a 'child of' but this is deliberate. Look, let us start with the fact that 'A Hat of Glass' was simply an investigation, myself in front of the mirror, therefore the text is very dense, concentrated, like, pardon the analogy, like a blood sample which was left standing and began congealing. It has many congealing factors, this book. I cannot read it today, I find it very difficult, very difficult. It hasn't got a breath of air. I was suffocated when I wrote it, but I didn't realise how suffocating it is to read it. Therefore I cannot read it today. In *Gershona*, I wanted to examine being a child of Shoah survivors in real time. Not retrospectively as in 'A Hat of Glass'. I mean, if I stood close to the mirror for 'A Hat of Glass', in the other books a process of distancing begins and I look at the reflection from other angles too.

Becoming Gershona (Gershona Shona):

'Not knowing in real time'

Gershona Shona (*Becoming Gershona*), (1988, 1990), a novel for young adults, is the story of a young daughter of survivors living in Tel Aviv, who makes friends with a blond boy, whose Israeli name, Nimrod, and his pretence to be a *sabra*, fools her despite the tell-tale signs about him being a survivor, a new immigrant from Poland. This is very much a story about the construction of 'native' Israeli identity.

It interested me to examine not knowing in real time, to examine Gershona, who does not know, the moments when non-verbal information begins to be filed away and when there is a gap between today's reader, who knows exactly what she is locating and her innocence and her defence in not knowing and on the other hand, her curiosity to link things, and that includes the mistaken connections she is making. And to examine the obvious. I mean, as a child I thought that all parents go to bed with sleeping pills. I started from the naive premise that all parents are like this. With Gershona – this is the kind of obviousness that I wanted to locate – the tattoo on her mother's forearm is obvious, the pills by the bed and the glass of water are obvious, but on the other hand, there is a vague fear that one day, the mother will swallow too many pills by mistake.

'The seam of Israeli identity'

I mean, she knows, in her own way, but at the same time she wishes to examine the beginning of the seam of the Israeli identity. Gershona's yearning for identity is so huge that she refuses to recognise Nimrod who arrives in the neighbourhood, she refuses to see or read, because she has enough tell-tale signs, that what he is selling her is a false Israeli identity. And all the same it's important for her to fortify herself within this identity.

'We all refuse to carry someone else's name'

There is the issue of names, which is very significant. We all refused to carry someone else's name, particularly a name of someone who died. Particularly someone who died in the Shoah, particularly someone about whom we knew nothing. And we had to carry another identity on our shoulders and to carry the expectations for that person who had died before her time and we had to actualise not only our own expectations, but also other people's expectations. This was more or less what interested me in Gershona.

Flying Lessons (Maurice Havivel Melamed La'uf):

'A "macho", peasant moshava' versus 'uprooted biographies'

Maurice Havivel Melamed La'uf (*Flying Lessons*), (1991, 1995), a novel for young adults, is the story of the friendship between Maurice, a new immigrant from Tunisia, and Hadara, a young girl whose mother had died, in an Israeli co-operative settlement (moshava) in the early 1950s. This too is a story about the construction, by new immigrants, of Israeli identity.

With *Maurice* I was interested in something quite different. I was interested in the encounter with the old *Yishuv*. It was not only Hadara. Hadara represents a whole moshava of people who did not absorb, not only Maurice, but also the uprooted Tova, about whom it is not clear whether she was saved, or whether her parents died in Transnistria. She is a Shoah survivor, it does not matter whether she had been to a concentration camp or not. No one is aware of her loneliness. Both Maurice and Tova are lonely and are not absorbed by that 'macho' Israeli moshava, that peasant moshava. And therefore it was very important for me to differentiate between that settlement which makes no effort to understand that they have come from another place and the survivors themselves who arrive with uprooted biographies.

'Night Games' (Rali: Masa Matara):

'The Shoah as internally structured'

Rali: Masa Matara ('Night Games') (1993) is a novel about a group of
Haifa school friends who are playing treasure hunt on a Day of Independence eve in 1987, six months before the *Intifada* (Palestinian
uprising). The book is structured in ten stories-chapters, each dealing
with one couple and with one stage of the treasure hunt.

> In *Rali*, which I have just finished, that book about the forty-something
> Israelis who are playing a game in Haifa, there are several very casual
> mentions of the Shoah. In this book there is a macro-examination of
> Israeli identity in general, because it is a group of people, each of whom
> has a different biography, and I examine what unifies them, why they
> can no longer stand the Zionist ethos which they carry on their shoul-
> der. It's 1987, the decisive year in which the *Intifada* broke out, in which
> the reverse of the Six Day War reached its peak. From now on the state
> of Israel would be different. The process of the sinking of the Likud, or
> of what I call the fascist face of Israel, has also begun in 1987. Today we
> have reaped the benefits, but these are always long processes. I have so-
> called casual mentions of the Shoah in that book.

RL
In other words the Shoah has been sufficiently worked through to be
able to be mentioned only casually?

NS
Sort of casually. It's part of what you said at the beginning of our conversation, I examine the Israeli historiography and the Shoah as a structured element. In this book the Shoah is internally structured. It comes
out in a sentence here and there, in a riddle they explore, the riddle of
the Templars.[11] In that chapter I examine how Nazism can exist by
remote control. The Templars settled amongst the Jews, they advised
Bilu[12] and the first settlers in Rishon LeZion, on how to be farmers in
that desert hole. Their leader Christoph Hoffman gave detailed practical
advice on agronomy and on communal settlement building. Nevertheless, in the 1930s, when Nazism began, and particularly between 1939
and 1941, Nazism flourished amongst the second-generation Templars.
I mean it was possible to activate it by remote control. And most of them
returned to Germany to enlist. Do you understand? It's easy perhaps to
say to people in Germany that Jews are sub-human, but to transmit that
message across thousands of miles, to people who live amongst the Jews
as a minority, and to succeed in it, says something which I wanted to
examine. Is Nazism transmittable in certain historical circumstances?
  In the story of the Templars, the woman who solves the riddle is a
daughter of survivors whose parents came to Israel. She knows the
story of the Templars from her parents who joined a settlement and got

a house in Waldheim, a Templar moshava in the Izrael Valley, and got their first house after the Shoah, at long last their first home in Israel, and found out they had entered a Nazi house. It was full of Nazi arte-facts and their first action in Israel was to collect all these artefacts and light a bonfire and burn them all. It's almost surreal.

In one of the other stories, a mother has a fight with her young daughter before she leaves for the treasure hunt, because her daughter loves sleeping in a sleeping bag on the floor. And because the parents are going to be out the whole night, it is Independence Day, the daughter is going to stay at her grandmother's. And the grandmother is not pre-pared to allow the child to sleep on the floor, and suddenly it occurred to me that the grandmother had been to Ravensbrück. And the whole thing becomes clear. Why is it so difficult for the grandmother to see her granddaughter sleeping on the floor? She says 'the floor is dirty, and there are beds in the house, and there is a clean sheet, why should any-one choose the floor when there is a clean sheet and a bed'. The story of Ravensbrück sneaks into that chapter in several ways.

The Shoah is mentioned throughout. There are many Arab charac-ters that group members meet through the night and there is one Israeli man who is clearly a fascist. He is anti-Arab, he is almost a Cahana[13] supporter. And at some stage, with no connection to the Arabs, they mention a grandfather and a grandmother and then he says: ' I don't have grandparents; of my family no one was left'. And suddenly it puts him, even his fascism, in a different light. I mean, this is not the theme of the book, but the Shoah comes in through the seams.

The new book

'How did the process of repression begin?'

The book I am writing now is about new immigrants, not necessarily survivors of concentration camps, rather people who migrate from home to a hostile, alien environment, with a great sense of loss. And they are coping with loss, not with the trauma of the Shoah itself, not with their memories, but with that awful sense of deprivation, of what they lack, home, family, climate. The book is set on 4 February, 1950, when it snowed everywhere in Israel. And I have three families, one Pol-ish, one a Romanian woman who meets another lonely Romanian, who comes from Gura Humora [laughs],[14] and a father and son from Morocco who are stuck on a ship in Haifa port, where they are held for two days because of the snow. For all of them snow is an amazing trigger.

I am in the middle of writing so I don't yet know what will happen. I am dealing mostly with loss and lack. Not really with direct memories, but with the lack of memory. One of the members of the [Polish] family is a girl who cannot remember. How did the process of repression begin? Throughout the story she reconstructs the city of Rovno, in Poland. She is not even clear about whether she was born there or not. But she reconstructs an imaginary Rovno. She is collecting the pieces and constructs a false world, and it is very sad, because this would be the world with which she would live. And it is a world based on repressing memory and not on remembering.[15]

Ceremonial versus intimate memory

In this section Semel develops a central theme for her: finding a place for intimate Shoah memory in a country which up until very recently allowed only the existence of ceremonial, nationalised memory.[16] Here, issues of nationalised memory are linked to the personal experience of carrying a dead relative's name, the appropriation of people's names by state institutions (Semel describes this process as 'stripping'), and the adoption of new, Israeli, as opposed to Jewish, models. I begin by suggesting to her that she is proposing that the state of Israel was constructed on the repression of memory and, on the other hand, built on the memory of all the persecutions of all times.

'Israel was constructed on the repression of memory'

Without a doubt. But remember what sort of memory we are remembering. We remember a ceremonial memory. We have never had intimate memory. If you want to summarise everything I do on this subject, the book I am working on now will be my fifth book which mentions the Shoah, I am trying to bring back intimate, individual memory. Israeli society has dealt only with heroic memory, with memory that was far too big for us, and with a kind of ceremonial memory which would serve the Zionist ethos.

'Changing identities as fast as possible'

A kind of memory which was to be a tool, a tool which would first of all change identities as fast as possible.

I remember that when I arrived at *Galei Tsahal* [the IDF radio station], and it was not a million years ago, it was in 1972, there was a rule in the station that everyone whose name was to be broadcast, producers or presenters and so on, had to have a Hebrew name. A woman whose name was Yael Horovitz enlisted on the same day as I did. She was given exactly three minutes to change her name. Poor girl. Do you know how it feels? So she changed quickly, the first name that came to her mind was the name of her kibbutz, Dan. And she is called Yael Dan to this day. And I witnessed it, and saw how a person had to change her name in a second. I was lucky to have arrived protected, because I was called Nava Artzi,[17] Artzi was already Hebraicised. And I remember my relief that they did not do it to me. I felt as if they stripped her naked. [I was] protected from this terrible process of stripping, when they tear off your clothes and dress you with something else. Do you understand? It's very traumatic.

When we were children, the burden of names was so heavy. Because when you scratch the Israeli names of the 1950s, you discover Yiddish names. I am Sheindl,[18] what do you think? But my son is Iyar. He has an Accadian-Sumerian-Assyrian name. The root is not clear, but it is probably one of the versions of *Or* ['light' in Hebrew] in the Sumerian-Accadian language, I mean, pre-Canaanite, you understand. How far did I get away from Jewish names? It is not accidental.

The direction came from above, I don't mean it negatively, because I am trying not to attack. I have a deep understanding of why things were done. I don't think there was someone, an ideologue, who said we should direct this society to be something else. But there was apparently an instinct, a protective reflex of building a new identity. It was clear from our circumstances in a piece of land where, a year after the survivors, after my parents arrived, they already faced another war. My mother claims that the birth of my brother Shlomo was delayed until after the end of the War of Independence. She was scared to give birth.

New (Aryan) models

In order to turn the Jew, the lamb to the slaughter, the diaspora type, the passive type, who accepts his fate resignedly, to turn him quickly to Mordechai Anielewicz, it was necessary to change names, and find very clear and quick models for identification, including, in my opinion, physiognomic models. The model was always blond, with blue eyes, tall and erect. I am talking about Aryan models, in fact. I don't think that it's accidental that the first line in Moshe Shamir's *Pirkei Elik* (1951) is: 'Elik was born of the sea'. He did not originate from anything Jewish. Nothing of the sort, but rather came from the sea, a Venus born from the waves, from the Greek mythology. I am saying it sort of cynically, but things had a huge significance then. And therefore the memory was very ceremonial and very channelled to one purpose – changing the diaspora identity, which had betrayed us, abandoned us, into an identity of a fighter, which is why there is such extensive use of the Bible as a source of models. In this transition intimate memory was abandoned and this is what I wanted to examine in my work.

Again, I return to something a researcher said to me. One of the researchers who wrote about 'A Hat of Glass' pointed to the fact that the word 'Shoah' appears throughout the 250 pages only once. And it appears only in the title of the story 'Private Shoah'. And look at the combination – 'Shoah' and 'private'.

Gendered images

At this point I return Semel to my research question, but although she describes the moshava which fails to absorb Maurice and Tova as 'macho', and while she does agree with the gender divide I am suggesting, saying that men told more heroic stories than women (an observation supported by Zvi Dror, member of kibbutz *Lochamei Hagetaot* and editor of survivor testimonies, [Dror, 1984]), she argues that

the heroic models were not gendered. She does, however, concede that
the women who fought also served as female 'heroic, fighting models'.
While gender does not seem to be her primary concern, her narrative
displays clearly the construction of her gendered identity. She also
makes a clear distinction between her father's 'heroic' tales about the
Zionist struggle and her mother's stories about the Shoah.

RL
Do you think that intimate memory is the domain of women, in contrast with the memory which constructs warriors?

NS
Yes. I cannot negate the fact that because it is my mother who is the
concentration camp survivor, in this case a woman, my link is more to
women survivors than to men survivors. I am always playing with the
idea of what would have happened had my father been the survivor. In
the case of Renana, in the book *Rali*, the daughter of those survivors
who came from Berlin and who knows about the Templars, it is her
father who is the survivor. And he is the one who tells her the story, perhaps the more ideological story, of Nazism.

RL
But your father told more at home, no?

NS
Yes, but not so much about the Shoah as about heroism. And in particular about the Zionist struggle.

RL
Yes, but what I want to ask: it's clear that the Israeli ethos is an ethos
supposedly constructed for survival, war and so forth. Do we as women
collude, or do we resist? Is it an act of resistance or an act of collusion?

NS
In the first few years of course we colluded. Undoubtedly. That's why we
have Mordechai Anielewicz and Haike Grossman by his side. And what
about Hanna Senesh?[19] The models were constructed as heroic and at
the same time a feminine model was also constructed. An equally
heroic, fighting model of a woman. I remember that in all the stories
about Anielewicz and the Warsaw Ghetto uprising, the part played by
the women was very important. Perhaps also because women joined
the [Israeli] army.

RL
But ... when we begin taking this myth apart, you know exactly what
sort of equality it is.

NS

But the models were equal, I believe.

RL

But it is a masculine model, no? A heroic woman, using firearms? It is not a Jewish model, of a woman.

NS

Anielewicz too was not a Jewish model.

RL

You said that in the first years we colluded. Where are we now?

NS

Look, in the first years, we went along with it. Again, it's worth examining: look at the models of *Yom HaShoah* ceremonies from the early years. There was not one *Yom HaShoah* ceremony in which we did not read Hanna Senesh, 'My God, my God, let it never end', and 'Happy is the match', and [the poet, Nathan] Alterman, who is Israeli born. In my opinion these ceremonies are the key ...

Yom Hashoah as an isolated island

This is another evaluation sequence, in which Semel contextualises her own book within the 'stone wall' reception for earlier Israeli Shoah literature. She acknowledges the role 'A Hat of Glass' played in introducing the Shoah onto Israel's cognitive map ('if it played a part in opening something, I am glad'), despite the negative reception when it was first published. Semel contextualises the initial reactions to the book in the general climate of negating the Shoah and maps its gradual acceptance. She also links her protective attitude towards her mother's privacy and her own privacy with the book's initial 'secrecy'.

NS

Understand, *Yom HaShoah* was an isolated island. No one ever spoke about the Shoah on any other day of the year.

RL

Until the Eichmann trial.

NS

Afterwards too, in my opinion. *Adam Ben Kelev*,[20] which was published in 1969, and is one of the most important books in Hebrew literature, and *Lizkor veLishkoach*,[21] which was published in 1968, after the Six Days War, were isolated islands. And after them there were thirteen years of silence, in which the Shoah was not present in Israeli cinema, in Israeli theatre, or in Israeli literature. It was non-existent.

Appelfeld[22] did not deal directly with the Shoah, he dealt with the before, or with the after. Therefore it was easy to publicise Appelfeld without saying he was dealing with the Shoah. I am talking about two Israelis, *sabras*. Dan Ben Amotz – in 1968, no one knew he was a Shoah survivor himself – embodied the *sabra* myth. And Kaniuk is Israeli-born. Why was he writing such a book, which penetrated the soul of a Shoah survivor who loses his sanity? These books met a stone wall. The Shoah was an isolated, once-a-year ceremony, in which we fulfilled our duty, and that was it.

'A Hat of Glass': *'Israeli society was not ready for it'*

NS

'A Hat of Glass'had one response. It was published on a Thursday. On the following Friday *Ha'aretz* published a small box, not even in the literary page, interestingly, but in the paper proper, which carried the by-line of someone who I know today was 23 at the time. He wrote something like, 'Yesterday 'A Hat of Glass' by Nava Semel was published. From what it says on the cover, this is a book about children of, about the second-generation, sons and daughters of Shoah survivors. I for one have no intention even of reading it. Haven't we had enough with Shoah survivors and their problems, do their children too need to tell us they have problems?'

That was it. Now, I was prepared for it psychologically because when I took the manuscript to my publisher, my editor Natan Yonatan told me: 'I hope you know you are committing suicide. But we are prepared to commit suicide together with you'.

RL

What about your mother?

NS

It was not a small victory for her, some symbol of survival, me publishing the book. I continued to protect her very much. The silence around the book emanated from two things. First, from the fact that Israeli society was not ready for it. I know of one critic who wanted to write about it. He asked the Israeli mainstream newspaper *Yediot Aharonot* to let him write about the book and the answer was the following, and I quote verbatim: 'don't write about it, because we do not know how to "eat" it'. The 'we don't know how to eat it' is a key phrase. Most people did not know how to eat it, which is why they chose to ignore it.

The second factor, I think, is my own obsessive need to protect my mother. I was so afraid she would be hurt and that there now was a physical hand grenade, that I wasn't available to anyone. I almost refused to give interviews. I reacted very aggressively. I remember that at some stage a woman, who used to write for *LaIsha* [a women's magazine] said to me 'I want to write about the book'. But she added, 'but I am going to verify the things in the book with an investigation we are conducting on your mother's life. From all sorts of people from her town and so on'. And I became hysterical. Because I was terrified that the things that she had chosen to keep secret would find their way to *LaIsha* magazine. And I threatened that I would commit suicide if she published the article. I am ashamed to tell you, but I had no other way. It got to a point that whenever anyone mentioned my mother, I begged the journalist not to write about the book.

Since then many things have been written about the book, first in the US. The second serious thing was by the journalist Sarit Yishai-Levi, who is Israeli-born, whose parents come from Morocco, or Iraq, from a completely non-Shoah environment. She read the book and did not leave me in peace, saying, 'I will interview you. It isn't possible for this thing to be forgotten'. And it was very easy for me to talk to her. She didn't nag me about my mother, or about Shlomo, and she didn't say she would examine my life and cross-check informations, all sorts of things people said to me which made me very cautious. And she opened it up. Afterwards there were other articles. I have no doubt that it was because Sarit was committed to it as an Israeli. I mean, her commitment to the Shoah is because the Shoah is part of her historiography, not part of her biography.

Many people say to me, what a pity you didn't publish the book after Grossman.[23] It was a different climate. Poliker[24] did something. David Grossman did something. Should I say I feel discriminated because the book was published in the wrong time, when the climate was not yet ready, as opposed to today? But if it played a part in opening something, I am glad. It was re-printed three times [and was re-issued in 1998]. It has been reviewed throughout the years, which means it has a real life, because there is hardly a month I don't get some reaction to it ...

'Israel is growing in leaps and bounds'

Here again I stop her flow, asking her to evaluate Israeli society's reaction to the Shoah. She begins with a short evaluation, and generalises about what she calls the 'metaphysical clock', (probably meaning a biographical clock), which compels survivors to tell and their children – who have become parents themselves – to listen. This leads her to a more personal narrative, about how her own anxiety about her children is a replica of her mother's anxieties ('I was the embodiment of my mother'). This is followed by another short evaluation, which links the 'metaphysical clock' with the Jewish tradition of 'reckoning' and atoning for our sins by 'opening the gate' (to the survivors' stories). I begin by asking her if as a state Israel is coming to the end of its adolescence.

NS
The state of Israel is growing in leaps and bounds, and there are undigested bits. But I believe that things, for better or for worse, have to come out, at some stage, at the right time. This is also valid in relation to confronting the Shoah. It did not happen in real time, it happened in another time. This morning, a minute before you came in, I received this

in the mail [she shows me material relating to a second-generation con-
ference]. Look how many established bodies support it. *Amcha* and *Ella*
are two bodies offering psychological support and welfare to survivors
and their children. None of this was available in the early 1980s. I wrote
'A Hat of Glass' in 1980. The thirteen years that have passed are very significant. In the US I met Helen Epstein. Helen wrote *Children of the Holocaust* [1979], the very first text which was written about children of
Shoah survivors. And she too wrote it after she had a child. And this is
very significant. I certainly didn't know about her and she didn't know
about me. This means that something in the metaphysical clock was
working. And this is the product of two biological factors. First we have
grown up and became parents and many of our behaviours, against
which we rebelled as children, in particular the banana and sweater syndrome, we have found ourselves doing exactly the same to our children.

I fought with my son hysterically last Friday because he was late
home, not because I mind him coming home late, but because he didn't
telephone, and I was lucky not to have known that a terrorist was roaming freely in Ramat Ef'al, because had I known it, I think I would have
gone crazy. And I patrolled the windows and the house, just like my
mother used to, and I knew I was doing it and you know what? It didn't
bother me I was doing it. And I screamed at him as my mother used to
scream at me. I was the embodiment of my mother. The second factor is
our parents' ageing.

Look at the interview that arrived five minutes ago. It's time for us to
talk a little and get to know each other, and why so late? As it says in the
Yom Kippur [Day of Atonement] prayer book, 'Open a gate for us now,
while a gate is being locked'. It is not accidental that the article mentions *Yom Kippur* ...

'The process of repression'

I return Semel to my research question, gender differences – is there a
feminine element in daughters of survivors breaking the silence and
telling their parents' stories, and their own stories? Semel explicates
this in the context of the differences between women and men as parents, another example of her perception of the construction of gendered identities. Again, 'trigger' is a key word. However, she uses this
question as an entry point to a long narrative sequence about personal
experiences relating to her childhood eating problems. Food is a 'sub-
text of survivorship' in many Shoah survivors' families (key words are
'guilt', 'responsibility' and 'control'). As we agreed, I have deleted
much of this sequence, leaving only the bare references to elucidate
the meaning of the story in relation to her transformation, from feeling weak, the classical 'lamb to the slaughter' in her words, to finding
peace and closing the circle, through writing.

This is significant in relation to the general story of the place of the Shoah in the Israeli psyche, from being secret, shameful and stigmatised, to a more respected place in the national ethos; from the definition of the Israeli ethos as hegemonic, masculine and ceremonial to a more intimate, feminine identity, aided, I would argue, by the narrators' books and films.

'The process of repression regarding the Shoah was very deep with me'

I think that the experience of parenting, for a woman, is a far greater trigger than for a man. It's an immediate trigger. Let's say that for a man the experience of parenting, when he examines himself versus his parents, may happen later, when his children are older. I think that with women this trigger acts very fast, when they have a baby. I'll give you an example of something I was aware of when Iyar was born. I was obsessive about food from the start. This was an exact copy of what happened to me as a child. I think that the process of repression regarding the Shoah was very deep with me.

The doctor's recipe was to feed me only when I wanted to eat, never to force me, and to insist I ate only two things, a boiled egg and a chopped tomato. With this I would be able to survive. And leave the rest. I did the same with Iyar. Food was a nightmare at home, my mother would cry ... why did she deserve such a thing. Why did she deserve such punishment. Now, I didn't control it, I can say this with certainty.

The woman is the one who is responsible for feeding the child. I think that in many families of Shoah survivors life's focus is food. There are many sub-texts of survivorship, of mutual guilt apportioning around this business of food. And it goes: how can you do this to me? The passing on of the guilt ball is very, very problematic in these families. The sense of responsibility you receive as a child, becoming adult before your time, and being able to control your parents. There is something in the basic structure of the family, like who is the source of authority, who is the source of responsibility, who is the source of control. To a certain extent this balance is shaken, and you too assume a source of authority, and a source of responsibility, for your parents' well-being. All these reverses, this game of reverses is often happening around the table and around the plate.

'It was easy for me to retreat to the position of the rejected'[25]

Semel begins the narrative of the second part of her trajectory – of finding an alternative to 'the position of the rejected' – with an incident which happened when her son was in kindergarten. From guilt and having to 'fulfil expectations' and 'fill the gap of the people who died', she begins her journey towards asserting herself and, through her writing, taking her place in contemporary Israeli society. The beginning of this journey, however, is full of anger and violence, two key words. I try to develop the topic of anger, but before speaking of the irritation she felt through her mother equating every catastrophe, large or small, with Auschwitz and the Shoah, Semel speaks of the Gulf War, the one time when her parents did not resort to Shoah codes.[26] Interestingly, Semel too uses Shoah metaphors of passivity and heroic pride to describe her own choices during the Gulf War. She was in New York at the time and felt she was abandoning her 'old parents in the ghetto and going out to the forests as a proud partisan'.

> One of the triggers to the guilt feelings you carry is undoubtedly because you fill the gap of the people who died, and because you are meant to fulfil expectations, and you cannot always fulfil them, and then you become a greater disappointment. This business of guilt weighs very heavily on me. Therefore it was easy for me to retreat to the position of the rejected, because it answers a basic need in me.
>
> Because we are talking about life's strange triggers, when the writing is on the wall, it was written on the wall in something very accidental, again in relation to my child ...

She narrates an incident that happened when her first-born was four, when she was rushing to pick him up from kindergarten. Anxious about being late – she is anxious about being late to pick up her twins as we talk, and keeps looking at her watch – she was accused by a woman of crashing into her parked car, and Semel assumed responsibility immediately:

> I immediately volunteered guilt. I apologised grovellingly, I said, pardon me, and I am sorry, and I was in a hurry, and my child is in the kindergarten, and I am very sorry, and I will pay anything you want. I felt the aggression towards an oppressor [laughs] who is standing in the street and spitting on me and I accepted it all and nodded ...

When the woman left, Semel realised, from the way the car was parked, that it was not she who had crashed into the woman's car.

> It was the first time in my life. I called her back and I was burning with anger. It was not anger. It was something abnormal, it was all my anger at having volunteered to be a victim. All these volunteering acts were collapsed on to that stupid scene, that accidental scene. And I screamed at her. I think I was capable of hitting her, physically. I had such violence in me that I didn't even know existed. And within a minute she apologised and said 'I beg your pardon' and she gave me back my piece of paper, and I tore it in front of her with hysterical ceremony. And when I got into the car, and drove, I felt that a huge level of violence remained in my body, all my muscles contracted. I mean, what I off-loaded was one-sixteenth of the iceberg of the violence stored in me. That situation helped me later. Of course I worked it out in my head, it was clear to me where it came from.

'I have no doubt that I have stored anger'

RL

Anger is one of the things that are very well documented in the lives of children of survivors. A very deep anger at their parents.

NS

I have suppressed it very much. I have no doubt that I have stored anger about this business of food. Because it wasn't my fault …

But I feel no anger towards them. Certainly not towards my mother. On the contrary, I have a high degree of understanding. Truthfully. A high level of understanding. What I do find difficult today is the equation of everything with Auschwitz. I mean every catastrophe is Auschwitz-scale catastrophe. Excluding one thing – the Gulf War. During which my parents were a source of calm and serenity. I was abroad and here my sense of guilt was a thousand times greater than if I hadn't been a daughter of survivors. The sense of abandonment, of having abandoned my old parents in the ghetto and going out to the forests as a proud partisan, was very difficult. And on the other hand, all my friends, my age group, my generation, whether they were children of survivors or not, fled the city [Tel Aviv] hysterically, while my parents remained in their empty street, alone, exuding calm, un-hysterical.

On the other hand, throughout my life, any and every catastrophe, illness, everything became equivalent to Auschwitz and this did irritate me. Today too. Suddenly it seems that the concentration camp returns. And these are small things. And in relation to the [Gulf] war, which was a huge, existential thing, there was suddenly calm and security, which they radiated towards me. They never gave me the slightest feeling that I was a deserter, a traitor, that I 'have abandoned my old parents in a sealed room in Tel Aviv'.

RL

Perhaps it came from the same place as having jumped from the train?

NS

It also came from a feeling that the worst had already happened, this couldn't be as bad, it doesn't come near that other evil. On the other hand, in the everyday, there are things that trigger some catastrophe, some ultimate catastrophe.

'I had spoilt the Israeli stereotype'

One reaction to 'A Hat of Glass', among the other hostile and alienating reactions, was the claim that I had 'spoilt the Israeli stereotype'. How dare I describe, underneath the macho, a trembling Israeli [man], frightened, scared, diaspora-like? I was criticised for having spoilt the beautiful ethos. In *Gershona*, I was criticised for writing that when she didn't come home and her mother said to her, 'the Nazis didn't kill me, you will kill me. They didn't kill me, you will kill me'. Many people spoke to me about this text, I mean, 'this is what I survived Auschwitz for?'[27]

'You had to be strong – I was the classical lamb to the slaughter'

Positioning herself as 'the classical lamb to the slaughter', Semel offers a key evaluation of Israeli society, where you 'had to be really macho ... women too'. Again, mixing Shoah past with Israeli present, she judges that she would not have been able to take up arms during the Shoah, not even to escape the Mengele selections. She uses this judgement of her own personal abilities to generalise: we were being 'lied to', we are not at all 'new Hebrews', but rather 'frightened, scared' and 'diaspora-like'. Ironically, this understanding helps her make peace with her identity, helps her 'stop being ashamed that it was always I who was the frightened child'.

> My work includes deciphering many things. Walking in front of the mirror in varying angles makes me stop rebelling, like I did in my childhood, and stop being antagonistic. Accept them [my parents] on the human level, as people with a private, intimate life, connect with their intimacy, make peace with my identity, stop being ashamed that it was always I who was the frightened child, though I always had to mask it, because in Israel then you had to be really macho, and not necessarily masculine, women too. You had to be strong. And I always knew inside that I was very weak. That I was a naturally born victim, that I volunteer. And I often wonder what would have happened had I been in that situation with Mengele? I would possibly not have escaped. I am telling you the truth. With my givens as Nava? Not at all. I was the classical lamb to the slaughter. I, an Anielewicz? Not at all. This I already knew when I was little. I knew that I was being lied to, because I knew I would not have been heroic. How could I have been heroic? I, who tremble at every shadow in the house? I never go to sleep, delaying sleep as much as possible. [But I] would never use sleeping pills, of course, I would eat the ceiling first, I would go out for a walk, but I would not take a pill ...

'Hiding behind my books'

I ask her about having chosen, like her brother Shlomo, the public forum and again, she gives shame and guilt as reasons for 'hiding behind her books', which she calls her 'satellites'. Later she returns to the topic of anger, which, she claims is directed against herself, not against her parents. Food as a problem has been overcome, she no longer has the urge to force her children to eat and has achieved the most difficult feat for a Jewish mother. She is able to throw out uneaten food (which both she and I understand, from our common memory bank, as a huge personal victory).

> Yes, but Shlomo is risking much more than me, he is exposed bodily. I, because of my shame and guilt feelings, launch satellites. The books. And I can also hide afterwards at home. Shlomo always says to me 'you are actually saying that you haven't written it. That someone else has

written it. You don't give interviews, of course, great, so that you can put it onto someone else. So that you do not stand behind things like an adult, because you are so scared'. I tend to retreat fast, I retreat *a priori*, from the start. I say I don't want people to hurt me, so I retreat. So they won't know who is the writer, she won't be available. And the book will not look attractive, yes? The cover of 'A Hat of Glass' is grey, and this hat looks so monk-like, with its ash cloth. It was my choice, how to colour it so that it would look grey as a little mouse. I know it is happening and I cannot get over it. And I say to myself fuck off, why should I get over it? At 38 I will not get over it. That's me and that's it. What can I do? I want the books to come out. But I detach myself from the books all the time.

Unless someone arrives intimately, like you. I have no problem with intimacy. I have a problem with public exposure. I also don't mind giving lectures, because it isn't me. In lectures it is another entity who is speaking, looking on. Exposing myself is more difficult and has to do with the fact that the media and the public have burrowed into our family, and with the fact that Shlomo is so exposed.

'I have learned to live in peace with what there is..'.

I have learned to reconcile, and to generally live in peace with what there is and not to demand what isn't there. Including living in peace with my childhood. At the end of the day, childhood is a very crucial part of our adulthood, but when we are kids, we don't pay it any attention. Today, I have accepted it. I no longer pester my children with food. I am very proud of it. Very very proud of it, Ronit. They eat what they eat. There is always a moment, and then I take the plate, and I throw all the leftovers into the bin. And I am very happy.

RL
It's hard. To throw leftovers into the bin.

NS
No, it's one of my greatest pleasures today.

RL
But to reach the moment in which it becomes a pleasure ...

NS
Ach, it's a struggle. It's really a compulsive pleasure. I clear the plates and throw out the leftovers immediately. And I don't make the children eat them. And when someone like my mother says to me, they haven't eaten, I say yes, so they didn't eat. So they were not hungry. I immediately have these aggressive lectures. And it's all very aggressive, so they didn't eat. Look, I am a good mother, they didn't eat.

[We both laugh nervously, wildly: I know exactly what she is talking about].

RL

It's a battle. I mean, the aggression is still there.

NS

Look, the aggression is against myself. Today I no longer think it's against my parents. I suppose I would have done the same thing if I had been a Shoah survivor and I had a girl [with eating problems]. I may even have strangled her. Seriously. I believe my mother should have had a huge amount of aggression towards me. I tortured her. My anger is against myself. How did I do such a thing?

'Writing is the closing of circles'

The interview came to a close when Semel had to pick up her twins from the neighbouring kindergarten. The final section is a summary that brings together all the themes of the narrative, mixing narration and evaluation. In it, Semel links life and literature. Literature, ultimately, is a channel for anxieties, guilt and shame, and a method through which she can cope. Many earlier key words recur ('loss', 'anger', 'aggression', 'violence', 'bubble', 'guilt', 'shame', 'uprooted', 'Zionist ethos') to link biography and literature. The evaluation sequences evaluate literary strategies, but also chart, once again, the change of emphasis from the Shoah taking centre-stage to being more subtly integrated into the texture of the text. Writing is a way of 'marking territories' and channelling feelings of guilt and shame. Semel's writing has changed from being compulsively carried out in a 'bubble', to a routine of a working writer-mother, 'split, scattered through my life'. Writing her stories, by 'taking apart the bricks of her life', has enabled Semel to 'make her self'.

The final part of the narrative locates her in contemporary Israeli literature ('my books could have been written only here') but argues that 'uprootedness' is ultimately 'a collective Israeli experience'. Moving from what Karmit Gai describes as being 'the *other* of the *other* of the *other*', Semel's narrative confirms Gai's contention that 'no one fitted the mould', and reports being in the process of 'acceptance', 'peace making', and 'the closing of circles'.

> The circle was closed. In many ways. In 'A Hat of Glass' there are many concentrated materials, derived mainly from my anxiety level. I located, I think, my anxiety levels, and each level became a story. The school outing, leaving home, food, travelling to a foreign place [Fayum], meeting strangers who threaten you. In 'Private Shoah', London, the story, the threat of someone who can do something terrible to you and no one would have known that you ever existed. I don't know. In almost all of the stories you can see a parent's death, grief, an *a priori* loss. I tried to

locate this type of anxiety. When I work them through literature, through the literary channel, something is healed within me. There is, undoubtedly, a therapeutic act in writing. Beyond the literary needs. And specifically a closing of circles and an acceptance and peace making, which happen to me immediately after a story is closed.

Literature channelling guilt and shame

I very much like using literature as a channel for the polarising, extreme emotions. Because when you build a new system, you reshuffle the same aggressions, violence and angers, a terrible disappointment, and a terrible shame. Guilt and shame are the two things that are the most difficult for me, to this day. But I can see them. Not that they have become less difficult. When a catastrophe occurs, or a situation in which I feel shamed, or guilty, I still feel it as acutely. What allows me to breathe between the situations, is the fact that I am aware of it occurring, that I mark their territory the whole time, and that the marking of territories is done through the writing.

RL
Do you have a sense of relief when you finish a story?

NS
Today less so, because I am writing with much longer breathing spaces. Writing has become part of my life. It's no longer done in a bubble. 'A Hat of Glass' was written in a bubble. Just so. I didn't leave the house, I looked after the baby and I wrote, I looked after a baby and I wrote. And as you know, in the first few months a baby sleeps. I would stick bottles in his mouth, warm them, I was a functional mother and that's it. And I wrote the whole time, all the hours I was on my feet. Today it's a different sort of writing routine. Another form of discipline. It's split, scattered through my life differently. Do you understand? Therefore these emotions, the intensities which characterised the writing of 'A Hat of Glass' are different. It's also typical of first books. Later you learn techniques, discipline and in particular, your right emotional doses.

When you live in the very intensive emotional doses of another world, you must watch them, so that they do not, God forbid, seep in. This is precisely the axis around which one loses one's sanity. I certainly think that in 'A Hat of Glass' there was something very obsessive, very borderline. After which I learned to arrange the two worlds so that they live in peace with one another, feed each other, enrich each other and not clash with one another. I don't say that there are no situations in which writing is difficult, when I don't succeed in getting out what I want. But I think that this is a matter of technique, training, and many years of work.

'Taking apart the bricks of my life'

RL
So you are speaking of writing as therapy?

NS

No. It's not writing in lieu of therapy. Last night I read Milan Kundera, and he quotes Nabokov as saying that every writer takes apart the bricks of his life, because he thinks that his life is not worthy of being written as a book, he takes apart the bricks and builds afresh. And that's why there is no point, in Nabokov's opinion, in looking for the writer's biography, because from the beginning there is no connection. I always say that all I do is use my biographical materials. But it is no longer me. Gershona was a little bit me, but Hadara is not at all me. Maurice is certainly not me. In *Rali*, there are twenty-two characters none of whom is me, in any way. In contrast to 'A Hat of Glass'. The person who said that there was only one character in that book was probably right. There is one mother and one male/female hero.

'My books could have been written only here'

Today I feel that using the same bricks, my gaze is far less direct. It's me versus these bricks. I like moving materials around, but there is no doubt that I am working in a circle which still interests me. But this circle has certainly widened greatly. In *Rali* you will certainly see it. It is happening here and now. It deals with the Zionist ethos. More so than with the Shoah, it deals with the Zionist ethos. And with issues of children of uprooted people, more so than with children of Shoah survivors. The uprootedness is already an Israeli collective experience. And what I am writing now deals only with new immigrants and the experience of uprootedness. The Shoah stands, for a situation of uprootedness in general.

But I no longer feel like justifying myself when people say to me, you keep returning to the early years of the state of Israel, to new immigrants, to uprooted people, to Shoah survivors. Personally, I do not want to write about Sheinkin.[28] What can I do? There is a certain fashion in the last few years in Israel, and because I am always out of sync, now too I am out of sync, and today's fashion is the type of literature which deals with the me, the private, the here and now, representing what I call 'Sheinkinism'. The individual in the large urban space, Tel Aviv dressed up as New York. My own books could have been written only here. What can I do? I do not pretend to be like someone who lives in New York. I am not contemptuous of it, I am just stating what I am not. Do you understand? I could not write a book about fucking in Tel Aviv. I may be saying it out of jealousy because I would have liked to be able to. To be free of the duty; perhaps I have a duty to continue to deal with these things the whole time? Perhaps it is my duty. I do not find the strength to refuse [to translate Shoah-related plays, for instance]. And I know what it compels me to do. And despite it I continue to be attracted to it. However, I think that *Maurice*, and *Gershona* and *Rali* as well as what I am writing now are really different. The density is different. Do you understand? These are texts with more air. But I can't say that I would not have been happy to write something more fun, freer. In *Rali*, by the way, I did think I had written something different, but didn't the Shoah crop up at least four times? I really didn't think it would come in with the Templars' story, but it did, and how. And Ravensbrück? I didn't know a thing about that place. Only after I had written the word I checked it in the books. What did I know about it? I possibly only knew that it was a women's camp.

Although well structured and ordered, the interview has no coda. The time came to pick up her young twins from kindergarten, and although the domestic help offered to do it for her, Semel decided to pick them up herself and asked me to accompany her. Gendered domestic duties take over, as they punctuate her life and her narrative. We spent another couple of hours, chatting, while she fed the children.

Conclusion

Nava Semel's narrative is a 'key story' to the interpretation of all nine narratives and to the understanding of the complex relations between Israel's second-generation and the Shoah and its survivors. It is a well-ordered and structured auto/biographical account where self, life and discourse mesh to demonstrate how, in making our stories, we make our selves. Like Pines's patients, Semel 'knew and did not know' about the Shoah at the same time; the Shoah and its aftermath were a dark presence at home and in society at large. Semel made her story, literally, by learning to listen to her mother, beyond the silences, when her mother became ready to talk, gradually, partially, leaving many 'memory gaps'. When the mother's story was first told, through a stranger (Semel's boyfriend), it was heard, but not consciously digested. Life – the ontology of the daughter of survivors – was experienced, but no discourse was available to represent it. The road, however, was paved with tell-tale signposts: the school commemoration ceremonies which privileged heroic acts of resistance which the daughter could not equate with her 'passive' mother; the Shoah book she was not allowed to read; the quick name (and identity) change in the army (though not her own). It took becoming a mother for the stories to formulate in the daughter's head and to find their way onto paper. The representational discourses were becoming available and as the daughter began 'making her stories', she went in search of her self, via her mother's stories, which she chronicled as daughter, therapist, and chronicler, all the while writing her own chronicle, making her own self: stories-within-stories.

Semel's narrative charts the process of closing the gap between ontology and representation and signals the very Israeli trajectory from complete silence about the Shoah to an active voice telling, persistently and obstinately, the story of the 'second-generation'. The narrative juxtaposes the heroic versus the (allegedly) passive, Shoah versus *gevurah*, Israel versus the diaspora, the individual versus society.

Semel highlights, with great understanding and mercy, not only Israelis' incomprehension but also the survivors' great strength and tenacity, and with her stories, she helps shift the boundaries of self and society, Israeli and survivor. The themes she brings up in this perfectly structured and ordered 'key story' narrative, are picked up by the other narrators who highlight, perhaps more so than Semel, the central theme of stigmatisation, which is developed in chapter 6.

Writing, according to all the narrators, 'is not a matter of choice'. Seeking out a discourse to make the silences talk, to 'break the conspiracy of silence', was and is 'necessary' (see Stanley, 1996) in order to bridge the gap between ontology and representation. Silence may be the only option – for some – to respond to the Shoah; but for Israel's Shoah daughters, discourse, writing (or making films) was their way to reify their own, and their parents' Shoah and post-Shoah experiences in contemporary Israel, and to begin the process of reckoning, and mourning, for that hitherto unacknowledged '*a priori* loss'.

Notes

1. Israeli publishers tend to insert an English title of books published in Israel on the copyright page, often in preparation for publication in English. The English titles are not necessarily a translation of the Hebrew title. I list both in the cases of all Hebrew books cited.

2. Semel pointed out in her comments that although Hebrew was spoken at home, her parents, just like mine, spoke German, their mother tongue, when they wanted to 'talk about things not intended for the ears of the children'.

3. Adolf Eichmann, an SS *Sturmbahführer*, played a central role in the transportation of Jews to the extermination camps. After the war he escaped to Argentina, where he was captured by the Israeli Mossad (secret service) in 1960, and taken to Israel to stand trial, which ended in his execution (Segev, 1991: 307).

4. Katzetnik 135633 is the pseudonym of the Shoah survivor writer Yehiel Dinur, whose identity was revealed to the Israeli public only during the Eichmann trial in 1961, when he gave evidence and collapsed on the witness stand. The trial was broadcast on Israeli radio. *House of Dolls* is the very explicit, very painful story of a young girl, Daniela, who is a prostitute in a concentration camp. It made a huge impact when it was published, although, as Semel says later in the interview, nobody thought of Katzetnik in literary terms, but in survivorship terms. Today, many children of survivors who write would agree with Irena Klepfisz (1990a: 46) that *House of Dolls* represents violence and sexuality in a manner which borders on the pornographic.

5. For information about Mordechai Anielewicz, commander of the Warsaw Ghetto uprising, see chapter 4.

6. The word, according to Semel's later comments, is actually in Polish, but her mother thought it was Russian.

7. *Shiv'a* means 'seven' to denote the seven-day mourning period Jews keep, sitting at home on wooden stools, and receiving those who offer their condolences, hence the expression 'sitting *Shiv'a*'.

8. Professor Sasson Somech is an Israeli researcher in Arabic literature and studies and a translator of Mahfouz's work.

9. The actual first sentences in the story 'A Hat of Glass' (which is the first story of the collection of that name) are: 'This isn't the whole truth. Only pieces of it have fallen in the passing years. When I collect them, they are like crumbs of mouldy bread' (Semel, 1985: 9).

10. The heroine of *Flying Lessons*.

11. The Templars were Protestant German settlers, motivated by Christian faith to settle in Erez Israel, and who believed that by encouraging the Jews to return to their land, they would bring about the second coming of the (Christian) Messiah.

12. *Bilu* is an acronym for *Beit Israel Lechu veNelcha* (The house of Israel, let us go forth), a Jewish student organisation founded in Kharkov, Russia, in 1882, with the aim of establishing collective agricultural settlements (*moshavot*) in Erez Israel. In 1882 several scores of pioneers immigrated to Palestine and founded several *moshavot* (Dubnow, 1956: 680).

13. Rabbi Meir Cahana was a racist US-born Israeli member of Knesset whose re-election was prevented by an anti-racism law. He was murdered in New York, but his followers are still active: Yig'al Amir, who assassinated Prime Minister Yitzhak Rabin in November 1995, was one of them.

14. My father's birth place. Nava and I had exchanged biographical details.

15. As it happens, Semel's next book after Rali was not 'Snow in Tel Aviv', the book she was talking to me about, but *Isha al Neyar* (Bride on Paper, Semel, 1996), a love triangle between an Erez Israeli man, a new immigrant from Poland, whom he brings to Palestine by fictively marrying her in order for her to gain an immigration certificate, and a major in the British army in pre-war Palestine in the 1930s. Semel wrote to me later that she had decided not to publish the book she was talking about for the time being.

16. See chapter 4 for a detailed discussion.

17. Interestingly 'Artzi' means 'My Land' in Hebrew. It was probably chosen because it sounds like 'Herzig', Semel's father's original surname. This was one way Jewish surnames were Hebreicised; another was to translate the European name into Hebrew.

18. 'Beautiful' in Yiddish. A literal Hebrew translation would be 'Yaffa'. 'Nava' – 'comely' in Hebrew, is a more modern version.

19. Hanna Senesh was a Hungarian-born Israeli paratrooper, parachuted behind Nazi lines during the war and killed by the Gestapo. See chapter 4 for a discussion of her role in Zionist history.

20. Yoram Kaniuk, *Adam Ben Kelev (*Son of Dog*)*, 1969.

21. Dan Ben Amotz, *Lizkor veLishkoach (*To Remember, To Forget*)*, 1968. See chapter 4 for a discussion of the centrality of Dan Ben Amotz in the construction of the *sabra* identity.

22. Aharon Appelfeld, an Israeli writer born in Bukovina, who wrote many novels centred around the experiences of Jews before and after the Shoah.

23. David Grossman, whose *Ayen Erech: Ahava (See Under: Love)* 1986, is an acclaimed novel about the implications of the Shoah in contemporary Israel. *A Hat of Glass* was published a year before Grossman's novel.

24. Yehuda Poliker, the rock artist and son of survivors, featured in Orna Ben Dor's film *Because of That War* (1988).

25. In a later comment, Semel said she really meant to say 'the position of a victim'.

26. Which Israeli society did, as discussed in chapter 4.

27. In Aaron Hass's *In the Shadow of the Holocaust: The Second-generation* (1990), there is a chapter titled 'For this I survived the camps?' This, apparently, is a common reaction by many survivors.

28. The name of a street in downtown Tel Aviv, which has become yuppified in recent years. Together with this gentrification, a new trend in literature has evolved.

CHAPTER 3

BREAKING THE CONSPIRACY
OF SILENCE

Introduction

In deciding to write publicly, the narrators, Israeli daughters of Shoah survivors, are challenging the stigmatisation of their Shoah survivor parents and their exclusion from the Israeli story. This stigmatisation and exclusion continues: in several cases, the narrators' work is reviewed and criticised as the work of daughters of survivors, not merely the work of writers and film-makers, and questions are being asked by some critics as to their 'right' to appropriate Shoah materials in their creative work.

The complex relationship between language and silence regarding Shoah materials is discussed in chapter 4. In this chapter I examine the balance of language and silence in relation to Israeli children of survivors and the narrators' attitudes to that silencing. I then examine the different ways mothers and fathers communicated the Shoah and the gendered differences between men's 'heroic biographies' and women's 'black holes'. All the narrators spoke about the discursive stigmatisation of the survivors and the symbolic dichotomising of gender in the creation of the Israeli State – this chapter documents both this and the narrators' own continuing stigmatisation. By writing and making films, Israel's Shoah daughters have not only put themselves on Israel's cognitive map, they have also attempted to break what they call 'the conspiracy of silence' and the isolation involved in being a daughter of survivors. Despite the fact that the narrators do not all confirm simplistically my assumptions about the masculinisation of Israel versus the feminisation of the Shoah, they make revealing gendered observations, some of them triggered by the inter-view process. By anchoring their narratives to the gendered roles of daughter, mother and wife, narrators confirm women's personal nar-ratives as useful resources in the construction of gendered identities. The chapter concludes by questioning whether the narrators' works were instrumental in, or the consequence of, the shift in the relation-ship between Israel and the Shoah. Above all, the chapter makes trans-parent the complexity of using personal narratives to tell a 'collective story'. The narratives – besides offering a back-cloth to theorising Israel's multi-layered, and gendered, relationship with the Shoah – demonstrate the multi-faceted diversity of people's lives.

Israeli daughters of survivors between language and silence

Dori Laub, child survivor and co-founder of the Yale Video Archive for Holocaust Testimonies, a psychoanalyst who specialises in working with trauma victims, believes that silence is always part of Shoah testi-monies. Historical truth, according to Laub (Felman and Laub, 1992) and Bar On (1994) must not concern listeners to Shoah testimonies. In his work with Shoah survivors and their children, Laub stresses, it is more important to recognise the victim's silence. He can then become a listener who can meet the 'gaping black hole of the unmentionable years', which is how Nadine Fresco, on the basis of her work with chil-dren of survivors, describes the silence that swallows up the survivors' past: 'to speak up and thus to realise the grip of death, which was the grip of silence, seems to have represented for these parents too grave a danger for such an action to seem possible' (Fresco, 1984: 417–27).

Children of survivors often speak about that silence, that 'black hole', 'the black hole' of the Shoah years in Nava Semel's mother's biography. Dina Wardi quotes a child of survivors saying 'I think my parents' problem was that they could not feel again what they had experienced there. They were also unable to speak openly with the children about what happened there' (Wardi, 1990: 37). Child of sur-vivors Helen Epstein says: 'For years it lay in an iron box buried so deep inside me that I was never sure just what was there ... whatever lived inside me was so potent that words crumbled before they could describe' (Epstein, 1979: 9).

The silence about the Shoah might have been a continuation of the power and the victory of its delusional quality. It has taken a new gen-eration of 'innocent children' (as in 'The Emperor's New Clothes'), removed enough from the experience, to be in the position to ask ques-tions. It is often through questioning by the second, even the third,

generation, that survivors were enabled to tell their story. The narrators attest to their parents' silence and to their parents' response to
their sometimes tenacious and obstinate questioning.

The initial Israeli reaction to the Shoah was silence. For years it
seemed that the events of the Shoah were disappearing from Israeli
memory. Yael Feldman (1992) argues that while so much talk about
silence is ironic, when it comes to second and third-generation writers,
the limits of representation are most acutely felt. Indeed, it is in the 'forbidden' realm of Adorno's (misunderstood) dictum about poetry after
Auschwitz (Adorno, 1949: 362) and of Elie Wiesel's (1984) decree that
all those who were not 'there' must remain silent, that most Israeli
Shoah literature is located. For most Israeli Shoah literature, from the
start, is the work of writers who are not survivors. Commentators (e.g.,
Ezrahi, 1980; Roskies, 1984; Mintz 1984; Young, 1990) emphasise the
'otherness' of survivors' testimonials and measure it against the native-
born Israeli Shoah narrative. This norm tends to be mythicisation, col-
lectivisation and ritualisation, adapted to Zionist perspectives and
focused on the conflict between the native Israeli identity and the diaspora 'Jew' they were raised to reject (Feldman, 1992: 229).

Most accounts of the silencing of survivors or of Israeli Shoah literature do not take gender into account. However, there have been
several studies of Israeli women's literature (e.g., Fuchs, 1986; Feldman, 1990; Rattok, 1994). Rattok, for example, argues that the
female voice in Hebrew literature did not wish to replace the male
voice, but rather to join it, albeit modestly. This modesty is forced upon
women by Jewish culture, which does not allow women a public role in
the synagogue. Israeli women writers were therefore neither 'tribal
sorcerers' (Oz, 1979: 22) nor 'community chroniclers' (Appelfeld,
1965: 14). Rather, they were reduced to relative silence in a society in
which novelists and poets are political interpreters, instrumental in
shaping not only the perception of reality, but also reality itself (Gover,
1996: 28–9). The fact that these interpreters were mostly male is
another facet of the masculinisation of Israel. Only in the 1980s
(when this study's narrators started to publish), did Israeli women's literature begin to introduce the 'missing portrait of the woman author'
(Rattok, 1994: 270). Rattok suggests that perhaps the fear of male
criticism of women writers as producing 'empty aesthetics' prevented
Savyon Liebrecht's heroine in the story 'Enduring the Great Beauty'
(Liebrecht, 1986: 143) from publishing her poems: 'The price she paid
for her silence was living at the edge of madness, in increasing isolation... Without a supportive environment ... some women remain
completely silent' (Rattok, 1994: 268).

According to Feldman (1990) Israeli women writers, unlike men,
seem to shy away from telling their life stories directly. I would argue

that this has to do with the construction of the Israeli female subjectivity, subordinated by a guise of equality nurtured by a state intent on constructing a 'new Jew', a construction which, allegedly, included women (as in conscripting women to the army and the attendant images of gender equality). According to Rattok, 'Israel of the 1950s was a young state, fighting for its survival and emphasising the masculine elements in its culture' (Rattok, 1994: 272–4).

Until the 1980s, Hebrew literature was mostly the domain of male writers. The women who wrote fiction mostly wrote short stories and novellas, rather than novels (Feldman, 1990: 494–5). This lack, or silencing, and the reluctance to tell their life stories, may go some way towards explaining the relatively negative reception by the literary mainstream of some of the Israeli writers and film-makers who are daughters of survivors (e.g., Nava Semel, Lea Aini, Rivka Keren, but also Lily Perry-Amitai and Dorit Peleg), and who have tried to escape the constraints created by the Zionist ideology. By comparison, David Grossman's post-Shoah novel *See Under: Love* (1986) was well received, perhaps because he has 'consciously tried to undermine [the constraints] from within' (Feldman, 1992: 227).

'My home was a silent home'

On the screen is an old photograph of three young women, dressed in prewar European style, short tailored jackets, flared knee-length skirts, smiling at the camera. Subtitled, but the voice is barely heard:

> I knew...
> what camp...
> Karola was in...

The picture changes to that of an elderly woman sitting at a kitchen table, writing in a school copybook. The sound is still very muted as the subtitles continue; the film is so quiet that your hand moves to adjust the volume control of your video recorder, but nothing happens:

> So I...
> begged...
> begged him...
> that German officer...
> to send...
> send me...
> to Parsnitz ...
> in the Sudetenland ...

> When I met ...
> Karola ...
> when I met Karola ...
> Karola burst into tears.
> Karola asked me ...
> asked me ...
> 'What?
> You're here too?
> sent here ...
> as a prisoner?'

This scene goes on for a long two minutes and fifteen seconds, a long time for an almost silent scene in a film. Then the telephone rings. The woman looks up. It rings again. She answers the telephone and speaks to her sister, telling her how busy she is with her husband's illness, with making doctor's appointments for him 'until I am out of time... I've let myself go...' The sisters go on to discuss their husbands' illnesses, their own illnesses, and their third sister who is in an old people's home.

Three Sisters (Reibenbach, 1998a) is Israeli film-director Tsipi Reibenbach's second film about her parents. Her first film, *Choice and Destiny* (Reibenbach, 1993), discussed later in this chapter, documents her father telling his Shoah 'story' against a background of mundane domestic activities. *Three Sisters,* supposedly her mother's story, turned out to be a different project to her first, the story of the minutiae of old age, illness, disintegration, spun very carefully from the silent beginning of Reibenbach's mother attempting to write her story in that school copybook. *Three Sisters* is the story of silence. This is how Reibenbach describes the film:

> 'Life has passed and we have achieved nothing', that's what Esther, the youngest (of the three sisters) says. The eldest, Karola, keeps quiet. Fruma, who is also my mother, tries to write what she remembers. Three sisters in their seventies, Holocaust survivors. More than fifty years have passed and still they can't talk of their memories. This is a film about trauma... Three sisters talk on the telephone occasionally but never meet. The film follows their daily lives – three women who, in their old age, devote most of their time to caring for their sick husbands. The camera follows them in the shower and during intimate medical examinations, exposes the wrinkles and varicose veins which will not go away, and the taboo of the naked bodies of the elderly. They are forced to deal with the weakness, loneliness and anger of old age. The Nazis stole not only their youth but also their ability to grow old in serene fulfilment. (Reibenbach, 1998b)

The complex relationship between language and silence in relation to Shoah materials in the Israeli context emerges in the narratives in various contexts. Narrators relate to the silence prevalent in their own families, silenced in turn by a society reluctant to listen to their Shoah experiences.

Savyon Liebrecht, born in Germany in 1948, her Polish survivor parents having been on transit to Israel, is a writer of short stories ('Apples from the Desert', 1986; 'Horses on the Highway', 1988; '"It's Greek to me"', She Said to Him', 1992; and 'A Love Story Needs an Ending', 1995), novels ('A Man, A Woman and A Man', 1998a), television plays ('Deadline', 1989; 'Spears and Orchids', 1992 and 'A Touch of Magic', 1992), and stage plays ('Sonia Mushkat', 1998b; and 'Ducks', 2000, both produced by Habimah National Theatre). Liebrecht argues that Shoah survivors often 'keep total silence, or talk obsessively. I suppose that those two abnormal ways of addressing the subject arise from the fact that the phenomenon is abnormal'.

Indeed, according to psychologist Dr Yitzhak Mendelsohn of the Jerusalem branch of *Amcha*, the National Israeli Centre for Psychological Support of Survivors of the Shoah and the Second-generation, although there seems to be a fundamental difference between those parents who told their children about the Shoah and those who did not, in essence all 'were not able to tell' (personal communication, Jerusalem, November 1992).

Narrators juxtapose familial silences with the public act of commemoration, manifested in Shoah Day ceremonies at school. Liebrecht says it took a long time before she realised that these ceremonies were about her own parents:

> My home was a silent home. They really didn't talk about the Shoah at all. And the first information I had about the Shoah was at school and then I didn't yet understand it was directly connected to my history, to my biography. And I think in some very strange way, this silence somehow sank into unconscious layers and from there begins the creative act. At school they talked about it very generally, like they spoke about the destruction of the Temple. It took me a long time to realise that the Shoah survivor is my father.

Liebrecht has never spoken to her parents about the Shoah. Her parents have remained 'silent' even after the screening of a television film she had scripted, 'Deadline', about this very silence. The film tells of an elderly Shoah survivor who decides to make a video tape telling her story to her children. It takes place a year after her death, when her children are watching the video of the things their mother had not been able to tell them during her life. It is, according to Liebrecht, who was not able to break her own family's silence, but who did it in public, 'the story of the extraordinary breaking of the conspiracy of silence'. Silence, which begins as self-protection, often becomes second nature:

None of us wants to shake the defences and they continue to protect me and I them, and it is convenient for us. This topic remains a taboo topic, we don't talk.

Narrators speak of knowing and not knowing about their parents' Shoah legacy at the same time. Batia Gur, born in Israel in 1947 to Polish Shoah survivor parents, is a writer and critic, who has published several thrillers ('Murder on Saturday Morning', 1988; 'Death at the Department of Literature', 1989; 'Cohabitation', 1991; and 'Orchestral Murder: A Musical Case', 1996) and novels ('Afterbirth', 1994; the story of Yoela, a gynaecologist and daughter of survivors, and 'Stone for Stone', 1998, the story of a bereaved mother who battles the minister of defence for the right to commemorate her fallen soldier son in her own way). She says:

I don't remember when I became aware, I don't know if I was ever actually aware and I think that when the question of reparations from Germany came up, it was mentioned directly. Somehow there was a feeling of war at home all the time, but I don't know when they talked of it with me for the first [time].

As a result, some daughters became ambivalent about listening to their parents' Shoah experiences, as Gur explains:

My mother never talked at all, but my father would say from time to time things like 'you don't know, you don't know what I experienced', and so on. And then I would say, 'yes, what, what, for instance?' and they would not tell. In the last few years she began to tell and I am ambivalent. I am not sure, I mean, on the one hand I sort of really want to know but I get really nervous every time she talks.

Others, on the other hand, were not ready to listen when their parents did talk. Orna Ben Dor, born in Israel in 1954 to Romanian-Bukovinian Shoah survivor parents, is a film maker, whose films include several works on the status of women in Israel (Ben Dor, 1984, 1986, 1991, 1992) but who is mostly acclaimed for her Shoah related films 'Cloud Burst', screened in 1988 on Israel Television, dealing with the reception of the survivors upon arrival in Israel; 'Because of That War', 1988, the story of two rock musicians who are sons of survivors; *Shoah Tova*, 1993; and 'Newland', 1994, discussed below. She says:

Father talked most when I was in my teens. If I said something, no matter what, a 'Shoah hour' would begin. So I would switch off, and I didn't concentrate. Later I realised I had heard it all.

Lea Aini, born in Israel in 1962 to a working-class Sephardi Greek Shoah-survivor father, the youngest of the narrators, has published poetry ('Portrait', 1988; 'Empress of the Imagined Fertility', 1991), short stories ('Sea Horses' Race', 1991; and 'Oleanders, or Poisoned Stories about Love', 1997) and novels ('Sand Tide', 1992; 'Someone (f) Must be Here', 1995; *Ashtoret*, 1999). She too, describes the syndrome of silent versus talking parents, categorising her father in the talking parents category. By talking, he shared what Aini calls 'his yuk' with his family:

> As far as I have read on the subject, I know that there are parents who talk and parents who don't talk. So my father talked from the day that I could hear, he has nothing you could call delicacy. And this coarseness meant he simply shared all of his internal 'yuk' with everyone, whether it was necessary or not. Now, a dominant part of it was the Shoah, of course, which found expression in nightmares, and all sorts of behaviours that, that originated from it...

The silence enveloped Israeli children of survivors not only at home, but also in society at large. However, for narrators who grew up abroad and emigrated to Israel as children, while there was silence at home, the social environment allowed the Shoah to seep through. Naomi Ben Natan, born in Romania in 1947, to Hungarian camp-survivor parents and who went to Israel as a child, is a film-maker whose films deal with political topics (e.g., *40 Jahre Israel*, 1988a, for the fortieth anniversary of the State of Israel; a film about the Palestinian Gaza Communist activist Mary Khas, 1986; 'The Investigation', 1995) and Shoah topics (e.g., 'The State of Israel vs John Demianuk', 1988b; and *Born in Berlin – Three Women*, 1992, a film about three extraordinary Shoah-survivor women, born in Berlin, who have chosen to make Jerusalem their home). According to her:

> the norm was that everyone had experienced the Shoah, everyone I knew had experienced it. How did I find out? It's blurred – my parents didn't talk about it directly, [there were] rumours that there had been a great war and awful things happened. I had terrible dreams in which the question was whether I would commit suicide before they came to take me away. My mother had a number tattooed on her arm, I knew she had been in a camp, a *lager*, but I didn't know details. It was the same with most of my friends. There was a number, or there were other pieces of knowledge. My story was not exceptional. I found out that it was not the norm only many years later.

Breaking the familial silence came much later and often involved a definite approach by the daughters:

> My mother did talk, because I asked, at the age of fifteen or sixteen. I wanted to know. Somehow she told me mostly the human experiences, the better experiences, the lucky events, when she was saved, with a lot

of humour. She didn't tell the really difficult things, until I was much older. (Naomi Ben Natan)

Another reason for the silence that reigned in narrators' homes was the lack of support for survivors in a society intent on nationalising the Shoah. In a more ideologically centred milieu, such as *Yad Hannah*, the kibbutz where Karmit Gai was born in 1949, speaking about the Shoah was part of the political education given to kibbutz children. Gai is a radio and television broadcaster, and in 1992 she published the story of her kibbutz ('Back to Yad Hannah'), which, amongst other things, tells of the struggle of this group of Communist Hungarian Shoah survivors for a place in Israeli society, in which their kibbutz is the only Communist kibbutz. She has published several other books, including a biography of the renowned Habimah actress Hanna Rovina (Gai, 1995) and is also a translator and editor. According to Gai, the Shoah was transmitted as a set of political messages, not as intimate memory:

For me as a child, the Shoah existed as information. I knew my parents' story because I asked questions and got informative answers, not as terrifying descriptions. And it wasn't merely a Jewish matter, but rather a matter of war, a war against Nazism and fascism and because of this, one needed to side with the Soviet Union.

Tania Hadar, born in 1947 in a displaced persons camp in postwar Germany, to parents who spent the Shoah in the Bernowicz ghetto in Belarus, is an ultra-orthodox poet, whose collections include 'There is No Other Mercy' (1975) and 'In the Lands of the Living' (1991). Her father, another 'talking parent', also used the Shoah to transmit a political message, albeit a different, more 'conventional' one – that after the Shoah, Israel is the only place for all Jews:

This was so from a really young age. Because in our home the parents talked of the Shoah, mainly my father, and it was mainly about Israel being the only place, for every Jew. And a Jew who, after the Shoah, doesn't understand it, is wrong... I grew up with this business of choice and price – but not price in the sense of I lost, but on the contrary, I won.

Rivka Keren was born in Hungary and arrived in Israel at the age of eleven. Her books include works for young people ('Kati: a Young Girls's Diary', 1973, about her childhood in Hungary; and 'Sad Summer, Happy Summer', 1986, about her first years in Israel), and novels (the trilogy 'A Taste of Honey', 1990; 'Mortal Love', 1992; and 'Anatomy of Revenge', 1993; and 'Tita and the Devil', 1995). She broke the silence only after her father's death. Four months prior to our meeting, in May 1992, she had visited the Hungarian cemetery where her baby brother had been buried. On her return, she persuaded her mother to talk:

> It wasn't spoken about, nothing said, nothing mentioned, it was taboo. So much so that one day my brother and I dragged Mother to a coffee house and virtually made her talk. What happened in the ghetto? What happened to her? How was the day of liberation? How did Father come back? What did they do, how did she look? And dreadful things came out, things I never knew. So, you may ask, why had she not spoken of it twenty years ago, why had she not spoken of it when I was fifteen?

Beyond the silence at home, narrators stress the silencing of their survivor-parents by Israeli society. Naomi Ben Natan recalls her mother's first encounter with Israeli relatives and the ensuing silencing:

> I remember my mother's meeting with her family in Israel, with her sister from Beit She'an. I will never forget the first meeting of the two sisters. They stood and cried for half an hour – a terrible crying – their whole childhood, everything they had lost – it all ended with this hug. I stood by their side in the yard. After this there were no more questions, no more talking. Nothing. For years. This did it, sort of ... I don't know to what extent it bothered her. It seems natural to me today that if I had met a sister I had not seen for years and in the meantime everything that happened, happened and their mother had died – and I would not have been able to talk to her – I suppose it would have choked me. But it was a complete refusal to listen by those who were here.

Mother tongue – father time

Most studies of children of Shoah survivors do not take gender into account. When the survivor was the narrator's father, talking seemed to come more easily. Fathers, however, tend to talk about facts and, in some cases, to emphasise heroic deeds and acts of resistance rather than suffering, thus epitomising the victim versus hero gendered role division imposed by the Israeli Shoah commemorative machinery.

'Black holes' versus 'heroic biography'

Stressing the heroic element of Shoah survival contrasted with unacceptable diaspora Jewish images, despised by the Israeli-born, who nationalised the Shoah and the murder of the six millions. State discourses coupled the terms 'heroism' and 'Shoah' in the official naming of the catastrophe and of the day Israel set aside to commemorate it, the day on which the Warsaw ghetto uprising started, as discussed in chapter 4. While the dates of the deaths of the millions remain unknown, the armed resistance of the few is commemorated, and nationalised: commemoration precedes mourning.

According to Zvi Dror, male Israeli Shoah survivors tend to give general, factual testimonies in the spirit of Israeli hegemonic masculinity: 'the world of occupation is a world of men and it translated itself to the Israeli army, which is governed by a masculine set of rules, while women testify more emotionally' (Dror, personal communication, December 1992).

In Bar On's study the women he interviewed spoke more openly than the men about the dialogue between fear and hope (Bar On, 1994: 274).

Survivor fathers, unable to look after their families during the Shoah, often became passive and introverted, while survivor mothers often became family spokespersons. Fathers were therefore often at a disadvantage in later years. Psychologists see the survivor father as a victim on the one hand, and as a hero, saved miraculously for his children, on the other, as posing an identification problem for his children, who find it difficult to identify with him as either victim or aggressor (Lieder, 1985: 7–8). Many survivor mothers, on the other hand, became mothers when they were very young, in the displaced persons camps, in transit to Erez Israel, or while trying to adapt to the new state. Although each experienced the Shoah differently, many women survivors had experienced sexual humiliation, which often made telling their experiences near-impossible (Wardi, 1990: 48–50).

Some men find telling Shoah experiences easier. Reibenbach's first film 'Choice and Destiny' (Reibenbach, 1993) documents the almost banal life of her Shoah survivor parents. As they shop, clean, prepare, serve and eat food, her father Yitzhak tells his Shoah story. He tells it factually, unemotionally, although the story itself is heartbreakingly horrific. All the while Fruma, Reibenbach's mother, continues her domestic chores, a silent witness. Thirteen minutes before the end of the two-hour film, she speaks, for five minutes, about her unwillingness to remember, her inability to tell:

> What do you think? How can I tell everything? I lie down at night and I can't fall asleep ... I lie there with my eyes open and I see it ... I lie down for hours and when nobody is at home, sometimes I walk around and I call out loud 'Sarahle, Shimshele, where are you? Where are you? Where? I don't even have a tombstone for you ...' That's it. Tomorrow I can tell you a lot, a lot, a lot. I'll remember again. That's it. (Reibenbach, 1993)

Fruma's outburst is followed by a long silence, as her husband and grandchildren look on. She then repeats the names of her lost relatives. Daughter-director allows her survivor parents to tell, but even in telling, her father seems to find it easier to speak while all her mother can do is mourn. The daughter continues filming as her mother talks about the value of talking, after the long years she had refused to talk, unable to remember:

> Heshik – he didn't live to tell. To get it off his chest. Maybe it would have been easier for him. Maybe he wouldn't have become so sick. Maybe it'll be easier for me too. I'd be able to fall asleep at last. [All those years] I didn't want to talk. I didn't want to. I have told you nothing. Leave me alone, let me be. I don't want to remember. [But] now, you see I'm talking. I could talk all day long ... So many events! So many! I never talked before and now maybe I'll feel better if I let everything out ... (Reibenbach, 1993)

It is perhaps not surprising that the fathers of several of the narrators seemed to concentrate their Shoah accounts on facts, rather than feelings, and more specifically, on acts of 'heroism'. Mothers, on the other hand, spoke, or more often remained silent, about their private suffering. Semel, for instance, characterises the biography of her father, who was not a survivor, but who was active during the Shoah in smuggling Jews into Palestine, as 'a heroic Shoah biography', while her mother 'had a black hole in her biography'.

To comply with Israeli celebrations of heroic acts during the Shoah, narrators often felt they had to re-write their parents' Shoah biographies in accordance with the masculine heroic model:

> I constructed my father as a partisan, in my utterly mistaken opinion. My father was actually a child in a concentration camp, not a partisan, nothing of the sort. But he *was* a partisan, he saved his family, he killed Nazis, in short he was a hero. I couldn't hide the fact that he was a Shoah survivor. I very much wanted to, I mean, I very much wanted to have been a *sabra* third generation and from the *Palmach*, from the youth movements, and so on. But I was always different. I mean I felt more and more 'other'. So I invented stories. This was my weapon, because the real stories about my family scored very low points. I mean it was a great shame. (Orna Ben Dor)

Rivka Keren too, re-invented her biography, but unlike Ben Dor who invented a 'heroic' biography for her survivor-father, Keren re-invented her parents' and her own biography completely:

> I had a very vivid imagination and I used this imagination to compensate myself and to cheat on my friends. I would invent all sorts of stories about myself. I mean I invented for myself another history, another childhood, almost other *parents* I'd say, only to escape this attachment to the Shoah, extermination, guilt feelings, a sort of trap one cannot escape. (Rivka Keren)

This contrast between the victims 'going to death like lambs to the slaughter' with the heroic Anielewicz myth, images taught at school and transmitted in public commemoration ceremonies, led to relief when parents did not carry the outward sign of survivorhood (the tat-tooed concentration camp numbers):

> There were messages on every level, as in 'don't mind her, because her mother came from the Shoah and she is crazy'. This didn't relate to my parents. Because first of all I was terribly happy that my parents didn't have numbers [tattooed] on their arms. I mean it was very, very impor-tant to me. And I remember that when there were numbers, when friends of mine whose parents came from 'there' with a number on their arm and so on, displaying strange behaviours and what-not, that we had to forgive them, to feel sorry for them, not to be angry at them because they were 'crazies' who came from the Shoah. (Orna Ben Dor)

In some cases father-speak was also employed to convey more com-plex political messages about the existential necessity for Israel to be strong and never to lose a war. For Tania Hadar, who stresses the nationalistic, rather than the universal message, the establishment of the state of Israel is 'the most important thing that happened after the Shoah; if it hadn't happened, it would have been a terrible disaster'.

Indeed, survivors often internalised the heroic myths in wishing their children to be different from their own diaspora past:

> [despite absorption difficulties] ... there was a feeling of gratefulness about having a life, and a world and I think that part of it resulted from the fact that they were young, and got married, and loved each other, and were saved, generally, from it all. And their baby daughter was healthy, lived, was a *sabra* and had a big future. I would be different, I am other, I will be free and liberated from all the terrible things. (Batia Gur)

The project of turning their children into a new model of Jew was even more emphasised in the kibbutz where Karmit Gai grew up. Most kibbutz members refrained from talking to the children about their suffering, preferring to stress heroic acts, with the kibbutz assuming the father role:

> it was always partisan heroic stories, and heroic Soviet war films, not the terrors of the concentration camps. But the concentration camp terrors always served as an illustration of how terrible the Nazis were and how you had to be a horrific hero in order to win over them and defeat them.

Dina Wardi argues that in Shoah families, one child is often given the role of 'memorial candle'. These children, not necessarily the first-born, are not only expected to fill a huge emotional void, they are also expected to reconstruct, single-handedly, family and national history (Wardi, 1990: 35). Lea Aini's and Orna Ben Dor's fathers, both obses-sive talkers, appointed their daughters to the role of 'memorial can-dles'. Aini played the role willingly:

My brothers and sisters, and my mother, were deaf to [his stories] ... and
I, I remember, from a terribly young age, because I loved listening ...
and cross-connecting all sorts of things, he perceived very quickly ...
that he had a partner here.

Howeer, Aini's father did not convey a simplistic nationalistic message. His stories were more complex and allowed for victimhood and
suffering, conveying a different, food-related, very strong Shoah message, usually conveyed by survivor mothers:

during my teens, I was dieting and I didn't eat bread [but] it wasn't
allowed not to eat bread. What would have happened if you were in
Auschwitz now, every piece of bread, here one doesn't waste bread.

Fathers often talked of the Shoah to their daughters primarily
because of their own need to talk. In telling me about her father telling
her, Aini mixes her voice with his:

It was a sort of a need of his to off-load and at the same time to get what
he called 'mercy', yes, have mercy on me, how miserable I was ... He is a
very nervous man, very difficult. So it isn't that I am simply nervous and
so on, it's because I have dreamt again that they had come to take us, to
take us all, yes, so you must understand and ... all these stories.

At a certain age, Ben Dor interpreted her father's obsessive need to
relive his Shoah experiences as having neglected her needs as an adolescent. Now she understands his 'need to mobilise enormous dramas'
in order to be able to feel:

I would come to him with a grade and he would say, at your age I was
already after death. So I said to him, look, this was what you did ... and he
said, 'I had already died. In order to feel alive again, I need to mobilise
enormous dramas. Because if it is in a minor key, I can't feel it'. (Ben Dor)

If fathers either spoke about their heroics or used their daughters as
audience, mothers not only said less, and later, they often protected
their daughters from the real horrors:

She told me somehow mostly the human experiences, the better experiences, the lucky events when she was saved, with a lot of humour. She
didn't tell the really difficult things, until I was much older. I knew that
she arrived in Auschwitz by train with her mother and family, that she
understood already then, a few weeks later, when she moved to another
camp, that on that night her parents had been gassed... When they get
off the train and there is a selection and her mother and the adults go to
one side and the young [female] cousins go together and one wants to

join her mother and is forcefully prevented. And that her mother looked at her as if to say goodbye and my mother wrote, 'what did she try to say by this look?' That's all. It's powerful. But this she told me only when I was 35. It isn't something I grew up with. (Naomi Ben Natan)

'Children have a secret task to protect their mothers'

Since mothers seem to have been the parents who transmitted the less heroic narratives (even when their bravery was implicit), it may not come as a surprise that narrators felt protective towards their mothers. By comparison, some sons of survivors express doubts as to what their mothers 'had to do' (implying a sexual price) in order to survive. Throughout her narrative, Semel protects her mother's biography. We negotiated carefully as to which sections of the narrative to omit in order to protect her mother's biography.

Ultimately, however, a daughter's task is to tell her mother's story. For Nava Semel, writing her first book coincided with discovering her mother's 'real' biography, beyond the 'black hole' that was Auschwitz. Writing becomes a danger zone. A few months after writing her first story and consigning it to the bottom drawer, she is tempted to re-read it and is filled with fear for her mother, as she wrote in a magazine article:

What have you done? Where have you gone? Are you crazy? You have approached that word, the word that if you only dared ask about it, God knows what would have happened. She would cry, she would burst out, she would collapse, all would be your fault. What would happen? Children have a secret task to protect their mothers. (Semel, 1986: 44)

But writing, despite the danger to her mother, and therefore to herself, is stronger than her and the image used to excuse it (burnt zone) is a Shoah image:

What right have you to pick other people's wounds? So what if she is your mother, think of the others too. It is not you, it is not only your shadowed childhood, it is the burnt zone of her soul ... It is an existential need, it's under my skin ... (Semel, 1986: 44)

Some narrators protected their mothers from having to worry about them:

I wasn't allowed to be sick. That's true, if I was sick it frightened her ... If she thinks that I am sick, to this day, [if] she thinks I don't feel well, she loses her mind. I mean, this caused me, from a very young age, to hide anxieties, mental and physical. Not to burden her in this way. But I burdened her instead in other ways, without knowing I was doing it. (Batia Gur)

Other narrators knew intuitively that re-inventing themselves as Israeli-born (which entailed having to deny their diaspora origin) would mean betraying their mothers:

> I saw people around me doing it, people who seemed like 'our *sabras*', healthy and wholesome, a myth which was rather a fabrication. I did not do this. Perhaps it was not only intuition but a certain moral duty towards my mother? That I would be betraying her if I felt ashamed of her. I would not do it – denying the past meant being ashamed of my mother. (Naomi Ben Natan)

Some were unable to fully protect their parents, since being a daughter of survivors was shaming in the Israel of the 1950s.

> For instance when I invited friends home, it was terrible. I had a father who didn't speak Hebrew. There is an age you are ashamed of these things most extremely, without any proportion. So I was ashamed of it. Being a new immigrant, and I am speaking of the late 1950s and early1960s, always went together with the Shoah. (Rivka Keren)

Psychoanalytic literature argues that of all the roles transmitted from mother to daughter, the most significant are those transmitted on the eve of the daughter becoming a mother herself (Wardi, 1990: 49). Several narrators said their mothers spoke of their Shoah experiences only when they became mothers themselves. Over the years, however, most of the narrators became able to reach out to their mothers. For some, becoming mothers was the turning point:

> I had to arrive at an age, with a little forgiveness, perhaps to be a mother myself, in order to understand, to have empathy for my mother who was 23 when I was born, after everything she had experienced, to think about her fears. Which, on the surface, she coped with quite well. (Batia Gur)

'I'm actually alive and he died'

Maturity and dealing with Shoah materials helped the narrators understand, and in some cases, forgive, their parents, even when they had been extremely angry, or hurt by not having been told things during their childhoods. Both Tania Hadar and Rivka Keren had brothers who had died young during the Shoah. In both cases they were only told about it later on, and these family secrets had shaped their childhood. Tania Hadar speaks of the brother who had died before her birth as a great loss and a cause for anger at her parents for not having told her:

> I had a little brother who was born at the end of '38. He passed away of pneumonia at the beginning of 1939. I learned of the existence of this

little brother only a short time before I got married. At twenty. They did-
n't talk about it. And I was very angry at my parents. I found out from
my step-grandmother.

For Rivka Keren the death of her brother remained a source of grief
and anger for a long time:

My older brother died as a baby in the ghetto. He starved to death. He was
a baby of ten months and this subject of my brother's death was sort of
half, half-hidden. And I would grieve quietly so they wouldn't realise the
pressures of the grief and didn't talk about it properly to work it through...
I turned it into a real ritual, a secret ritual between me and me. For
instance each evening before going to bed I would pray for him to be resurrected. I mean it was at the age of six, seven, eight. At [the age of] eight
I stopped because I understood it wasn't working. But these were the years
in which I tried to resurrect him and he was, it was, a sort of a myth.

Her brother's death was a source of guilt, identified by many survivors as 'the guilt of the survivor', nurtured by her family's silence:

Something awful was happening here, terrible. Today I admit it, to this
day it is that I'm actually alive and he died. I mean there is something
improper here, that shouldn't have happened. And although no one of
course blamed me directly, it was implied by the silences, by the education I got, where joy, or competitiveness, or striving for excellence and
simple everyday pleasures, were not obvious things with us. The death
of my brother was so fatal to the relationship at home that it was
unbridgeable. It was completely irreversible. It became a real fixation.
And with all my knowledge and with everything I've done, with all my
work on myself, I haven't been able to get over this feeling that ... if I had
not existed, he would have.

Daughters of survivors often find it impossible to harbour anger at
their survivor-parents, and although Keren had always been angry at
her parents for not allowing her brother's death to be spoken about
and worked through, she understands that family secrets do take time
to come out. Having 'made' her mother talk about her experiences
after her visit to Budapest in May 1992, where she found her brother's
grave (as part of a communal grave), Keren admits that 'it's a very
slow process':

It appears that the soul isn't capable of confronting it any faster. It takes
its time. And perhaps it's tragic that it happens to us after fifty years,
because after all, how long do we live, you know, limiting ourselves to
doing it faster, I mean giving us the freedom to breathe sooner, but no.
It stays in there, the heaviness stays inside for years, until it is released.

The narrators' own generation too, must arrive at a certain maturity in order to work the materials through and make peace with their mothers' generation. But importantly, in some cases daughters must wait to make sure that writing about Shoah subjects will not hurt their mothers:

> There is a certain slowing down of the biographical tempo, and a certain acceleration in our spiritual development. Although my mother doesn't read Hebrew so well, there was a very very significant psychological barrier. I am sure I am not the only one, I heard other women writers say exactly the same. For instance [YR] who is dying to write a novel, and she is 53, or 54, and she hasn't written to this day, only for that reason, what will happen if her parents read the book. (Rivka Keren)

'We had to be worthy of these parents'

Having spent months researching her kibbutz past, Karmit Gai insists that she feels no anger towards her parents' generation. Despite the fact that they were politically and socially isolated, even ostracised; and despite constantly feeling an 'other' both inside the kibbutz (because of her parents' separation) and outside it, she kept reminding herself how much more difficult it had been for her parents and their colleagues.

> They never talked then, never expressed doubts [about the Stalin-Hitler pact]. There were no cracks, at all. I found myself, while working on the book, saying to myself, more and more, oops, these are survivors, don't forget. Perhaps it was because they really were twenty, and our son is 22 now, and all the time I was saying to myself, for heavens' sake, they were such children then. As children, first of all their world began to break in that they weren't allowed to go to high school, and they were taken away from Hungary to the camps and all. Their families were finished, and most of them returned, alone. Their world had been burnt. They returned home. Hungary was no longer theirs, Hungarians were physically in their homes. So they joined the Zionist movement, they uprooted themselves, physically, from Hungary and they came here, established a new kibbutz and then all the political mess began. And I remind myself of this all the time, to explain their fatigue later, their 'Leave me alone, I don't want to hear of it any more', that we internalised as children.

Feeling and expressing anger was not on. The children of *Yad Hannah* felt they had to protect their parents from more suffering, or at least not exacerbate their suffering: 'We had to be worthy of these parents. This is a universal syndrome. To be worthy of the parents who survived'.

Making peace with survivor parents entailed putting one's suffering in proportion to theirs. Orna Ben Dor recalls this 'grading' of proportional suffering as she tells of an abortion she had at the age of sixteen and a half:

My father took me to have the abortion. I was afraid, one of these deadly, existential fears when you are sure you wouldn't survive. And I remember saying to myself – what's wrong with you? He was in a concentration camp when he was ten, he got potato skins for his mother, and you are afraid of an abortion?

Savyon Liebrecht, who admits she had taken upon herself the 'memorial candle' role (Wardi, 1990), finds an understanding for her parents' unbroken silence:

I think that my parents remained silent in order to let me grow up normally and not burden me with their history. And I presume they were right. Because a child who grows up in such a new ethos and at the same time is burdened by other ethoses, grows up in great confusion.

Batia Gur, who expressed much anger at the nationalisation of the Shoah and its memory and at what she calls 'the syndrome', can also understand her mother's difficulties:

Look, she was 23 when they came to Israel. For years I lived with guilt and all the other relevant things without thinking it was connected to my mother's [survivor] personality, without understanding it was part of the syndrome. And when I heard of the syndrome of the second-generation, I became apoplectic. I mean I hate being part of a syndrome in general and I didn't like it, because, among other things, I have to be different and exceptional.

For Lea Aini, however, there seems to be no forgiving, no peace making, because her father's pain has nurtured dependence and precluded intimacy. Ultimately, she knows, she cannot make peace with herself or accept herself because of her father's view of life:

It is surely from the same attitude to life he transmitted to me. To us all. Perhaps to me more so, because I was more sensitive. He transmitted [the message] that one mustn't be joyful and one mustn't forget the suffering and mustn't forget the fact that today you have bread and tomorrow you may not.

'We are the *other* of the *other* of the *other*'

My central argument is the conflict between the newly created masculine Israeli normality and the despised, feminised Shoah-surviving diaspora, whose worst 'sin' was having allegedly gone to its death passively during the Shoah. This brought about the stigmatisation of the survivors and their families, a stigmatisation expressed by the narra-

tors and extending to their present lives, and at times, affecting the
reception of their works. Karmit Gai uses the English term 'other'
when she describes the double otherness which *Yad Hannah* members
experienced in Israel as Communists and as Shoah survivors. '*Yad Hannah*' she says, 'was really the *other* of the *other* of the *other*; you could-
n't be more than that'.

'No one fitted the mould'

Karmit Gai's parents and their kibbutz colleagues coped with their otherness by imprisoning themselves within their new kibbutz bubble;
but this didn't help and they never ceased feeling 'other':

> They organised for themselves a little Hungarian bubble that was the
> kibbutz. The fact is that Israeli society didn't accept them ... because
> they were Communists ... because they were different, not necessarily
> because they were survivors. They felt alienation all the time, although
> they were ultimately very Israeli.

Gai's parents' otherness became her personal problem. Her book
was an attempt to answer a question which gnawed at her throughout
her life, the question of being an outsider, an 'other', a difficult thing to
be in the early, conformist, days of Israeli society, but a near-impossible
position in the enclosed kibbutz society:

> The question ... on a personal level, was why was I different? Why did I
> have the feeling of being different? Being different in a kibbutz is the
> most terrible thing, it's a terrible curse.

Gai's book, she found out through readers' reactions, helped many
Israelis legitimise their own 'otherness'. Israelis no longer attempt to
hide their 'otherness'.

> The excitement was linked, ultimately, I think, to some sort of legitima-
> tion of the *other*, of being different ... If it's so, then there are many other
> *others* ... and this feeling of the other is a feeling which is very much
> sharper now, because after all, no one fitted the mould. And only now,
> when everything begins to crumble, these people and the children of
> these people understand that they had invested all their lives either try-
> ing to fit the mould or hiding the fact that they didn't fit. And the chil-
> dren realise that the return they got for the investment wasn't worth it.
> Who wants to be a *sabra* model? What is it, what is that model worth?

If for Karmit Gai the otherness was compounded by growing up in
a Communist kibbutz, for Orna Ben Dor (and to a lesser extent for me
too) it was compounded by her parents' Romanian origin:

I was very very ashamed of my parents' 'Romanian-ness' and I was ashamed of their survivorship and refugeeship... Mother [was part of] a group of survivors who were in a *moshav*. And they called them RIF, the name of that soap.[1] And they would steal from them the few things they had and they evacuated all the people of their age group because there was a war on, and left them to work. This stemmed from the fact that they hadn't learned Hebrew, being ashamed of their language and their inability to be part of the group ... My parents lived in Giv'at Shmuel. It was an army neighbourhood and Gandhi[2] was our neighbour. I had just been born. One night he gave a banquet for Meir Harzion[3] who had just returned from some (adventure) ... and they made a terrible noise, and Mother sent Father to ask them to be quiet so Gandhi said to him, I am either going to shoot you, or send you back to Romania.

'My roots are "there"'

This feeling of 'otherness' resulted in uncertainty about narrators' Israei identity:

My roots are 'there', sort of, and not here. I very definitely don't see myself as an Israeli. It's sort of silly to say this, because I am very Israeli, my way of speaking, my behaviour ... but I am not. I think I have fixed my identity at a late age and I think my identity has to do with my parents' refugee-ship and not with them finding a home here. (Orna Ben Dor)

Israeli-born Lea Aini also does not see herself as an Israeli and links this to her father's Shoah history:

I have a problem with this Israeli identity. Because the truth is that I have a love-hate relationship with this place. I have never belonged here, to anything.

'I am always inside-outside'

Although they are all central figures in Israeli literature, narrators speak of feeling both inside and outside of Israeli culture and society:

It will never be different. I am always inside-outside. The more I am inside, the more suspicious I am towards what I am inside of. I simply want to be outside all the time as well, and to examine what is happening, and I can't. I can't avoid seeing the truth. (Batia Gur)

'I knew I wouldn't be like them'

The narratives chart clearly the tension between Israeli and Jew. Not surprisingly, the children of survivors who express their 'otherness' most vividly are those who arrived in Israel as children, and were not born in Israel, and experienced the stigmatisation personally. The Israelis' unwillingness to accept their survivor parents marks their

'otherness' in contemporary Israel and at the same time marked them
as 'Jewish', not 'Israeli'.

> I think there was a difference – even today – between me and the *sabras*.
> It was definitely because I came from 'there'... I know that my *sabra*
> friends absorbed the fact of being Jewish only when they went abroad
> for long periods and lived there among non-Jews. To me it was clear *a*
> *priori*, my otherness was the consequence of coming from 'there'.
> (Naomi Ben Natan)

Because refugeeship, as well as widowhood, prevented her mother
from becoming fully acculturated, Ben Natan's mother's story is a classic story of migration, 'otherness' and alienation:

> My mother never really acclimatised. When she arrived she had no time
> to learn Hebrew. She had to face becoming a single bread-winner and
> being culturally cut off as an immigrant, although she knew she had
> done the right thing – for me. I don't think she thought she was doing
> the right thing for herself, as it meant emigration, living as a stranger in
> a strange place, cut off. For her Israel never became her own landscape,
> compared with the European forests, and autumn wasn't autumn. She
> remained an immigrant, although she knew she would not be perse-
> cuted here. (Ben Natan)

However, Ben Natan herself absorbed the dominant Israeli ethos
and made it her project to become one of the *sabras*, although she
knew she would never fit the *sabra* mould (although, ironically, she *is*
blond and blue-eyed ...)

> I had a clear aim. To be absorbed here. Completely. But I knew I would-
> n't be like them, our beautiful *sabras*, the blond, the rooted, with the
> blue-eyed gaze, whose parents served in the *Palmach*. But I wanted to be
> absorbed, so I threw myself into the language, learned the songs,
> adopted childhood memories from here, went on hikes, everything ...

Because of the efforts she made to become 'Israeli', being reminded
of her 'otherness' hurts, to this day:

> What does it mean, 'other'? It had to do with nothing apart from the fact
> that I had had another life, I didn't have a normal family exactly. I was hurt
> once, when I met someone I hadn't seen for several years and she said to
> me, oh, you no longer have an accent, or something like that. Because as
> far as I was concerned, I never *had* an accent. And it offended me.

To compensate, and in order to fit in, Ben Natan too changed her
biography:

I would make myself a little younger, I lowered the age at which I came here, it was sort of getting closer to the date of birth, from eleven I would go down to ten and then nine-and-a- half and I blurred it somehow so it would become sort of insignificant.

Today, perhaps because she never felt that in order to become one of the gang she had to deny her past, Ben Natan no longer feels an outsider.

Fortunately, all this didn't entail denying home, language and childhood pictures – I didn't feel that in order to be absorbed one had to erase, so I didn't erase. I felt I could be absorbed without denying.

Ultimately, Naomi Ben Natan regards the dichotomy between 'heroism' and 'lamb to the slaughter', employed to divide Israelis from survivors and to stigmatise survivors, as meaningless:

I talked about it with my mother and she said, it's very difficult to understand or transmit the complete powerlessness. What are we talking about – lamb to the slaughter? Uprising? These arguments seemed to me artificial already then. All the symbols. So there is an uprising here and an uprising there, so what? All the rest, what was it?

'Buying a place in society'

For Rivka Keren the memory of being 'other' is still vivid and unassuaged and she talks of it haltingly, yet emphatically and with great pain. Having experienced acute antisemitism and hostility during her Debrecen childhood, and coming from a Zionist home (the family obtained legal emigration papers only in 1956), going to Israel was the fulfilment of a dream. The reality, however, was a great disappointment.

I came with a different internal world to a completely hostile environment. I took into consideration that there would be language problems. I knew no Hebrew, only a few words. And I had images of the children of Israel as tanned, and healthy and eating oranges all the time. So *I* too wanted to be like that, but I was pale and I was sort of dressed in those shoes and that track suit, I was a classic new immigrant. So of course I felt foreign in my looks. But *this* was not the important thing. Inside, a terrible thing was happening. Because, gradually, my world started to collapse. I arrived with the Hungarian language, the Hungarian culture, while children in Israel knew nothing. They gloated in a sort of vacuum of orange groves and sand and, and marshes,[4] and I fell into this environment, and inside there was a great confusion. I suddenly found myself between two stools, on the floor ... And this makes a mess of your identity and your self-image at this sensitive age.

Her sense of alienation was directly linked to the Shoah, but she found it impossible to share her Shoah past with her new Israeli friends. Her family's suffering only stigmatised her further: 'It was very shaming to have a Shoah background. It wasn't a thing I could pour my heart out about and buy a respected place in society'. Instead of telling her school friends scary Shoah stories, Keren coped with her stigmatisation by using her talent for painting to draw posters for the teachers and decorate the copybooks of her school friends, in order to 'buy a place in society'. But it did not fill the emptiness inside. 'I never had any [school] breaks. They would queue up with their copybooks ... and I would draw the covers. It was literally bribery. It sounds terrible'.

However, this did not prevent her teachers from wishing to re-invent her diaspora identity by attempting to change her surname, Friedländer, to a Hebrew name, a common nationalising strategy reported by many immigrants to Israel. But she insisted on keeping her name.

> There was no anchor, no altar one could ask for 'help, help'. Among the teachers ... were some who literally hated me ... they would mock my name, I was still Friedländer then, to a point that I really hated my name and it took me years to understand that it's a ... respectable name like any other, that one didn't have to be ashamed of it. They said what is it, this diaspora name? What is it, a German name? Are you from Germany? And the association was immediately the Nazis ... It created a certain [person] who had come from 'there' and now we have to sort of make her one of us. I had to fight for my place terribly hard. I tell you, I simply had to use tricks to ... buy myself ... a certain position, a certain place in society, I really needed it.

'I didn't feel anything special'

However, the experience of 'otherness' and alienation was not reiterated by all the narrators. Tania Hadar grew up in Lod, a small mixed Arab-Israeli town near Tel Aviv, among immigrants from all areas:

> I didn't actually feel anything special about being a daughter of survivors. Not at all. Yes, I mean an awareness from home, yes, as part of the parents' past, but not as something different in society.

Savyon Liebrecht too, lived in a heterogeneous neighbourhood of Shoah survivors and Mizrahi Jews and 'very strangely, I was somehow taught a certain superiority over them. So I didn't, I didn't grow up with the feeling of the discriminated Shoah survivor'.

For her, becoming Israeli 'wasn't a project. I didn't see it as a mission to become something I was not. My language was Hebrew, the landscapes I saw were, were Israeli. I had no memory of another place and if I am asked to define myself, I am Israeli'.

'I am also different in the way I write'

For many children of survivors, the legacy of their parents' otherness has developed into a full-scale personal otherness, especially regarding the reception for their books or films. Their works have often been reviewed as the works of daughters of survivors, not on their own merit. According to Zvi Dror, writers of the second-generation, who, he argues, are often 'obsessed with the Shoah', tend to regard themselves as 'better', due to their proximity to Shoah experiences, and therefore demand a more sympathetic approach to their books. He criticises them for valorising, rather than negating, the diaspora, a very Zionist reading:

> Since the topic became acceptable, members of the second-generation ... have become marketable. What their parents sought to conceal, they expose. Moreover, they even adopt ideologies connected to the diaspora, which their parents who are living in Israel have criticised ... The pioneering-pragmatic Zionism has become a Zionism of memory ... legitimating the diaspora despite what happened to our nation in the diaspora. Readers must differentiate between reading a book by a member of the second-generation and literature written by the generation who experienced the Shoah. (Dror, 1992: 41–2)

Despite the initial dismissive critical response to Nava Semel's 'A Hat of Glass' (1985), it has become a 'second-generation' classic. In 1988, Semel was awarded *Massuah*, the Institute for Holocaust Studies Award for the book. The writer and critic Zvi Herman said at the award ceremony that Semel 'is an exception in the young generation of Israeli writers, not merely because of her themes, her emotional depth and her richness of thought ...'

But the initial response still hurts. The following section deals with the narrators' response to the critical response to their work.

'A very one-sided film'

Orna Ben Dor's films got a mixed reception. While 'Because of That War' (Ben Dor, 1988) was acclaimed,[5] the documentary 'Cloud Burst' (Ben Dor and Kaplanski, 1988), which dealt with the reception for the survivors, was heavily criticised. Israelis refused to acknowledge that the survivors were stigmatised and discriminated upon their arrival.

> It was a very one-sided film, some sixty articles were written against the film. People attacked me in the street, it was very difficult, especially the *Palmach* generation, because I actually attacked them directly. There were awful headlines in the newspapers like 'I was an SS officer in *Sha'ar Ha'aliah*'[6] and the like.

Ben Dor's short television drama 'Shoah Tova' (Ben Dor, 1993) was not shown in Israel for almost three years because its title, meaning

'Good Shoah', which Ben Dor refused to change, was banned by the Israeli film censor. This is an example of how not only commemorating, but also naming had to fit the official version of nationalised memory. In 1995, she won her appeal against the censor and the film was broadcast on *Yom HaShoah* in 1995. 'Newland' (Ben Dor, 1994), depicting the stigmatisation of the survivors, this time in dramatic form, was also slated by most critics, who refused to accept this stigmatisation, although some reviewers found the film 'beautiful and moving' (Megged, 1994b).[7]

The hostility towards Ben Dor's version of the Israeli reception for the survivors continued when she took part in a television debate after the television version of Tom Segev's *The Seventh Million* (Bruner and Segev, 1995). *Ha'aretz* criticised Segev for being a 'hostile foreign correspondent' (Tal, 1995: A3), and Ben Dor for 'repeating the basic clichés of that mythic fact' (of the hostile reception for the survivors) (Bronowsky, 1995: B8).

'I am not part of the establishment'

The narrators not only continue to live as 'others'. They also ascribe the hostile reviews of their books (which have also received good reviews and sold extensively) to this otherness and to the inability of the Israelis to cope with them as daughters of survivors, who tackle the sacred topics of the Shoah, and of nationalised grief and loss in their own individual ways.

Lea Aini's 'Sand Tide' (1992) is a 'counter narrative' in Israeli terms, the story of an army widow who refuses to follow nationalised grief procedures and insists on pitching a tent on her dead husband's grave.[8] Aini spoke about being hard to categorise – she is neither well-schooled and middle-class, nor a product of the working-class, Mizrahi 'second Israel'. Reviewers found both 'Sea Horses' Race' (Aini, 1991), a collection of short stories about people who live on the margins of society, both geographical and social, and 'Sand Tide', difficult to digest. She identifies shades of classism and racism in the reviewers' attitude:

> Perhaps they were a little scared that here was someone who dealt with slums and so on without a political viewpoint. I sort of penetrate their middle-class living-rooms and make a mess. I am not part of the establishment. I am not an intellectual, I haven't studied literature and haven't got a clique behind me. Apart from that I am not at all Polish [referring to her Sephardi origin]. In all the interviews I give they return again and again, like a damn curse, to my childhood, and they don't understand how a young woman whose father sold fodder can write, people can't accept it.

Aini's stories are in complete contrast to the *sabra* heroic narrative. But although she has never felt discriminated against, her feeling 'other' has persisted since childhood. She attributes it all – being different, coming from a home where there were no books, music, or carpets – to her father's Shoah experiences.

> I think that had he not been a Shoah survivor, the home would not have been so ascetic in the sense that what was important was to have food in the fridge. The rest was unimportant.

Aini internalised this otherness to such an extent that she resolved, at a young age, to be different from her parents, even if she had to pay the price for it; apart from belonging to an 'other' family, she also was uncompromisingly 'other' at home and in society. And the price was high.

> I have always rebelled. I was actually very lonely. I was always isolated, I would look different, dress differently, but not like the children at school. Because there too I was not one of the gang. I wasn't one of the family and wasn't one of the gang.

And now, battling with an uncomprehending press, she is resolved not to follow any literary school:

> I am different in the way I write too. From the beginning, already in 'Portrait' [her first collection of poems, 1988], in the first reviews, no one could have said I had taken from anyone. And this too, by the way, is hard to swallow. Because it's much more convenient to categorise you.

'Otherness' has been a part of Lea Aini's life to such an extent that she finds it near-impossible to enjoy her success. The price she pays is internalising her stigmatisation.

> Look, of course if the reviews had been less reserved, I would have been happier. But, this is only secondary. The main thing is that I don't accept myself. No, it starts from me. What happens is that I minimise the praise and exaggerate the reservations.

The result is a near total alienation in contemporary Israeli society:

> I don't like it. I don't like that Israeliness of the songs. I don't like Israeli literature. I hated the army. I simply hated it. I served in the army, but I very much hated it. This finds expression in everything.

Ultimately, Aini's literary success and her present fulfilment cannot make up for the legacy of despair, otherness and the existential combination of pain and yearning, willed by her father and which she conveys in her writing. Nothing can make her forget the pain, forget the legacy of the Shoah.

I definitely think that there is no meaning. To anything. This was what they tried to teach me at home, that the only things which have any meaning are food, and clothing and health, and such things. And it wasn't enough for me. So I went looking for other meanings. But this too isn't enough. I am trying to soften that pain, which is there all the time, in things which are very important to me, such as my family and my home and the things I love doing. But I don't think for one moment that these are the things that would take the pain away. And I also don't really believe in anything. I don't know how to say it, but the whole business has a huge price, because the fact is that you can't deny the pain. This is how I live.

'A racist attitude towards anyone who is not from here'

For Rivka Keren too, the pain of otherness and stigmatisation have not diminished. She too, speaks of the hostile reaction to the first books in her trilogy, 'A Taste of Honey' (1990) and 'Mortal Love' (1992).[9] The third novel in the trilogy, 'Anatomy of Revenge' (1993), published after our meeting, also received mixed reviews, but won the Kugel Award in 1996. Some critics, such as Eleonora Lev, herself a daughter of survivors, who has written a book about her journey to Poland and about her Shoah past (Lev, 1989), takes Keren to task for writing about what she calls 'a sacred topic' which one should refrain from touching:

> Rivka Keren's novel deals – as we understand from its oh-so-delicate title which relies so heavily on the reader's sensitivity – with an archetypal fantasy of revenge, very common in Shoah survivors and their children, but also in many who were not 'there': the impulse to close the broken circle, plug the cracks in the world we had known, not allow the horrible sin to pass without compensation ... This book, like its title, is tasteless, awkward, cliché-ridden and repulsive. Reading it, one yearns for the days ... when most of the writers, in Israel and elsewhere, treated the Shoah like a sacred topic and refrained from touching it.(Lev, 1993: 13)[10]

Keren attributes this critical hostility to her unorthodox way of dealing with the lives of Shoah survivors in contemporary Israel.

> If one delivers messages which don't touch the right place in the *sabra* body, one is rejected. There were people who simply hated 'A Taste of Honey'. But the reaction was so visceral, so amazingly powerful, that I understood that I did something big. I asked myself why, what am I describing here. There are intensities, of course, it's built on intensities, it's a book which has a strong cathartic process, but an adult who has done some work on himself can go with it without carrying such burdens of hatred.

'Mortal Love', the second of the trilogy, was criticised because of its non-linear, associative structure. Does this mean that the male *sabra* logic is linear and incapable of coping with a different, diaspora thought pattern? And has the legacy of the Shoah and therefore of its survivors and their children fractured that linear memory? [11]

> Just as life isn't linear, but associative, so I feel the need to construct my books. People with linear thought patterns find it very hard to cope with the structure of my books, and even the psychic structure of my characters is different from what exists here in Israel. But these are living people, these are people I knew. I didn't make them up. But they weren't absorbed, because maybe something in their psychic climate threatens the Israeli-born, I don't know how to define it, but there exists in Israel a certain blindness to any 'foreign' penetration.

Keren rages against this blindness, this refusal by some (male) Israeli writers to accept any 'other', including the otherness of 'there' and the Shoah, and implicitly, Judaism itself. To her, this is another facet of the Israeli arrogance towards the diaspora, the Shoah and its survivors.

> Their arrogance, their denial of all that business of 'there' and Shoah and the different heritage, implies something so, élitist, no, worse than that. It is cruel. Very cruel. It's possible to understand the people who were captivated by the idea of returning to the land of Canaan and becoming Canaanites[12] and not Jews at all. But they are denying Judaism as Judaism. It's not only in literature or art. This roughness, the prejudices, a certain racist attitude towards anyone who is not from here and not from now.

Earlier I have linked the silence about the Shoah to the silence about the expropriation of the Palestinians (see Laor, 1995; Ram, 1999). Keren identifies the Israeli arrogance towards the diaspora with an Israeli tendency towards power and control (over the Palestinians? she doesn't say).

> It is certainly a power society, a society which admires control. People openly step on corpses and do awful, hard things. It's like a terminal illness. It's something very tough, very closed, very blocked off, a complete lack of flexibility. Here we are, a minority within a minority, a minority within ourselves, so we crush each other all the time because we are endlessly frustrated.

'The message is that I'll remain different'

Keren believes that people do not understand her, but although she feels this gives her a sense of vocation 'through my ability to influence the consciousness of a group of people', the pain of not being accepted is hard to bear and no publishing success, no support by academics and some critics, can assuage that pain of being forever 'other' in her chosen country.

> Look, the message is that I'm different and that I'll remain different. And perhaps it even gives me a position of strength, but it means a lot of pain. I don't know whether to link it to the Shoah and to my background and to what I am carrying with me. It's a fate I carry with me. But what can we do? What can we do that we have the Shoah in the background?

Writing about the Shoah is her fate, her 'personal identification mark', or stigma:

> It's a personal identification mark, the characteristics of which are unfortunately amongst the most horrifying events known in human history. But what can we do that this is what happened to us? It isn't I who have chosen it. So why do I keep returning to it? Not because I am a masochist, [but] because these are uncomparably *strong* materials. Because what is stronger than the Shoah?

'Accepting ourselves as other'

Otherness may be assuaged by the creative process. Things have changed since the mid-1980s and Israelis seem to be in a process of learning to accept themselves as weak, to accept themselves as Jews, and therefore accept the Shoah. After years of silence, 'Now, strangely enough, over the last two or three years, this past has come back into Israeli consciousness in the most vivid way' (Friedländer, 1988: 288). For the narrators, writing or film-making has gone some way towards answering questions of why they had always felt 'other'. It helped expiate this legacy of acute otherness, replacing it with an ability to accept their parents' generation, other outsiders, themselves. As Karmit Gai puts it:

> I told myself the story and I said to myself, it's all right to be different. Regarding the other, there was a legitimisation to being different, to differing from the mould... And this in my opinion is something Israeli society has only recently begun to confront.

'Breaking the conspiracy of silence'

To find out how the narrators attempted to put themselves on Israel's cognitive map, I asked each of them when, how and particularly why they began to write or make films (I use 'writing' to mean both). All the narrators link the creative act to being Israeli daughters of Shoah survivors, and personal histories as writers are backgrounded by the silencing by Israeli society which made them want to write and by the effect of the dominant ethos which they needed to change and make their own.

Apart from the narrators' personal reasoning of how they became writers or film-makers, there have been several national triggers which influenced their awareness of the Shoah and therefore their creativity. These triggers are closely linked to the history of the state (see chapter 4) and resonate with my own increasing awareness of the Shoah. The first was the 1961 Eichmann trial and the most recent was the 1991 Gulf War when Israeli Jews were forced to remain in sealed rooms, threatened by Iraqi chemical warfare (gas). The fact that the gas was produced and sold to Iraq by Germany added to the irony and anger, pressing all the buttons of the Shoah codes (Segev, 1991; Zuckermann, 1993). Some narrators list Katzetnik's writing as their first encounter with the Shoah in Israeli literature.

Narrators gave various reasons for starting to write. The most poignant reason was the compulsion to break the conspiracy of the silence by which the narrators were surrounded at home. And although the Shoah is rarely the main theme, its presence looms large. Savyon Liebrecht, for instance, demonstrates what Semel calls the 'seeping' of Shoah materials into her writing, somewhat unconsciously:

> For instance in a story like 'Room on the Roof' [1986]. It's a story about the relationship between a woman who is building a room on the roof and an Arab construction worker. Now, this story does not seem to have any link to the Shoah, at all, at all, but there is one sentence there when she brings them coffee in a china service her grandmother had brought from Germany. I find Germany or the German topic saying hello almost in every story. Or take the story 'Apples from the Desert' [1986]. That woman, Victoria, who has nothing to do with the Shoah, who arrives at the kibbutz to bring her daughter back. And the young man her daughter lives with is called Doubie and when she asks what sort of a name it is, he says he is called after his grandfather who was killed by the Germans during the war. In some way, it's planted, very indirectly, in every story.

Other reasons for starting to write can be categorised as follows: writing as a compulsion, writing to escape or 'talk to someone', writing or making films because narrators 'did not belong', writing as a reaction of having 'deserted the family memories'. And writing in order to influence, or to 'take the Shoah out of the museum'.

'Writing is not a question of choice'

The narrators often refer to their writing as a compulsion, a no-choice act of self-expression, or the only way of coping. Nava Semel writes about this compulsion in terms of 'forced labour':

Writing is not a question of choice. One should rather liken it to forced labour, when you, the writer, don't know who is the obstinate entity who is pushing your hand onto the paper, demanding that you make contact with the materials of your life. It won't allow you to sink into pleasantness, it hits you and pushes you into the hard, burning materials which you have hidden with secretly clenched fists. They flood all the dams you had laboured to build, they splash you and wash you into the sewers. Have I not protested against it umpteen times? In the four years during which I wrote 'A Hat of Glass' I shouted many times 'Enough!! Why me?' As if someone pointed at me with his finger and compelled me to do it. It wasn't a duty, perhaps a bond, the payment of which was due. I wasn't even conscious of the cunning process in which the strange entity pulled me into the trap (Semel, 1986: 44).

Other narrators too speak of writing as a compulsion. Rivka Keren:

I don't think I can stop writing. That's it. With me there is a constant accumulation of materials that I have to get out in this very specific way.

Lea Aini:

Writing chose me. No one sort of sent me writing. I mean it certainly comes from somewhere. Because I didn't have any stimulation, or encouragement at home to write. On the contrary. But I also chose *it*, there's no doubt.

Tania Hadar, on the other hand, speaks of poems 'emerging', suddenly, at a young age, out of definite Shoah dreams:

I had nightmares at a later age, when I was already deep into my writing, there was a period of nightmares in which I am being shot at and that I die and that I, there were all sort of dreams, very, very difficult dreams, during that period. But on the other hand, they also helped me later with my writing ...

She describes a dream, like a Chagall painting, with people gliding up and down glass hills, 'like Jacob's ladder'. This dream inspired a poem, 'linked to Jerusalem and the Shoah', as are many of her poems, which link Shoah images with Biblical and contemporary Jewish images.

'Writing in order to escape'; 'writing in order to talk to someone'

Lea Aini has always been writing at the threshold of great pain and yearning:

It seems to me that the yearning, the pain have always existed and will always exist, something existential. As an ongoing thing. And I don't believe it will become any better.

Like Aini's, Rivka Keren's writing was a reaction to loneliness and unhappiness:

> Writing grew out of unhappiness, loneliness, a wish to talk to someone. So one talks to the paper. Why writing and not something else? Because intuitively I felt that I was strong verbally. I mean ... I can create a world with words. Therefore it was words ... I have always painted too, but, the verbal expression was stronger. So I started writing because it was a saving. It really was an anchor. At the start in Hungarian and later in Hebrew.

'I didn't belong, so I went to see films in the dark'

Orna Ben Dor has known that she wanted to make films since she was ten:

> There was a cinema near us at which films changed every day. I would see a film every day. I wasn't sociable apart from being able to tell horrifying stories to my classmates. I somehow didn't belong. So I went to see films, in the dark. I knew I would make films from the age of ten. Really. I knew that this was what I wanted, you can say, the freedom.

'I have deserted my memories'

Writing as a way of expiating Shoah memories and exorcising Shoah presences underpins the reasons given by most of the narrators as to why they write. Mediating Shoah memories is most directly apparent in both Nava Semel's and Tania Hadar's narratives. While Semel talks about the need to solve the riddle of the 'black hole' that was Auschwitz in her mother's life, for Tania Hadar writing is a reaction to feeling she had deserted the memory of those who had died.

> While I was writing, I was reading Elie Wiesel's *Night* [Wiesel, 1960] which shocked me enormously. I was alone at home and I simply cried, so I wrote a sort of a diary in which I referred to this business of having run away, sort of deserted the memories of the parents, the relatives who passed away, who were murdered. I saw it as a sort of betrayal, you know? I felt awful, I actually cried. And, and I remember afterwards, a flow of poems came out, mainly featuring family figures, my grandfather, my grandmother, not yet in a structured form. I even created a structure for the book, which I called 'The Family Album'.

Hadar did not publish these first poems and re-started writing four or five years later although her first published poems had nothing to do with the Shoah.

> Writing about the Shoah came later. There are allusions to the family, but indirectly. The subject I tried to tackle was war, but there was no direct reference to the Shoah. Yes, in the background were the barbed-wire fences, the babies. It was in the atmosphere, but not directly like in this [her most recent] book.

In 1978, Hadar visited Germany and the Jewish cemetery in Frankfurt, her birth-place. This led to tackling the Shoah in her poetry, and, less directly, to her return to orthodox Judaism:

> I remember seeing at the entry to the cemetery 'I shall walk before God in the lands of the living'.[13] And with the double meaning, that is both a cemetery and the land of Israel. I remember seeing these Hebrew letters in Frankfurt, inside all the noise and the industrialisation. I didn't feel any closeness, although I was born there, I felt very alienated. The whole feeling of Germany was very difficult. But it was a great gift. And I think that from that journey on, I mean it took some more time, but I started to write. And these poems were written differently. Link upon link. The connections were very difficult ... but I knew that I mustn't give up.

Karmit Gai wrote her book in order to understand her own otherness, but also to give her parents' group an opportunity to exorcise their Shoah past. Instead of asking them directly about the Shoah, she preferred to start with 'the day after the war before' because she did not want them to 'start telling me all their stories' and because she didn't 'so much want the horror but the life born out of the horror'. In a way she too was writing in order to compensate for deserting her parents' memories. Her book helped her parents and their colleagues to talk about things they had never been able to talk of before. When she finished taping the individual testimonies, Gai assembled them and played back the interviews. Some kibbutz members used rape imagery such as 'open legs', and 'penetration' to argue that in the very public kibbutz environment, their Shoah memories were their last bastion of privacy.

> They heard many of the stories for the first time. And they said that they hadn't been able to talk about it because they couldn't talk about it. Not because they didn't want to disclose it, but because they couldn't talk about it, to themselves, because it would have meant that they would simply not have been able to do anything else in life. Only talk. The other thing was their fear of banalisation. They'd say to me, what can I tell you? And the interesting thing was that in the kibbutz there were no secrets and everything is so open that they wanted to keep at least their personal history to themselves, and not talk about it. Because this would have meant that really, you open your legs and everyone can come and do whatever they want. They had a feeling of penetration into their privacy, in their Shoah accounts.

'I had a wish to influence'

The most public motivation for writing or making films is the wish to use the creative product in order to change things, to influence opinions and events. 'Doing meaningful things' is perhaps more easily achieved by making documentary films for television than by writing novels, short stories or poems. Naomi Ben Natan expressed this wish most clearly and openly:

> I had wishes – beside the wish to express myself – to influence. I grew up in a period in which if you didn't do something meaningful for society, you were wrong. Perhaps I don't mean influence, but meaning. Have someone else hear it. That's why I do what I do.

Ben Natan has always been involved in public causes, primarily because of her fear of Israeli society becoming a 'rhinoceros' society.[14]

> I started by researching news reports. This brought me to the occupied territories, to the Black Panther movement,[15] to reading political and social background material, I have never made archaeological or nature films, but I've made several films on Shoah subjects – a film called *Transport,* the story of a deal between a Dutch Jew from Bergen-Belsen and the Templars in Israel; a film about the Demianiuk trial – and other political topics, including a film about the Communist Palestinian activist Mary Khan in Gaza. This has been my direction all along.

However, Ben Natan realises that her early wish to change things, to influence, had perhaps been too ambitious. The *Intifada* disillusioned her and she makes the inevitable link with Nazism.

> I didn't despair but I understood that my ability to influence and do things is minimal, and everything became complex and I had no energy to do things really forcefully. Perhaps I didn't see the point and I tormented myself. Here we are all becoming rhinoceros, and this is exactly what happened to them, there, in the 1930s. And if I do nothing, I am part of the process. After a certain time I gave up. Everyday life, children and so on, distract you ...

Ben Natan sees her politics and concern about the nature of Israeli society as the legacy of her survivor mother, whose

> critical attitude to prejudice and racism was very sharp. And she didn't think Jews were exonerated by their past. She saw even there, during these events, some very dark things. The fact of being a victim doesn't make you a better person, it only means suffering. She transmitted this clarity to me in relation to other things too.

Ben Natan regards 'Born in Berlin'as a dialogue with her mother:

> Why did I sink myself into it? I found that in many ways it connected to my life and to my mother and through it I could touch things which were truth and not clichés. It was important to me, I understood only at the end of filming that through it I actually held a dialogue with my mother and discovered things and it was important for me to negate

clichés and prejudices. I slanted the statements by the three women because they are my own statements. There is a link between a form of self-expression and a wish to change things. Perhaps less declamatory and political than at the start – today it's on a more minor key.

'Taking the Shoah out of the museum'

Nava Semel and Orna Ben Dor, although initially not motivated, like Ben Natan, by a wish to change things, believe that their work has contributed to changing Israeli attitudes towards the Shoah. Ben Dor's 'Because of that War' (1988) played a major role in changing Israeli attitudes to the Shoah. The film is the story of the Israeli rock icon, Yehuda Poliker and his lyricist Yaacov Gilead, whose music is immensely popular, and who are at the centre of Israel's masculine consensus, but who are also sons of survivors. Linking rock and Shoah, Ben Dor believes the film took 'the Shoah out of the museum'.

When Ben Dor met them through Poliker's father Jacko, a survivor from Saloniki who took part in 'Cloud Burst', Poliker told her about their 'Shoah album', 'Ash and Dust'. The film features Poliker and Gilead as well as Jacko Poliker and Gilead's mother, Halina Birnbaum, a survivor who teaches school-children about the Shoah. Through these rock icons Ben Dor allowed young Israelis a way into the Shoah, previously perceived as belonging to the past, and to an older genera-tion. As a result, their song 'Here is Treblinka Station' is sung by groups of Israeli school-children as they visit the camps, the words are accompanied by drums and electric guitars, buzuki, bass guitar and keyboard. The tune is ever-repetitive and the pupils hum it along with the cassettes, almost religiously (Segev, 1991: 461). It is also danced to in Poliker's gigs. Ben Dor comments:

> This is the ultimate cutting-off point. When the kids came to see Poliker in the film, they did absorb the other facet of 'Here is Treblinka Station'. This is also what happened with older people who came to see the film because of the Shoah and started to buy Yehuda's albums, because they made the link in the other direction.

Gendered subjectivities

Like other nationalist ideologies, Zionism, a modern meta-narrative, has appropriated the masculine (and the masculine pronoun) to con-struct the new entity in the process of constructing and consolidating itself. At the same time it feminised the homeland (*moledet*), the nation (*umma*), and the land (*aretz*), all feminine nouns, in keeping with cast-ing woman as symbol of the nation (Yuval Davis and Anthias, 1989) and in the process silenced women's voices. In the Israeli construction of identity and gender, the Shoah was used rhetorically to strengthen the new active, fighting masculine self-image of the new state.

The stories women tell are influenced by our gendered experiences. Working with their parents' Shoah materials and against the dominant Shoah-silencing Zionist discourse, the narrators created new narratives which privileged 'intimate' versus 'nationalised' memory, but which also negotiated a 'written' gendered 'self', reflecting a gendered 'life', the necessary components of women's auto/bio/graphies.

Although not all the narrators agreed that there is a specifically female turn of events, or set of responses, to what I see as the masculinisation of Israel versus the feminisation of the Shoah, their narratives did reflect the juncture of gender, ethnicity and 'Shoah daughterhood'. None of them, judging from their narratives and from their written and cinematic works, could have been anything other than women, Israeli Jews, and daughters of Shoah survivors.

In keeping with the complex, diverse and multi-layered data achieved by auto/biographical narratives, the narrators' discursive responses to my argument ranged from the private, by being the specific daughters of specific families, to being the consequence of public textually mediated discourses and ideologies promoted, perhaps through necessity, by Zionism and the Israeli State, as examined in chapters 4 and 6. Moreover, in organising their narratives, the narrators referred to their gendered roles as daughters, mothers and wives. Women's personal narratives, even when narrators do not give feminist researchers the satisfaction of speaking in 'feminist theory', often point to the construction of gendered identities (Personal Narratives Group, 1989).

The range of gendered responses as to the role that the narrators and their work play in shifting the Israeli gendered binaries in relation to the Shoah indicates a certain tendency towards essentialising women's societal roles (as in arguing, for instance, that women are 'more connected to complexities' than men and that women have a 'specific contribution to make'). Another tendency was to accord women greater responsibility in shaping Israeli society's hardened response to the Shoah and its survivors. Ultimately, however, the narrators identified their work as offering a forum for intimate, rather than nationalised Shoah memory and linked it to the gendered stigmatisation of the survivors, an argument developed theoretically in later chapters.

'Women find it easier to connect to complexities'

Homogenising women and essentialising early Israeli responses to the Shoah as masculine and therefore childish, the narrators argue, rather unproblematically, that women find it easier to connect to complexities and weaknesses.

Perhaps the feminine part of one's personality is more ready to accept complexities. In our country's history the war period was a sort of childhood. When I read about 'human dust' and so on,[16] I become deeply angry. This is where my forgiveness ends. It isn't possible that people here were so blind, so narrow-visioned and so focused on their immediate aims that they couldn't see beyond it. (Naomi Ben Natan)

Karmit Gai argues that if Israeli society has only recently taken on being an individualistic 'other', then most of the creation in this area is by women:

Women are more connected to complexities. That's what I feel. Women are more connected to weaknesses.

Men who deal with the Shoah, Gai argues, tend to pathologise their stories (she is referring primarily to David Grossman's *See Under: Love*). When they depict the cracks of Israeli masculinity, their protagonists are always soldiers, since Israeli masculinity is defined by men's military roles. Referring to Israeli cinema, Gai argues that:

the film-makers deal very well with the problems of Israeli masculinity. But it always has to be through the army. If you want to tell a story of someone who is going to die, he has to be a pilot. Because, otherwise, how would you show a man who is the world's most macho facing the fact that he's going to die? Why can't he be a bank clerk?

'Women have a very specific contribution to make'

Referring to the question of whether women writers have a specific contribution to make as children of survivors in Israeli literature, Savyon Liebrecht agreed that women, who form the majority of second-generation Israeli writers, have a very specific contribution to make, constructing what I maintain are counter-narratives to the Zionist narration of nation:

What happened in Israeli literature is that there was a generation whose spokespersons were mostly men, who shaped a certain image of the new Israeli man, who is secular, who is usually not urban. And then the Shoah survivor arrived, who is actually the antithesis of the new man. And what is happening now is really that we [females] are turning back the wheel. I mean, we've lost a certain link in the chain somewhere. And we hopped from phase to phase without working through the data properly. And we [females] are returning, yes, crawling back to the place, in order to connect better. And I think that we are really a bridge, because the fact that we are so busy with the old materials, means that it's part of us, we've taken it from home.

According to Liebrecht there is a direct link between 'breaking the conspiracy of silence' regarding Shoah materials, and breaking the conspiracy of silence in relation to women:

> With all the change in the status of women in Israel and elsewhere, women today dare to do things they hadn't said before. But this is linked to the business of maturing, we are ripe to deal with this subject and this is linked somehow to women making themselves heard, and this finds expression not only in literature of course.

'A focus on the feminine'

Another manifestation of the gendering of the relationship between Israel and the Shoah is a choice of women as protagonists. Several of the stories in Savyon Liebrecht's collection '"It's Greek to me" She Said to Him' (1992) focus on women in relation to the Shoah.

> I think the main difference between these and previous stories is that there is a focus on the feminine. And I think that what happened in the Shoah was a certain blurring of the feminine element. That creature, the Shoah survivor, had always been sort of asexual. There was a reduction of the gender subject and here, suddenly, specifically, I am talking about women, the experiences of women at that period. And it's not only that, but, 'Morning with the Childminders' speaks of women who were used, who were used for the pleasure of the Germans. I mean, a woman's most feminine element, a woman's eroticism. From my point of view this is a turning point, looking at something I haven't examined up until now.

Another of her stories, 'The Berries Girl', told from the point of view of the German wife of a Nazi concentration camp-commander, received a sceptical critical reception.

> One of the critics opposed my writing in the first person through the mouth of a Nazi officer's wife. I suppose that in the field of Shoah stories there are things which can't as yet be spoken about. And a story, in the first person, of a German woman, is harder for the Israeli public to accept in Hebrew, now.

Just as she understands the Israeli inability to accept a story told from the point of view of a Nazi wife, Liebrecht also understands the unwillingness of the *Palmach* generation to accept the survivors when they first arrived. Having re-read 'The Days of Ziklag' (Yizhar, 1948), a seminal early Israeli novel about male soldierly brotherhood, where the 'new man', that 'glorious Hebrew- speaking creature' is valorised, she asked the author, S. Yizhar, how come the soldiers had more sympathy for every Arab than for the survivors, for her father.

He apologised *terribly* and said that if you examine it from the point of view of these young people, terrified, defenceless, who were facing destruction, you understand that they were really preoccupied, not just out of self-indulgence. He told me that every second friend of his fell... If I ignore my need for Yizhar to acknowledge my father's pain, I can understand that it wasn't possible to absorb the survivors any differently.

Tania Hadar, although she believes that putting survivors in danger again, by enlisting them to the pre-state fighting forces during the 1948 war shortly after their arrival, was totally unacceptable, expresses her support for the Zionist ethos of a 'no choice' ongoing war and in doing so, she uses the masculine pronoun. When I point it out, she reiterates her defence of the importance of the existence of Israel after the Shoah. For Hadar, fighting for the state of Israel is an entirely male affair, although the lesson she draws from the Shoah, that Israel needs to be forever strong, is a lesson absorbed and practised by women and men alike:

> Yes, OK, endangering the survivors was atrocious. On the other hand, if I am in danger, I don't move [m – *zaz*], I fight [m – *nilcham*]. I mean, this is my place.

> RL
> Have you noticed that you've used the masculine form? ... Would you say fight in the feminine form [f – *nilchemet*]?

> TH
> Ah, yes. But of course, in that sense women are not so active, but in the sense of, say, leaving Israel, and living in other places, it was very clear to me that one must live here.

'The greatest sinners were the women'

As they see women as colluding with the Israeli power and control ethos, the narrators refrain from making simplistic male-female distinctions. Nava Semel speaks of collusion and of the shame involved in having been less than the Israeli male heroic stereotype, arguing however that the fighter model was not really gendered. Batia Gur is the strongest voice regarding the collusion of Israeli women in the Zionist ethos. Speaking of her third detective novel 'Cohabitation' (1991), she accuses Israeli women of much more than just collusion. While ostensibly a detective story about a murder in an established kibbutz on the eve of the passage of the children from cohabiting communally to living with their parents, 'Cohabitation' is an indictment of the kibbutz ethos, and indirectly, the Israeli ethos. The book, which has had a controversial reception, answers my research question, although the person who speaks about the flawed kibbutz ideology is a man, Moish, the kibbutz secretary. But Moish was once a frightened child, whom the ideology did not take into account.

> This is what I tried to say. Apart from the masculine-feminine issue, which I was not aware of. In my opinion the greatest sinners, if we can express it thus, were the women. Because I would have expected them to rebel. The men do not rebel, when they work they bury their wishes under their ideology. But the women could have done it, when it is their children who are concerned, when they are babies. And they camouflage the whole thing in ideology which enables them to see their babies for only half an hour a day, not because they wanted to, but because this was what the public good dictated and they pretended to believe in it, and thought that this was the right way. I suppose that this is why the murderer in my story is a woman from that generation.

Gur goes on to speak about kibbutzim moving on to family living as if the whole idea of real Communism, which 'people died for' had meant nothing, and about breaking families apart for the sake of an idea. And she blames women, whose function it is 'to expose such lies. Because they have no pay-offs'.

Speaking of why her Shoah-survivors protagonists, Fania and Gouta, are women, Gur ties together stigmatisation and gender, and links the position of women and of Shoah survivors in the kibbutz, the epitome of early Zionist ideals:

> Shoah survivors joined kibbutzim and allowed their children to cohabit. I don't understand how they could stand it, what did they abandon their children for? How could they, I wonder, let their children cohabit, where were their anxieties? How could they? You are asking why women? With women, such strong women, they must have been strong to be able to go from that experience and join a kibbutz. The characters were based on real people I heard about. How can you explain that women who arrive from the Shoah join something like this, that demands such conformity? I can tell you: for security they were prepared to do anything.

I suggest that she, as a woman, has performed an act of resistance by writing what she wrote. She agrees, and although she distances herself from feminist labels, she expresses a deep commitment to 'real' feminism. This is an example how narrators, while not identifying with researchers' theoretical constructs, often display in their narratives our very argument.

> Yes, as a woman I believe this is the role of women. Always. I don't recognise the feminist revolution at all. I mean, I'm not *women's lib*. Women have nothing to lose anyway. Apart from their femininity. I

understood already at the age of 39 that I will not be nice any more. So *I might as well* say the truth. I don't know if as a woman ... I mean if I was a man, could I have not written such a thing? I am very pleased to be a women, I have never regretted being a woman, and I always thought being a woman was very powerful [italicised words were spoken in English].

'I link my femininity and my feeling as a daughter of survivors'

Orna Ben Dor's narrative brings together the Shoah, the stigmatisation of the survivors, gender and film-making. She not only links her personal life with her creative work, she also tells, in her 1994 feature 'Newland', the cinematic narrative of that link. Some of her films attempted to solve her dilemmas about the status of women and men, which she links directly to the status of survivors in Israeli society. Our conversation helps her to construct a link between refugeeship and femininity: an example of the research process facilitating narrators' transformation.

> Because I was confused about this business of men being strong and women being weak, because I do view myself as a strong woman, I decided I would find a solution by making films about women who fulfilled masculine roles. Mania Shochat was very masculine, she founded the first army and then the first peace movement, but it was all within very masculine, political areas. It may all be linked, because if refugeeship and weakness are feminine, then I was going to connect to these things because I have taken the masculine role in my personal life. And it may be that this link to refugeeship is also a link to what I define as femininity.

If being a woman links with being a daughter of survivors, Ben Dor's films can be read as acts of resistance, 'not against the six millions but against *Yom HaShoah.* I don't know. It's as if I link my femininity, which is very troubled by being Israeli, with my feelings as a daughter of survivors, who is very troubled by being Israeli'.

There is indeed a link between otherness and femininity, particularly in 'Shoah Tova', although the protagonist is a male Shoah survivor:

> Now what you are saying about the link between refugeeship and femininity and anger sounds really very logical.

Ben Dor regards her films as very angry, very masculine and ultimately, despite her success as a documentary film-maker, her dissatisfaction is linked to being a woman and to being an outsider, a daughter of survivors:

> I had awful troubles with the funding authorities [about 'Because of That War']. They didn't give me money because [they said] 'you are too

angry, you do not transmit the pain, you transmit the anger'. 'Because of That War' is very aggressive, very masculine. Deliberately so... But I am at a different stage now. I mean, one side is already developed and I know now that I will live, I will survive, so I can afford to be less angry. In this respect I am a very successful product of Israeli society.

'Intimate memory versus nationalised memory'

According to Zvi Dror the testimonies of male survivors and female survivors are quite different.

> It seems to me that women's testimonies are more personal testimonies ... they speak about what is in their heart. Men tend to see things more generally and they often locate their personal experience within the general story of the war. They tend to deviate more often from the personal story to other topics, but ultimately what we want to get in an interview is the personal story as testimony. (Dror, 1992: 11)

The narrators, some more vehemently than others, insist that official Israeli Shoah commemoration practices did not allow survivors a forum for expressing what Nava Semel calls 'intimate memories'. Privileging heroism over personal memories of victimhood and suffering is part of Israel's masculine ethos:

> We remember a ceremonial memory. We have never had intimate memory. I am trying to bring back the intimate memory. An individual memory. Israeli society dealt only with heroic memory, with memory which is far too big for us, and with a kind of ceremonial memory which would serve the Zionist ethos. (Nava Semel)

Naomi Ben Natan, on the other hand, views the emphasis on heroism over suffering as an inevitable, if childish, reaction by the state of Israel.

> The need to emphasise heroism was the only way in which the state, which wanted an army of brave men, could get over its problematic self-image. How could we be heroic paratroopers if we follow the lamb to the slaughter? So we must follow, if not the Maccabeans, then the Warsaw ghetto insurgents. It's a type of teething problem – the whole *sabra* myth ... A lack of confidence that we were able to face only by constructing a 'new man'.

Gendered stigmatisation

Ben Dor's first full-length feature 'Newland' (1994) is an important statement on the gendered link between Israelis and the Shoah. 'Newland' is the story of an eight-year-old girl, Anna, who arrives in Israel from Poland with her older brother Jan to a *ma'abara* (a transit camp for survivors and other new immigrants) in 1949. In her arms Anna cradles a tatty teddy bear and a yellowing picture of her mother. Their father was killed by the Nazis. The film's gaze is Anna's. Through her eyes we see Rosa, a pregnant survivor from Saloniki, who overhears the Israeli doctor say: 'Poor woman, you know what they had to do in order to survive in the camps' and she burns the number the Nazis had tattooed on her arm with a hot iron, so she is never called a Nazi whore in Israel again. We see Marushka, a blond Christian German who had to sleep with a Nazi officer in order to save the life of her Jewish husband. In the *ma'abara* her husband is dying of TB and the camp un-crowned black-marketeer king, the Moroccan Bardugo, will give her medicine if she sleeps with him. She refuses, but one night, when she can bear her husband's cough no longer, she goes to Bardugo and kneels before him, unbuttoning her blouse. Overwhelmed, Bardugo gets her to her feet and gives her the medicine. In the morning, she wakes up to find her husband, who had found the medicine by his bed-side and assumed the price his wife had paid, hanging from a tree.

Through Anna's eyes we see her brother Hebraicise his name to Dan and join the neighbouring kibbutz, leaving her in the *ma'abara*. Through her eyes we see Uri, the *ma'abara*'s youth worker, who pre-tends to pass for a *sabra*, though he is really Shloime, the diaspora boy whose family had been exterminated. Through Anna's gaze we hear Uri's survivor girlfriend Betty shout: 'You think all survivor women had to be whores in order to stay alive, your mothers, your lovers, your sisters. Do you know what that makes you? Sons of whores'.

Survivor, woman, both are subordinated by the heroic masculine *sabra* fictions. In the end the *ma'abara* is closed down and Anna has no option but to join her brother's kibbutz. In the children's communal home they re-clothe her, take away her smelly teddy and rename her Ilana, a good Hebrew name. Motherless, nameless, Anna is awakened by her brother's tap on the children's home window and together they recover their old clothes and Anna's teddy bear from the kibbutz rub-bish heap and fly to the full moon over the sleeping kibbutz, a flight of fantasy away from the pain of silence and stigmatisation.

Israel of the mid-1990s appeared to have come of age, but the myths of masculine *sabra* versus feminised diaspora victim still prevail. Orna Ben Dor's film was largely rejected by Israelis, unable or unwilling to remember, and apologise for the way they silenced the survivors.

Conclusion: 'The writing is the consequence, not the causative factor'

Ultimately, the narrators write or make films for their own reasons. It is a contested issue: was the shift in Israeli attitudes to the Shoah brought about by the passage of time and the readiness to confront Israel's Shoah legacy, or by the counter-narrative type of intervention by writers of the second-generation? Savyon Liebrecht argues that books, and films, but particularly books, cannot change attitudes:

> I don't believe writing can change anything, perhaps only on the personal level. But on the social level, I don't think a book can change anything. Unless it's political things that expose things, but literature? Or poetry?

The opposite process exists, Liebrecht argues. The writing did not change the relations between Israelis and the Shoah, but was a consequence of the process of maturation:

> The writing is the *consequence*, not the causative factor. Because the second-generation started to come out, forty years is a generation, it's not accidental, and just as we have matured, so has the Israeli public and a sufficient historical perspective has been created, in order to examine things. Things which are of their time find their right expression. Things which come before their time wait until the atmosphere is ripe to absorb them. But I don't believe that literature can change things. Not on the social and political level.

Other narrators also argue that the shift in attitudes about the Shoah was a matter of time and of the survivors' ageing, rather than merely a reaction to the imposed silence. According to Karmit Gai, by beginning to be able to deal with the Shoah, Israel is beginning the process of departing from its masculine obsession with heroism and becoming more able to legitimise weakness.

> The grandchildren who are asking the questions are getting the answers and parents who haven't told their children are now talking to their grandchildren. And because the survivors themselves are retiring now, they feel the end is near and they know that if they don't tell it now, it will be lost and it is beginning to worry them. Apart from which, they feel their children are strong enough to absorb it. Apart from which they can no longer, they can no longer not talk.

Israel and the Daughters of the Shoah is an attempt to link the 'masculinisation' of the 'new Hebrews' with diaspora-negation and the stigmatisation of Shoah survivors. By making this link, and by working auto/biographically with personal narratives of daughters of survivors, I am better able to make sense of the relationship between contemporary Israel and the Shoah. If the construction of the masculine 'new Hebrew' subjectivity discursively stigmatised the survivors and feminised the Shoah, the works of the narrators have acted as counter-narratives and played a central role in shifting the emphasis towards greater complexity and inclusiveness in the parameters of Israeli 'normality'. The narrators' works are eloquent acts of coming to terms with the legacy of the Shoah in Israeli society, as are their narratives. In them, narrators make real and present their parents' past experiences and their own memories. Telling me their auto/biographical 'stories within stories', is part of a process of 'accounting', or 'reckoning', which, I argue, is the first step towards bridging the gap between experience and discourse, and towards beginning the process of mourning.

The narratives suggest the dichotomous nature of Israeli Shoah commemoration. The commemoration privileged, until very recently, the few acts of armed resistance over passive victimhood, as discussed in chapter 4, which deals with the appropriation by the Israeli state of the Shoah as part of constructing itself as the antithesis of diasporic Judaism. The narratives also suggest the pathologisation of the survivors and the construction of a convenient, yet disputable, discourse of a survivor and a 'second-generation' syndrome, as discussed in chapter 5. The stigmatisation of the survivors, posited so eloquently by the narratives, is discussed in chapter 6, via an examination of Zionist and Israeli state and nation-building discourses of that stigmatisation and employing Goffman's (1968) and Bauman's (1991) theories. Chapter 6 also discusses the feminisation of that stigma, my central theoretical assumption.

Notes

1. Shoah survivors were nicknamed, among other names, *sabonim* (soaps). This was based on the common belief that the Nazis produced soap from human fat. In fact, *Yad Vashem*'s research proved that the Nazis did not produce soap from Jews. During the war there was a shortage of soap in Germany and soap was rationed. Soap bars carried the initials RIF (Pure Industrial Fat) but the rumour that this meant RJF (Pure Jewish Fat) spread. In the last months of the war the Germans began experiments in Danzig into the possibility of producing soap from human fat, but according to *Yad Vashem* Jews were not murdered for this purpose (Segev, 1991: 167). Soap, however, has a deep significance in Shoah mythology and several community graveyards in Europe, including my mother's home town Vatra Dornei in Romania, have tombstones for that soap. The issue was raised in August 1995, when Ben Dor participated in a studio discussion after the transmission of Tom Segev's film 'The Seventh Million' (Bruner and Segev, 1995). Her story about her mother and her colleagues being called 'RIFs' was negated by the *sabra* writer Haim Guri, who argued that 'soap' denoted a feeble quality, rather than a reference to 'that soap'. The survivors, in other words, were seen as weaklings. Naming, as argued in chapter 4, is of essence in relation to the Shoah.
2. The nickname of the former IDF general Rehav'am Ze'evi, now an extreme right-wing member of Knesset.
3. A legendary paratroopers commander, famed for his secret and illicit excursions into Jordanian territory in the 1950s.

4. A reference to the Zionist myths we grew up on of the pioneers having 'paved the roads and drained the marshes'.

5. Some quotes from the reviews are: 'It is a film that should be shown as widely and as often as possible'; 'The film's emotional intensity is rare and a mountain of handkerchiefs will not soften it' (Meir Schnitzer, *Ha'ir*, 1988); 'Ben Dor Niv's film is one of the most moving Israeli films for years' (Yehuda Stav, *Yediot Aharonot*, 1988).

6. A transit camp for new immigrants and Shoah survivors in Haifa in the early 1950s.

7. Some examples of reviews: '"Newland", a beautiful and moving film, joins the "new historians" in constructing its own inaccuracies and distortions' (Aharon Megged, *Shishi*, 30.12.1994b); 'Ben Dor Niv's first feature film turns the difficulties of Shoah survivors in Israel ... to a sentimental spectacle ... It is a collection of plot formuli and dramatic clichés which do not make for ... a historical statement of any weight' (Uri Klein, *Ha'aretz*, 10.1.1995); but also 'I was moved by the film – and this is no everyday occurrence' (*Ha'ir*, 6.1.1995); and 'despite the problems [of this film] it is well worth seeing' (Shmulik Duvdevani, 1994). Despite its success in the US, the film was taken out of circulation in Israel after only four weeks. In 1995 the film won several awards at international film festivals.

8. There are about 172,000 widows in Israel, many of them war widows. Widows constitute 29 per cent of Israeli single mothers (Katz, 1991: 124). War widows are a national institution, they are under the financial and moral protection of the Defence Ministry, which assigns a social worker to each widow until she remarries or dies (Waintrater, 1991: 120).

9. Many reviews focused on the sex life of Keren's Shoah survivor protagonists. Some examples: 'A taste of a contagious disease: kitsch and death, sex and Shoah – Rivka Keren falls into every possible pitfall' (Avi Lan, *Yediot Aharonot*, 1990); 'An Israeli variation on the temptation of monks' (Batia Gur, *Ha'aretz*, 1992); 'The Jewish fate as a romantic novel' (*Davar*, 1990). Keren showed me these reviews in her house; they are not included in the reference list.

10. Other examples: '*Anatomy of Revenge* is an anatomy of tunnels of pain and unforgivable suffering, but at the same time it is also a fascinating journey to present-day memory and its depths' (Sa'ari, *Ha'aretz*, 1993). '*Anatomy of Revenge* is ... a flowing text, full of erudition and culture. It's well-written, perhaps too well written. The many analogies ... are beautiful ... but too transparent, and at times forced ... The "formula" seeps through the lines one millimetre too much..'. (Miran, *Ha'aretz*, 1993: 6).

11. Writers on survivors' testimonies talk about the fragmentation of memory. Dror, for instance, says that often, while telling, a survivor feels 'as if events, hitherto unavailable, are floating back into his memory' and about memories skipping, forwards and backwards, and about mixing places and historical occurrences (Dror, 1992: 19).

12. A movement comprising an influential group of Israeli writers and artists, during the 1940s and 1950s, who ascribed the Israelis' origin to the pre-Judaic Canaanites who inhabited the land of Canaan, which was later conquered by the Israelites. By aligning itself to the Canaanites, the group disassociated itself from Judaism.

13. 'The Land of the Living' (Hadar, 1991) is the title of one of her books.

14. This refers to Eugene Ionesco's anti-fascist play *Rhinoceros*, which was shown at the Haifa Theatre in the early 1960s and which had a profound effect on Israelis of my generation.

15. A militant movement of young Mizrahi slum-dwelling Israeli Jews in the early 1970s, who campaigned against ethnic discrimination.

16. Refers to the descriptions of the survivors upon their arrival. See chapter 6.

CHAPTER 4

ISRAEL'S NEW HEBREWS 'MEMORISE' THE JEWISH SHOAH

When did the journey begin? ... You could have been a child from there, but they did all they could so you would be a child from here, a strong, earth-smelling *sabra* ... Did they, secretly, think you wouldn't have survived had you been born there? (Lentin, 1989: 13)

In Israel then you had to be really macho ... You had to be strong. And I always knew inside that I was very weak. That I was a naturally born victim ... I was the classical lamb to the slaughter. I, an Anielewicz? Not at all. This I already knew when I was little. I knew that I was being lied to ... (Nava Semel)

My perception of the Shoah has changed over the years, partly due to living outside Israel for much of my adult life. I remember being pre-occupied by Shoah 'stories' from a very young age, while at the same time sharing with many of my generation a certain contempt for the alleged passivity of diaspora Jewry. From casting myself exclusively as an Israeli, different from the diaspora Jews whom I met upon my arrival in Ireland in 1969, I have come to embrace Jewish customs and values which my generation was taught to reject. When I came to writing *Night Train to Mother* (Lentin, 1989), I 'knew' I was not the strong 'new Hebrew' my generation was told we were. I knew, as did Nava Semel, that the Israeli coupling of Shoah and *gevurah* (heroism) was a fabrication, constructed in order to downplay our existential fear and differentiate us from the allegedly passive, weak, diaspora Jewry.

In the mid-1990s Israeli historians, sociologists and journalists began heatedly debating the appropriation or 'Zionisation' of the Shoah by the Israeli state. While the debate hitherto was largely gender-blind, as were most studies of the relation between Israelis and the Shoah (notably Segev, 1991; Zuckermann, 1993; Hacohen, 1994; Yablonka, 1994; Grodzinsky, 1998, but with the exception of Shapira, 1992, and Zertal, 1996a), my analysis (en)genders the Israeli appropriation of the Shoah.

This chapter discusses the main themes of Israeli commemoration and 'memorisation' of the Shoah: the silence of the survivors and their silencing by society, and the debates surrounding questions of silence in telling and re-telling the Shoah; the link between the early Israeli silence about the Shoah and the negation of the diaspora; the discourses surrounding naming the Shoah; the Shoah and Israeli historiography; the gendered meaning of Shoah versus *gevurah* (heroism) in official Israeli discourses; the nature and stages of Shoah commemoration in Israel and present-day new figurative metaphors employed to re-member the Shoah in contemporary Israel. Throughout, my analysis privileges gender as a focus.

Language and silence: the 'memory gap'

One of the consequences of the Shoah was the survivors' determination to remember. However, the search for a discourse for telling, writing and re-writing the Shoah, required establishing a balance between silence and the duty to tell. There was indeed a temptation to succumb to silence, or avoidance. The debate on the balance between language and silence regarding the Shoah (see, for instance, Adorno, 1962; 1965; Langer; 1975; 1991; Steiner, 1969; 1984; Celan, 1968) asks, on the one hand, whether art can express the inhuman suffering during the Shoah without deriving pleasure and thus doing an injustice to the victims (Adorno, 1965: 125–8). On the other hand, there is the question of what 'Shoah texts' can teach us about historical, biographical and political realities. Against the claim that the reality of the Shoah addresses the mind most effectively with the authority of silence (Steiner, 1969: 22), Paul Celan (1968), the Bukovina-born poet and survivor, wrote that although there were no words to describe what happened, language did survive these horrific events.

It may seem absurd to speak of silence on a topic about which so much has been written and published, by survivors and others. Lagerwey (1998: 20), for instance, counted 160 entries for Shoah diaries listed by the *World Catalogue*, and 2,744 accounts of survivors of Auschwitz alone, listed in 1990 in the Archive of the Auschwitz memorial. However, because the Shoah was an event that 'had no witness' and did not 'exist' and thus signified its own death and reduction to silence, its survival inevitably implied the presence of an informal discourse, a degree of unconscious witnessing that could not find its voice during the event. Diaries and other attempts to record it were doomed to fail: the event was not transmittable at the time. Grunfeld (1995) posits a 'memory gap' that separates the material, bodily, immediate knowledge of the traumatic experiences of the Shoah and the discursive, mediated memories that followed. Similarly, psychoanalyst Dinora Pines (1993) documents the 'knowing and not knowing' about the Shoah, a dissociation reported by several of the narrators.

It is not accidental that Shoah testimonies became receivable only in the last two decades of the twentieth century, a whole generation after the catastrophe itself. Writing about the Shoah must involve struggling with silence, and the narrators have battled against this silence in their lives and work. My task here is an 'archaeology' of that silence (see Foucault, 1967: xi), although it must be said that in recent years the Israeli silence about the Shoah has begun to be broken, mostly by the third generation and by the almost-mandatory school visits to the camps, problematic as these may be. In some ways, silence has been replaced with obsessive talking about the Shoah, arguably a form of Israeli 'banalisation'.

In relation to Theodor Adorno's famous edict (1949: 362) that 'after Auschwitz it is no longer possible to write poetry', the question must be asked about the 'barbarity' of writing footnotes after Auschwitz (Hilberg, 1988: 25). I agree with Saul Friedländer that although we are dealing with an event which tests traditional conceptual and representational categories, an 'event at the limits' (Friedländer, 1992:3), the Shoah must be as accessible to representation and interpretation as any other sociohistorical event, as argued by Bauman (1989) in relation to the dearth of sociological studies of the Shoah. A further crisis in representation lies in the tension between historical 'facts' and interpretation. Historian Raul Hilberg, argues that despite the 'success' of his own historical accounts of the Shoah, 'historiography itself is a kind of fiction', (Hilberg, 1988: 273).

The enormous difficulty of writing about the destruction of the Jews is one of the reasons why Shoah texts have tended to focus on the victims, as if the history of the Shoah is the history of its victims, outside the broader contexts of history, society, politics, fascism, racism and sexism. Shoah memory and its representations were shaped by and in turn shaped twentieth century society, and in particular Jewish and Israeli society, where the 'memory gap' between personal testimonies and nationalised discourses shaped the very nature of Israeli identity formation.

The initial Israeli reaction to the Shoah entailed survivors silencing themselves and being silenced by Israeli society. During the 1948 War of Independence survivors were silenced not because they did not

want to tell their stories, but because their story was not really acceptable, being very different from the heroic myths constructed around
the European Jewish partisans and ghetto fighters on the one hand,
and around the war fought by Erez Israeli youth on the other. The only
heroism Israelis valued was armed resistance, but survivors often felt
that merely surviving was heroic. This is how the binary oppositions of
Shoah versus *gevurah,* and of the ghetto uprisings versus the 'lamb to
the slaughter' myth were constructed. Survivors report resenting the
way Israelis attempted to get them to speak and in particular, being
asked 'how come you stayed alive?' which they interpreted as being
blamed for surviving (Yablonka, 1994: 60). Theresienstadt and
Auschwitz survivor writer Ruth Bondi has this to say:

> The number on my arm, exposed during the long summer months, lays
> bare my life, people know about me more than I know about them...
> they don't hesitate to ask, in the bus, in the shops, on the beach, if I had
> met their relatives in the camps, and how come I stayed alive when
> they were murdered. Before long I concluded (I wrote about it in
> November 1950) that Israelis prefer not to hear about the Shoah.
> (Bondi, 1997: 43–4)

Silencing the survivors also stemmed from the Israelis' fear of being
damaged by their accounts. Yablonka quotes survivor Marek
Dvorszky: (Dvorszky, 1956: 102–4): '[Israelis] were not prepared to
listen and at the same time we were not ready to tell ... usually the new
immigrant found only very few people in the settled population who
wished to placate him, console him and give him attention'.

However, the fear went deeper than being damaged by survivors'
testimonies. Idith Zertal (1996a) examines the encounter between the
Yishuv's illegal immigration organisation and the survivors after the
Shoah. She argues that *Yishuv* leader David Ben Gurion allocated the
one-and-a- half million survivors, transported by illegal immigration
organisations to the Erez Israeli shores, a crucial role in the Zionist
struggle to establish a state. However, the Israeli-diaspora encounter
uncovers the mysterious, paradoxical terror felt by the strong, patronising Erez Israeli subject vis-à-vis the vanquished, victimised survivor-
object which he (*sic*) carried on his shoulders from ship to shore. This
terror was not a fear of the unknown, but rather the opposite – the fear
of the repressed familiar – a terror of that part of the Israeli subjectivity that *was* the diaspora Jew (Zertal, 1996a: 498).

The struggle between Israeli and Jew continues. Ram (1999) quotes
former Prime Minister Shimon Peres, after the 1996 elections he lost
to the Likud's Binyamin Netanyahu, as saying that 'the Israelis' lost
the elections to 'all those who don't have an Israeli mentality, i.e. the
Jews' (Ben Simon, 1997: 13). Ram posits the struggle between Israeli-

ness as a civic-political identity ('post-Zionism') and Jewishness as an ethno-cultural identity ('neo-Zionism') which, he argues is 'a struggle for the collective memory and the map' (Ram, 1999: 349).

The US Shoah scholar James Young (1993) argues that there is an inevitable partnership between a nation and its memorial monuments, between figurative language and the memory of the past. Depending on where and by whom Shoah memorials are constructed, these sites 'remember' the past according to national myths, ideals and political needs. Artistic expressions – literature, theatre, film – as well as history, testimonies, educational and official commemorative discourses, can shape a nation's (and a person's) access to memory.

While silence, or 'forgetting', is 'a crucial factor in the creation of a nation' (Renan, 1990: 11), silence about a person's, or a collectivity's calamitous past can be conveyed only through language, even if language expresses only the inability, reluctance, or refusal to speak or to listen. According to Passerini (1992: 2), memory – linguistically expressed in spoken exchanges, oral history, survivors' testimonies and other textually-mediated discourses – is the tool which gives meaning to our lives. But what is required is not merely a simple and spontaneous memory, nor memory that stems from a need for vengeance, but a memory of a memory. We can remember only because somebody else has remembered before us. Yet, there is nothing to transmit if there is nobody to receive the message. Memory also depends on the ideological frameworks which shaped and dictated our access to that memory.

Feelings of guilt and complicity impact on memory in different ways. The issue is further complicated when the victims of oppression become its agents, and endeavour to justify oppression by 'memorising' events transmitted through national or collective memory, which is what has happened in the history of the Israeli occupation of Palestinian lands. Linking individual memory to collective memory, Passerini argues that Fascism accentuates the gap between the political sphere and daily life, thus creating wounds in the tissue of memory, which cannot easily recompense what had been forcefully separated. Another 'memory gap', arguably bridgeable only through personal narratives of survivors, or children of survivors.

I would like to suggest that past conflicts, catastrophes and genocides are not only remembered, but 'memorised', through a multiplicity of discourses, from one generation to the next, playing a central role in the ways collective memory shapes a collectivity's 'story'. Israeli collective memory and the role it allocated to the Shoah has been mediated and shaped by official discourses and artistic representations, and their interaction with personal testimonies.

Silence and 'the negation of exile'

Not surprisingly, the Shoah is memorised and commemorated differently in Israel than anywhere else due to the special relationship between the Israeli state, the Jewish diaspora and the Shoah. As a daughter of 'the first generation to redemption' and at the same time of a family of survivors, my examination of the Israeli politics of transmitting the memory of the Shoah is also about me and my generation.

In negating the *galut* – exile – diaspora, and constructing a new Hebrew type of (male) Jew – *ha'ivri hakhadash* (literally meaning 'the new [male] Hebrew') – the state of Israel used the Shoah to define itself and strengthen its self-image as other than the diaspora. A host of contradictions is implied in the ongoing existential debate between Israeli and Jew. On the one hand Israeli society had a need to memorise and commemorate the Shoah in order to create a sense of continuity with the Jewish past and thus justify its existence. On the other, it needed to distinguish between itself and the diaspora and therefore the Shoah.

In the early years of the state, Zionism, which demanded 'realisation through *aliyah*' (immigration to the Land of Israel), positioned the Jew's country of birth versus the Jew's 'homeland', thus complicating the already fraught relations for contemporary Jews between 'homeland' and 'diaspora' (Lentin, 1999b). The only Jewish homeland was to be Israel, constructed as the state of all the world's Jews which, ironically, negated the Jewish diasporic existence.

There is a deep gulf between Israel conceptualising itself as a 'Jewish state', which 'belongs' to all persons defined by the Israeli authorities as Jews (Shahak, 1994), and the insistence on a sense of discontinuity with the diasporic Jewish past of Israeli Jews. This gulf was at its most pronounced in relation to the Shoah. The causal continuum between the Shoah and the establishment of the Israeli state does not, according to Zimmermann (1999: 489), pass the critical test. Zionism existed prior to the Shoah and its success did not depend on the Shoah. The argument, by the Israeli education system, that Israel is the only logical response to the Shoah – *a priori* and *a posteriori* – is in fact not accepted by all Jews, most of whom have chosen not to emigrate to Israel. Zimmermann argues, furthermore, that the criticism of the instrumentalisation of the Shoah and its positioning at the centre of the Israeli-Zionist consciousness is not 'post-Zionist' but 'post-Shoah' and only one of the possible explanations of the link between the two major events in twentieth-century Jewish history. In searching for an acceptable form of Jewish continuity, Israeli society, and Zionism before it, had a need to negate the notion of 'exile' and contrast it with the Zionist notion of 'returning to the land'. However, despite its search for new discourses, Israeli society, when memorising the Shoah, had no option but to anchor its memory in a Jewish continuum. But, by linking the Shoah to the state's *raison d'être*, early Israeli leaders located it at the centre of the national identity.

Young (1993: 212) asks whether it was possible, on the one hand, to negate the diaspora and put it behind the 'new Jews' of Israel, while basing the need to 'invent' the new Jews in memory of the Shoah, and, on the other, to remember the Shoah without allowing it to constitute the centre of one's Jewish identity? The dilemma could only be solved by making a clear distinction between Israeli and exilic Jew.

Despite this distinction, the Shoah has become a central ingredient of contemporary Jewish identity. More than ever the future of the Jewish nation depends on the relation to the worst Jewish calamity in living memory. Jewish tradition is the opposite of Israeli nationalism, yet like all 'civil religions', which need myths in order to empower society, Zionism needed the Shoah as its central myth. In the words of the Israeli Defence Force's chief education officer: 'the Shoah shaped our national consciousness and the way we understand ourselves and our world' (IDF, 1976). The Shoah myth, based on the biblical perception that all gentiles hate all Jews, was rejected by several pre-state Zionist leaders, who believed that once the Jews had a homeland, the gentiles would change their tune. However, the Shoah remained a central Zionist tenet, not only in interpreting the Shoah ('the world saw and remained silent') but also in justifying the continuous state of war and privileging a 'national security' discourse.

Constructing a new type of Jew, the opposite of the diaspora Jew, and memorising the Shoah accordingly, was an inevitable, albeit understandable, part of a policy of silence. There was silence about Jewish victimhood during the Shoah, and silence, initiated by Prime Minister David Ben Gurion, regarding the 'true story' of the pre-state violent return to Zion, which entailed expelling Palestinians and dispossessing their lands during and after the 1948 War of Independence. With the years, the silence deepened. However, new historical studies, using newly available archive material, shed light on the silenced facts of the 1948 expulsions and the 1950s murder of thousands of so-called 'infiltrators', Palestinian refugees stealing across the borders in an attempt to return to their villages (Morris, 1987; 1993).

A silence also enveloped the survivors as they began arriving. And the monopoly on memory, appropriated by the Israeli state, assisted the 'state generation' in nationalising the memory of the Shoah. Nationalisation meant that the inconceivable events of the Shoah were re-conceived so that the nation and the state became their lawful owners. At its worst this meant 'the projection of the murder of the six millions onto the Arab-Israeli conflict' (Wasserman, 1986: 6–7).

'Zionising' the Shoah affected the naming of the catastrophe as well as official Israeli Shoah commemoration. It also affected the memory available to Israeli children of Shoah survivors by not allowing individual, intimate memory to gain legitimisation.

The Jewish past, long denied as part of the Zionist nation-building effort, is gradually coming back into Israeli consciousness via, among other things, studies of the attitude of the pre-state *Yishuv* and of the state to the Shoah and its survivors (Porat, 1986; Lerner, 1994; Weitz, 1994; Eshkoli, 1994; Grodzinsky, 1994a; 1994b; 1998). Israel, according to Friedländer (1988: 289), is becoming a more mature society, and is therefore better able to face the 'truth' about the ruling *sabra* élite refusing to confront the Shoah and welcome its survivors. Perhaps that 'truth', like the 'truth' of exiling and expropriating the Palestinians, has no option but to return to haunt us. The encounter between Israelis and survivors signals the return of the diaspora as Zionism's repressed, or unconscious 'other' (Zertal, 1996a: 499), as discussed in chapter 6.

The 'negation of exile', and therefore the Shoah, was at the heart of the construction of the state of Israel, which viewed the reality of Jewish diaspora life as doomed to destruction and Zionism as the only answer to the plight of the Jewish people. Zionism's founders, who had fled the diaspora and rebelled against their parents by emigrating to Palestine, burnt the bridges to their diasporic past. By negating exile, Zionists rejected the status of Jews as an eternal minority within a hostile 'host' people. Unfortunately, what has become known as 'the negation of exile' often translated into the negation of diaspora Jews themselves, perceived not as living people, but as an abstract concept. The term 'diaspora Jew' came to symbolise everything Erez Israeli youths were not. To this day, one of the worst things an Israeli can be said to have is a 'diaspora mentality'.

At the same time, the Shoah was employed to strengthen and encourage Israeli ideologies and self-images. 'State-generation'[1] novelist and essayist A. B. Yehoshua (1984: 61–2) sees exile as 'the neurotic solution' to the Jewish problem and the Shoah as 'the ultimate proof of the failure of the diaspora'. Exile answers the age-old Jewish need to be different, a need negated by living as a sovereign nation on its own land. If exile has proved a source of suffering, the appalling sacrifice of the Jewish nation during the Shoah had, according to Yehoshua, been 'in vain'. It proved how dangerous exile is for Jews.

The subordination of Jewish memory in favour of newly created Israeli memories — to a certain extent a conscious process — affected the ways in which the Shoah, its memorisation and commemoration, and its very naming, were politicised in the cultural construction of the state of Israel.

Naming the catastrophe

In deciding how to name the massacre of Europe's Jewry, Jews had several options. The Yiddish term *khurbn* (*khurban* in Hebrew, meaning destruction), unlike the term 'Holocaust', linked the events of the Second World War with the first and second destruction (of the Temple). Yet the Shoah was not simply a third *khurban*. This would suggest that the events were in direct succession to previous Jewish destructions and involved divine retribution, employed to explain previous destructions. It would also deny the uniqueness of the Shoah, a much-debated issue. Even though the Shoah was an event like no other, as soon as we speak of it or represent it in any fashion, we contextualise it in relation or in opposition to other events (Young, 1990: 88). If what happened to the Jews was unique, then the Shoah happened outside of history; it becomes a metaphysical event. If, on the other hand, it is not unique, what are the precedents or parallels (Bauer, 1978: 31)? The problem is essentially that of language and its means of representing discontinuity and uniqueness.

The term *Shoah* (catastrophe, cataclysm, disaster) was first used in Hebrew newspapers in Palestine-Erez Israel as early as 1933, when the Nazis rose to power: Jews were reported as destined for destruction and their fate was described as a 'Shoah'. The term was adopted as a deliberate Israeli alternative (to the Biblical *khurban*) to designate the specific, unprecedented murder of Jews. *Shoah*, although still resonating a Biblical order, allowed for a new meaning, echoing Zionists' view of the Jews' situation in exile, particularly during the War. It still implied elements of divine retribution for the sin of remaining in exile (a very Zionist interpretation), which cast the Shoah as another link in the chain of Jewish persecutions, for which Jews relinquishing their religion are blamed by the orthodox establishment (Sassar, 1995: 10).

While *khurban* figures the events in a Jewish way which creates specific Jewish understanding and memory of this period, *Shoah* figures it in a uniquely Israeli way, in contrast to both the Yiddish *khurbn* and the English-language *Holocaust*, only used to refer to the annihilation of Jews since the late 1950s. The Israeli poet Meir Wieseltier sums up the naming dilemma in his poem 'Words':

> Two years before the *khurban* / the *khurban* was not called *khurban;* two years before the Shoah / it did not have a name. // What was the word *khurban* / two years before the *khurban*? / A word describing something bad / that we wish would not happen. // What was the word *Shoah* / two years before the Shoah? / It was a word signifying a big noise / something to do with commotion. (Wieseltier, 1984: 189)

The survivors had already been named *she'erit hapleita*, 'the remnant of the deliverance', another Biblical expression (Genesis 45:7;

Chronicles I 4:43), in the early 1940s. This was another device that distinguished the survivors from the Israelis.

The Nazis succeeded in preparing both killers and victims for the Jews' literal destruction through their linguistic abuse of the Jews. For example, would the use of Zyklon B roach gas to exterminate the Jews be imaginable without first repeatedly describing Jews as vermin (Young, 1990: 93)? The Nazis understood Jewish traditions sufficiently to delude them into thinking that the Shoah was 'only' a repetition of past destructions, an interpretation taken up in Rabbinical writings (e.g., Fuchs, 1995) about the Shoah, some of which blamed Zionism and Zionists for the destruction (Sassar, 1995). In reinstituting the Renaissance ghetto, the medieval yellow star and the seventeenth- century Jewish councils, the Nazis created a world that was as terrifying, yet familiar, to Europe's Jews, as it was alien to Israel's 'new Hebrews'.

Names mould events in the image of a particular culture's understanding of events. What makes the Shoah unique is its intentionality and its meaning. Bauman (1989) argues that sociology, and society, must find a way and a language to figure the Shoah, not as an aberration of European civilisation, but as the consequence of that very civilisation. Until the Shoah is named, compared and interpreted, the events will continue to exist outside history.

By locating the Shoah in the 'Jewish grammar', Israeli society, keen on viewing itself as other than 'merely' Jewish, had placed the Shoah outside, and even in opposition to, Israeli existence. Israeli society figuratively created a 'new Hebrew' and then discursively stigmatised Shoah survivors as passive, less brave, less masculine, less heroic than this new construction. Yet, at the same time, due to the negative place of the Shoah in Zionist ideology as the ultimate consequence of *Jewish* exile and vulnerability, the Shoah began to figure rhetorically in relation to all pre-Shoah catastrophes and became a standard by which all Jewish and non-Jewish catastrophes were now measured in Zionist speak. PLO (Palestinian Liberation Organisation) terrorists were perceived as extensions of Hitler, for example (Young, 1990:134), as was Saddam Hussein (Zuckermann, 1993). Segev quotes a letter to President Reagan, in which Prime Minister Begin wrote that liquidating Arafat's Beirut headquarters had felt like sending the IDF (Israeli Defence Forces) to liquidate Hitler in his bunker (Segev, 1991: 375).

Survivors had to make do with the nationalised memory of the Shoah to represent their suffering, using the only language to hand. By silencing the survivors, whose experiences they were unable, and unwilling to hear, and nationalising the memory of the Shoah, Israel confiscated the Jewish nature of the catastrophe, subordinating it to Zionist goals. According to Nava Semel: 'Memory was ceremonial and channelled to one purpose only – exchanging the diaspora identity that has betrayed us, for a fighter identity ... The intimate memory was abandoned'.

The battle to incorporate Shoah memory into the Israeli discourse is still on. Orna Ben Dor's *Shoah Tova* (Ben Dor, 1993) tells the story of a survivor giving a *Yom HaShoah* lecture. On the way he runs over a dog and identifies the vet as a former concentration camp fellow-inmate. The survivor and his wife take the dog to the kibbutz where the lecture is taking place. The lecture is not his customary piece, but the story of a dog he once had before the Shoah. In the morning a kibbutz child names the dog 'Shoah' and pats it: '*Shoah tova* ' – 'good little Shoah'. The film's title, *Shoah Tova*, was not passed by the censor. Ben Dor refused to alter the title and the film was not broadcast until 1995. Naming remains a central issue in the Israeli-Jewish identity and memory stakes.

Shoah historiography: the 'Zionisation' of the Shoah

Initially there was resistance in Israel to researching the Shoah.[2] Historical research on the relationship between the *Yishuv* and the Shoah began towards the end of the 1960s. Later studies (notably Bet Zvi, 1977; Porat, 1986) criticised the *Yishuv* for its lack of ability and will to attempt to save Europe's Jews. Yosef Grodzinsky argues that Bet Zvi's book was deliberately 'boycotted, silenced, criticised and almost forgotten' in the same manner that the Zionist leadership silenced the 'truth' about the events of 1948. Here is another dichotomy between diaspora Jew and Zionist Israeli: 'The Shoah – the strongest justification for the establishment of the state – was presented as a Jewish, but mostly a Zionist event. Bet Zvi ... and others ... looked on as the Zionists took over from the Jews, linking the catastrophe of Europe's Jews to the Zionist movement. Thus a "Zionisation of the Shoah" was constructed' (Grodzinsky, 1994a: 5).

In his book *Good Human Material: Jews Versus Zionists 1945–1951* (1998), Grodzinsky documents the story of Jewish survivors, targeted in the displaced persons camps by pre-state and Israeli immigration officials who were determined to take the survivors to Erez Israel, but only the 'good human material' among them. At times, the survivors were not enthusiastic and in 1948, the officials used force to take them to Erez Israel so that they joined the fighting forces in the 1948 war. One example of the Zionisation of the Shoah was the omission by Israeli historiography of the role of the non-Zionist *Bund* in the Warsaw Ghetto uprising. Furthermore, attempts to organise Bundists at the displaced persons camps after the war were sabotaged by the Zionist representatives (Grodzinsky, 1994a, 1998).

The political commentator Israel Shahak, who survived the War-saw Ghetto 'to the end' and then spent two years in Bergen-Belsen, writes that Bet Zvi was the only historian who showed that Zionist leaders, despite explicit information on the extermination, did nothing to warn Europe's Jews to save themselves. The only way the Zionist leadership was interested in saving Jews was by emigration to Erez Israel: 'thus sabotaging even the scant possibilities of saving Jews else-where' (Shahak, 1994: B9). Shahak is a lone voice celebrating staying alive as the only heroic act, and he rejects Israelis memorising the Shoah exclusively in terms of victimhood versus heroism.

The debate in Israel on the re-interpretation of Zionist myths by historians, political scientists, sociologists and political commentators became known as 'the new historians' debate'. It was triggered by an article by Aharon Megged (1994a), a 'State generation' novelist. Megged bemoans the exploding of Zionism's myths by historians and sociologists (e.g., Morris, 1993; Kimmerling, 1983; Shafir, 1989), and accuses 'the new historians' of Shoah denial. On the surface, the debate seems to be between historians and sociologists favouring pos-itivist, objective historiography (e.g., Ahronson, 1994) and those viewing Zionist historiography as a set of relativist narratives (e.g., Pappe, 1994). It is, however, a debate about Israel's very soul, between those privileging Zionist readings of the Shoah and Zionist history and those critiquing this exclusive interpretation.

Although the debate is conducted mostly between men, none of whom links the Zionisation of the Shoah with the masculinisation of Israel, I would argue that the two are closely linked. To start with, there is a direct link between the debate on the relationship between Zionism and the Shoah and the debate on Zionism and its relation to the Palestinians. Israelis often explain the Arab-Israeli conflict using models based on antisemitism and on the Shoah while negating, or ignoring, the existence of the Palestinians. Both debates, that of the masculinisation of Israel, and that of the Zionisation of the Shoah, are related to the Zionist notion of the negation of exile, and the result-ing construction of the 'new Hebrew' whose right to 'the Land' was seen as indisputable.

Zionism constructed the 'new Hebrews' as different from the dias-pora but also, like all other national movements, as based on 'manly strength and beauty, represented through a well-proportioned, steeled and muscular body' (Mosse, 1992: 325). It erased the role of the anti-Zionist *Bund* in the Ghetto fighting, and discriminated against Shoah survivors upon their arrival in Israel. All this in the name of a survival strategy perceived as necessary and directly linked to the Arab-Israeli conflict and to the ensuing hegemonic 'national security' discourse, which was masculine in essence.

Another debate has featured in the Israeli media since the mid-1980s, between those who see the Shoah as justifying the existence of the Israeli state and those who prefer to draw more universal lessons from the Shoah. There are ongoing arguments as to whether Israel can afford to stop feeling endangered by a 'new Shoah', and therefore end the influence of the Shoah on Israel's political life, or whether Israel is still traumatised by the Shoah. However, Shoah memorisation, learning the Shoah by rote, stripped of its humanitarian lessons, was nationalised and tagged onto a masculinised imperative of Israeli versus Jew. At the same time this nationalistic memorisation is pitched against personal, intimate memory, which has not always been allowed space in Israel's society and polity.

As distinct from the national Shoah commemoration in Israel, Baumel (1998) documents the individual and communal commemoration culture, undertaken primarily by survivors and emigrants from Europe. This commemoration culture concentrated on producing memorial books to extinct Jewish communities; 90 percent of these memorial books were produced in Israel, some in Yiddish and European languages, some in Hebrew or English, for the benefit of survivors and their children who live abroad. Some of these books idealise pre-Shoah Jewish life and gloss over painful questions such as the behaviour of the *Judenräte*. Most of the books minimise the role of acts of armed resistance in opposition to the Israeli tendency to over-play physical acts of resistance over spiritual resistance (Baumel, 1998: 25). This commemoration culture has also constructed scores of communal and individual memorials, with communal memorials featuring synagogues, pictures of the deportations, stones and other artefacts from the home community, scrolls with the names of the victims and the dates of the deportation. Baumel stresses that 98 percent of the memorials do not feature acts of physical resistance:

> The iconography of Israeli communal memorials attests to a culture clash. On the one hand, they are influenced by the Israeli bereavement culture, expressed in the 900 memorials for the fallen in Israel's wars...
> [On the other] communal memorials are devoid of any ideological signifiers, either Zionist or Israeli. (Baumel, 1998: 29)

Official Shoah discourses: the gendered meanings of Shoah versus *gevurah*

My generation grew up on institutionalised official Israeli Shoah discourses which stressed the active over the passive, revolt over 'going like lambs to the slaughter', *gevurah* over Shoah. This has gendered connotations: the Hebrew word *gevurah* derives from the same root –

g-v-r – as the word *gever* – man. Pitching Shoah versus *gevurah*, armed resistance versus extermination and active Israel versus passive diaspora, linked to the construction of Israel as a nation of soldiers, also articulated by the narrators, is the central gendered meaning of Israeli Shoah commemoration and memorisation.

In order to facilitate the nationalisation of the memory of the millions, whose only sin was their alleged passivity in the labour, concentration and extermination camps, this passivity had to be identified by the new state as 'weak' and therefore, I would argue, stereotypically 'feminised'. Heroic accounts were obviously more acceptable.

Heroism has a pride of place in the Israeli myth-making and personal and national responses to losses in wars and in the Shoah are channelled into bereavement and commemoration as the dual face of the national myth (Witztum and Malkinson, 1993). One explanation for the emphasis on the heroic deeds of the Ghetto fighters is the inability of Israelis to endure the intense pain of the Shoah, among other things, because of the alleged passivity of Europe's Jews (Falk, 1990). Intent on commemorating its dead soldiers (and when we say soldiers we mean male soldiers, because women soldiers do not participate in combat), Israel coined the phrase 'the bereavement family'. The term represents double heroism: that of the sons, who fell for their motherland, and that of the parents, who had brought up the sons for sacrifice and who mourn their loss (Witztum and Malkinson, 1993: 243). Not surprisingly, Shoah victims are not part of the Israeli 'bereavement family'.

However, the Jewish nation whose history is paved with its sons' losses, finds it hard to mourn; instead it perpetuates mourning by commemorating heroism (Falk, 1991). The question must be asked whether the glorification of death in battle through the commemorative acts of the 'bereavement family' has diminished the ability to mourn the Shoah, commemorated as part of the narrative structure which includes *Yom Hazikaron*, the day commemorating Israel's fallen soldiers, and the Day of Independence. This narrative structure tells a compelling story: the nation, which was almost annihilated, fights for its survival, defeats its enemies and constructs, for the first time in two-thousand years, a state of its own. War is men's business, but it also demands of them the highest price: their lives. But as far as Israelis are concerned, the Shoah was not a war, and its victims did not fall on the battlefield, like men, but as lamb to the slaughter, like women.

The Israeli education system is aware of issues of balance between Shoah and *gevurah*. It began allocating time for Shoah studies in 1953: the topic was given two hours per annum in total. In 1963, after the Eichmann trial, it was given six hours. Until the 1973 war, teachers and pupils alike identified with *gevurah* and rejected the Shoah. In

1977 a Shoah syllabus, no longer representing the Shoah as an anathema to the state of Israel, allocated 30 hours per annum to the topic. Another syllabus, introduced in 1979, stressed the emotional value of the Shoah rather than its historical context (Segev, 1991: 432–6). The historian Haim Schatzker (1998), one of the instigators of the Shoah syllabi, posits five crucial dilemmas facing educators teaching the Shoah. The first and central dilemma is to what extent the Shoah is unique. The second is whether the Shoah can be compared with other 'holocausts', and the third asks whether the perpetrators should be seen as ordinary people or as demons. The fourth dilemma is whether the Shoah should be taught cognitively or emotionally – Schatzker argues for a synthesis. Finally, he asks whether the Shoah should be taught as a Jewish or a universal event (Schatzker, 1998: 87–92).

The effect of teaching the Shoah is debatable: in 1982 the sociologist Uri Farrago questioned 400 Israeli secondary-school students about the Shoah. Most said they derived their information from films, television programmes and books (notably *The Diary of Anne Frank*), school commemoration ceremonies and workshops at Shoah museums. School history lessons came last (Farrago, 1982). Most respondents in Bilha Noi's (1990) study of Israeli children's attitudes towards the Shoah said that the information gained in primary schools was inconsistent, terrifying and inconceivable. Students were given negative messages about the diaspora compared with positive messages about Israel. However, the binary opposition of *sabra* versus diaspora Jew was perceived by respondents as a stereotype. According to Noi, 'the metaphor of the [Aryan] blue eyed and blond *sabra* is not based on real Israelis, but on an ideal type... this may have its roots in a basic feeling of insecurity here, passed on by adults' (Noi, 1990: 8).

Commemoration

In this section I follow critically Tom Segev's (1991) charting of the process of the Israeli Shoah commemoration culture becoming part of the Zionist secular national symbol system, and privileging *gevurah* over Shoah. As early as 1950, a law to establish the Israeli monopoly on the Shoah proposed that all Shoah victims would become, posthumously, Israeli citizens. According to this logic, the Shoah was seen as the murder of potential Israeli citizens. After long debates in the Knesset the proposed law was rejected in favour of selling, for $12, 'memorial citizenship' to all the victims (Segev, 1991: 421).

The debate, in 1953, on the enactment of 'The Shoah and Heroism Memorial Law – *Yad Vashem*', was, according to Segev, a battle for Israel's very soul. The then Minister for Education Benzion Dinur argued in the Knesset that the Shoah was a consequence of the Jews being dispersed in the diaspora. The Nazis wished to erase Israel's name, he said, deliberately using the term 'Israel' to denote the Jewish nation, and implying that the Shoah was a sin against the state of Israel. Dinur stressed the heroism of Europe's Jews – for him the War of Independence was a direct sequel to partisan and underground fighting during the Shoah.

Segev does not comment on Dinur's gendered description of diaspora Jewish communities as 'ideal women', 'young and joyful', 'life-loving and vibrant', 'chaste and modest'. Figurative descriptions determine our view of events. Israel, the masculine construction, was taking over the memory of the feminine, Jewish diaspora catastrophe.

To give the day commemorating the Shoah a meaning for young people, Menachem Begin, then leader of the opposition, proposed to separate the day commemorating the Shoah and the day commemorating *gevurah*. He proposed setting *Yom HaShoah* (Shoah Day) on *Tish'a BeAv* (the ninth day of the month Av, which commemorates the destruction of the first and second Temples) and thus giving it a religious meaning. And he proposed setting *Yom Hagevurah* (Resistance Day) on the same day as *Yom Hazikaron* (Remembrance Day, the day commemorating Israel's war dead). According to Friedländer (1988: 288), Begin believed the Shoah would be remembered only if set within the Jewish calendar and the *Gevurah* within a Zionist worldview.[3] Begin's proposals were not taken up and the day commemorating the Shoah was set on 27 Nissan, in the middle of the Warsaw Ghetto Uprising, which fell on 19 April 1943, on the eve of Passover, when Jews celebrate their liberation from Egypt, 'the house of bondage'.

The day, originally named by the Knesset, on 21 April, 1951, *Yom HaShoah UMered HaGetaot* (the Shoah and the Ghetto Uprising Day), and subsequently named, in April 1959, *Yom HaZikaron LaShoah VeLagevurah* (Shoah and *Gevurah* Remembrance Day), falls one week before *Yom HaZikaron* and eight days before Israel's Independence Day. The day recalls and links Biblical and recent liberation, modern resistance and national independence, but not mourning and destruction. Grief and metaphors of death and destruction are subsumed as secondary to images of resistance and redemption in the Zionist commemoration repertoire. By linking the Shoah and *gevurah*, that is the Jews' and not God's attempt to deliver themselves, the Israeli government has pulled it out of the Jewish religious continuum in order to nationalise remembrance (Young, 1990: 185). According to Wasserman, 'The choice of date ... corresponds with the rejection of ancient historiosophical Jewish norms in favour of explicit nationalist norms ... another nationalising mechanism by a state which wishes to educate its sons [*sic*] properly' (Wasserman, 1986:7).

By linking Shoah and *gevurah*, the Israeli state also separated them. According to the writer Haim Guri, one of the pre-state independence fighters, who documented the Eichmann trial in his book 'The Glass Cage: The Jerusalem Trial', 'We were ashamed of the Shoah as of a horrible, visible handicap while adopting the *gevurah* with pride, as something which has allowed us to carry our heads high' (Guri, 1963: 247).

Shoah historian Yehudah Bauer disputes this very Israeli dichotomy between Shoah and *gevurah*:

> Israeli society suffers from a Shoah trauma ... To cope with the trauma we have invented falsehoods, consciously and unconsciously. Take the very name ... *Yom HaShoah veHaGevurah* ... these were not two things, one Shoah and the other revolt, or heroism. There was a Shoah and there were many displays of heroism, heroism without weapons ... and heroism with weapons ... Because we did not know how to deal with the memory, and were unwilling to face the truth, and because of the renewed Jewish power syndrome, we viewed the fighters as the precursors of our present military, and left the Rabbis to say *El Male Rachamim* [the Jewish prayer for the dead] for the rest. (Bauer, 1993: B5)

In the best tradition of masculine-military hegemony, the annual semi-military Shoah commemoration ceremony is held in *Yad Vashem* in Jerusalem, in the presence of heads of state, with a guard of honour, complete with military fanfares and torch-lights. Prayers are said by uniformed IDF rabbis. Public Shoah ceremonies give politicians an opportunity to reiterate the isolationist message that today, as in the past, Israel and the Jews stand alone against their enemies, the rest of the world. The ceremonies also reinforce Israel's military superiority, arguably another masculine message. In recent years there has been a move away from nationalised ceremonies to more individualised commemoration. In 1990 stands throughout Israel invited passers-by to read aloud the names of survivors (Segev, 1991: 428).

Yad Vashem is the most sophisticated, multi-layered Shoah memorial in Israel. It was founded in the early 1950s in the spirit of the national vow, articulated by the poet Avraham Shlonsky: 'remember it all / remember and never forget' (Shlonsky, 1971: D, 84), institutionalising and codifying the perpetual topicality of Shoah commemoration in Israel. A mandatory stop on the itinerary of every official visitor (a rule revoked by Ehud Barak's government in August 1999), *Yad Vashem* attracts one and a quarter million Israeli and foreign visitors each year. Memorising both heroes and victims, it embodies the Zionist contrast between passive 'old' Jews and fighting 'new Hebrews'.

When *Yad Vashem* was founded, its philosophy was that there should be no analytical writing about the Shoah. *Yad Vashem* staff were to concentrate on collecting data and gathering documents.

Although this initial impulse soon vanished, its existence in the first place is significant (Hilberg, 1988:22). [4] Apart from the mostly photographic exhibition, giving Shoah and *gevurah* equal weight, *Yad Vashem* acts as a memorial for the victims by storing on microfilm the names of victims. Visitors can locate their relatives' names and if they cannot find them, they are invited to add them to special forms, free of charge. In 1996 *Yad Vashem* began collecting every-day items belonging to survivors in order to construct an exhibition to illustrate the actual lives of camp and ghetto inmates. This approach, influenced by the Washington Holocaust Memorial Museum, will give the Shoah a human dimension, which the documents and photographs currently exhibited in *Yad Vashem* fail to convey fully (Winkler, 1996: B7).

Nations erect memorials not to replace memory or to reshape it according to their self-image, but to allow the whole community to take part in the commemoration process. There is an inevitable partnership between nations and their memorials. Commemoration is not only about symbols, but also about the interaction between the symbol and the event, and between the symbol and the public (Young, 1990:139). Liebman (1981:110) regards *Yad Vashem* (where male visitors must cover their heads according to Jewish religious custom) as a religious shrine. Others see *Yad Vashem* as merely a memorial, not a centre for education about the Shoah and its lessons. Is this a case of the monumentalisation of memory when memory itself is not always accessible?

Arieh Barnea, chairman of the *Lapid* ('Torch') organisation, differentiates between commemorating the Shoah and teaching its lessons. His organisation is committed to transmitting the lessons of the Shoah, beyond memory. Barnea, a son of survivors and member of the *Yad Vashem* Council, is committed to the intimate, not merely the Zionist-institutionalised lessons of the Shoah. 'We are not god-like', he told me in Jerusalem, 'and a survivor who says he was scared should not be alien to us. *Lapid* 's main aim is to shape Israeli society with the Shoah in mind, facing history and ourselves'.

Both Barnea and Segev criticise the aggressive marketing policy of Avner Shalev, appointed in 1993 to head *Yad Vashem*. According to Segev,

> It is presented like some Jurassic Park ... The reason why Israel adopted the equation of Shoah and *gevurah* may have its roots in the difficulty of digesting the truth; but the fact that *Yad Vashem* continues to nurture this equation is problematic. *Yad Vashem* is enshrined in stone. It should release the Shoah from its myths and re-link it to history and facts. (Cited by Prat, 1993: 36)

Barnea would like to see *Yad Vashem* link the Shoah to contemporary political events, such as the *Intifada*, or Bosnia. Shalev, in response, insisted that the most important lesson of the Shoah was 'the ever-topical Zionist message' (Prat, 1993: 36). *Yad Vashem,* it seems, remains a monument of nationalised memory, giving equal weight to Shoah and *gevurah.*

Another Shoah memorial is *Bet HaTfutsot,* the Diaspora Museum, on the Tel Aviv University campus. It relegates the diaspora clearly to the past, locating the Shoah between the pre-Shoah Jewish past and the post-Shoah Israeli present – another void. The sociologist Dafna Izraeli, in a feminist critique of *Bet HaTfutsot,* points to the absence of women from the depiction of diaspora life:

> What we see in *Bet HaTfutsot* is not a historical document, but a cultural representation selected by the curators ... *Bet HaTfutsot* deals with the life of diaspora Jewry ... but a short glance reveals that the presentation is of Jewish men, while Jewish women serve as mere background ... The Jewish calendar is represented by men only ... *Yom HaShoah* [is represented by] an old man grieving by a tombstone. Independence Day [is represented by] young men parading with Israeli flags ... Were women not murdered in the Shoah? Is the State not celebrated by girls and boys alike? ... *Bet HaTfutsot* is a metaphor of the marginalisation of women, of their exclusion from honour, money, power. Like other memorials in Israeli society, *Bet HaTfutsot* reinforces the stereotypical world in which women are nameless, voiceless, and are not represented as contributing anything to society. (Izraeli, 1989:47)

There are several Shoah memorial-museums in Kibbutzim: *Tel Yitzhak, Giv'at Haim, Yad Mordechai* and *Lochamei Hagetaot. Yad Mordechai,* founded by young Polish socialists in the 1930s, was named after Mordechai Anielewicz, commander of the Warsaw Ghetto uprising, who was adopted by the Israeli Shoah commemoration establishment as symbolising *gevurah* as opposed to Shoah (hence Nava Semel's reference to Anielewicz in the quote at the beginning of this chapter). Kibbutz *Tel Yitzhak,* founded by members of the Zionist Youth underground, has established the Masu'a Institute for Shoah Studies whose main aim is to teach Israeli youth about Jewish youth in Europe and who publishes annual essay collections on Shoah topics.

While *Yad Vashem* is a memorial and a shrine, kibbutz *Lochamei Hagetaot* ('The Ghetto Fighters'), founded by the Warsaw Ghetto fighters themselves, aims, through its workshops for young people, soldiers and foreign visitors, to transmit the lessons of the Shoah. Not all the founding members were Ghetto fighters – some were 'mere' survivors – but the heroic myth weighed heavily. The work done by the *Lochamei Hagetaot* Shoah museum aims to bring Israeli youth to love bygone Jewry. The Shoah is presented in the context of Nazism's genocidal ideology, but also in a Jewish, not merely Israeli, context according to kibbutz member Sara Gashmit (1988: 159–61).

The museum, built as soon as the survivors arrived, presents the extermination of the Jews as a backdrop to its main story – that of the Ghetto uprising. In the early days, when labour and resources were scarce, the kibbutz allocated members to commemorative work. It also invested considerable resources in publishing survivors' testimonies, releasing one member, Zvi Dror, on a full-time basis to collect, edit and publish members' testimonies, published in several volumes (Dror, 1984). For members, the existence of the kibbutz side-by-side with the Shoah museum is the best sign of victory over the Nazis. The survivors' children, now in their forties, live daily with their parents' memories. It is a relentless burden.

It is fitting that the Acco Alternative Theatre's five-hour show *Arbeit Macht Frei vom Toitland Europa* ('Work Liberates from Europe, the Land of Death') begins with a tour of the *Lochamei Hagetaot* museum, led by Zelma, an elderly survivor who turns out to be a fictive character played by the actress Smadar Yaron-Ma'ayan. Rokem (1999: 389–99) examines the multi-layered meanings of the term 'work' (*Arbeit*) of the title as referring to the Zionist edict 'work is our life' and also to theatrical 'work' that can lead to liberation from the shame of 'exile' or from Europe, 'the land of death'. Zelma presents the Nazis' rise to power using terms familiar to Israelis, such as 'annexation' and 'occupation'. She sums her experience as a victim by saying that 'our contribution to this century has been the death camp'. Rokem argues that Zelma's message, contextualised in contemporary Israel, is clear: 'these things can happen again, here and now, in 1990s Israel; the first stages of the oppression of the Palestinians are already behind us' (Rokem, 1999: 395). The tour ends with a view of a model of the Treblinka concentration camp guided by Haled Abu Ali, an Israeli-Palestinian actor, who presents it from the point of view of the Jewish victims, a stance reserved in Israeli discourse for Jews only. When I attended the show, Abu Ali was observed by the incredulous, embarrassed thirty-strong audience who were not sure whether he had a right, as a Palestinian, to present the Treblinka model, and thus appropriate 'our' Shoah.

The show consists of several experiential scenes, illustrating the painful relationship between Israelis and the Shoah, beginning with a re-enactment of nationalised school Shoah commemoration ceremonies (which we had all attended), in which Haled tries, in vain, to participate. We are then moved into a bunker-like narrow corridor, where the actors ask us to relate our own Shoah links. The next stop is a low-ceilinged room where Zelma is a survivor mother typically chasing her *sabra* child with a banana and a warm sweater, while Haled, her *Araber* (Yiddish for Arab, one of the stigmatising names for Israeli Palestinians) cleans her obsessively spotless home. During this scene she competes with her survivor neighbour as to who suffered more during the Shoah – this is how some survivors created hierarchies of suffering.

In the next scene Smadar Yaron-Ma'ayan traces the German (Nazi) musical origins of supposedly Israeli 'folk' music, accompanying herself on the piano. This scene moved me to tears, evoking for me, an exile, both the proximity and the remoteness of my early nationalist musical memories.

The low-ceilinged room then becomes a meal scene, at which Moni Yosef, playing a macho ex-army officer husband, justifies Zionism's conquests while Yaron-Ma'ayan, playing his survivor wife, argues a more appeasing point of view, dismissed by her 'new Hebrew' husband. The argument usually begins with that week's current political developments. When I attended in October 1993 it began with the recent Palestinian attack on Israeli targets and the husband used it to rubbish the 'peace process' while the wife begged him, in vain, to allow us, the 'dinner guests', to 'dialogue' about peace. The argument then went back in time through the Israeli-Arab wars, the destruction of the Temple and finally to Adam, whose 'rationality' the husband contrasted with Eve's irrationality. The gendered meaning is clear: the argument, you realise, is ultimately between male *sabra* fighters and female peace-loving survivors. The final devastating scene is set in a surrealist psychiatric hospital, where actors-survivors lie in foetal positions or flagellate themselves mercilessly in a contemporary post-Shoah Israel, where survivors' nightmares remain hidden away, a secret hissing whisper.

Rokem deepens the gendered reading of this incredible play, which crosses between contemporary Israeli reality and the surrealist regions of collective memory. In his reading, the Shoah is another *Dibbuk*, which, according to the Habimah play (first shown in 1922 in Russia and which continued to run in Israel until the 1960s), is the ghost of a dead young man who was not buried or mourned properly and who tries to return to life by penetrating the body of a young woman, Lea:

> Israeli society is still terrified that the six million victims who were not properly buried (or mourned), will return to haunt the survivors. That is why I think Zelma is a possible contemporary version of Lea. (Rokem, 1999: 391)

Rokem relates this to a later scene in which the near-anorexic Zelma lies naked and takes out of her vagina a piece of bread, hidden, supposedly, by a Musulman in the death camp:

> Zelma thus shows us where the food and the energy for survival was hidden, and what is the source of her own life, as opposed to the tattooed number she 'inherited' from her father, and also her own effort –

the work and the birth – through which the actress playing Zelma turns herself into a work of art. (Rokem, 1999: 397)

Like the other spectators, I felt transformed. But official Israel felt threatened: when the company performed in Germany, it was attacked by the Israeli press and a plan to stage the play in London was foiled by embassy officials.

Balagan (mess), a documentary film based on the show, made by the German film maker Andres Veiel (1993), who describes himself as a 'child of perpetrators-murderers', attracted considerable audiences in Germany and was shown at the Berlin Film Festival. Veiel made his film in order to engage the second-generation of perpetrators in a debate about the Shoah. The film follows the stories of three of the actors, the Palestinian Haled Abu Ali, who demonstrates for Palestine 'with blood and fire', yet works in Acco with Jews; Moni Yosef, torn between his readiness to give up the Golan and his love for his settler-brother; and Smadar Yaron-Ma'ayan, who says her survivor-father would turn in his grave if he knew she was singing the Nazi anthem in the film.

The filming provoked strong reactions: Abu Ali's family, viewing him as a collaborator, refused to take part; his friends told him to make films about the murder of Palestinians, not Jews. Abu Ali is convinced, however, that until Palestinians understand the Shoah, there will never be peace. The Shoah, according to the Palestinian-Israeli writer Emil Habibi in 'Your Shoah, our disaster', 'is viewed by the Palestinians as an '"original sin" used by the Zionist movement to convince millions of Jews of the right of its way' (Habibi, 1986: 26–7; see also 'Universalizing the Holocaust' by Saghiyeh and Bashir, 2000, in which they argue that the Palestinians need to understand the Shoah, but also that both Israelis and Palestinians need to assimilate each other's history).[5]

Stages of commemoration

My own biography corresponds to the various stages of the Israeli Shoah commemoration trajectory. From familial silence and disavowal – the 'knowing and not knowing' experienced by me and by many children of survivors – Israel moved through a series of attempts to bring the Shoah and its Zionist lessons into the national consciousness by conducting first the 1954 Kästner trial and then the 1961 Eichmann trial, to the present stage of the near-mandatory school trips to the concentration camp sites.

As a militaristic society, Israeli history tends to be periodicised according to its wars. The 1967 Six Day War (aptly named after the six days of creation), the 1973 Yom Kippur War, the 1982 Lebanon War, the

1987–1993 *Intifada*, and the 1991 Gulf War also mark stages of Shoah commemoration. The Rabin-Peres 'peace process' and the school visits to the concentration camps in recent years spell the integration of the Shoah into a post-masculine-hegemony Israel. Nevertheless, what Zuckermann (1993) calls the 'Shoah code' tends to resurface regularly. The most notable use of the Shoah code was in the posters of Prime Minister Yitzhak Rabin in Nazi uniform prior to his assassination in 1995 by an orthodox opponent of the peace process. This image was one of the discourses said to have legitimated his murder.

Segev (1991) has been influential in examining the complex web of relations between Israelis and the Shoah. While his analysis, which dichotomises between the humanitarian and the nationalistic implications of the Shoah, is gender-blind, I see the trajectory in gendered terms, as part of the shifting binaries masculine Israel versus feminine diaspora-Jew, and therefore Israel versus Shoah and Shoah survivors.

Silencing: constructing the 'Shoah code'

At the end of the Second World War, the Zionist settlers in Erez Israel expressed contempt both for Shoah victims, who had allegedly gone to their deaths 'like lambs to the slaughter' and for the survivors, of whom it was said that 'only the egoists were able to stay alive' (Segev, 1991:104–6). This stage was characterised by a refusal, or inability, to listen to the survivors' experiences and by the silence in which Israelis enveloped the survivors, leaving memory in the realm of the private, and at the same time legislating to nationalise and 'Zionise' that memory. According to Ruth Bondi (1975: 20):

> No one wanted to listen ... the listeners lowered their eyes, as if they were told things which were too personal, not fit for public memory. We learned very quickly to be Israelis outside and survivors at home. Not even at home – why burden your loved ones – only in your heart.

The Israelis did not want to listen, but the survivors too were motivated by a desire to make a new start and a wish to protect their children from the horrors. Their reluctance to speak and the unwillingness of the Israelis to listen deepened the gap between Israelis and survivors. This gap, and the resulting initial lack of social integration between Israelis and survivors, coupled with the chasm between the new Hebrew's self-image as heroic, active and masculine and their view of the survivors as cowardly, passive and feminine, meant the silencing of Shoah experiences up until the 1961 Eichmann trial.

At this stage memorial days had been fixed and commemoration ceremonies instituted in schools; Shoah memorisation was set in train. Segev (1991: 167–8) writes that the uneasy ideological alliance between Zionism and Shoah was based on four main assumptions: the Shoah 'proved' that the only solution to the 'Jewish problem' is a Jewish state; it proved that 'Jews are alone in a hostile world' and that the world 'saw and remained silent'; it assumed that the Shoah must be coupled with *gevurah*; and that the less the Shoah was spoken about the better.

At this very early stage, according to Zuckermann (1993: 20), it became clear that while the Shoah became enshrined as the ideological legitimisation of the existence of the Israeli-Jewish state, the state itself – as collective subject and political entity – did not 'remember' the Shoah. Rather it repressed it *a priori,* adopting its mythical image as the secular historical 'proof' for its right to exist (and to occupy Palestinian lands). Zuckermann differentiates between memory and the representation of that memory, and posits a 'Shoah code', which conceives the inconceivable and articulates the indescribable.

If individual Shoah survivors, having emerged from the Nazi hell, needed to repress their past in order to stay alive, the Israeli collective had an *interest* in repressing the past so that the memory of that hell did not mar the 'new leaf' it wished to turn in its history, and the 'new Jew' it aimed to construct. But both individuals and the collective could only repress the Shoah, not banish its effects from their sub-conscious. As a result, although the Shoah was not part of Israelis' everyday consciousness, it was 'used', mythologically, to create an existential, ever-present anxiety, as Zuckermann argues:

> The Zionist collective demands ... on the one hand to eradicate the Shoah ... in order to turn a new leaf and on the other, to ... remember so as to anchor the ideology of that new leaf. The 'Shoah code' had to be nurtured without the Shoah itself becoming part of the collective's self-definition. (Zuckermann, 1993: 21–22)

The Kästner trial

In 1954 the state of Israel prosecuted Malkiel Grünwald for accusing Dr Rudolf Kästner, one of the leaders of the Budapest Jewish community, of having collaborated with the Nazis in exterminating Hungarian Jewry. Four-hundred thousand Hungarian Jews were deported to Auschwitz. At the same time Kästner managed to save 1,685 Jews he sent to Switzerland. Grünwald, a Hungarian survivor who lost most of his family, accused Kästner of sacrificing the many to save the few. The 'Kästner trial' was conducted very publicly, amidst fierce debates regarding German reparations, negotiated by Ben Gurion's government, as to whether it was right to take money from the murderers. The debate was won by the pragmatists: Israel took the money and its economy was transformed. The trial was underpinned by the struggle between Shmuel

Tamir, the young right-wing defence lawyer, representing the Erez Israeli fighters, and the 'diaspora Jew' Dr Kästner, presented as the utter opposite of all *sabra* symbols, who negotiated with the Nazis in a 'lorries for blood' deal, which eventually fell through. It highlighted the dichotomy of Shoah versus *gevurah*, Israel versus the diaspora. In his play *The Kästner Trial* (1994) Motti Lerner has Tamir accuse Kästner of having a 'diaspora mentality', the worst sin of all, because he dealt with the Nazis rather than take arms against them. Bilski (1999) argues that the Kästner trial, which dealt with the past, became a debate about Israel's political present and future. Despite the defence's claims that it aimed to give survivors a chance to 'tell the truth', Tamir's questioning was only meant to accuse the Zionist leadership of having known about the Shoah yet not warning the world and the Jews (Bilski, 1999: 129). The controversy lives on: in June 1998 I attended a conference at Haifa University, where Tamir's children raked up the same argument against survivors of the Budapest Ghetto as to whether Kästner, who did save 1,658 Jews, was morally justified.

The verdict, which stated that Kästner had 'sold his soul to the devil', divided Israel. During the course of the trial many Israeli myths were shattered, including that of the heroism of the Erez Israeli paratroopers who parachuted behind enemy lines into Hungary in the hope of assisting Jews, but who were either captured or killed.

It is interesting to note the shift in the image of the paratrooper Hanna Senesh, who was captured by the Nazis and was reputed not to have betrayed her comrades. Senesh was the female epitome of the masculine Israeli soldier, proving that women too, complied with the heroic myths. She became a legend and was commemorated in school ceremonies, books and plays (e.g., Megged, 1958). Lerner's televised play of the Kästner trial (1994) alleged that Senesh betrayed her comrades under pressure.[6] The dichotomy between the heroic myth and the difficulties faced by the paratroopers was emphasised by Hanna Senesh's mother, Katarina, who testified for the defence, accusing Kästner who she had been unable to see in order to give him a parcel for her imprisoned daughter. Bilski (1999: 129) notes the irony in the construction of the Israeli heroic myth in the Kästner trial via the stories of two women, the mother, Katarina Senesh, the symbol of (diasporic?) sacrifice, and the daughter Hanna Senesh, the symbol of (Israeli?) heroism.

In 1957, soon after the verdict, Kästner was assassinated by a right-wing activist. In 1958, the High Court reversed his conviction and cleared him posthumously.

The Kästner trial signalled a change in the Israeli perception of the Shoah, although, with the debate focusing on victims versus heroes, it barely touched upon the fundamental issues of the relationship between Israel and the Shoah (Weitz, 1993: 143). Indeed, the image of

the Shoah itself, according to Dalia Ofer (1993: 152–8), began changing only later, with demographic changes (the increase in the number
of Israelis with no personal connection to the Shoah), the increasing
volume of Shoah research, and the 1961 Eichmann trial.

The Eichmann trial

Like other Israeli secondary-school children, I too, was glued to the
radio during the teachers' strike of 1961, when the Eichmann trial,
held in Jerusalem, was broadcast live on national radio. Although
Adolf Eichmann was in the dock, it was the Shoah itself which was on
trial. For Ben Gurion, the trial had two objectives – to remind the world
that the Shoah meant they had to support Israel, and to teach Israelis
the lessons of the Shoah (Segev, 1991: 311). Segev cites Hannah
Arendt (1956) who argued that Eichmann was only a medium – it
was the trial of the Jewish nation, and Israel took it upon itself to speak
on its behalf, in the spirit of Zionism.

The trial forced witnesses-survivors, for the first time, to expose
themselves and their past: 'the impulse to speak became stronger than
the impulse to remain silent' (Segev, 1991:321). It was a turning point:
the horrifying testimonies wrenched out from the depths of silence,
brought about the identification by Israelis, including Israelis of non-
European origin, with survivors and victims. The trial was staged as an
emotional pageant. In his opening and closing speeches, state prosecu-
tor Gideon Hausner linked the Shoah to the long chain of antisemitic
persecutions but at the same time highlighted its meaning to each and
every survivor. Although the Eichmann trial was, according to Segev, a
national group therapy session, the evidence evoked familiar Israeli
contempt towards the down-trodden diaspora Jewish victims, as is evident from Haim Guri's account of the testimony of Maurice Fleis-
chmann, one of the leaders of the Vienna Jewish community: 'I don't
want to hear this broken, small man tell, and retell, of his suffering, of
his sickness, of his humiliation ... I would prefer to be today at the
Nakhal [the acronym for 'Pioneering Combative Youth', the IDF's kibbutz corps] display, to see strong, beautiful people' (Guri, 1963: 33).

This contrast between 'strong, beautiful' Israelis and 'small, broken' survivors could not have been expressed more poignantly. However, the trial, aimed to establish Israel's supremacy over the entire
Jewish nation, began the move towards a greater Israeli understanding of the Shoah. In May 1961, Guri wrote: 'How long is it since we
first sat in this hall? A month. Yes. But none of us will come out of here
resembling himself' (Guri, 1963: 73). And in September 1961: 'We
have to apologise to those we had judged, we who were outside that
circle. And we judged them, not once, without asking ourselves what
right we had to do so' (Guri, 1963: 247).

Zertal (1999) argues that in spite of claims that the Eichmann trial changed Israelis' self-perception, it was more a nation-building history lesson, or a national passion play, than a properly conducted trial. It also aimed to restore the Israeli (and the *Yishuv's*) hegemony over the collective memory, a hegemony severely damaged by the Kästner trial. But while the trial persuaded Israel more than ever of the justification for its post-Shoah existence, Hannah Arendt (1956) wrote an uncompromising indictment of the trial. Arendt objected to the propagandist and pedagogical tone of the trial and deconstructed the Manichean mythical meaning of the Shoah as presented by the trial. Her book, *Eichmann in Jerusalem: a Report on the Banality of Evil,* presented disturbing theses about the ease with which mass murder was 'normalised' and with which collaboration with a genocidal regime, also by some of the victims, was routinised. The amazing thing, Zertal argues, was the near absence of debate in Israel on Arendt's book, which was never translated into Hebrew, an absence explained by the difficulty of looking the Shoah in the eye, and by the Israelocentrism of the 1960s. The contemporary debate on Arendt's work, Zertal concludes, is about Israel; Arendt is only the medium (Zertal, 1999: 159–67).

While bringing the Shoah in to Israel's collective consciousness, the trial also distanced it. The most memorable testimony was by Katzetnik, the writer Yehiel Dinur, identified and named for the first time during the trial, when he called Auschwitz 'another planet'. I had read Katzetnik's books as a young adult. A series of auto/biographical novels about the camps, they were signed by the pseudonym Katzetnik, 'he who was in the camp', a pseudonym Dinur hid behind until the Eichmann trial. His books were hugely influential.

The trial enabled Israelis to perceive the Shoah as a one-off, demonised event, unrelated to universal, humanitarian messages: we perceived Auschwitz as indeed, 'another planet'. It took Dinur, and us, years to accept that it was not another planet. After lengthy psychotherapy in the Netherlands, when, under the influence of LSD administered by his therapist, Dinur imagined himself in SS uniform, he realised the most horrible of all truths, that as a human being, he must share the blame. In 1987, in a television interview, re-broadcast in the documentary film based on Segev's book, *The Seventh Million*, Dinur reversed his 'other planet' claim: 'Auschwitz was not another planet as I had thought. Auschwitz was not created by the devil, nor by God, but by humans ...' (Bruner and Segev, 1995).

The 1967 War

Before the 1967 war, the talk was of the danger of Israel being 'annihilated' by the Arabs. Not conquered, not destroyed, but annihilated. Only a nation which 'memorised' mass annihilation could prepare thus for the next Shoah: the existential fear was still too close to the surface. The war broke out in June 1967. Within six days the IDF captured the Gaza Strip, the Sinai and the West Bank, including East Jerusalem. Within a week it became clear that the IDF was more powerful than all the Arab armies. The anxiety about 'annihilation' had been unfounded, but it was this Shoah-rooted anxiety which brought about the war. The Israeli victory was attributed, among other things, to Shoah awareness. Segev cites member of Knesset Arieh Ben Eliezer: 'we were not as few as we thought; the six millions fought by our side whispering the eleventh commandment: thou shalt not be murdered' (Segev, 1991: 368).

Israeli-born *sabra* soldiers, educated to believe that Israel was the only safe home for Jews, the only guarantee against another Jewish Shoah, suddenly felt threatened, as expressed in *The Seventh Day: Soldiers Talk About the Six-Day War*: 'Suddenly there was talk about Munich, about the Shoah, about the Jewish people left to its own fate..'. (*The Seventh Day*, 1970:20).

Segev comments on *The Seventh Day*: 'It is impossible to know where speakers expressed their own feelings and where they repeated clichés meant to enshrine the fighters as beautiful souls who "shoot and cry" in a just war. It seemed that the Shoah was used by some of them to shape their own image' (Segev, 1991: 366 fn). Thus, the Israeli soldier was compelled to fight by the memory of what had happened in the diaspora, precisely and paradoxically because it could also happen in Israel (Young, 1990:136).

The 1973 War

The 1967 war, like the Shoah and the establishment of the state, was seen by many Israelis as a new beginning of Zionist history. The years after 1967 were years of complacency, despite a continuing war of attrition. These were also the first years of the Israeli occupation of Palestinian territories. But it was the 1973 war, in which the Arabs surprised Israel during *Yom Kippur*, the Day of Atonement, the holiest day of the Jewish calendar, and in which the Israeli victory was a close shave, which reinforced the perception of the Jews as eternally isolated and hated (Liebman, 1981: 110). The 1973 War did not put an end to Arab attacks: in the following years Israelis found themselves time and again in situations which reminded them of the Shoah.

Lomsky-Feder (1997), who collected 63 biographies of Israeli Jewish men who served in the army during the 1973 war, argues that contrary to the traumatic meaning the 1973 war assumed in the Israeli collective historical memory, the fighters memorised it as a 'normal' experience. This interpretation supports what Kimmerling (1993b) calls Israel's 'cognitive militarism', according to which Israeli society accepts as self evident the centrality of war. Lomsky-Feder uses her findings to chart the changing cultural discourse about war in Israeli society from the 'heroic youth' ethos to the more vulnerable image of soldiers, from a reality in which military service is an integral part of Israeli men's lives, to a different reality in which the 'cultural debate on war and the fighter ethos has become, since the 1970s, more critical than ever before. It deals with the traumatic facts of the military experience, while debating the moral values of the fighter ethos, stressing private pain over public bereavement' (Lomsky-Feder, 1997: 76). These shifts cannot but have a crucial effect on the relationship between Israel and the Shoah.

The Lebanon War

Menachem Begin, Israel's first non-Labour Prime Minister, came to power in 1977. The 15 years of his Likud Party reign saw the most cynical appropriation of the Shoah in public discourses for political purposes.

The 1982 Lebanon War, the first non-consensual war, began as 'Operation Peace for Galilee', ostensibly aimed at defending Israel's northern border, and ending with an invasion of Beirut and the ensuing occupation of a 'security zone' in southern Lebanon which still continues. During the war Begin used Hitler and Shoah images to justify the invasion. In response to Begin's use of the Shoah to justify the bombardment of Beirut, the novelist Amos Oz wrote: 'But Mr Begin, Adolf Hitler had died 37 years ago ... Hitler is not hiding in Nabatieh, Sidon or Beirut. He is dead and burnt' (Oz, 1983: 71). Begin also compared the Palestinian leader Yasser Arafat to Hitler and argued in the Knesset that no one can make moral demands on Israel after the Shoah.

However, after Lebanon, for the first time, the suffering of others, particularly of Palestinian children, not Jewish suffering, was the principal subject of Israeli literary and poetic discourses. The death of Palestinians was described using Shoah images; their fate was equated with the fate of the Jews as Israeli poets and playwrights (collected in Kafri, 1983; Hever and Ron, 1983) reflected and compelled Jewish understanding of the suffering of the Palestinians.

The Intifada

The longer the occupation lasted and with it Palestinian resistance, the more Israel moved to the right and the more the Shoah was used by politicians as moral justification for the occupation and its excesses. The *Intifada*, the Palestinian uprising, began in December 1987 and led to oppressive measures by the Israeli army. Several months later, in March 1988, the Israeli historian Yehuda Elkana published an article calling on Israelis to forget the Shoah. Elkana, deported to Auschwitz at the age of ten, linked the excesses of the Israeli occupation to the Shoah and argued that Israeli society's relation to the Palestinians is motivated by 'a deep existential anxiety, fed by a particular interpreta-tion of the Shoah and by a willingness to believe that the whole world is against us and that we are the eternal victim'. Elkana concludes his article by saying: 'it may be important for the wide world to remember [the Shoah] ... we, on the other hand, must forget' (Elkana, 1988: 13).

Commenting on Elkana, Segev asks: 'How should Israeli children have interpreted the horrifying Shoah pictures shown to them time and again, if not as an imperative to hatred?' (Segev, 1991: 471). Elkana's daring is not in pointing to the link between the Shoah and the Israeli occupation (a link made by other Israeli figures, notably the philosopher Yesha'ayahu Leibowicz, who enraged many by calling Israeli occupiers 'Judeo-Nazis'). Rather it is in his call to un-link the establishment of Israel from the Shoah, and to stop justifying the occu-pation by Israelis' existential anxiety or by the Shoah.

If the Lebanon War began the watershed in the relationship between Israelis and their wars, the *Intifada* made it clear that a con-clusive military victory was no longer possible in a war against a civil-ian population. On the one hand, soldiers' visits to Shoah museums and memorials sometimes achieved a nationalistic, rather than a uni-versal, purpose, with soldiers initiating units to liquidate Arabs which they called 'the Mengele Unit' or 'the Auschwitz Regiment' (Segev, 1991: 381). On the other hand, the *Intifada* and its excesses shattered the accepted images of a fighting Israeli manhood. Male IDF recruits, often as young as eighteen, had to fight against Palestinian women and children. Many felt brutalised by the encounter and the number of psychological problems and suicides within the IDF increased. A grow-ing number of reserve soldiers refused to serve in the territories.

The *Intifada* also politicised Israeli women peace activists. Early in 1988 'Women in Black' began holding weekly vigils in the main town squares and conducted meetings with Palestinian women (see Lentin, 1995; 1998 for a review of Israeli and Palestinian women's peace activism). The *Intifada* was also a turning point on Israel's way to peace – the 'peace process' gained momentum during the *Intifada* and led to the 1993 Oslo Accords.

At all stages Israeli society appropriated the Shoah as uniquely Jewish and therefore uniquely a diaspora (not Israeli) experience, though with different degrees of identification. The IDF's excesses during the *Intifada*, even more so than during the Lebanon War, moved Israeli poets, novelists and playwrights to compare the suffering of Palestinian children with that of Jewish children during the Shoah (Young, 1990: 145).

The Gulf War

The 1991 Gulf War, the first war in the history of Israel in which the IDF did not take an active part, re-awakened the 'Shoah code' like no other war. Israelis, sitting in sealed rooms, equipped with gas masks against the threatened German-manufactured, Iraqi chemical scud missiles, have never had such a 'Jewish' experience. Nor have Israeli men ever felt so emasculated. Women working with victims of family violence reported that during the Gulf War there was a huge increase in violence against women because families were locked in sealed rooms with all the accompanying fears, which were expressed, violently, against women and children (*Noga*, 1993: 3; Lentin, 1998: 338).

Saddam Hussein was compared to Hitler by Israeli politicians and media who highlighted the irony of a state of Shoah survivors being threatened by German-manufactured Iraqi gas. According to Moshe Zuckermann (1993), who surveyed the Israeli press during the Gulf War, the 'Auschwitz code' was activated during the Gulf War by public figures in order to further silence any discursive debate beyond the sealed wall of survivors' emotions. Interestingly, survivors and their families were shown to be the least anxious during the Gulf War, as Nava Semel recalls of her own parents (see chapter 2).

Another code, that of the 'classic Jew', also emerged during the Gulf War. In a symposium held two weeks after the war broke out, about the mass escape of the inhabitants of Tel Aviv from their scud-missiled city, the journalist Meir Uziel evoked the heroism part of the Shoah equation: 'I am fascinated by the human quality called courage. How come Hitler did not manage to kill us? Simply, people who did not behave like Jews, not like the 'classic Jew' whose main aim is to return home to mother, fought him to his bunker' (*Iton Tel Aviv,* 1991: 7). Uziel represents Israeli Shoah instrumentalisation which appropriates the 'classic Jew' while denying the very memory of that Jew (Zuckermann, 1993: 220–1).

The 1992–96 'Peace Process' and Rabin's assassination

Yitzhak Rabin's labour government came to power in July 1992, and embarked vigorously on the so-called 'peace process'. Official government discourses have changed somewhat and the Shoah was no longer invoked as a justification for wars, but the right kept appropriating it in its opposition to the peace negotiations. At the 1993 Likud AGM, its leader Binyamin Netanyahu attacked Rabin's peace policy: 'We may wake up one morning and find ourselves suddenly within the 1967 Auschwitz borders'. Right-wing Knesset member Ariel Sharon, speaking at the same AGM, defended Likud's objections to the establishment of a Palestinian state: 'some say this is not democratic. Perhaps, but our grandparents did not come here to establish a democracy, but a Jewish state' (Tal, 1993: 1).[7]

Rabin was assassinated on 4 November, 1995 at the end of a peace rally in a Tel Aviv square, by Yigal Amir, a young orthodox Israeli Jew, for his part in the Israeli-Palestinian peace negotiations, in the middle of handing back Palestinian towns. The assassination, preceded by displaying posters of Rabin in SS uniform at anti-government demonstrations, unsettled several Israeli norms around military masculinities, and around the Israeli versus Jew dichotomy. Rabin, the first Israeli-born Prime Minister, was also a celebrated army commander, whose military career had begun in the pre-state army, the *Palmach*, and who, as chief of staff, had been responsible for the 1967 War victory, which resulted in occupying Palestinian territories. He was indeed the epitome of the 'new Hebrew' whose roots were in 'the Land'. At the same time, he made a U-turn regarding Israel's relations with the Palestinians and won popular support for his peace policies precisely because of his impeccable military, *sabra* credentials.

Media commentators interpreted the huge grief expressed by young Israelis as emanating from regarding Rabin both as father figure and as the first Israeli *sabra* son, who had fought in all of Israel's wars but had the courage to fight for peace when the goals and objectives changed (Segev, 1995a; Samet, 1995; Zertal, 1995).

The opposition to the peace process comes from what can be termed as the 'Jewish' element of Israel. The peace process is seen by ultra-orthodox Israelis as 'anti-Jewish' in that it involves the return of 'Jewish lands' to 'enemy hands'. In the months prior to the assassination, the ultra-orthodox weekly magazine *Ha'shavua* published scores of articles criticising Rabin and his government and suggested Rabin should die for his work for peace. Terms such as 'traitor', 'madman', 'non-Jewish', and 'anti-religious', recurred. Several articles, making a direct link with the Shoah, called Rabin and his foreign minister Shimon Peres *Judenrat* (Nazi-appointed Jewish ghetto-leaders) and *Kapos* (Nazi-appointed concentration camp block-heads). These articles did not cease with the assassination, and the magazine, closed in late November 1995, renewed publication under a different title in December 1995 (Ilan, 1995: 3).

In contrast to these gender-blind interpretations, Tamar El-Or, in a book on literacy and identity among religious Israeli women (1998), (en)genders Rabin's assassination by likening it to murdering a woman to preserve the family honour, as practised among Israel's Palestinian population. According to El-Or, in holding talks with the Palestinians, Rabin had alienated sections of the Jewish Israeli public, therefore a member of the (Israeli Jewish) family had to avenge the family honour by assassinating him. Like a woman or girl who transgresses sexually, Rabin transgressed by negotiating with the Palestinians and shaking Yasser Arafat's hand on the White House lawn:

> The Prime Minister made love with the forbidden, he broke the rules of morality and chastity and damaged the national family honour ...

the picture of the girl who was caught in the act was distributed in the right's demonstrations ... wearing a *keffieh* headdress... [8] her fate was sealed.

As in cases of murder for family honour, where the murderer is a son, brother or father who knows his duty, Rabin's assassin came from the heart of religious Zionism. The murder, like the mourning, was an (Israeli Jewish) family affair: someone saw to it that Arafat would not be invited to the funeral (El-Or, 1998: 80–4).

El-Or's interpretation triggered a heated debate on the Israeli feminist internet discussion list (reproduced in *Noga*, 1998). Several discussants criticised her for using a 'brilliant' feminist argument to diminish the seriousness of the assassination, which achieved the immobilisation of the peace process. Others criticised her for considering the assassin as a family member. My own response (in *Noga*, 1998) supported El-Or's view of Rabin as a wayward daughter who had damaged the extended family honour. Rabin was racialised (dressed in Nazi uniform) and feminised (his military career was mocked, he was called a traitor). The murderer, though convicted, was adopted by ultra-religious and ultra-nationalist Jews as defending 'our honour' and 'our land'. Meanwhile, 'we', peace-loving Israelis, allowed 'them' – Netanyahu and his religious-nationalist supporters – to kill the peace, demolish Palestinian homes and rhetorically justify their suicidal policies.

The binary opposition of Israeli versus Jew is less clear-cut in the post-Rabin era than ever before. Binyamin Netanyahu, elected as Prime Minister by a small majority in June 1996, got to power with the help of the ultra orthodox parties. His own Likud party, opposed to territorial compromise, never hesitated to employ Shoah discourses to justify the ongoing occupation. Journalist Orit Shochat (1996: B8) views Netanyahu's victory as the victory of 'Jews' over 'Israelis'. His reluctance to deal with the Palestinians or to return Palestinian territories is hailed, by his followers, ironically, as the victory of the 'Jewish nation'. But there is a contradiction here because Netanyahu, like Rabin, is an Israeli-born *sabra*, whose family has a celebrated military record and who prides himself as an anti-terrorism expert (Netanyahu, 1986; 1993). It is clear, however, that his election signalled a return of masculine discourses and practices: during his election campaign, Netanyahu did not bother to address women, not even as lip-service (Ostrowitz, 1996: 13). In May 1999, after three years of stalemate in the 'peace process' and of economic and political stagnation, Netanyahu was defeated in elections by the former chief of staff Ehud Barak, hailed as Rabin's political successor. Amidst hopes for renewed progress in negotiations with the Arabs, Barak has managed to alienate both his women voters and his Palestinian voters. During his first year in office, Barak seemed intent on a heavy-handed military-style government. In spite of successfully withdrawing from Lebanon (in the face of demonstrations by mothers whose soldier sons serve in Lebanon in favour of withdrawal in view of the many Israeli casualties), despite some progress in negotiating with the Syrians, and despite having handed back small tracts of land to the Palestinian National Authority, the general tone of Barak's government is that of masculine militarism.

New figurative metaphors

The contemporary stage of Shoah commemoration is epitomised by 'the new historians' debate' and by the school trips to the concentration camp sites. The shifting relationship between Israelis and the Shoah is best characterised by this stage. The school trips began in the late 1980s and during the 1990s twelve thousand Israeli youngsters visited Poland and the concentration camp sites. During the early journeys, the encounter with economically depressed Poland strengthened the young Israelis' accusation of all Poles for collaboration with the Nazis. Nili Keren (1998: 93–100) documents the detailed training given to teachers and students prior to the trips, but argues that the young Israelis fail to appreciate either pre-Shoah Jewish life or contemporary Polish life and tend to concentrate on the Shoah element of the journey, which serves to strengthen their Israeli identity. She also bemoans the commercialisation of the trips and the confusion, for many students, in relation to the 'fun' element of the school trip. Segev (1991) argues that the young Israelis visit the scene of the Jewish massacres as Israelis, for whom the Shoah is but a backdrop against which their distinction from diaspora Jewry can be re-rehearsed and views this as Zionist irony:

> One generation after the establishment of the state of Israel, it sends its sons to the Jewish past deserted by its founding fathers, who had dreamt up the 'new [Hebrew] man', to find what the secular Israeli reality cannot offer them – identity plus roots. The journey is a ritual full of symbols and emotions ... deriving from two sources, one national, the other religious. It has a distinctly political character, transmitting closeness, almost xenophobia, instead of openness and humanity. (Segev, 1991: 452)

Laor (1999: B14) writes in relation to what he calls Israel's 'monstrous Shoah culture', that:

> the grandchildren who go on 'The March of Life' in Bierkenau listen to the large story, but erase their grandmother's small story – how she hid under the canvas on a tank carrier beside a coupling pair, how she paid the Russian officer for this lift, how he left her some of her money to buy

bread, how the coupling pair gave her some after they came – such grandmothers' tales are far less 'national' than 'The March of Life'.

Laor calls for the isolationist myth to be re-visited and argues that it is important to remember those of Poland's Jews who did not adopt the Zionist narrative, such as members of the *Bund*, whose stories were erased by the Zionisation of the Shoah:

> Jews had lived in Poland for a thousand years. We mustn't allow the genocide to erase these lives... Polish Jews who did not immigrate to Israel 'stain' the ideological picture. Any story... which is not part of the prevailing [Shoah] kitsch, is far more important than the 'automatic' narrative which erases far more than it commemorates.

Aware of the Israelocentrism displayed by the students, *Masu'a* dedicated its 1999 annual to preparing teachers and students for their journeys in a collection of articles on pre-Shoah Jewish life, on the Nazi occupation and on post-Shoah Poland (Rappel, 1999).

The school journeys have produced their own literary expressions (e.g., Levin, 1990; Bar El, 1992). Bar El's *They Also Shot the Crows* is a nationalistic teenage novel, mixing the 1973 war, army emblems and nationalistic popular songs with concentration-camp experiences, and presenting Poles and Polish culture as the antithesis of Israeli nationalism. When Rabin's education minister Shulamit Aloni called for an examination of the rationale behind the school trips to Poland, she was attacked from all directions. If Bar El's book is an authentic portrayal of these trips, there is indeed reason to re-examine their message (Talmor, 1992: 23).

The contemporary commemoration stage is also characterised by a re-examination of past school Shoah ceremonies, where images intended to enrich our spirit, frightened us instead. Journalist Gideon Samet, critical of the thick symbolism fed to Israelis each year during the 'commemoration season', realises that 'these symbols are hard to control ... In their very contradictory ways they will continue to shape us more than we are prepared to admit' (Samet, 1993: B1).

Other critics of Shoah commemoration school ceremonies call for a universalist rather than a nationalist focus, but what seems a logical demand is seen by the Israeli education establishment as subversive. Barkay and Levy (1999: 433–9) tell the story of *Kedma*, a progressive secondary-school founded in 1993 in a Mizrahi working-class area in Tel Aviv, which decided, on *Yom HaShoah* 1995 to change the conventional ceremony and stress racism and human suffering as universal aspects of the Shoah. Students lit a seventh torch in addition to the six torches commemorating the six million victims. Media coverage of the ceremony aroused protests from government ministers, parliamentarians and members of the public alarmed by the message *Kedma* wished to stress. The alternative ceremony, which also aimed to protest at the Ashkenazi appropriation of the Shoah, spurred a debate about the meaning of these ceremonies. However, the debate was about more than the Shoah, it was about ethnic and class hegemonies and about universalism versus particularism.

A much more subversive approach to *Yom HaShoah* ceremonies is expressed by the punk artist Avi Pitchon who writes, in keeping with 1990s spirit:

> It's clear we must abolish the sirens on *Yom HaShoah*... this totalitarian ceremoniality belongs in the past. There is no room for mourning by order in a democracy that presumes its citizens are thinking people... A more honest answer to this question is: as long as I don't have a kid who goes to school, I don't give a fuck. And even if I have a kid, I'll wait for him to come home from the ceremony and together we'll laugh at those children who want to be loved and who stand on the stage in a dusty jacket and a cardboard yellow star... (Cited in Yahav, 1999: 385).

The memory of the Shoah was nationalised in Israel in the mode of the masculine construction of Israeli-ness, which valorised *gevurah* over Shoah and 'mere survival', and which excluded the less-than-masculine feminised Jewish memory and stigmatised Shoah survivors in this discursive process. At the same time Israel took on board its Jewish past, extending the memory boundaries. Memory was monopolised by the ruling Zionist discourse, dictated to by a 'security imperative', which shaped the more recent Israeli past. The history of Israel is a masculine-military history of wars, seen by many as an inevitable mode of existence. The struggle to combine the two parallel channels – that of the Jewish diaspora past and that of the more recent Israeli past – has created a tension between Israeli and Jewish identities.

Young (1990) quotes Ba'al Shem Tov, the eighteenth century founder of the Hassidic movement: 'Forgetting lengthens the period of exile! In remembering lies the secret of deliverance!' The question is whether breaking the silence and transmitting the memory of the Shoah has further negated the exilic diaspora, or enabled Israel to begin committing itself to its Jewish past. The Shoah has been systematically 'memorised' by inscribing it onto the Israeli consciousness. The Zionist founding fathers wanted to construct a 'new man', 'new Hebrew', 'new Jew'. But the heritage of the Shoah 'returns the Israeli to the roots of his [*sic*] Jewish identity without committing him morally or personally' (Segev, 1991: 472).

Re-reading Elkana's article, Uri Ram (1999) writes about the struggle between Israelis and Jews and cites Elkana as differentiating between two kinds of collective memory and two kinds of collective relationship to the past – democratic and fascistic. 'If we want freedom and peace, Elkana states, we must forget, side with the living, build our future instead of dealing morn and night with symbols, ceremonies and the lessons of the Shoah' (Ram, 1999: 356–7). However, while Elkana calls upon Israelis to forget (the Shoah), Zuckermann (1993: 31), as a leftist 'post-Zionist' (rather than a right-wing 'neo-Zionist'), argues that 'after Auschwitz, the Jewish nation isn't allowed to forget'. Ram reminds us that the new academic historical paradigm, including debates about silence and silencing, born in the 1980s, has become part of the public discourse in the 1990s. However:

> the debate on remembering and forgetting must affect both remembering and forgetting themselves. In the 1990s the conflict between Zionism, post-Zionism and neo-Zionism as to who controls collective memory and forgetting is central to Israel's political culture. (Ram, 1999: 357)

The only answer, sociologically speaking, to illuminating, and breaching, the dichotomy of Israeli versus Jew, is observing and documenting the development of new discourses. During the 1992–1996 Rabin-Peres regime new figurative metaphors were beginning to replace the siege and anxiety discourse as official Shoah discourses were changing, but only somewhat. In April 1992 the then Chief of Staff General Ehud Barak headed an IDF delegation to Auschwitz. Although his speech was redolent with heroic, masculine *sabra* rhetoric, he did acknowledge the martyrs, albeit using masculine grammar and imagery and binaries such as 'our fallen brethren' versus 'the sons *[sic]* of the redeemed generation':

> We, the soldiers of the Israel Defence Forces, arrived here fifty years too late. Our fallen brethren, we, the sons of the redeemed generation who grew under the deep blue skies of the state of Israel, we who did not stand in your place, know that we cannot judge you. We are proud of your struggle to maintain your humanity in the realm of Satan and we are proud of your acts of resistance and struggle, limited as they were. The Israel Defence Forces salute you. (Barak in Auschwitz, April 1992, in Bruner and Segev, 1995).

A year later, Yitzhak Rabin's 1993 speech at the fiftieth anniversary of the Warsaw Ghetto uprising used much more elegaic, more 'Jewish' imagery:

> Here, on this square kilometre, there once stood the Warsaw ghetto ... housing the 400,000 Jews who lived here. And the city is empty. Where are the writers? Where are the rabbis? The doctors? The musicians? Where is *Amcha* [ordinary Jews] and where are the children? Scorched

eårth. Scorched people. My people is no more. (Rabin in Warsaw, April
1993, in Bruner and Segev, 1995)

The 'peace era' hopes that Israelis might relinquish the 'Auschwitz
code' and its symbolism and learn to forget (Segev, 1995b: B1) were
dashed during Netanyahu's visit to Auschwitz in 1998 – his speech
linked nationalism, power, religion, and, implicitly, masculinity – no
universal lessons here:

> [During the Shoah] the Jewish nation did not have any power... neither
> military nor political. [But now] the Jewish people have a home, a flag,
> an army... the lesson of the Shoah is that the existence and rebirth of
> the Jewish people is dependent on Jewish sovereignty, a Jewish army,
> and the power of the Jewish faith. (Horowitz, 1998: 10)

It remains to be seen whether official Israel follows unofficial
'counter-narratives' in relation to the Shoah. For the film version of his
book Segev interviewed a group of young Israelis with whom he had
travelled to Auschwitz five years previously. Their camp visit affected
their Israeli identity deeply. Segev does not refer to the striking gender
differences. Adam Max relates his visit to the camp to his army service:

> When I served in the territories ... when you don't know who is your
> enemy ... many guys lose control ... and I thought several times when I
> saw it happening ... all the time I remembered what I saw in Poland, this
> subject of an army working with civilians, that it was important not to
> lose my humanity.

Shira Gal, on the other hand, draws a broader lesson:

> [it's important] to be aware of other people's Shoahs, which we don't
> even study in Israel ... The Armenians, the Kurds, almost everywhere
> there are horrible things and it does not have to be called 'the Shoah',
> because then it becomes exclusively Jewish. But genocide is a broader
> term ... (Bruner and Segev, 1995)

Jewish memory and tradition depend on the capacity of figurative
language to remember the past. The naming of the Shoah, its historiography and commemoration indicated a break with Jewish memory.
At the same time, according to Young (1990: 84), by placing the
Shoah in a Jewish continuum, it initially enabled Israelis to distance
themselves from it. However, unable to invent a new Israeli grammar
of Shoah memory (as they had invented an Israeli discourse of war
memories, with expressions such as the 'purity of the weapon', and
with intense Hebraicisation and biblicisation of Palestinian place
names),[9] Israelis had to resort, inadvertently, to Jewish memory when

naming, memorising and commemorating the worst Jewish catastrophe in living memory.

I agree with Young's argument that, in learning to confront the legacy of the Shoah, Israelis are beginning to resort to a Jewish grammar. For some, this has spelled a positive process of being enabled to position their intimate memories in the public domain, as the narrators of this study have done in their stories and films. On the other hand, Israel, still traumatised, has not yet begun working through Shoah memory and grief. The battle between monumental and intimate memory continues.

Notes

1. 'State generation' is a term reserved particularly for Israeli writers born in Israel in the 1930s.
2. A resistance reiterated in 1998 in the US in the attack by Gabriel Schoenfeld, senior editor of *Commentary* magazine, in *Commentary* and *The Wall Street Journal* (cited in Lipstadt, 1998), on academic studies of the Shoah, said to diminish the catastrophe and aid Shoah denial. Not surprisingly, Schoenfeld centred his attack on feminist academic studies of the Shoah.
3. Begin, though not a Shoah survivor, saw himself as having been personally liberated from Auschwitz, and therefore a proud, fearless Jew. After receiving the Nobel Peace Prize in 1978, he described himself as a member of 'the Shoah and redemption generation' (Zak, 1991: 49–56).
4. In 1958 Hilberg's important study of the perpetrators of the Shoah (Hilberg, 1983) was rejected for publication by *Yad Vashem*. The letter of rejection, quoted by Hilberg in his autobiography (Hilberg, 1995), cites Hilberg's reliance on German sources, his comparisons with other 'holocausts', and the fact that his study focuses on the Nazi perpetrators and not on the Jewish victims of the Shoah. But the main reason given was that Hilberg did not emphasise Jewish acts of resistance and heroism, contrary to Israeli Shoah commemoration principles (Hammerman, 1995: 5).
5. Another film based on *Arbeit Macht Frei, Don't Touch My Holocaust* (1994) was made by the Tangiers-born Israeli film-maker Asher Tlalim, who filmed the cast being harassed in Germany by neo-Nazi youths and the reactions of children of Nazis.
6. In the debate following the screening of Lerner's play, one of Senesh's comrades, Reuven Dafni, sued the Israel Broadcasting Authority for alleging that Senesh did break under pressure. He said: 'I don't understand why we are so anxious to explode myths. Hanna withstood very severe physical torture ... I would not have lasted, she did. My only consolation is that in fifty years, when everyone forgets Motti Lerner, Hanna Senesh will still be remembered' (Melman, 1994: B5).
7. See Ghanem et al., (1998) on the debate over whether Israel can be termed 'democratic'. With particular reference to Smooha, (1998) who argues that Israel is an archetypical 'ethnic democracy', Ghanem et al. argue that Israel breaches several fundamental principles of democracy, chiefly equal and inclusive citizenship, minority rights and consent, and the demarcations of clear boundaries of sovereignty. The authors argue that a state that facilitates an ongoing process of ethnocentric colonisation and domination cannot be considered an 'archetype' of ethnic democracy.
8. Also clad in SS uniform.

9. Just as many Shoah survivors and other immigrants were pressurised to Hebraicise their names, Palestinian place names were erased and given Israeli or Biblical names once their inhabitants were dispossessed and were thus Hebraicised, as argued by Benvenisti (1997). See also Ziv (1998) on Shoah survivors settling on abandoned and demolished Palestinian villages and on the refusal of the central settling authorities to allow them to call their settlements after European communities, destroyed by the Nazis.

CHAPTER 5

ISRAEL'S 'SECOND-GENERATION'

Introduction: beyond 'the survivor syndrome'

Having worked with Shoah survivors, the Norwegian psychiatrist William Niederland described what he called the 'survivor syndrome' (Niederland, 1968). Symptoms included anxiety, depression, inability to experience pleasure, nightmares, psychosomatic disorders, withdrawal, irritability and a profound alteration of personal identity. These symptoms were a consequence both of the traumas experienced during the Shoah and of the defence mechanisms required in order to cope with the trauma and survive. Despite the caveat that these symptoms were neither unique nor exclusive, there is a tendency, when compiling the psychological profile of Shoah survivors, not only to view survivors as a unitary category, but also to psycho-pathologise them. Psychiatrist and son of survivors Aaron Hass argues that the tendency to distort the composite picture of survivors occurred because almost all therapists working with survivors used a psycho-analytic perspective 'notorious for its emphasis on and assumptions of psychopathology' (Hass, 1990: 17).

As it was only survivors who sought psychotherapy who were studied, most of the literature on survivors and their children, in Israel and elsewhere, is derived from psychoanalysis and psychotherapy. It tends to disregard the fact that the majority of survivors have not sought any form of psychotherapy (Hass, 1990: 18), probably because 'their trust in organised society has been shaken to the extent that survivors avoid seeking the support of social institutions' (Dasburg, 1987: 99). There is also a tendency to forget that in continuing to live and in bringing up families, Shoah survivors have 'achieved remarkable success and, perhaps because of their need for continuity and compen-

satory life-affirming attitudes, have inspired their children to be ener-
getic and dedicated' (Bergmann and Jucovy, 1982: 11).

In recent years there has been a proliferation of interest in Israel
and elsewhere in what has come to be called the 'second-generation'.
This chapter reviews briefly the psychological literature about children
of Shoah survivors in Israel and the scant sociological literature on the
topic. I would argue that the tendency to 'medicalise' and 'pathologise'
the survivors is part of the uniformity self-imposed upon Israeli society
that negated the diaspora and stigmatised the survivors and nationalised the Shoah as part of the Zionist discourse. This is part of the
masculinisation of Israeli society, although gender is not always implicated directly but rather intrudes and overlays other meanings.

I examine the construction of a 'second-generation syndrome'
which regards children of survivors as a unitary group, although the
psychological profile of Israeli children of survivors is not radically different from that of their age cohort. Positing gender as an important
variable in studying the Shoah, I explore the gender angle of the existing literature on children of survivors. I seek to situate the psychological literature in the study's overall argument, the stigmatisation and
feminisation of survivors in Israeli society. In their attempt to understand the inconceivable, clinicians who dealt with the small proportion
of survivors (and children of survivors) who presented for therapy did
not contextualise their findings within societal silencing and stigmatisation. By seeking to make this context visible, I argue that by pathologising the survivors, Israeli society sought to de-pathologise itself.[1]

'Normalising' the survivors

Conventional theoretical models of the psychopathological study of
trauma (including psychobiology of post-traumatic stress, psychoanalysis, cognitive psychology of stress and the psychohistorical model
of 'numbing'), which stress individual symptoms, are inappropriate
for the study of Shoah survivors. Dasburg argues that none of these
models takes into account that victims of organised social violence
suffer from social pathology, and that their (new) environment reacts
pathologically with the resulting negative interaction between the victim of violence and the absorbing society. Dasburg suggests that issues
facing children of Shoah survivors should fit into a 'post-organised
violence syndrome' rather than into the more conventional 'post-traumatic stress syndrome' (Dasburg, 1987: 99).

In the Israeli context, identification with the victims and a sense of
collective responsibility should have prepared the Israeli 'bystanders' –
themselves often 'near misses' – to answer the victims' question as to

where they had been when 'we were there'. Instead, the absorbing society reacted to the victims' silence with accusatory questions.

Psychotherapists, influenced by the society in which they live, tended to be conservative and wished to 'normalise' survivor-clients. Several studies (Davidson, 1980; 1981; 1985; Lifton, 1978; Moses, 1977) demonstrate clinicians' awareness of this problem of viewing psychotherapists dealing with victims of organised violence in isolation from society in general. Unfortunately, Israel has had wide experience of mass death: hundreds of thousands of Shoah survivors live in Israel and some twenty thousand Israeli families have suffered losses due to war (Davidson, 1985).

Dasburg's critical starting point is, however, psychotherapeutic. Apart from a few sociological studies (e.g., Boldo, 1983; Yuchtman-Yaar and Menachem, 1989) and a more recent psychiatric study by Levav et al., (cited by Eldar, 1994), there has been little articulate critique of the pathologisation of Shoah survivors and their families in Israeli society. Pathologising the survivors in Israeli society has been part of the construction of a masculine Israeli 'normality', which privileged Israeli-born *sabras* and stigmatised diaspora-born survivors, as I argue in chapter 6. Stigma is one way of social control, and another is medicalisation or pathologisation. Turner argues, after Foucault (1973; 1977), that 'a disease entity is the product of medical discourses which in turn reflect the dominant mode of thinking within a society ... disease is not a pathological entity in nature, but the outcome of socio-historical processes'. Furthermore, 'the clinical gaze (as Foucault called medical power in *The Birth of the Clinic)* enabled medical men to assume considerable social power in defining reality and hence in identifying deviance and social disorder' (Turner, 1987: 11).

Foucault argues that we understand human beings through the effect of knowledge/power relations in which medicine and social science have played an important part as agents of control. Modern disciplines, systems of surveillance and control, and contemporary forms of knowledge about humans are, according to Foucault, focused on the body and its reproduction. Turner argues that distinguishing between illness and health depends on general cultural values: 'the notion of sickness is fundamental to the ways in which we evaluate things (people, experiences, societies or events) as desirable, important or appropriate' (Turner, 1987: 216). The medicalisation of certain sections of society in the interests of a discourse which identifies and controls that which is normal, parallels Goffman's (1968) classification of the 'normal' versus the 'stigmatised'.

Pathologising survivors should be seen in the context of the medical model, which assumes that disease can be 'cured' by intervention. In the case of Shoah survivors, their 'disease' – their difficulties in 'overcoming' their Shoah trauma and adjusting to their new society – could be 'cured' by stigmatisation on the one hand and by therapy on the other. The ultimate aim was assimilation into Israeli society through 'absorbing'[2] the survivors. Dasburg argues that because clinicians are part of a defensive Israeli society, which does not necessarily wish to confront death, survival and fear, they may have become partners to societal denial and were therefore unable to prevent the stigmatisation of the survivors, and may have overlooked the survivors' existential and spiritual strengths (Dasburg, 1987: 102).

The fact that many studies assume that 'the survivor syndrome' refers to the general survivor population derives from the proliferation of clinical studies, but also from the fact that many survivors referred themselves to doctors and psychiatrists in order to gain higher compensations paid to survivors by Germany. This made the problem more transparent but also presented the symptoms as more extreme. However, survivors are not homogeneous, their heterogeneity derives from age differences during the Shoah, from the different experiences after the Shoah, and from personality differences (Lieder, 1985: 4–5).

The 'second-generation syndrome'

The mostly clinical literature on children of Shoah survivors, based on those who sought clinical help, assumes that the parents' Shoah trauma was transmitted to their children and manifested itself in mental-health problems. According to Wardi (1990) the question is whether the specific 'second-generation syndrome' identified by clinicians – and consisting of symptoms such as the guilt of the survivor, dealing with parental over-expectations, compulsive symbolic return to Shoah experiences, difficulties in personal relationships, death identification, victim/aggressor identification, defective sexual identity and low self-esteem – is common to all children of survivors or only to those experiencing psychological difficulties. This question is particularly relevant in the face of the high achievements of Israeli children of survivors in all areas, from politics and business, to literature and the arts. In order to answer this question we have to consider variables such as the parents' age and whereabouts before the Shoah, their experiences during the Shoah (were they, for instance, resistance fighters, 'collaborators' or 'passive' survivors? Were they in camps, ghettos, in hiding?), but, primarily, their lives and their children's lives after the Shoah (Wardi, 1990: 14).

Reports on the treatment of children born to survivor families began appearing in the literature in 1966. Much of the early literature (Rakoff, 1966; Sigal, 1971; 1973; Trossman, 1968; Krystal, 1968; 1978) found disturbances in children of survivors due to the conflict arising out of the need to fulfil the expectations of their over-protective parents (Bergmann and Jucovy, 1982: 19).

Another important factor was the 'pact of silence' in survivor families in order to protect the children from the horrors, as argued in previous chapters. Israeli children of survivors had to confront the silence with which survivors enveloped themselves and which enveloped the survivors in Israeli society. Pines argues that in some survivor families, disavowal of the Shoah experience, in which the trauma is 'known but not known', leads to confusion for the children. This can be repeated in analysis with the second-generation, when what is not known cannot be dealt with until the secret is exposed (Pines, 1993: 211).

A symposium held in 1973 on children of the Shoah raised the methodological question of whether, without statistical analysis, we can conclude that psychic scars carried by people who survived the Nazi ordeals affect the mental health of their children (Aleksandrowicz, 1973: 385–92). Bergmann and Jucovy describe a study Klein conducted in Israel between 1967 and 1969 on 25 survivor families living in kibbutzim (Klein, 1973: 393–409). Significantly, Klein speaks of survivors' fears of being aggressors. They were made uneasy by their role as defenders of the state of Israel because they had been victims rather than victors. Mothers in Klein's study expressed fears of giving birth to monsters, internalising the Nazis' attitudes towards them. Children shared parents' fears and they all had fears about separating from each other. Survivor-parents spent much more time with their children than did other kibbutz families. Klein describes the function of collective mourning in survivors' lives. While Bergmann and Jucovy (1982: 22–4) maintain that 'collective rituals undertaken at various levels can allow families and individuals to work through feelings of shame, anger and fear', my research argues that collective rituals tended to silence, rather than enable, intimate Shoah memories.

The Shoah is fundamental in the context of the return of the Jews to Zion as manifest in modern Zionist ideology and inspired by a number of social myths and images of martyrology, sacrifice and the victory of the few over the many. The 'Shoah trauma' has stamped an indelible mark on the Israeli national psychology (Ayalon, 1981). Witztum and Malkinson (1993: 231–58) describe the place heroism plays in myth-making in Israeli society. They examine the interweaving of personal and national response to losses in wars as reflected in memorisation vis-à-vis personal grief. They also examine stages of personal grief in analogy with trends in the development of a 'national bereavement culture' involving memorisation and commemoration after the Arab-Israeli wars.

The Israeli educational system's emphasis on heroism aimed to overcome the image of Shoah victims as 'going to their death like lambs to the slaughter' vis-à-vis the heroic *sabra*, who sacrifices 'himself' for his homeland. Davidson (1985), theorising the psychological and sociocultural meanings of the Shoah and its survivors for Israeli society, described the *sabras* as 'victims of the Shoah' who paid the price by denying the extermination and avoiding the pain caused by the systematic destruction of a whole nation (Witztum and Malkinson, 1993: 236–7).

'Second-generation' – a contested term

Criticising the global use of the term 'second-generation', Hazan (1987) refutes the very existence of a second generation to the Shoah. Contextualising it in the Biblical metaphor of the exodus from Egypt, Hazan argues that the term is a code, which facilitates a dialogue between survivor parents and their children. While the children's generation continued its journey to the promised land, the parents' generation died in the desert, but because both generations were partners in the exodus, continuity was achieved only through rebellion. In our generation, the children's rebellion would have been to reject the term 'second-generation' and to fight to be a first, free generation. Rebelling against the term will, paradoxically, offer continuity with the parents' generation. If we understand the term as expressing an inter-generational conflict, Hazan argues, we can carefully prophesy that the term would disappear when the Shoah becomes a historical, not a personal event: 'It is possible that the children's promised land is that emotional territory free of any stereotypes and labels ... Ultimately there will be no "second generation to the Shoah", because only one generation was there' (Hazan, 1987: 107).

Ravnitsky (1986) argues that naming children of survivors the 'second-generation' stigmatises them and perpetuates the trauma. Psychologically, the Israeli 'second-generation' is not radically different from its age cohort, though naturally the Shoah plays a central role for those children of survivors who present with psychological difficulties. Israeli society must assist children of survivors to forge an independent identity by encouraging an open discussion of the trauma. The question of identity is central not only to children of survivors but to Israeli society as a whole. Retaining the sense of persecution (such as in the dictum to retell the story of the exodus from Egypt every Passover as if he [*sic*], the narrator, was 'personally' freed from Egyptian bondage), was sharpened by the Shoah, but it prevented an open discussion of Jewish identity in the state of Israel. In its search for identity, Israeli society vacillates between denying and re-living the past. Zionism, rooted in creating a 'new Hebrew man' and negating the diaspora, resulted in a young Israeli generation searching for a contemporary Jewish identity. One way was a nostalgic return to Jewish isolationist roots. Thus in Israeli society the death myth (living the past) is stronger than the life myth (planning the future). The Shoah was the fulfilment of an ancient prophecy about the threat to Jewish existence: that prophecy, part of the Jewish identity, produces anxiety, which the Shoah has augmented. Both denying the Shoah and compulsively holding on to it limit Israel's freedom to choose and be independent (Ravnitsky, 1986: 47–8).

In 1980 Israeli children of survivors who felt the need to meet and share information did, nonetheless, found the organisation *Dor Hahemshech Lemoreshet Hashoah veHagvurah* (The Second Generation to the Transmission of the Shoah and Heroism). Another organisation which works with children of survivors is *Amcha* – the National Israeli Centre for Psychological Support of Survivors of the Holocaust and the Second-generation. Its dominant discourse is therapeutic. *Amcha* employs social workers, psychologists, psychiatrists and psychoanalysts, and its activity includes recording survivor testimonies, home visits to survivors, personal and group counselling for survivors, and courses for medical and psychological professionals aimed at increasing their awareness of the effects of the Shoah. The organisation also offers personal and group counselling to children of survivors in order 'to increase their awareness and ability to cope', holds seminars and workshops, and gives legal and financial advice to survivors and their families.

The premise of both organisations that children of survivors are a pathological population, is rejected by Batia Gur, for whom the term 'syndrome' is so alien that she used the English word for it during our conversation:

> For years I lived with guilt and all the relevant things, without thinking it may be linked to my mother's survivor personality, without understanding that it was part of the syndrome. And, when I heard about the second-generation syndrome for the first time, I became apoplectic [...] It enraged me to such an extent, the use they were making of it, the attempt to build on it and to create some collective identity ...

However, Billie Laniado, the organisation's chairperson, told me in November 1992: 'We are not demanding the same rights as the survivors. On the contrary, hearing and knowing about the Shoah means we have to pass it on'. It is the third generation, she says, who can connect more easily: 'Grandparents find it easier to talk to their grandchildren; children of survivors find it harder to talk to their parents. We were not told much at school either but today there are many courses for teachers about the Shoah'.

'Memorial candles'

Although preceded by several studies by Israeli psychotherapists (e.g., Klein, 1972; 1973; Hazan, 1987; Davidson, 1972; 1980; 1981; Gampel, 1982; Natan, 1982; Lieder, 1985; Dasburg, 1987, among others),[3] *Memorial Candles* (Wardi, 1990) was the first book published in Israel dealing specifically with children of survivors. Wardi's main argument is that in most survivor families one of the children was designated as a 'memorial candle' for family members lost in the Shoah (as discussed in chapter 3). They were expected to take on their parents' emotional world more so than the other children, and to serve as a connecting link between the past and the future in order to fill the vacuum left by the Shoah. These children were supposed to be the connecting link, to repair the loss, and to fulfil the huge expectations of their parents, and perhaps even of the whole Jewish people. This duty was a huge burden but also a spur (Wardi, 1990: 15).

In a sense I too am a 'memorial candle'. My two younger brothers have never shown the same interest in family history as have I. As part of the legacy, 'memorial candles' were given the names of their parents' lost relatives. Like several narrators, who were named after dead family members, I too was given two Jewish-Yiddish middle names, Rivka and Gittel, in stark contrast to the very Hebrew name Ronit, and was greatly relieved, as an Israeli child, that they were never used.

Why do children of survivors agree to take on the 'memorial candle' role? There are covert messages transmitted by survivor-parents to their children regarding lost family members. If victims are perceived as heroic martyrs, survivors must be perceived as morally inferior, as people who, in order to survive, must have acted immorally. This was reflected in the masculinist Israeli attitude to survivors who did not take up arms. Wardi argues that survivor-parents demand that their 'memorial candle' children re-experience the Shoah and 'solve' its dilemmas for them. In some survivor families every family crisis is perceived as a new 'shoah', an expression of the compulsive need of both survivor-parents and 'memorial candle' children to return to the Shoah and survive it again and again. But, says Wardi, it is not enough to compulsively return to the Shoah and exit it in order to untie the knot (Wardi, 1990:47). In the final stage of the therapeutic process, according to Wardi, Israeli children of survivors learn to part with the role of 'memorial candles' and, having unloaded the family's unspoken grief, become a living, not dead, link between the family's past and its future. Nava Semel's narrative demonstrates such a trajectory as does Dvorah, cited by Wardi:

> Yesterday I felt so clearly that I'm fed up being the symbol of Shoah and *gevurah* ... I shall share this burden with my sister and talk to my parents

openly ... I don't want to carry the dead single-handed, I don't want them all on my back ... I won't be simply a hearse any longer ... I have collaborated for forty years, enough ... (Wardi, 1990: 172)

Many Israeli children of survivors research their roots by travelling to their parents' birth-places as I did when I travelled to Bukovina in 1984. The Jewish past, eradicated by the silence imposed on the survivors by themselves and by Israeli society, becomes real again. In institutionalising camp visits by school children, Israeli society engages in a similar collective process of reifying the Jewish past, albeit on Zionist terms.

Gendered 'second-generation' subjectivities

Most studies of children of Shoah survivors are gender-blind, in line with the reluctance to include gender in Shoah scholarship, as argued in chapter 1. I asked Helen Epstein, whose study of children of survivors was the first to be published in the United States (Epstein, 1979), whether she found gender differentiations in the accounts of the sons and daughters of survivors she included in her book. As a daughter of a survivor-mother who became an electrician in the concentration camp and who experienced 'a broadening rather than a diminution of gendered roles', Epstein feels no sense of being limited by gender: 'I always felt I could do anything because my mother could do everything. There are several aspects of being second-generation I could live without but this one has proved invaluable'. (Epstein, letter to Lentin, 19 August 1993)

However, Epstein's observations of men and women children of survivors correspond to the narrators' tendency to homogenise and essentialise women as 'connected' and men as centred on issues of heroics:

> My general feeling about gender differences applies also to men and women and their relation to the Holocaust, here and in Israel – that is, women connect; men don't, unless it's around issues of courage and valour and pride, with which they can identify. My experience of male children of survivors is that they deny, repress, split off and identify only with resistance to Nazism ... At a recent meeting of children of Nazis and concentration camp survivors held in Boston, I noted that eighteen out of twenty participants were women. I think women have less at stake when they allow themselves to connect to pain [their own and other people's]. Most of the people I've encountered working in fields related to Holocaust commemoration seem to be women, although younger [under 40] men are getting more involved. (Epstein, letter to Lentin, 19 August 1993)

According to Hass, communication from survivor-parents affected daughters more adversely than sons. 'Daughters identified with their mothers and the role of victim. Sons were more likely to emulate their father, act "tough" and aggressively' (Hass, 1990: 80–1). Daughters of survivors tend to highlight fear as their predominant problem, while sons stress anger as theirs (Hass, 1990: 92–3).

Wardi quotes Heller (1982) as saying that survivor-parents tend to select daughters more often than sons as 'memorial candles'. As Judaism is carried through the mother, the 'memorial candle' daughter would be able to preserve the family's Judaism; furthermore, in Jewish families it is often daughters who are expected to deal with emotional problems (Wardi, 1990: 36). Even so, in her work with Israeli children of survivors Wardi did not find that the 'memorial candle' role was exclusive to daughters. '"Memorial candles" tend to be people who present for psychotherapy, and since more women than men present for psychotherapy, it seems that there are more female "memorial candles"', she told me. A random sample may find many more men who may function well externally, but who carry a heavy second-generation burden.[4] Wardi views the proliferation of books, articles, films and television programmes on the second generation in the 1990s as part of a maturation process 'from the frightened little boy, to a mature woman', of which the 'peace process' was also part (Wardi, in conversation with Lentin, December 1992).

This is in line with the construction of women as ethnic subjects (Yuval Davis and Anthias, 1989), above all, as mothers and sexual objects. In fact, women (both German and Jewish) were targeted by the Nazis primarily as producers of the next generation (Bock, 1993). Not surprisingly, the few studies of daughters of survivors that do make gendered observations (e.g., Marcus, 1986; Bienstock, 1988), focus on motherhood and on the relationship between survivor-mothers and their children, or on the functioning of daughters of survivors as mothers. Wardi distinguishes between adolescent survivor-mothers whose feminine identity was not yet formed during the Shoah, survivor-mothers who were at the end of their adolescence and whose feminine identity was already formed, and adult survivor-mothers who became mothers prior to the Shoah. The three groups confronted motherhood in different ways. Most of the survivors who gave birth immediately after the Shoah transmitted complex emotions to their unborn babies. This was the background to the birth of the first generation after the Shoah, the so-called 1946 generation (Wardi, 1990: 48–77).

Many survivor-parents, torn by the guilt of the survivor, longed to bring healthy children into a world no longer dominated by death, dehumanisation and terror. However, survivor parents who had lost their first families in the Shoah felt unable to provide a foundation of security for the second set of children. Pines argues that the loss of children in the Shoah may have affected a mother's capacity to empathise and be emotionally available to her child: 'we know from women's dreams that a dead child is always somewhere in the mother's mind'. However, Pines essentialises the mother as the primary carer and her clinical experience shows that 'second-generation children may be less affected if it is the father who sustained the losses rather than the first caretaker, the mother' (Pines, 1993: 209).

Two similar studies of mothering behaviours of daughters of Shoah survivors, one conducted in Israel (Marcus, 1986), and the other in Florida (Bienstock, 1988), produced contradictory findings. Marcus studied 34 mothers who had lost both their survivor-parents and compared it to a control group of 31 mothers both of whose parents immigrated to Israel prior to the Second World War. Her findings confirmed her hypotheses: daughters of Shoah survivors give high value to family values; their own experience of motherhood show evidence of emotional difficulties; they are more anxious, less satisfied, tend to suffer more and are less flexible in responding to their children's needs; the father and mother images tend to be more negative. Bienstock's data, on the other hand, did not support her hypotheses that 'daughters of female Shoah survivors can be expected to be particularly vulnerable to transmission of negative parenting behaviours'. In her study of fifteen daughters and granddaughters of Shoah survivors and an appropriate control group, the similarities between the two groups were greater than the differences.

Strong impetus towards achievement

Israeli scholarship on the 'second-generation' is dominated by clinical discourse. The Israeli sociologist Bella Boldo (1983) cautions against the tendency to generalise from clinical studies on all Shoah survivors. Her study compared 31 Israeli children of survivors, 31 control group members and fifteen children of ex-partisans. Her hypotheses were that the second-generation of Shoah survivors would demonstrate a greater impetus towards achievement and would demonstrate different personality traits (including family relationships, personal image and national and religious identification), to those of the control population. Her study confirmed her first hypothesis as far as sons were concerned: survivors' sons were found to have a higher achievement motivation than those of the male control group and of the ex-partisans' sons. However, comparing the average achievement tendency amongst daughters showed no statistical difference. Boldo's second hypothesis was not confirmed: she found no significant statistical differences regarding personality traits between children of Shoah survivors and children of parents from the same countries of origin who did not experience the Shoah.

Boldo concludes that Shoah survivors reached Israel with a higher moral strength than is generally believed and that the pathology associated with survivors, due to categorising all survivors as unitarily affected by the 'survivor syndrome' is exaggerated. She charts specific gender differences: while survivors' sons were encouraged to identify as 'fighters' and to strive for above-average achievements, daughters were encouraged to conform to accepted ethnic values, and to marry and have children. Boldo explains these differences by the demands made on young Israeli males in the army compared with the non-combative assignments for women in the IDF. Furthermore, since, according to many studies, the socio-sexual image of male survivors was more diminished during the Shoah than that of female survivors, encouraging sons towards high achievement may compensate for the father's humiliation. Jewish sons carry the family name, they say the prayer for the dead on their parents' graves, and their achievements reflect on the whole family. Daughters were required to 'undo' the effects of the Shoah on the one hand, and on the other, to act according to the female stereotypes of dependency and conformity. Daughters were encouraged to actualise the emotional aspects of survivors' identity, which correspond to the stereotype of the 'warm-hearted Jewish mother'. Survivors saw their daughters as their emotional partners and expected them to listen, to be considerate and family-oriented. This ambivalence may explain the lower self-image of daughters of survivors as opposed to sons of survivors (Boldo, 1983: 67–74). Boldo concludes that survivors' Shoah experiences have indeed influenced their Israeli children's lives, but not by bequeathing a pathology (Boldo, 1983: 77).

While ostensibly a sociological study, Boldo uses the psychological term 'achievement motivation' rather than measure children of survivors' actual achievements. Yuchtman-Yaar and Menachem (1989), on the other hand, examine the socio-economic achievements of two generations of Jewish refugees who emigrated from Europe after the War. Contextualising their statistical survey in theories of the adaptive capacity of first and second-generation immigrants, Yuchtman-Yaar and Menachem compared the achievements of these migrants with those of veteran Israelis of the same ethnic origin. Thirty years after arrival, the new immigrants of the older generation (immigrants from Europe between 1948 and 1954, mostly Shoah survivors) did not reach the same levels of success as the veterans. Survivor-immigrants 'lacked the entrepreneurial spirit and drive for success that often explain the economic achievements of migrants, including refugees'. They were unprepared for the difficult conditions of settling in the new country and usually had a 'diffuse positive attitude towards Israel but no strong identification with its aims and values', being 'more concerned with their personal problems' (Talmon-Garber, 1962: 482). In relation to the second-generation, Yuchtman-Yaar and Menachem's confirm Boldo's findings. Children of survivors, characterised as a generation unit 'driven by a syndrome of achievement orientation and economic adaptation' (Yuchtman-Yaar and Menachem, 1989: 1), showed greater individual achievements than children of veterans. This was due to the experiences of the parents prior to immigration and their high, sometimes unrealistic, expectations regarding the economic performance of their children.

Danieli (1980; 1982) documents survivor families' socialisation patterns and the achievement orientation that characterises children of survivors, and argues that the drive for economic and academic success instilled in these children is related to the centrality of the security motif in their parents' lives.

The most comprehensive clinical study to date, by Levav et al., (cited by Eldar, 1994), aims to put paid to the pathological labelling of the survivor generation. Levav et al., studied Israeli survivor families and concluded that survivors were model parents, who mobilised huge strengths in order to protect their children from the horrors they experienced. The study concludes that children of survivors are not different, mental-health wise, from other Israelis. They also found that even in relation to battle shock, there are no differences between the two groups. Eldar cites Levav as saying: 'It is time to put an end to all this. [Israeli] society should release this generation from the burden' (Eldar, 1994: B7).

While these studies put paid to the discursive pathologisation of survivors and their children, none of them used personal narratives. Nor do they foreground survivors' stigmatisation by an Israeli society intent on de-pathologising itself, as do historical studies (e.g., Segev, 1991; Yablonka, 1994; Hacohen, 1994; Zertal, 1996a; Grodzinsky, 1998).

'Staying here'

In the same year as Nava Semel's first collection was published, Israeli daughter of survivors Shoshana Zingal (1985) published a book of interviews with children of survivors. It reflects the complexity of the debate about the meaning of the Shoah: the victims versus heroes dichotomy, the survivors versus the state of Israel, the negation of exile, the alienation which children of survivors felt as a result of the official Israeli commemoration of the Shoah and the centrality of a strong Israel. Some of Zingal's interviewees expressed anger at the appropriation of the Shoah by the state, while reflecting the state's very negation of the diaspora:

One of the things I could not stand was the *Yom HaShoah* ceremonies ...
Me of all people ... They had a diaspora element. The ceremonies repelled
me because I felt they were forced on us ... Once a year they played the
same song, the same recording, the same poem ... And that was that. We
can return to normal and forget about the Shoah until next year ... None
of us is 'just' another child, 'just' another Israeli, 'just' another name. We
carry a heavy burden of death, of our parents' hope for a better future
here, in our country of refuge. (Tal Bashan, in Zingal, 1985: 57–9)

Arieh Barnea, chairman of *Lapid*, in a typically Israeli mixture of
nationalistic and universal meanings, problematises 'heroism' in relation to the Shoah:

People evade the topic of the Shoah because they have a problem identifying with the victims ... The diaspora Jew has a weak, passive, miserable image. But it's an erroneous image. I was taught at school about
the Warsaw Ghetto uprising, but they didn't teach me that in Poland ...
there were 44 Jewish uprisings ... I am proud of the Jewish response
during the Shoah. The majority did not rebel because they were not able
to. Shoah survivors fought in the War of Independence ... What happened to them during those three years? Did their character change? In
1945 they were passive and in 1948 heroic? No. What happened was
that they had an army and a gun ... (Barnea, in Zingal, 1985: 144)

The poet Rivka Miriam sees the Shoah as part of an antisemitic trajectory and argues that Jews have to remember the Shoah in order to
be aware of the persistence of antisemitism today. But ultimately, her
message is Zionist:

If the Jewish nation does not immigrate in its multitudes ... we may disappear. And then someone will say, there was once a state called Israel
... I don't see the Shoah as a deviation from human behaviour ... Jewish
history did not begin in 1939 ... I am not ashamed of my parents' dias-
pora-ness. I too am diaspora-like, but I am also Israeli ... I was influenced by my parents' Shoah traumas, but I was not damaged ... In
certain ways I was strengthened by it ... I love living here and feel I have
to be strong ... [because] such a Shoah can happen again. It's a fear ... I
have no more energy ... for this fear ... for this question mark ... (Miriam,
in Zingal, 1985: 162–5)

In her afterword, Zingal reiterates the universal, but also the national
message of the Shoah. Ultimately, children of survivors, despite their
deep existential anxiety, resist their stigmatisation and claim their place
in Israel, the country of refuge, because 'there is no other place':

Staying here. Planted on this soil. Holding on to the rock with all my
strength with the sun burning my face. This is my inheritance. This is
my testament. This is my duty to my grandmother ... to help form a bet-

ter, more moral, more loving world. This is the bloody, hopeful, lesson.
(Zingal, 1985: 175–6)

Another collection of testimonies of Israeli children of Shoah survivors (Fox, 1999) documents the parents' wartime experience and the
children's Israeli childhood, adolescence and adult life. Fox says she has
learned, through examining what she calls 'second-hand narratives of
children telling their parents' wartime experiences', 'not to try and catalogue, not to try and put to order the chaos', since hers is 'not a social
sciences study, and I do not claim to represent Israeli society'. Fox aims
at no more than charting 'a tiny sample of Israeli society which, perhaps with one or two exceptions, would not otherwise be represented
anywhere' and allow these 'second-hand inherited memories' to write
themselves into present lives and experiences' (Fox, 1999: 9–10).

'So I'm a Shoah child, that's all' – the 'syndrome' revisited

In 1994 ten Israeli children of survivors, including five well-known
writers and artists, participated in a series of workshops moderated by
psychotherapists Dina Wardi, Haim Dasburg and Shalom Littman. The
sessions were filmed and the resulting film *Dor Sheni* (*The Second-generation*) (Gonen, 1994), was broadcast on Israel television on *Yom
HaShoah* 1994.

Publicly 'coming out' about the Shoah, which began with rock
artists Yehuda Poliker and Yaacov Gil'ad in *Because of That War* (Ben
Dor, 1988), is part of the current process of legitimising the Shoah.
If the 'second-generation syndrome' identified by clinical studies was
contested, Gonen's film spells permission to return to the 'syndrome'.
Interestingly, having argued forcibly against the survivor syndrome
and the second-generation syndrome, Batia Gur surpsied me when I
spoke to her in 1993, a year after our first meeting, and she told me
about the new novel she was just completing, *After Birth* (1994). The
novel's Hebrew title, *I Didn't Imagine It Would Be Like This,* is more apt.
It is the story of Yoela, an Israeli woman gynaecologist, who has to
treat a young orthodox woman whose female reproductive organs
are missing. Yoela has to confront not only her own feminine identity, but also her identity as a daughter of a survivor-mother. In a
poignant scene, Gur juxtaposes Yoela's mother, very European, very
diaspora, very foreign, with a *sabra* woman teacher who Yoela has a
crush on. The scene epitomises the survivor-daughter dilemma. 'I
have written the syndrome', Gur told me. Writing for her, as for the
other narrators, was one way of working through her identity as a
daughter of survivors.

After years of silence and of hiding behind their successful public image, participants in Gonen's film admit to the centrality of the Shoah in their lives. The gender gap evident in my interview with the three *Lochamei Hagetaot* members (see chapter 6) is not present here. The men – popular musician Shlomo Artzi, actor and stand-up comedian Shmuel Vilozny, actor and director Yoni Lahav – join the women – theatre director Tsipi Pines, broadcaster and writer Karmit Gai, *Yad Vashem* PRO Billie Laniado – and four less public participants, in baring their souls for the television cameras. Among the things they said are:

> So I'm a Shoah child, that's all. (Artzi)
> Looking at everything I've done, I used the Shoah everywhere it was important for me to fail. (Lahav)
> Define myself? I am a Shoah survivor. All my school-books are full of drawings of German soldiers. (Vilozny)
> I lived with a sister called Shoah – she was much bigger and more important than me. (Mala Meir)
> Shoah and *gevurah* – Mother from Auschwitz and Father a partisan. They never talked about it until the third generation. (Billie Laniado)

The ten speak about the silences, about the anger at their parents' violent rages and the unending, often inexplicable grief, about their parents' violence, about their own inability to ask their parents to tell them about their Shoah experiences, about resenting being named after dead relatives, about their ambivalence regarding being Israeli and at the same time inheriting the Shoah legacy. The film was recorded over three intensive days and at another session, a week later. Towards the end of the first three days, participants attempt to put their second-generationship in perspective. Shlomo Artzi:

> We'll never understand what they experienced. Our parents are the best loved, we had no others. We didn't choose them ... I cannot think of my mother in Auschwitz. And I don't want to go there. There is no reason. I've seen it in pictures. The worst is that we're sitting here for three days and beating them ... as if they hadn't suffered enough. Saying 'so what if we are children of survivors?' was the closing of the circle for me. So what if we are children of survivors? They suffered the most ... My mother alone, alone, alone in Auschwitz ... But in the end we're sitting here, a group of so-called victims ... And they are mothers and fathers and they have feelings ... perhaps a little fucked up.

For Shmuel Vilozny the only way forward is to give up the second-generation label:

> I am sick. We're all sick here. And it's possible to get rid of it. Give up the pose ... For 39 years I woke up disgusted. Disgusted. And I blamed the whole world for my disgust. And my father and my mother ... No, it's my

own disgust ... What can I do, God gave me a father from Poland ... and such a mother. I must understand what it means, what it does to me.

A week later, the participants returned. They had all spoken to their parents in the intervening week. The film allowed them to relive their childhood, in public, but Artzi wonders whether they made real progress:

My feeling was that it was a marathon with children, not with adults. Because the whole time people spoke about their difficulties with their parents and I got the feeling that we were still chronologically little ... We were all stuck at a certain age, married or not, established families, careers, but underneath we are little children, still looking for answers.

Vilozny wonders whether his public soul-searching projects his pain onto others, onto society:

Why am I here? Because I'm stingy ... It would have been very simple to understand I am sick and pay someone ... What do I do instead? Give myself therapy in public. So I can say to the public, it's not I who is sick, it's you ... I'm not prepared to think of myself as crazy ... (Vilozny).

Conclusion: shifting the boundaries of silence and stigma

Ofer Gavish (1998), in the first study on Israeli Shoah popular music, argues that it took popular musicians who are children of survivors a generation until the music 'which *had* to come out' was written. Gavish dates Shoah popular music as beginning from Poliker and Gilead's album 'Ash and Dust' (the topic of Orna Ben Dor's 1988 film *Because of That War)*, and from Shlomo Artzi's work. After the initial burst of Shoah songs such as the famous 'Partisan Song' and other ghetto and illegal immigration songs, translated from Yiddish or Polish, and several Israeli 'Shoah poems' put to music, there was a long silence. He cites Nava Semel, commenting on poets and musicians, including her brother, Shlomo Artzi: 'The *sabra,* the new Israeli, had a problem to admit that you are linked to this problematic past, that you are a child of the lamb to the slaughter' (Gavish, 1998: 202). In fact, the first popular musician to sing about the Shoah was the survivor Hava Alberstein, whose album 'Immigrants' (1986) with the songs 'Like a Wild Flower', 'You'll be Walking in the Field', and 'Every Man has a Name' touched the Shoah and the stigmatisation of the survivors in Israel directly. Shlomo Artzi, despite appearing with Poliker in a *Yom HaShoah* concert in 1988, has only performed two 'Shoah songs', 'In Germany after the War', and 'Romania', although several of his songs allude to it. Gavish's article, written ten years after the ground breaking 'Ash and Dust', which influenced all Israeli musicians who wrote about the Shoah subsequently, lists several younger musicians whose work is inspired by the Shoah. Sharon Moldavi's 'Second-Generation Loser' epitomises the more relaxed, yet harder contemporary approach: 'I'm a second generation survivor / and a second generation loser... and I'll keep changing all the time / but I'll always remain the same child / insane inside' (cited in Gavish, 1998: 210, English in the original). Israeli popular songs have always accompanied, but also shaped events and, Gavish argues, 'Ash and Dust' and its successors helped to shift young people's attitudes towards the Shoah.

If words were unable to cope, visual images were even scarcer in Israeli representations of the Shoah. Haim Maor (1998) documents the gradual shift from total avoidance, through 'kitschy' visual representations, to more recent attempts by Israeli visual artists of the second-generation to 'come out' and attempt to represent the legacy of the Shoah:

> You are some sort of 'second hand instrument' who examines the memories... At least in my case... dealing with these materials – catalogued under questions of my identity as a man, as a Jew, as an Israeli and as an artist – the shadow of the Shoah looms over you and is carried behind you, like a relentless train. (Maor, 1998: 143).

Most of the artists Maor documents describe themselves as 'a different type of *sabra*' who deal with the Shoah obsessively, compulsively. He begins with a reference to Shamir's classic state generation novel *With His Own Hands,* (1951), as did Semel:

> They were not born of the sea, like Elik who came from the sea to the golden sands and fell like a mythological *sabra*. No, they were born from ashes and from dusty memories. They were their parents' mythological phoenix. They did not walk in the fields [a reference to another Shamir work], because their parents protected them with their orphaned nails and prevented them from going out hiking. Their parents came from across the sea, from across day and night, from the inconceivable 'there'. And they, the second-generation, were born with another chamber in their heart – like a black box, a hole – the genetic memory chamber. The chamber was locked for many years, hiding its secrets. With time, it cracked, the demons and fears were released and made room for artistic expression. (Maor, 1998: 144)

Maor, whose work illustrates the cover of this volume, has been working for many years with Susanna, a German woman whose family has a Nazi past. He describes the shift in his own work, from representing the Germans as demons, to being able to see them as human beings, and cites Susanna: 'Your work, like your personality, has developed and become open for possible dialogue. Like me, you recognise the need of the second and third generation for trust. We both understand that perpetuating hatred is a boomerang both for the hater and the hated'. (Maor, 1998: 152)

Ultimately, there is no escape from the silence. Unless Israeli society is prepared to take on the 'known but not known' legacy of the Shoah on a collective, and not just individual level, the only way for Israeli children of survivors to confront their 'private Shoah' is through the lies of the political messages (depending on your political affiliation), by being creative and hiding behind books, songs, films, or stand-up comedy, or, the most difficult and time-consuming way, by providing a forum for their auto/biographical narratives to be told and listened to. Shlomo Artzi ends the film with his back half-turned to the group:

> We had lived in silence all our lives, and for two days we spoke ... We spoke, but in a way we've returned to the silence ... because confronting the silence and the speaking and [Vilozny's] stand-up comedy, it's all a result of that crazy silence. Because what can you give people? You write songs because you cannot talk to people, so you give it to them through the back door. We have resurrected the dead here, haven't we? This is the first time they were moved from under the cement. It's all right, isn't it?

The symbolic commemoration of the Shoah in Israeli society has involved the stigmatisation of the survivors, and, like any symbolic ritual, has increasingly become empty of any real memorial content. In the symbolic structure, this stigmatisation has involved the feminisation of the Shoah and its survivors, as diaspora Jews, in relation to the masculinisation of Israelis. Stigma is not really evidenced in any of the positivistic clinical studies of achievement or of mental illness among survivors' children. Yet this does not detract from my thesis that second-generation cultural workers, as soon as they came of age creatively, began to produce meanings which challenged this symbolic stigmatisation and feminisation. Doing cultural work has been identified by my narrators as a strategy of resistance: writing as 'breaking the conspiracy of silence', or as a wish to influence. They produced these meanings through the dominant 'script' of the family dynamic (i.e. blaming parents for their silence, for their lack of emotion, and for burdening their children with guilt) because this was the only way in which their position could have been recognised and formulated by society. Most cultural workers (including myself) use this script to 'work through' to the position that it is not us, the second-generation, but our parents, who suffered and whom we must forgive, but also to re-capture a rightful place in Israeli society. Once the second-generation has worked this out, it will cease to exist as a psychological phenomenon. Once Israeli society has worked this out, it will invent ways of commemorating that connect more to private memory and pain, thus sharing the burden of the Shoah socially, in a more real (imaginary) way and less ritual (symbolic) way, and so ending the isolation of the second-generation.

The process of constructing counter-narratives to the Zionist narration of nation has already begun as argued in previous chapters and as will be developed further in chapters 6 and 7. Zertal argues (1996a: 28) that it is precisely the Zionist blindness towards the diaspora, which prevents us from doing real mourning work about the destruction of the Jewish diaspora in the Shoah. Telling auto/biographical stories is one way of beginning a process of mourning, not yet fully begun, according to one of Zingal's interviewees:

> Our worst omission as a nation is that we have not yet begun mourning the Shoah. And when you don't mourn something, you are not really aware of it. You continue to live and thus erase the death of the six millions. My family erased it. The state too erased it, replacing it with a symbol. We have *Yad Vashem* and we have to live *here*, because it happened *there* ... We have not felt the hurt ... If [we] say they were 'lambs to the slaughter', [we] did not feel the hurt. (Naomi, in Zingal, 1985: 109)

Notes

1. I am indebted to Robbie McVeigh (1992) for the idea that by pathologising the outgroup, society de-pathologises itself.
2. 'Absorption' is a central Israeli discourse and relates to the absorption of immigrants, regulated by the Jewish Agency and the Ministry of Absorption.
3. There is also a considerable body of work by psychotherapists working outside Israel dealing with the effects of the Shoah on survivors and their children. Some examples are the collection by Bergmann and Jucovy (1982) of psychoanalytic studies of 'the transmittal of trauma incurred during the Holocaust;' Barocas and Barocas, 1979; Danieli, 1980; 1981; Fogelman and Savran, 1979; Rakoff, 1966; Sigal, 1971; Pines, 1993). Most of these share a psychoanalytic perspective. Hass (1990) based his study on personal interviews and questionnaires presented to children of survivors; he used a snowball sample and presented himself as a professor of psychology and child of survivors and asked for their cooperation 'so that both laypeople and mental-health professionals could more fully understand the effects of growing up with such a background' (Hass, 1990: 3). Helen Epstein's *Children of the Holocaust* (1979) combines personal reflections on being a daughter of survivors with a review of the psychological literature and a series of interviews with children of survivors in America and Israel. Anne Karpf's *The War After: Living with the Holocaust* (1996) is a family memoir about her parents' experience as Shoah survivors in Britain and her own as a child of survivors.
4. Wardi told me that *Lochamei Hagetaot* refused to publish her book because it did not highlight the heroic image sufficiently. This also happened to Hilberg.

CHAPTER 6

THE FEMINISATION OF STIGMA IN THE RELATIONSHIP BETWEEN ISRAELIS AND SHOAH SURVIVORS

Introduction: Zionism as a re-imagined masculine community

The narrators told the story of the stigmatisation of their Shoah survivor parents and their own stigmatisation in Israeli society. They did not, however, fully or simplistically endorse my 'theory' of the feminisation of the Shoah by Israeli society. This chapter, therefore, completes the argument by employing another methodology. It draws on Goffman (1968) and Bauman (1991), on a critical feminist re-reading of Zionist and Israeli discourses and on theories linking masculinity and Zionism (Mosse, 1996; Boyarin, 1997a; 1997b; 1997c; Gluzman, 1997; Brod, 1998). This chapter argues that the construction of Israel as masculine in contrast to the despised and negated diaspora, and the stigmatisation and pathologisation of Shoah survivors upon their arrival in Israel, meant the feminisation of the survivors, by positioning them as the stereotypically weak, cowardly, passive antithesis of the allegedly strong, brave, fighting masculine Israel. The argument links with my auto/biographical split subjectivity: this construction influenced my generation's social formation and resonates with my own Israeli trajectory.

In his definition of nations as 'imagined communities' Anderson (1983) posits a shift from religious, dynastic communities, configured in ancient script languages, to modern political communities, brought closer together by print-capitalism and the development of national vernaculars. Zionist nationalism, conceived in Europe at the end of the nineteenth century, was deeply rooted in ancient Judaism, but at the same time sought to re-imagine an ancient religious community as a new political and cultural construct. Anderson and other modernist theorist of nationalism reject primordialism as does Barth (1969) in theorising ethnicity, which is one component in understanding nationalism as argued by Smith (1986). Barth theorises ethnicity in terms of boundary-construction via selected cultural markers of difference. Both Anderson's and Barth's theories are gender-blind: they neither theorise ethnicities or nations as imagined for and by men, nor do they interrogate the targeting of women as ethnic subjects (Yuval-Davis and Anthias, 1989), or the experiences of women in nation-making (Parker et al., 1992).

This chapter calls on post-colonial theory by positing Israeli Jews as the descendants of dispersed, exiled world Jewry, identified as passive, incapable of self-government and weak and therefore seen, as are the 'natives' in a colonised territory, as everything the dominant majority, or the coloniser, is 'not'. All subject people, long after self-determination is achieved, tend to observe rigid gender roles in order to assert the masculinity and right to power of the male (Nandy, 1983). The result, on the one hand, is a hegemonic masculinity, which, like imagined communities, implies a large measure of consent, in that the majority of men benefit from the subordination of women (Connell, 1987: 185), and, on the other, the feminisation of the colonised, the Other, the stranger (Nandy, 1983). Zionism is 'nationalism as narrative', in that it claims a privileged narrative of the nation and thus justifies its own capacity to narrate its story and construct its history in an assertion of legitimacy and precedent for present as well as future (Layoun, 1992). Zionism's military-masculine hegemony, and via its uneasy alliance with orthodox Judaism, guided by an ideology that openly rejects gender equality (Swirski and Safir, 1991), informs the specificity of Israeli masculine 'normality'.

The 'new Hebrew' hegemonic masculinity used nation-imagining discourses to stigmatise and discriminate against Shoah survivors and thus directly or indirectly contribute to its own dominance and to the subordinate position of the survivors. I examine that discursive stigmatisation of Shoah survivors as, arguably, a necessary pre-state and state strategy of defining itself by stigmatising the survivors. I argue that discourses of Zionist nationalism-as-narrative, attributing male characteristics to the re-invented 'new Hebrews', constructed Shoah survivors as less than the hegemonic masculine 'new Hebrew' norm, therefore as 'female'. Boyarin (1997a; 1997b) theorises the diaspora not only as 'female', but as fem(m)inised (with double 'm', to denote the femme in the femme-butch pair), the very opposite of the re-imagined Israeli masculinity. These masculine norms are exemplified by discourses of the political, literary and cultural Zionist élites. Set by the pre-state political élite and perpetuated during the state's history, these discourses played a central role in the construction of the Israeli subjectivity. The contested identities, created by the stigmatisation of Shoah survivors by the Israeli 'normality', form an integral part of my own 'split subjectivity' and that of the narrators, and have led to the construction of counter-narratives as will be argued in chapter 7.

Normalisation and stigma

Pre-state Zionist 'normality' affected the initial encounters between *Yishuv* representatives and survivors in the displaced persons camps prior to the survivors' arrival in Palestine. According to one *Yishuv* representative, Haim Yahil, the representatives' reports reflected their own value system and the Zionist sociopolitcal norms, stigmatising the survivors and defining themselves in turn: 'Our relationship with the survivors ... was ... dictated ... by evaluating their role in our own struggle ... We positioned the Israeli model of existence and the new Israeli man vis-à-vis the diaspora existence and the diaspora man' (Yahil, 1980: 36).

It also affected the encounter between the survivors and members of the Zionist illegal immigration organisation on the beaches of Erez Israel:

> The [illegal] disembarkation ... became a foundational experience for the Israeli-born, a central building block in the collective memory around the establishment of the Jewish state. It contained the main elements of the Erez Israeli discourse towards the Jews brought from the diaspora; a discourse full of pity and a classifying patronising Zionist rhetoric, which was also the other facet of the terror of that familiar stranger, of that near-far diaspora Jew who was arriving in the land. (Zertal, 1996a: 489)

Stigma, referring to any 'disreputable' person, group, activity, occupation or location, originated in ancient Greece to refer to bodily signs designed to expose the immoral status of the signifier – a blemished person, ritually polluted, to be avoided. Earlier Judaic tradition has Qayin (Cain), the murderous son of Adam and the woman Havva (Eve), 'the mother of all that is alive', marked, or 'stigmatised', by God, so that his killing of his brother Hevel (Abel) would not result in revenge (Genesis, C, 16). Today, the term, referring more to the disgrace itself than to the bodily evidence of it, is closer to the earlier, Biblical meaning.

Goffman's starting point in theorising stigma is the sociological version of the structure of the self. Normalisation as a form of power is central to his argument and stigma is seen as a way of categorising and socially grading individuals and groups. Grading someone is positioning her on a scale, defining her life chances. Society establishes the means of categorising, and grading is measured by ideal standards, completely beyond attainment for almost every member of society (Goffman, 1968: 2).

While the stigmatised is the archetypal 'marginal man' (Park, 1928), Goffman argues that all members of society are players in the stigma game. Stigmatics learn the standpoint of the normal, they are socialised into their disadvantage, or positioned in a protective capsule. They must learn a new way of being that is felt by those surrounding them to be real and valid by, for instance, changing their name, their accent, or taking on a new identity. Often and over various periods in the stigmatic's life, various 'affiliation cycles' are formed and often 'a life event can ... have a double bearing on moral career, first as immediate objective grounds for an actual turning point, and later ... as a means of accounting for a position currently taken' (Goffman, 1968: 52–3). The Shoah was such a turning point.

In some cases, stigmatics are ambivalent about accepting others with the same stigmas as their own. This ambivalence stems from an awareness of one's stigma with its perpetual threat of non-acceptance by normal people. This, Goffman argues, is to be expected, since what individuals or groups are, or could be, derives from their place in the social structure. The information about the stigmatised is reflexive and embodied – it is conveyed, among other things, by what Goffman calls 'stigma symbols' such as physical appearance, names, accents, all of which distinguished Shoah survivors from Israelis. The Israeli writer Yehudit Handel described this distinction poignantly, using binary racial terminology (godlike versus inferior, honour versus defective, privilege versus hunchback), in Orna Ben Dor's film, *Cloud Burst*:

> To say it quite bluntly – there were almost two races in Israel. There was one so-called godlike race, those who had the honour and privilege to be born in Degania or Schunat Borochov in Giv'ataim[1] ... And there was, how can I say it, an inferior race, people whom we regarded as inferior, defective, hunchbacks, and these were the people who came after the War. (Ben Dor and Kaplanski, 1988)

Managing stigma calls for special coping strategies, which, depending on the visibility or the known-aboutness of the stigma, include 'passing'. Goffman sees passing as the third stage in a process which begins with learning the normals' point of view and continues with realising one is disqualified according to this point of view. Other stigma management techniques include concealing or obliterating stigma symbols (e.g., name changing, a strategy which was imposed upon and sometimes selected by Shoah survivors, as in Nava Semel's narrative in chapter 2) and disclosing the stigma and thus transforming the situation, a strategy employed increasingly by Israeli children of survivors 'coming out' (see chapter 5). Passing has its dangers of being discovered by others, who include in their own biographies a knowledge of the stigmatic's undisclosed biography. Stigmatics can assimilate and thus purge their differentness or be militantly identified with the stigma, making it harder to assimilate. In stressing their distance from what society assumes as normal, they have to insist on their cultural affinity with their stigma. This strategy is employed by several of the narrators, who derive part of their cultural identity from being daughters of Shoah survivors. Goffman speaks of the 'stigma trap' into which militant stigmatics can fall unless there is a cultural alternative to the unified norms. One alternative is for 'well-known' members of a stigmatised group (such as several of the narrators), to 'come out' and therefore broaden the stigma boundaries.

Depending on how threatening a stigma is to its own 'normality', society finds it hard to cope with stigmas, which tell normals not only about their normality, but also about their own weaknesses. Information about marginal members of society gives us insight not only about them, but also about society as a whole. Stigma management is a feature of society, occurring wherever there are identity norms. The role of the normal and the role of the stigmatised, Goffman insists, are part of the same complex; they are not only complementary, but also parallel and similar.

Concentrating on face-to-face interaction, Goffman tends to view social structures and cultural systems as givens. Giddens' structuration theory (1984) is one sustained attempt to construct a theory using Goffman's work. Giddens argues that sociology must link face-to-face interaction and the organised pattern of role relationships that constitute a social system, because both face-to-face relationships and the relationships between different parts of social systems are produced and reproduced as individuals are constantly 'reflexively monitoring' social action. This 'double hermeneutics', or 'double consciousness', as members of a social system and as members of a stigmatised group in this instance, assists individuals in being constantly aware of 'normal' societal demands and at the same time managing their particular stigma. My own 'split subjectivity' and my *sabra* reluctance to associate with diaspora Jews or Shoah survivors is an example of such 'double consciousness'. Prejudice and discrimination are related to social and cultural norms. Without recourse to a contextualised, 'structurated' analysis of the individual in-herself and of the individual in-society, it would be difficult to analyse the co-temporal presence of both 'normalisation' and 'stigmatisation' in the position of Shoah survivors in Israeli society. The reproduction of anti-diaspora and anti-survivor prejudice, must be contextualised within the construction of new Hebrew norms, values, attitudes and ideologies (see van Dijk, 1993: 20).

Friends – enemies – strangers

Bauman's (1991) analysis of ambivalence as an inevitable existential condition of modernity offers another dimension to the study of stigma regarding the relationship between Israelis and Shoah survivors. Bauman posits 'friends' and 'enemies' as standing in opposition to one another, but they are not of equal status. It is the friends who define the enemies and the friends who control the classification and the assignment. But if the rift between friends and enemies guarantees their co-ordination, their cosy antagonism is disrupted by the *strangers,* who, unlike enemies, are a synthesis of wandering detachment and attachment and a union of closeness and remoteness (Simmel, 1971: 143–7), and who threaten sociation itself by their very existence. The strangers refuse to remain confined to the 'far away' or go away from our own land. They come into the life world and settle here, but, unlike straightforward enemies, they cannot be kept at a secure distance and thereby become a constant threat to the world's order. This union of closeness and remoteness – the stranger-survivor was close to the Israeli 'us' and at the same time remote from that 'us' – created an alienation whereby the survivors were objectified, as demonstrated later. Not belonging to the life world 'from the start', the strangers bring into relief the 'mere historicality' of existence; the memory of the event of their coming makes of their very presence an event in history, rather than a fact of nature. Thus the presence of survivors kept reminding Israelis of the implications of the Shoah: exile, Jewish suffering and supposed passivity in the face of adversity. Moreover, being theoretically free to go, strangers are physically close but spiritually remote. 'There is hardly an anomaly more anomalous than the stranger. He stands between friend and enemy, order and chaos, the inside and the outside' (Bauman, 1991: 61).

The modern nation-state collectivises friends and enemies, but, Bauman argues, it has been designed, above all, to deal with the problems of strangers, not enemies. Unlike a tribe, the modern nation-state extends its rule over a territory before it claims the obedience of a people. The next stage is promoting 'nativism' and construing subjects as 'natives'. Imagining themselves as communities, nation-states laud and enforce ethnic, religious, linguistic, and cultural homogeneity. They are engaged in incessant propaganda of shared attitudes and construct joint historical memories and do their best to suppress memories that cannot be squeezed into the shared tradition, now re-defined as 'our common heritage'. Thus Israel suppressed memories of supposed Jewish passivity, 'going like lambs to the slaughter', which did not fit its imagining itself as a nation battling for its territory and its future, privileging *gevurah* over Shoah (as argued in chapter 4).

The process of keeping strangers at a mental distance through locking them up in a shell of exoticism does not suffice to neutralise their dangerous incongruity. Goffman identified this process as stigma, which is not the way society deals with its enemies, but the way it conceptualises and deals with its 'own', its strangers (Bauman, 1991: 68). Stigmatics are those 'ambivalent third' strangers, anathema to the 'friends' versus 'enemies' binary order. Stigma, therefore, is at the heart of modernity. It is practically indispensable as a means of restoring some semblance of order into the disorder wrought on a neatly divided society. There is, therefore, a paradoxical parallel between stigma and the stigmatised.

By making the offer to assimilate, society reaffirms its superiority, therefore stigmatics-strangers have little chance of real assimilation. Often, the harder they try, the faster the finishing line seems to recede. The very efforts of the strangers to assimilate reaffirms the inferiority, undesirability and out-of-placeness of their form of life. The strangers cannot cease to be strangers – their strangeness is often defined for them by others, even when they themselves feel they have 'arrived'. And in some important ways, attaining an assimilated position within the native society means an ultimate elimination of the strangers' origin (or the origin of their ancestors). But, Bauman argues, the notorious restlessness of the strangers cast in the position of ambivalence, which they have not chosen and over which they have no control (a restlessness often cast by the natives and ascribed to the strangers' origin), is socially produced.

Despite appearances to the contrary, it is not the failure to acquire native knowledge which constitutes outsiders as strangers, but the existential constitution of the strangers, as being neither 'inside' nor 'outside', neither 'friend' nor 'enemy', neither included nor excluded, which makes the native knowledge unassimilable. Yet being outside positions the strangers in a vantage point from which the insiders may be looked upon and censored. The very awareness of such an outside point of view makes the natives feel uncomfortable (Bauman, 1991: 77–8). In other words, if the 'normals' exclude the stigmatics-strangers mostly in order to define themselves, the strangers, first by being positioned in the outsider vantage point, and then by attempting to assimilate the native position, assist the natives in defining themselves as 'normal'.

The feminisation of stigma

Goffman and Bauman's analyses of stigma and strangerhood are gender-blind.[2] There are several ways of incorporating gender into the stigma equation. One is by using the structuralist 'othering' of women, which theorises woman as Other and man as Self (de Beauvoir, 1949; 1993). According to this analysis, in the Jewish tradition woman has been stigmatised ever since the gendered story of Edenic post-knowledge. Having eaten from the 'tree of knowledge good and evil', Adam and Havva are assigned their respective roles by God. The ground is cursed for Adam, but 'the woman' is assigned a subordinate position (Genesis, B, 16–19). According to Adler (1991), Jewish tradition positions woman as Other through the very story of her creation. The account of the creation of humans in Genesis A: 'God created the human in His image, in the image of God, He created it, male and female He created them', can be taken to be a description of the creation of humanity. In Genesis B: 'The Lord God built the rib into a woman and brought her to the man', the account is re-written as the description of the creation of patriarchy. The Jewish male names himself *zakhar*, from the root z-kh-r – to remember. ('Female' in Hebrew, on the other hand, is *nekeva*, from the root n-k-v – 'hole'). In a patriarchy, the only memory is male memory because 'the only members are male members. They are the rememberers and the remembered, the recipients and the transmitters of tradition, law, ritual, story and experience'. Judaism, Adler argues, deconstructs 'dualistic, other-rejecting, patriarchal thought-structures' (though I would say that this is arguable in view of orthodox Judaism's argumentations regarding the Palestinians' right to 'the land'), but it 'stops short and leaves in place the foundational construction – the otherness of women, Judaism's most intimate others' (Adler, 1991: 45).

Hebrew, renewed and 'reimagined' after centuries of being relegated (in masculine grammatical renditions of God, 'the king of kings', 'the lord of hosts') to the prayer book, gives expression to the national symbolism of gender divisions. Meanwhile, the Jewish Eastern European street and home language was Yiddish, fondly called *Mame loshn* – mother tongue (see Lentin, 1996a). Several Hebrew roots link maleness with qualities valued particularly in the Israeli context. I have already mentioned the word for man, *gever*, also meaning rooster and deriving from the same root (g-v-r) as the word *gibor* – hero, and *gevurah* – heroism: hence the gendered connotations of Shoah versus *gevurah*. If heroism is purely masculine in Hebrew, weapons and fighting are more so. The sexual connotations of weaponry derive from the penis: the Hebrew word for penis is *zayin*, which also means weapon. Accordingly, the Hebrew word for 'takeing up arms' (*hizdayen*), also means 'having intercourse' (Cohn, 1987; Sharoni, 1992).

If we follow the man-as-self, woman-as-other analysis, we could argue, after Goffman, that women are always stigmatised in patri-archal society, or, after Bauman, that women are always the 'strangers' in any given binary opposition of (male) 'friend' versus (male) 'enemy'. Critiques of cross-cultural assumptions (Elshtain, 1981)[3] and biological essentialism (Tong, 1993: 215) notwith-standing, and despite the alluring comparisons which can be drawn between the 'othering' of women and the strangerhood of Jews in Gentile society (Rich, 1986: 202–3; de Beauvoir, 1993: xxxvii), the structuralist 'otherness' of women is less than theoretically satis-factory. Feminist theorists who emphasise difference, problematise different kinds of difference by arguing for a 'decentering' which abolishes the implicit norm which makes 'others' different. The notion of woman as 'different' risks presupposing an idea of man as the norm. Fox-Genovese (1994) cites Minow (1990) as convincingly arguing that recognising difference effectively stigmatises those who are labelled as different. 'To emphasise the difference between women and men is implicitly to accept men as the norm and to accept the male view of women as differing from that norm ... We cannot escape the dilemma unless we recognise difference as a rela-tionship which implicates both parties' (Fox-Genovese, 1994: 233). This supports Goffman's argument that stigma must be viewed as affecting both normal and stigmatised.

A more satisfactory way of incorporating gender into the stigma equation is the 'structurated' view of gender as a social structure that has its origin in the development of human culture, not in biology (Connell, 1987; 1994; Lorber, 1994). 'Social reproduction of gender in individuals reproduces the gendered societal structure; as individu-als act out gender norms and expectations in face-to-face interaction, they are constructing gendered systems of dominance and power' (Lorber, 1992: 6). Connell has developed the notion of hegemonic masculinity, 'a social ascendancy achieved in a play of social forces that extends beyond contents of brute power into the organisation of private life and cultural processes' (Connell, 1987: 184). Such hege-monic masculinity, embedded in religions, mass media, wage struc-ture, housing design, state power, welfare-taxation policies and a dominance-oriented military apparatus, does not assume the univer-sal 'othering' of women or their elimination, but it does assume their subordination within a social hierarchy.

The structural gendering of Zionism and Israeli society must be viewed in the context of the relationship between orthodox Judaism and Zionist ideology and of Israel as a militarist, settler-colonial society. This gendering has been produced and in turn reproduced the uneasy relations between Israel, its Palestinian citizens and the Palestinians in the occuppied territories, and between Israel and the diaspora, as well as a contradictory series of compromises between the Israeli state and its women citizens. Several analyses (e.g., Aloni, 1976; Hazelton, 1978; Izraeli et al., 1982; Swirski and Safir, 1991) illuminate the status of women in Israel, which is beyond the scope of this book. Yuval-Davis (1982), Shohat (1991), Sharoni (1992), and Shadmi (1992) analyse Israel as a masculine-military society. I do not argue that Israeli women are merely oppressed or totally powerless. I do argue, however, that conceptually, Israel is a paradoxical conflation of orthodox Judaism intent on denying gender equality, and masculine-militarist Zionism, which presupposes the state not only as a regulatory agency and a force in the dynamic of gender, but also as a fighting force.

The stigmatisation of Shoah survivors must be understood not merely in terms of the material discrimination against them (Segev, 1991; Yablonka, 1994; Hacohen, 1994; Grodzinsky, 1998), but also in terms of discourses which constructed the Israeli 'normals' vis-à-vis the less-than-normal Shoah survivors, and which objectified the survivors during the Zionist pre-state struggle (Zertal, 1996a). Like discourses of racism, perpetuated by 'symbolic élites' (van Dijk, 1993: 46), so discourses of the superiority of 'Israelis' and the discursive stigmatisation of Shoah survivors have been perpetuated by Zionism's symbolic élites, who both made and wrote history (Zertal, 1996a: 15), which has been incorporated into popular discourse.

The 'feminisation' (or fem[m]inisation) of this stigma derives from the internalisation of the masculine construction of the 'new Hebrew'. This feminisation must be understood in terms of discourses, just as gender, beginning from the site of actual individuals, must be understood as an effect of a complex of social relations defining femininity and masculinity and organising, across local sites of people's lives, a homogeneity of structured gender differences. A major part of the organisation of action in time is mediated by texts; discourses and ideology can be investigated as actual social relations ongoingly organised in and by the activities of actual people (Smith, 1990:160). 'Feminisation' may stem from the very notion of femininity, the actual social relations of a discourse mediated by texts, in which women are active as subjects and agents. In preserving the active presence of subjects, Smith displaces the central place given by Foucault to the textual, bringing into view the social relations in which texts are embedded, addressing femininity as a complex of actual relations vested in texts (Smith, 1990: 162–3).

Gendered post-colonial discourses

Memmi (1967 [1990]), who describes the image of the colonised as everything the coloniser is *not*, positions himself within the colonised-coloniser equation as a Jewish 'ambivalent third', reminiscent of Bauman's portrayal of Jews as 'the prototypical strangers in Europe ... "strangerhood incarnated" ... the epitome of non-territoriality ... a nomadic past in the era of settlement' (Bauman, 1991: 85).[4] Memmi's portrayal of the emulation of the coloniser's values by the colonised illustrates Goffman's claim that stigmatised and 'normals' are constantly negotiable perspectives of social interactions. It also illustrates Bauman's insistence on ambivalence as the only possible option for modernity. Not surprisingly, Shoah survivors, the strangers in the Israeli 'friends' versus Arab 'enemies' equation, were also described as everything the Israelis were *not*, as I demonstrate below.

Hartsock posits a way of looking at the world characteristic of dominant white, male, Eurocentric ruling class, a 'way of dividing up the world that puts an omnipotent subject at the centre and constructs marginal Others as sets of negative qualities' (Hartsock, 1990:161). The colonised cease to be subjects of history and become objects. According to Mohanty (1991: 81), out of the creation of the colonised, the Orient, the woman, there is a creation of a being who sees 'himself' as located at the centre and having all the qualities valued in his society. The result, as in Said's *Orientalism* (1978), is a *feminisation* of the colonised, the Orient, the Other, though Said himself seems unaware of the gender implications of his analysis.

The Indian political analyst Ashis Nandy describes the extent to which the culture of colonialism was based on patriarchy (Nandy, 1983: 4). To beat the colonisers at their own game and to retain self-esteem as Indians and as Hindus, many Indians sought a hyper-masculinity that would make sense to their fellow countrymen and to the colonisers. 'Anxiety about one's fitness for the (masculine) role of authority, deriving from a history of defeat or helplessness, is assuaged by the assumption of sexual dominance' (Meaney, 1991: 233). Similarly, a history of Jewish subordination in exile propelled the new Israeli state to reproduce the right to power of the male through privileging the military and through 'national security' discourses.

Although a settler-colonial theoretical approach to analysing Zionism in relation to the Palestinians (e.g., Ram, 1993; Abdo and Yuval-Davis, 1995) has become acceptable in Israeli critical sociology, postcolonial theories have hitherto rarely been employed to theorise the position of Jews rather than Palestinians in settler-colonial analyses of Zionism. I would argue, however, that we should be well able to analyse Israelis using a post-colonial paradigm, as the descendants of

Jews, who, in certain ways, usually not territorial, were 'colonised' in their diaspora countries of origin. Although the economic exploitation of colonised territories and peoples does not characterise the position of Jews in the diaspora, their discursive colonisation and their exploitation in terms of restrictive laws and levies should be analysed using similar theoretical tools to those used to analyse colonialism. After all, the memory, negotiated through discourses of what Bauman (1991) calls 'nation building', of having existed as a subordinate group was, and is, all too vivid. In constructing what it means to be 'Israeli', Israeli society, anxious about its own fitness for a role of authority, has negotiated assumed hegemonic masculine norms and adopted a complex process of classifying systems of domination and subordination. These systems discursively divided the male 'normals', Israeli- born or those who could 'pass' for Israeli-born, from the female stigmatised, newly arrived survivors (and, later, immigrants from Arab and North African countries) as will be examined later.

Daniel Boyarin (1997a; 1997b) seems the only scholar to employ a post-colonial theoretical framework to make sense and engender both European Jewish life and Herzlian Zionism, which he theorises as a colonisatory discourse in its intention to export 'white' European Jewish manhood to the Jews of the Orient and to 'Black' Palestine. Herzlian Zionism, according to Boyarin, was conceived as both nativist and colonialist in the sense of colonial mimicry (Bhabha, 1984): in the process of establishing the Jewish state and turning the Jews into colonialists, they would become white men, as I will elaborate later.

The 'new Hebrew man': the construction of 'normal' Israeli subjectivity

To understand the stigmatisation of Shoah survivors in Israel, a disturbing phenomenon, as Zionism aims to provide a refuge for all Jews (and has constructed Israel not as the state of its inhabitants or even its citizens, but as a *Jewish* state), one has to understand the masculine construction, both linguistic and conceptual, of Zionist-Israeli 'normality'. Conceptually, Zionist ideology resulted from Jews internalising the stigmatised position of the Jew in European society as a nomadic, homeless, weak stranger and consequently re-imagining a 'new Jew'. This and the ongoing 'no-choice' military conflict with the Arab states and the Palestinians, privileging the superiority of a 'national security' discourse, constructed a military-masculine hegemony.

Although it is impossible to discuss sociological aspects of Israeli society without taking into account the Palestinian-Israeli conflict as a social process which has had a great formative effect on the Israeli social formation, Israeli social formations and discourses have been informed by processes which started long before the establishment of the state. These processes originated in early Zionist ideologies and were concerned with the re-invention of Europe's Jews, in preparation for statehood. Long before the establishment of the state of Israel on 15 May, 1948, Zionist ideologues had posited and debated the need for the construction of a 'new Jewish person who will resemble, physically and psychically, his tall and strong (European) neighbours' (Shapira, 1992: 33). Shapira argues that European Zionism was born out of disappointment with the nineteenth century dream of progress and of Jewish assimilation into European societies. The deep insult at having been rejected, the anger and the resultant shame, were the building blocks of early Zionism (Shapira, 1992: 21). Having accepted, by necessity, their stigmatised position, Jews internalised antisemitic stereotyping. The way gentiles saw them played a large part in constructing the ideology of secular Zionists, who adopted stereotypical antisemitic images such as homelessness, weakness and cowardice in discourses about European Jewry. Late nineteenth century European Zionist ideologues attempted therefore to construct a new Jewish identity, which, in turn, though unforeseen by these ideologues, would stigmatise those who could not, or would not, adhere to its norms.

Early Zionist ideologues, such as Theodor Herzl (1896), Yehuda Leib Pinsker (1882), Max Nordau (1900 [1955]), saw the future Jewish State as breeding a new Jewish type, free of the complexes originating from living as a despised minority. Concluding *Auto-Emancipation*, Pinsker describes the Jews as 'everywhere aliens', who lack 'national self-respect and self-confidence' and who must find national regeneration to 'assure our people's future, everywhere endangered' (Pinsker, 1882 [1935]).

In *The Jewish State* (1896), Herzl envisioned a new and different Jewish youth, complete with national symbols such as army, uniforms and ceremonies. He borrowed the means with which he hoped to achieve this from the German national movement: patriotic songs stressing the bravery of past heroes, national 'honour' and military education. Images of Biblical heroes were invoked to construct this 'new Jew', a grammatically-masculine Zionist discourse. Herzl concluded his 1896 tract by evoking past heroes with confidence in a glorious future: 'Therefore I believe that a wondrous generation of Jews will spring into existence. The Maccabeans will rise again' (Herzl, 1936: 79). Jewish history was revised to alter the traditional conception of the Jewish nation as a lamb among the nations after generations of persecution and weakness (Shapira, 1992: 49). Hailing the trajectory from 'diaspora Jew' to 'new Jew' as a revolution in the Jewish image, to be brought about by Jews leading a free Jewish life on 'the land', Herzl used cowboy images to describe a Jewish horse-riding display in Rehovot in a diary entry in October, 1898:

> [our] eyes filled with tears as we saw these agile and brave riders, who could have been metamorphosed from the [diaspora] trouser sellers. Hurray! they cried and galloped on their Arab horses along the fields. I was reminded of the *far-west* riders from the American steppes whom I once saw in Paris. (Herzl, 1934: 176)

According to Boyarin's analysis (1997b: 136–40), the logic of Herzlian Zionism was that by becoming colonialists, the Jews aimed to prove they were as *virile* as the Germans. Zionism, then, is a parodic imitation of colonialism: 'feminine' Jews dressed up as 'men'. The ideal Jewish male as countertype to 'manliness', Boyarin argues, was not only imposed on the Jews by the gentiles, but was rather an assertive historical product of Jewish culture, which needed an image against which to define itself and produce a 'goy', a hypermale. Ultimately, Boyarin sees Zionism as anti-Jewish, if not antisemitic, but also as a cure for Jewish gendering: 'Freud ... had internalised the negative and pathologising interpretation of Jewish manhood and thus saw Zionism as the solution' (Boyarin, 1997a: 277). Boyarin analyses both Herzl and Freud, who saw Zionism as essentially masculine, anxious to re-make the 'new Jewish man' in the image of Anglo-Saxon white masculinity, an antithesis to the diaspora tendency towards passivity. Indeed, Freud, like Herzl, saw passivity as a sign of stagnation and humiliation (Boyarin, 1997b: 130) and saw Zionism as a mode of repressing and overcoming his own (homosexual) effeminacy. Seen in this light, Zionism 'is the most profound sort of assimilationism, one in which Jews become like all nations, that is like Aryans, but remain Jews in name' (Boyarin, 1997a: 276).

Theorising the diaspora people 'as a woman', Boyarin posits the fem(m)inisation of Jewish men, but not 'as women', rather as a cultural construction of the female as *femme* (not butch) (Boyarin, 1997c: 307). Boyarin finds both Freud's and Herzl's solutions flawed, in their political effects – on women, gay men, Jews and Palestinians. However, although his own solution to the 'Jewish problem' excludes a repudiation of Jewish male 'femininity', he ultimately fails to link the fem(m)inisation of the diaspora with the stigmatisation of the survivors, which, I would argue, implies their fem(m)inisation, not 'as women' but as the stereotypical *femme*-stranger-third in the Zionist binary (male) friend versus (male) enemy.

According to Max Nordau's 'Muscle Jewry' (first published in 1900), the antisemites stigmatised the Jews for their 'Jewish attributes': sharp intelligence, intellectual flexibility and quickness of thought. At the same time they mocked the Jews for their physical weakness, which resulted from their living conditions. The future would see a new, masculine, physically trained Jew: 'Let us renew the link to our ancient tradition: let us be again deep-chested, hard-limbed, straight-gazing men' (Nordau, 1955: 187). Nordau expresses the wish for a physical rehabilitation of the Jewish body in terms of nationalism worded as manhood. Gluzman (1997: 148), who bemoans the dearth of a gendered discussion of Zionist discourses, cites Mosse's (1985: 17) 'manly idealisation as a basis of nation and society', and argues that Nordau's call to toughen European Jews is an example of the moment when the masculine body becomes the symbol of a new society and a nation-building discourse.

Meira Weiss (forthcoming) embodies the argument further by positing Zionism as the eroticisation of the Jews. According to Weiss, Israel has been regulating bodies for the purpose of its ongoing armed struggle, which resulted in a society deeply concerned with territorial borders and body boundaries. Weiss discusses the pioneer and his symbolic heir – the *sabra* soldier, soldiers' screening, child-care, body impairment, war poetry and media coverage of 'terrorist' attacks to posit an emblematic Israeli (masculine) 'chosen body' for the 'chosen people'. Ultimately, she argues, Israeli and Jewish identities, although sometimes discursively (and politically) separated, are closely tied in non-verbal practices in relation to the body.

Images of the new generation of Jews who would grow up in the land of Israel feature prominently in Hebrew poetry at the turn of the century, dominated by Shaul Tchernichovsky and Haim Nachman Bialik. In 'Facing Apollo's Statue' (1899), Tchernichovsky rejects Judaism: the rebellion against the light, the stagnation, the old age, the lack of vitality, in favour of Greek Paganism: life, youth and beauty, which were to be the symbols of the new Hebrew generation. The masculine qualities of physical force and heroism are manifested in the conquest of 'the land' for the nation of Israel. In Bialik's 'The Dead of the Desert' (1902 [1960]), the desert generation, forced to end its life on the way to the promised land without reaching it, wakes from death and shouts: 'We are heroes! the last generation for bondage and the first for redemption are we'. God may have bid them stay in the desert, but they rebel and climb in the conquest of the mountain. These were the new Jews, rebelling against the Jewish fate and taking their lives in their own hands. In 'The City of Slaughter' (Bialik, 1904, 1960), an epic poem about the Kishinev Pogrom, Bialik rejects not only the perpetrators, but also the Jewish victims, exposed in their weakness. 'The trauma following the Jews' inability to defend themselves ... is linked to the ... process of the "negation of Exile" ... and the rebellion against the diaspora national entity' (Schweid, 1983: 172).

'Conquering the mountain' became a prevalent Zionist discourse. The poet Yaacov Cohen made extensive use of mountain-climbing metaphors. He acquired a pride of place in the national ethos with his poem '*Birionim*' (Hebrew for hooligans), in which he glorifies not victory but the struggle itself. Stressing motifs of 'blood' and 'fire', the poem centres on the new 'proud and powerful ... master generation' of *birionim*:

> We have returned, we, the *birionim*!
> We have come to redeem our stolen land -
> We demand our right with a mighty hand!
> Yehuda [Judea] fell in blood and fire
> In blood and fire Yehuda shall rise again. (Cohen, 1903)

I was one of this 'first generation': we, the first generation to be born close to or around the establishment of the State, were told by our parents and teachers, borrowing Bialik's phrase, that we were 'the first generation for redemption', one of the discourses around which our Israeli subjectivity was constructed. These discourses expressed the growing belief that only a military victory over the resident Palestinian population would bring about a Jewish state in Erez Israel/Palestine. Thus, military might and the 'masculine' qualities of soldiering plus an implied ideological devotion to the values and ideals of Zionism were the discourses which shaped the generation of our parents, most of whom were relatively new arrivals from Europe, who in turn shaped us, the 'first generation'.

What about Zionism's female counterparts? The seeds of hegemonic masculinity were sown regardless of the attempts by Zionist women to forge a space in the emerging 'new Hebrew' subjectivity. The self-defence organisation, *Hashomer* (the Watchman), founded in 1909, adopted a coarseness of demeanour, copied, together with power symbols such as horse riding, firearms and the *keffieh* head-dress, from the Bedouins, and followed the behaviour patterns of the Cossacks – another role model. This resulted in a patronising attitude towards women, although two of its founders were women, and despite heated debates on the role of women within the organisation. Although women members wished to take equal part and although they infused the concept of role equality into the national psyche, they made it clear to the men that they would settle for less than what they had asked for (Bloom, 1991: 129).

While Zionism centres on the discursive construction of a 'new Hebrew man', the definition of Judaism is matrilineal. We were brought up with myths of gender equality, which originated in pre-state images of women pioneers working alongside their men 'paving the roads and draining the marshes'. The reality, as studies by Hazelton (1978), Bernstein (1992, 1993), Izraeli (1981) and Bijaoui-Fogiel (1992) have argued, was more sobering.

Bernstein (1993) argues that in *Yishuv* society public issues such as Jewish immigration, land purchases settlement, and the conquest of labour from the local Palestinians, played a central role and brought about a denial of the importance of the private domain. *Yishuv* women, identifying with the priority given to public goals, were trapped in the contradictions between their own experiences and dominant perceptions. The demands of the private domain and the lack of awareness by male public institutions of women's lives resulted in their marginalisation (Bernstein, 1993: 88–9). Bernstein cites Shiloh (1980), and Izraeli (1984) to argue that *Yishuv* men viewed their female colleagues as 'different human beings'. They did not welcome female participation in the labour market, which they saw as threatening not only male employment, but also 'femininity', 'gentleness' and 'softness' which they wanted their women to possess (Maimon, 1972). Attempts by pre-state labour Zionism to re-define traditional family and sexual identities were not supported by economic, political and social transformations which would have addressed the tensions between 'woman as person' and woman as wife and mother (Bernstein, 1993: 101). This highlights the deep contradictions inherent in the construction of the 'new Hebrew man'.

Israeli militarism

The organised violent confrontation between Palestinians and Jews which began in earnest in 1936, saw the construction of the Jews as 'friends' and the Palestinian Arabs as 'enemies' (see Bauman, 1991). The resultant power ethos employed discourses such as poems, prose writings and slogans. Ancient historical Jewish models were reinterpreted: the contrast between ancient heroic models such as Modi'in, Gush-Halav, Masada, Bar-Kokhba and the passive, weak diaspora Jews who put their necks on the block and extolled passive heroes who died to sanctify God, was highlighted during the formative years of Zionism.

Motifs such as 'blood' and 'soil', the former fertilising the latter, which originated in Germany and in the national liberation movements of Eastern Europe, proliferated in the 1930s and were to remain prevalent Zionist discourses long after the establishment of the State. One such discourse was Yaacov Lamdan's 1927 epic poem 'Masada', which described the experiences of the third *aliyah* (1919–1923) and the destruction of East Europe's Jewish world in the wake of pogroms, wars and the Bolshevik revolution. The poem's protagonist is a pioneer who emigrates to 'the land', the last refuge. Lamdan uses Masada, the last fortress to fall in the rebellion against the Romans, in 73 AD, whose 960 Jewish inhabitants, according to the accepted belief, chose to commit suicide rather than surrender to the Romans, as a metaphor for his present-day Erez Israel, the refuge for Jews 'escaping the fire'.

In *The Masada Myth: Collective Memory and Mythmaking in Israel,* Ben-Yehuda (1995) demonstrate how, after 1,800 years, the long, complex and largely unsubstantiated narrative by the Romanised Jew, Josephus Flavius, was edited and adapted in the twentieth century to a simple and powerful myth of heroism. Ben-Yehuda looks at how this new narrative was created and maintained by pre-state Jewish under-ground groups, the Israeli army, the archaeological establishment, mass media, youth movements, textbooks, the tourist industry and the arts. Ben-Yehuda reads Josephus's original narrative to show that the Sicarii, the Jews who perished, were far from freedom fighters, they were rather a group of assassins who committed acts of terror and massacre (against other Jews in Ein Gedi, amongst others); that the 'rebels' did not fight the Romans for the alleged three years, that they did not fight the Romans at all; and finally, that they needed a lot of persuasion to commit suicide, they did not kill themselves willingly (Ben-Yehuda, 1995: 9). Despite these falsehoods, the Masada heroic narrative was a construction, to be used by Israelis to nurture their self-image as brave new Hebrews. 'Masada will not fall again' is the most eloquent rhetoric of the heroic Jewish national renewal project in the land of Israel. Like generations of youth movement members ever since my father's youth movement days in Jerusalem of the 1930s, I too recited it. Combining metaphors of heroism and fire, we sang repeatedly as we danced: 'Go up, the flame, go up in dance/ Masada will not fall again'. Youth movement pilgrimages and official army ceremonies held in the Masada site in the Judean hills presented it as a model of patriotic behaviour central to the education of the 'new Hebrew man'. The mass suicide was erased from memory as the dead Jews of Masada were re-cast as 'heroes who died in battle', enshrining the event as part of Israel's heroic memory.

During the Shoah, the Masada myth, a model of activism and mili-tant resistance, was contrasted with diaspora passivity, and the Masada 'heroes' were presented as the antithesis of Shoah victims (Zerubavel, 1994: 48–51). Brog (1996: 203–227) argues that the Masada myth and the construction of the Warsaw Ghetto armed struggle as an 'uprising', or 'rebellion', were appropriated by Zionist discourses in order to construct norms of resistance 'to the last bullet' for pre-state Erez Israeli youth. In 1942, at the height of the Shoah, the youth move-ment *Hano'ar Ha'oved* (Working Youth) held a leadership seminar in the Masada fortress. At the end of the seminar participants signed a scroll which laid the foundations of the Masada worship, combining hikes in the Judea desert and up the ragged Masada mount with impressive ceremonies in the fortress itself (Brog, 1996: B7).

During the 1930s, as (male) poets such as Natan Alterman coupled armed defence with working the land in their poetry, Rachel (Blovstein) wrote personal, lyrical poetry devoid of heroic slogans such as 'To My Land' (1921), and 'And Perhaps' (1922), which, put to music, became two of the most popular Israeli songs of all times. Her message was patriotism without aggression, in sharp contrast to the heroic messages projected by the other current myth of the period, that of Tel Hai. In March 1920 five Jewish defenders of the northern settlement of Tel Hai, including Yoseph Trumpeldor, a one-armed former Russian soldier, having determinedly stayed put despite tensions in the area in the wake of the transfer from French to British rule after the First World War, were killed by Palestinian villagers. It was the first time that the sanctity of the land, 'soaked with the blood of Hebrew workers' (Soker, 1920), was articulated. Trumpeldor had allegedly said, seconds before his death, 'it's good to die for our land' and his words became a powerful Zionist slogan which every school child recites on 11 Adar, the day commemorating Tel Hai. According to prevailing myths, in Tel Hai Jews did not retreat, but fought heroically, and the message sanctifying death for 'the land' lives on. The 1920s discourses contrasting the 'pointless' deaths of pogrom victims with purposefully dying to defend 'the land', were replicated in the 1940s. In 1943, commemorating the fallen of Tel Hai, Ben Gurion contrasted the 'pointless deaths' of 'hundreds of thousands women and children, old people and babies' during the Shoah with the 'new art of dying, inherited by the defenders of Tel Hai – a heroes' death of the ghetto fighters' (Ben Gurion, 1955: 121). It was universally agreed that the diaspora was cowardly, powerless and submissive, and the Erez Israeli *Yishuv* brave, powerful and uncompromising. Shapira seems the only Israeli historian who articulates the gender component in this dichotomy between diaspora and *Yishuv*: 'the diaspora had a feminine image and the *Yishuv* a masculine image' (Shapira, 1992: 239).

The determination to live with danger as part of the existential reality became another dominant discourse. 'There is no choice and no escape. The historical duty will be done' is how Bracha Habas, one of the Zionist women leaders at the time of the Palestinian rebellion, ended her book *The Events of 1936* (Habas, 1937). This discourse of 'no choice' and the consequent supremacy of the 'national security' discourse employed to justify the ongoing state of war, nurtured Israeli militarism (Waintrater, 1991; Bloom, 1991).

The transition from defence to offence, argued by Shapira (1992), entailed moving psychologically beyond Tel Hai. In the late 1930s, Jews no longer merely defended their settlements, but attacked Palestinian settlements. However, this produced a sharp contradiction between discourses such as the 'purity of the weapon' which claimed that Jews were not killing innocent Palestinian bystanders, and on the other hand, if you endangered yourself and penetrated a Palestinian settlement, the mere danger legitimised the killing, not just of armed gang members. This ideological conflict between the discourse of Jews as eternal victims, who, when cornered, used their 'pure' firearms to defend themselves, and Jews as forceful soldiers fighting valiantly for their land, prevailed for years to come.

Songs and poems glorifying the fighters, grammatically male, assisted in shaping the Erez Israeli youth, which was to be the epitome of the 'free men', new Hebrews, free of diaspora complexes. The pioneers rebelled against their parents and rejected the diaspora, fortifying themselves against the pull of their Jewish past by totally rejecting it and presenting it as undesirable. But they wanted their sons (and they were always articulated as 'sons', never as ungendered 'children') to be muscular, tanned, light of step and self-confident, brave and straight gazing. The sons were shaped through negating the diaspora but, unlike their parents, who had an inborn aversion toward the gentiles, they grew up with an arrogance, born out of a conviction that the world was theirs to conquer (Shapira, 1992: 359).

Ben Eliezer (1995) argues that although initially Israeli militarism was a response to the 1936 to 1939 Palestinian rebellion, the Israeli power ethos was shaped by the military actions of the 'pre-state generation', one of whose most prominent sons was the assassinated Prime Minister Yitzhak Rabin. According to Ben Eliezer, military commanders, later to become political leaders, such as Yigal Allon and Moshe Dayan, were captivated by their own myth of the *sabra* as superman. The pre-state army, the *Palmach*, the emblem of the Israeli *sabra*, founded in 1941, became the spearhead of the Zionist policy of establishing the Jewish state by force. Ben Eliezer posits the very lack of separation between nation and army, supported by discourses such as 'the nation's army' and 'all the nation is an army', as symptoms of that militarism. Ben Eliezer's analysis does not however, account for the military apparatus as a masculine structure. Gender must be the explanation of the way the military reproduces the ideological structure of patriarchy 'because the notion of "combat" plays such a central role in the construction of "manhood" and justification of the superiority of maleness in the social order' (Enloe, 1983: 12). The IDF is central to socialising men in Israel, where the use of violence is viewed as a legitimate way of resolving conflict. One consequent social problem is the high incidence of violence against women in Israel. In the history of Israel, wars, left firmly in the hands of men, are a daily reality. Wars necessitate a large defence industry, managed primarily by men. Political power tends to be won by former soldiers and officers, therefore the representation of women in politics is unequal (Swirski and Safir, 1991), as exemplified by Prime Minister Ehud Barak, a former general, who surrounded himself with military men and largely kept women (and Israeli Palestinians) out of power.

The IDF, one of the only armies to conscript women, was gendered from its inception. Constructing women as mothers, in the spirit of religious Judaism, it exempts married women and mothers (and women whose religious beliefs preclude their serving) from military service. The conscription of married women has never been raised, not even by feminists (Berkovich, 1993: 26). The IDF women's corps is named *Chen*, an acronym for women's corps, but literally meaning 'charm', denoting women's function in the IDF, 'adding charm and grace which makes [the IDF] also a medium for humanitarian and social activities' (Yuval-Davis, 1982: 17). It was modelled on the British ATS (Auxiliary Territorial Services) model, rather than on the pre-state *Palmach* model, which integrated women soldiers into all army units. Working within Jewish parameters, women have never been allowed to participate in battle. [5] Only 15 per cent of the Israeli army goes to battle and women participate in the image of the IDF as a fighting army by freeing men for 'the important task of killing men who wear different uniforms' (Niv, 1989: 35).

Ben Eliezer argues that the Shoah had a strong influence on the formation of Israeli militarism:

> The young [pre-state] generation believed the Shoah happened because the Jews were weak. It was antisemitic, and hated the diaspora ... This generation used the Shoah consciously in order to propagate military power, which was seen as a basis for the solution of the *Yishuv*'s political problems. When news of the extent of the extermination reached them, the [Zionist] leadership hesitated as to its response, but the Israeli-born generation hastened to use the Shoah in order to strengthen the *Palmach* and the use of force in order to solve political problems (Ben Eliezer, in Karpel, 1995: 36).

Sharoni (1992: 457) (en)genders the analysis and argues that the social construction of Israeli manhood has its roots in the Shoah and the re-assertion of masculinity through the establishment of the Jewish state. Israel's self-portrayal as a 'nation under siege' made 'national security' a top priority, offering Israeli men a privileged status, and resulted in legitimising national, ethnic and gender inequalities.

After the 1948 'War of Independence', militarism became a general norm. The power discourse continues to prevail in school and youth movement hikes, characterised by unnecessary risk taking and informed by the Zionist dictum of 'dying or conquering the mountain'

(Milner, 1994). I can still remember my own difficulties, as an asthmatic child, during these tough mandatory four-day hikes, which clearly signalled me as being 'weak' – another 'new Hebrew' stigmatising strategy. These hikes are rituals of conquest and occupation.[6] Risk taking and dangerous itineraries make these school hikes a way of sifting the 'strong' from the 'weak'. 'The hike cancels out diaspora characteristics. The hiker is the embodiment of the "new Jew"' (Shapira in Milner, 1994: 21). Commenting on these high-risk school hikes, Labour Knesset member Avraham Burg uses rape metaphors to criticise the Israeli conquest of 'the land:'

> Isaiah the prophet said: 'as a young man knows a virgin, so your sons will know you' and we returned to the land at the end of our exile and we penetrate the land, without limit, with quavering weaponry – bulldozers and excavators. This is rape which does not take into account the victim's pain. Only the great masculinity, awaiting to satisfy its egotistical lust. (Burg, 1994: 62)

The *sabra* generation

The highest form of the 'new Hebrew' was the *tsabar*, the *sabra*, named after the cactus fruit known as 'prickly pear' and refering to the fruit's prickly exterior but tender flesh,[7] a name given to Israeli-born Jews. The term was first coined in 1931 and consolidated in the 1940s. In her study of Israeli cinema, Shohat (1991) views the construction of the *Sabra* generation by the immigrant generation of pioneers who saw their children as the hope for Jewish salvation, as reversed Oedipalism in which the *Sabra* was born into a vacuum in which the ideal figure was not the father, but the son:

> The mythological *Sabra*, posited in genderised language as the masculine redeemer of the passive diaspora Jew, also signified the destruction of the diaspora Jewish entity ... The Zionist stereotype of the diaspora Jew as a passive victim and the *sabra* as an active redeemer has subliminally perpetuated a genderised discourse in which masculine toughness has been highly cherished, undermining the possibility of a revisionist feminist perspective. (Shohat, 1991: 31–2)

Incarnating the same nationalist features that oppressed the diaspora Jew, the *sabra* hero was portrayed in 'Aryan' terms as healthy, tanned, often with blond hair and blue eyes, confident, proud and brave, presumably cleansed of all 'Jewish' inferiority complexes. Ironically, this conception was partially influenced by the 'youth culture' fashionable in Germany at the turn of the century, especially the German youth movement *Wandervogel* (Elon, 1971).

Almog (1997) defines the *sabra* culturally rather than biologically in his definitive study of the *sabra* generation and argues that the *sabras'* cultural significance far outweighs their actual number. Gluzman points out that Almog pays scant attention to the gender aspects of this cultural hero, although he does stress the *sabra*'s virile beauty and Tarzan-like strength (Almog, 1997: 133):

> Almog's discussion, which critiques the *sabra*'s ethnocentrism from an androcentric point of view, is an example of an un-critical approach to the social and cultural consequences of Israeli masculinity. Unfortunately, Almog is not the only one. Even the 'new historians' who supposedly explode Zionist myths, do not deal with questions of gender and sexuality (and do not link gender, sexuality and nationalism)'. (Gluzman, 1997: 160)

Unlike Almog, Hazelton does link Zionism and masculinity and argues that while the yearning for Zion was the basis for Jewish solidarity during centuries of exile, fulfilling this yearning was 'seen in terms of sons re-uniting sexually with their mother' (Hazelton, 1978: 75) or as a homecoming to Zion 'the bride'. Zionist labour leader Meir Ya'ari spoke of the land which the pioneers worked as their 'bride': they were 'a groom forgetting himself in his bride's body ... as we forget ourselves in the motherly womb of our purifying land' (Ya'ari in Elon, 1971). In 'First and Foremost Hands', Ya'ari (1918 [1947]) juxtaposes the new Israeli-born 'hard and strong generation' with generations of diaspora 'dreamers'. Linguistically, he contrasts 'hard' with 'softish', 'strong' with 'dreamy', 'heroes' with 'poets', and 'men' with 'angels of beauty and love'. Lehman points to masculine versus feminine linguistic stereotypes in his text:

> The contrast between masculinity and femininity is strengthened by Ya'ari's description of the redemption of the land: 'only a heroes' arm can do the work of fertilising the rocky, arid land, the sands and the deserts'. This description of a great masculine arm fertilising the feminine land is overtly sexual. Throughout, the text ... endorses a masculine (not to say macho) Zionist ethos. The new fighter will substitute the old dreamer, activity will replace passivity. The heart (and with it also 'femininity') has no room in the land of the Hebrews. (Lehman, 1993: 24)

The masculine metaphors of making mother-earth bloom, ploughing her and planting her, were influenced by a generation who had grown up in the Jewish *stetl* [8] and who stereotyped women as passive, polluting or sexual vessels. For the young Jewish pioneers, Zionism was a re-affirmation of Jewish manhood, which renewed their potency after a long period of impotence (Gonen, 1976). This did not take women into account; all women could do was become men, or stick to their Eastern European

Jewish traditional positions. Hazelton argues that the birth of the male *sabra* in 'post-coital sadness' after the 1948 war, replaced the early joy at the home-coming to the mother-bride (1978: 81).

Labour Knesset member Yael Dayan, daughter of one emblematic *sabra*, the 1956 Chief of Staff and the 1967 Minister of Defence, Moshe Dayan, exposes the *sabra* in her novels (1961; 1967) as reserved, emotionally frozen, trying to fit the myth. His highest value is power, military and emotional, which means not showing any emotions. This pragmatic dictum to hide your feelings resulted from the constant state of siege. The Israeli aspiration to an elusive 'normality', to being just like all other (preferably Western) nations, required adhering to strong social norms, which define that 'normality'. Hazelton (1978: 89) argues that the rigid adherence to gender stereotypes of men as pragmatic and emotionally tough, and women as feminine, emotional and needing protection, shows an underlying anxiety (see Meaney, 1991).

Another emblematic *sabra* was the writer Dan Ben Amotz, who became famous for embodying the uncouth, earthy, masculine, blond, blue eyed, womanising 'new Hebrew'. In fact, Ben Amotz was actually born in Poland as Musia Tehilimzeiger (a Yiddish name) and immigrated to Palestine in 1938, at the age of fourteen, leaving behind his family, who were to be exterminated. When he began publishing, he changed his name to the Hebrew-sounding Dan Ben Amotz (Dankner, 1992: 31, 80). Ben Amotz constructed for himself an 'Israeli' identity, which was to be model and metaphor for the *sabra*. His early writing gave his generation a base from which to construct an Israeli normality. He 'touched a raw nerve of a generation yearning for a root, a normality ... ' (Dankner, 1992: 166). While not actually hiding his diaspora origin, Ben Amotz preferred not to mention it. In his seemingly autobiographical novel *Remember and Forget* (1968) he re-invented himself as a German-born Israeli encountering an imaginary German past. More significant was a series of novels in which he charted soldiers' experiences. *Don't Give a Fuck* (1973) is the story of a young soldier wounded in the 1973 war and unable to perform sexually. A best-seller with young Israelis, it charted the rage of a young Israeli male, no longer able to fight, or fuck. Only when he was in his sixties, before his death in 1988, after a visit to Auschwitz, did Ben Amotz admit publicly his Polish origins. In 1988, Israel was 40 years old, the *Intifada* was a year old, and the consensus as to its continued existence as a fighter-nation was beginning to crack: Israel and its son Dan Ben Amotz were beginning to be able to take on their Jewish identity.

Ben Amotz's life story is almost the perfect Israeli trajectory from immigrant to re-invented *sabra*, including agricultural boarding school student, pre-state soldier, natural Hebrew speaker and collector and inventor of colloquialisms (Ben Amotz and Ben Yehuda, 1972;

1982). For me and my generation Ben Amotz was the epitome of the male *sabra*, complete with his compulsive womanising, characterising so much of what it was, and to a certain extent still is, to be an Israeli man.[9] The story of his life, his 'passing' and disclosure, illustrates Goffman's argument that stigma is a feature of society, occurring wherever there are identity norms. The roles of the normal and of the stigmatised are not only complementary, they are also parallel and similar, and through time, individuals can play both parts in the stigmatised-normal drama.

Zionism, and later the state of Israel, as re-imagined masculine communities, were determined to construct what Bauman (1991) calls 'nativism', which in turn constructed its own ethnic (Jewish) subjects. Once it became a nation-state, Israel did everything it could to laud and enforce the 'new Hebrew' entity as an ethnic, linguistic and cultural homogeneity. Not content with 'building the land', it engaged in active 'nation building' which, amongst other things, constructed newly shared memories, different from those remembered by diaspora Jewry. The attempts at a 'melting pot' were successful only up to a point, with the acquisition of a common language and the building of an independent economy. However, with Israeli uniformity actively promoted, and with the constant emphasis on the friends versus enemies binary, it is hardly surprising that when the 'ambivalent third' Shoah survivors started arriving, the new Israeli subjectivity rejected its Jewish past, making the task of assimilation extremely difficult for the stigmatised survivors.

Israelis and the 'remnant of the deliverance'

The Zionist establishment in Palestine, which was already aware of the extermination in 1942, used the Shoah, rhetorically, to strengthen existing ideologies and self-images, based primarily on the negation of exile. The Israeli belief that the 'new Hebrews' can count only on themselves contrasted sharply with perceptions of Jews as passive victims of antisemitic violence. In constructing a 'new Hebrew' normality, Israelis not only stigmatised Shoah survivors discursively, but also discriminated against them materially.

The Shoah and its after-effects, coupled with the isolation forced upon post-1948 Israel, resulted in discourses of pessimism, encirclement and utter insularity. The main lesson the Zionist leadership took from the Shoah was that Jews must never be weak again. During the early 1940s, Israeli Zionism saw the extermination of Europe's Jews as resulting from the 'Jewish sin of weakness' (Shapira, 1992: 442). Israel Galili, deputy commander of the *Hagannah*, a pre-state army, responded to the Shoah with a simplistic, direct, power message: 'Out of the crematoria and out of the graves, each man in Israel is ordered to become a force ... the Shoah orders us to become a Hebrew force in the land of Israel' (Galili, 1943). Several years later, during a meeting with Zivia Lubetkin, a female leader of the Warsaw Ghetto uprising, the Zionist labour leader Moshe Tabenkin stated: 'our horrible fate forces us to be strong. Being weak, being powerless, this we always knew; now we have no choice but to become powerful' (Tabenkin, 1946). This obsession with power is understandable: after their rendezvous with death, Jews everywhere felt compelled to reaffirm their identity. For young Israelis, the Shoah 'confirmed one of the basic tenets of classical nineteenth century Zionism: without a country of your own you are the scum of the earth, the inevitable prey of beasts' (Elon, 1971: 267). Israelis perceived the Shoah as European Jews 'dying like lambs to the slaughter'- a powerful metaphor created in 1941 by the poet and partisan Aba Kovner in Vilna Ghetto, when he urged the Jews to rebel against the Germans (Arad, 1978: 544). This resulted in young Israelis feeling emasculated by anger, insult and pain at the idea of Jews dying passively and not acting according to the code adopted by Erez Israeli Zionism.

Shoah survivors, neither 'friends' nor 'enemies', were neither inside nor outside the emerging Erez Israeli culture, which was not always sure of itself, despite the loud rhetoric. The normal and the stigmatised, according to Goffman (1968: 163–4), are not persons but perspectives. The new Erez Israeli masculine subjectivity contrasted itself with the 'feminine' diaspora, defining itself in this discursive process. The construction of that subjectivity was based on obliterating the 'Jew' in favour of the 'Israeli'. Strangers, Kristeva (1991) argues, are really ourselves: thus the *sabra,* the national ideal, was threatened by the Shoah and by Shoah survivors because many of the locals were themselves not long in Erez Israel:

> Patronising the survivors aimed to cover up what the locals themselves had been ... the gap between dream and reality made locals demand much of the survivors. They demanded a readiness to change and identify with the *Sabra* ideal as an oath of allegiance and a semi-ritualistic rite of passage. (Segev, 1991:164)

I can identify with it. My membership of the Israeli 'first generation to redemption' prevented me from acknowledging that I belonged to a survivor family. This split subjectivity harboured unconscious 'survivor guilt' towards those who came from 'there', and the only way I could cope with it as a young Israeli was to distance myself from survivor-relatives (Lentin, 1996a). 'Normal' Israeli society is still finding it hard to accept Shoah discourses because they threaten the carefully constructed 'new

Hebrews', but also because survivors uncover a Jewish facet of them-selves which Israelis do not necessarily want to confront, as Rivka Keren attests: 'If one delivers a message that doesn't touch the right place in the *sabra* body, one is thrown out ... but the reaction was so visceral, so amaz-ingly powerful ... that I understood I had done something important'.

As cynical as it sounds, the Shoah provided a 'moral' justification for the Zionist struggle and Shoah survivors were used as a powerful polit-ical metaphor by *Yishuv* leadership. Although nobody had planned to use 'those who had escaped from hell' as a political weapon, they assumed political significance and became a decisive factor in the estab-lishment of the state of Israel (Tzahor, 1988: 443; Zertal, 1996a).

The first wave of immigration after the establishment of the state in May 1948 was made up mostly of survivors (Yablonka, 1994: 9–10).[10] Although by 1949 one in three Israelis (about 350,000) was a Shoah survivor, the 'new Hebrew' Israeli normality described them in negative terms, and discriminated against them. Erez Israeli repre-sentatives to the displaced persons camps, as well as Israeli political leaders used terms such as 'refugees', 'uprooted', 'godforsaken', 'human dust' (a term coined by the writer David Frishman as early as the 1920s and was often used by *Yishuv* leaders to describe survivors, Almog, 1997: 143), 'a large band of beggars', to describe the survivors (Yablonka, 1994). Survivors were characterised by 'stigma symbols' (Goffman, 1968) such as physical appearance, dress style and accents, which the Erez Israelis found unpalatable. According to Netiva Ben Yehuda, the legendary woman *Palmach* commander:

> They, the new immigrants, were not even given a chance. Let's first see what happens ... and what happens meant how fast he divests himself of his diaspora appearance and adopts the image of a true *sabra* ... Not only could we not stand their diaspora habits, their style of dress, we also did not permit them to have even the slightest accent. If you cannot speak like us, shut up. (Ben Yehuda, 1981: 7)

Yishuv representatives to the displaced persons camps stressed the survivors' low human quality, implying that the Jewish élite had been exterminated first, and that those who survived were of lower quality (Yablonka, 1994: 56). Segev (1991: 106) cites Ben Gurion (1949) who said: 'amongst German concentration camp survivors were peo-ple who, unless they had been what they were – hard, evil and egotis-tical – would not have survived'. These discourses were influenced by the distinction Erez Israelis made between armed resistance and pas-sive death. Yablonka cites one Erez Israeli:

> How come the Jew, bid to dig his own grave, didn't pick up the spade and hit the German on the head ... The terrible grief was compounded, like

a burning ember, by a feeling of shame and humiliation. And when we heard of the uprising in Warsaw, we felt redeemed'. (Rabinowicz, 1947)

Eliahu Golomb, the *Hagannah* commander, spoke in a conference in January 1944 of the need to indoctrinate those who would survive with Zionist fighting ideals, in order to affect the future of political Zionism: 'who knows, our fate after the war may be decided by the will of the remnant of the deliverance to immigrate to Erez Israel ... meeting Jewish fighters may be the central, fateful factor' (Golomb, 1953: 369). According to Yablonka (1994: 62–70), there was not even one report by a Zionist representative to the displaced persons camps, which did not view the survivors negatively. Representatives spoke of the survivors' 'low cultural standards', their deep 'inferiority complex', their 'greed', their 'idleness and unwillingness to work', their lack of political acumen – all stigmatising features, not unlike those attributed to Jews by European antisemites.

Yablonka's research, however, disputes Erez Israelis' descriptions of the survivors as 'human dust'. She presents them instead as model immigrants: most were young, ideal candidates for economic and military activity, most were married, and, after a short period of a high birth rate in the displaced persons camps, most had small families,[11] thus not burdening the social services. [12] Survivors were also highly educated, despite the fact that many had been unable to complete their education because of the Shoah, Many survivors were trades people, industrial workers, administrators or professionals (Yablonka, 1994: 9–13). These data indicate a high potential for survivors' economic success.

Despite this potential, survivors were materially discriminated against in the early years. On their arrival, they were settled in transit camps and temporary housing. Survivors who immigrated between 1948 and 1949 poured into abandoned Palestinian settlements and Palestinian quarters (Gil, 1957): it is deeply ironic that post-Shoah Jewish refugees settled in the homes of would-be Palestinian refugees. This created a geographical, physical and cultural distance between survivors and Israelis; it also created confusion and isolation since they were promised the housing was temporary but the construction of new settlements was delayed and survivors were left with an extended temporary feeling (Yablonka, 1994: 18–43).

Although the Zionist leadership did not trust the survivors' fighting ability, 22,300 survivors were conscripted to fight in the 'War of Independence', a third of the IDF's military power by the end of 1948 (Yablonka, 1994: 80), because of an acute shortage of fighting personnel.

The fallen *sabra* was one of the dominant myths of the 1948 War, a politically significant dramatic story, true or false. In contrast, the *Gahal*

[13] soldiers, conscripted 'straight from the ships' without adequate training, were sent to fight in the battle of Latroun (outside Jerusalem), where many of them were killed. According to the historian of the 1948 generation, Immanuel Sivan: 'The sacrifice [by *Gahal* soldiers] is perceived as pointless, a waste of lives without military purpose; the political and military Erez Israeli leadership thus stands indicted' (Sivan, 1991: 74).

The Latroun battle symbolised the cynical exploitation of the survivors by Ben Gurion. A historical examination shows that survivors played their rightful role in the battle. While survivor soldiers spoke of fighting in Latroun without equipment, in bad conditions, without rations or water (Yablonka, 1994: 147–8), *sabra* discourses of the time speak of the *Gahalniks* as 'filth', and as 'hard, cowardly, obstinate people' (Gilead, 1957). The survivors' allegedly inadequate fighting ability derived from negative discourses of the Shoah constructed in parallel to the heroic myth of the 1948 War. The model of the Warsaw Ghetto uprising guided War of Independence myths: staying put in the face of the enemy, with your weapon, and unto death. However, the majority of the survivors were neither partisans nor resistance fighters. In the IDF they were faced with heroic myths against which their own experiences seemed inferior, and being 'allowed' to participate in the War was presented as a great privilege granted to them by the Erez Israelis (Yablonka, 1994: 145–6). This is another example of the Israeli Shoah versus *gevurah* dichotomy.

The discourse of turning survivors from 'human dust' to 'upstanding citizens' was replicated in the patronising treatment meted out to them by the IDF authorities. Yablonka quotes letters of survivor parents, whose requests that their only sons be released from combat duties, according to IDF regulations, were refused. For example, Rivka A. writes: 'I am writing to the national command as a mother of an only son (Y.A., age 23, mobilised in Bat Yam). I am requesting not to send him on combat duty. His father was killed by the Nazis and this left just him and me in the whole world and after what we experienced in Poland, this son is everything I have'. A curt comment at the bottom of the letter reads: 'Do not release' (Yablonka, 1994: 141).

Survivor soldiers often complained of loneliness. Danko, a former partisan and later an IDF soldier, the protagonist of a novel by Kovner (1955) says: 'like in the forest, there, here too we were lonely and foreign'. Sivan (1991) cites one agonising *Palmach* member: 'Perhaps it was our fault? We despised them and kept our distance. The girls rejected them totally and the boys patronised them, as in '*sabras*' and '*Gahal*', 'us' and 'them' ... there was no contact between us and them in the early months and they were hurt and insulted' (*Lezeher Haverim*, 1950).

The survivors never became part of the heroic myth of the 1948 War (Yablonka, 1994:151). Survivor soldiers were called 'human dust', 'refugees', '*Gahaleizim*' (a combination of *Gahalniks* and *leizim* – jokers), 'human material' – a classic stigmatising strategy. Those who claimed they had been partisans were asked mockingly: '*parti-wus?*' ('Parti-whats?' in Yiddish) and this name, *partiwuses*, stuck (Nevo, 1994: 14).

The attitudes of the Zionist leadership are debated in the context of the 'Israeli versus diaspora Jew' dichotomy. Ushpiz quotes Hacohen (1994) who describes the 1948 to 1953 mass immigration as ultimately the story of the 'violent shaping of Israel's national myths, our "Israeliness" which ... externalised hatreds other nations express towards foreign immigrants ... Here was a state whose immigrants were members of its own nation' (Ushpiz, 1994: B5). Survivors, ambivalent 'strangers', disturbed not only the carefully constructed balance between Israeli 'friends' and Palestinian 'enemies', but also the friends' very identity.

One of the consequences of this stigmatisation and discrimination was that about ten per cent of the survivors left Israel. Many others enveloped themselves in silence. They paid a high price for this silence, 'going to the clinic to remove the numbers the Nazis had tattooed on their arms' (Nevo, 1994: 14); but they wanted above all to assimilate as fast as possible and become Israelis.

Conclusion: the return of the diaspora as Zionism's unconscious 'other'

Several discourses and cultural products illustrate my argument. The film *Mission Tel Aviv*, made in 1947 and funded by the United Jewish Appeal, focused on the 'new Jew'; it featured citrus fruit, tomatoes and strong men who bare their chests in the sun, shot at a low angle which emphasises their strength. Another film *Do You Hear Me?* funded by *Hadassah*, another international Jewish organisation, featured a woman as the emblematic Shoah survivor, shot from behind, trying desperately to contact someone in outer space. Her message was that although she herself was not able to participate in the redemption, all efforts must be made so that there is a state and her death would not be 'in vain' (Fercek and Klein, 1994: B8–9).

However, the best illustration is 'My Sister on the Beach' (1945) by *Palmach* commander Yitzhak Sadeh, one of the most widely read poetic-journalistic pieces of the 1940s, which was published several times in *Palmach* journals and became a regular text in youth movement activities (Almog, 1997: 143). It describes an encounter between Sadeh and a young female illegal immigrant survivor on an Erez Israeli beach. It is worth quoting it in its entirety (the translation is mine):

Darkness. On wet sand my sister stands before me: dirty, dishevelled, matted hair. Her feet bare and her head lowered. She stands and sobs. I know: she is tattooed: 'for officers only'.

And my sister sobs and says:

Friend, why am I here? Why was I brought here? Do I deserve to have young and healthy men endanger their lives for me? No, there is no place for me in the world. I don't deserve to live.

I hug my sister, I hug her shoulders and say to her:

There is a place in the world for you, my sister. A special place. Here, in our land, you must live, my sister. Here you have our love. You are black but comely my sister. You are black, because your torture has scorched you, but you are comely, comely beyond all beauty, holy beyond all that is holy.

Darkness. On wet sand my sister stands before me: dirty, dishevelled, matted hair. Her feet bare and her head lowered.

I know: the evil have tortured her and made her sterile. And she sobs and says: Friend, why am I here? Why was I brought here? Do I deserve to have young and healthy men endanger their lives for me? There is no place for me in the world. I don't deserve to live ...

I hug my sister, hug her shoulders and say to her:

There is a place in the world for you, my sister: a special place. Here, in our land. And you must live, my sister. Your feet walked the tortured path, and tonight you have come home, and here is your place. We love you, my sister. You carry all the splendour of motherhood, all the beauty of femininity. To you is our love, you shall be our sister, our bride, our mother.

Before my sisters I kneel down, bow down, kiss the dust of their feet. And when I get up, I straighten my body, lift my head and I feel and know:

For these sisters of mine – I'll be strong.

For these sisters of mine – I'll be brave.

For these sisters of mine – I'll even be cruel.

For you, everything – everything. (Sadeh, 1945: 725)

Several writers (e.g., Elon, 1971; Almog, 1997) cite Sadeh's account, but only Anita Shapira (1992: 451–2) and Idith Zertal (1996a: 490–6) appear to give it a gendered reading. Shapira argues that representing the Shoah as a young woman taken to prostitution was not accidental. Prostitution represented the height of humiliation and impotence of Jewish men during the Shoah. Although Sadeh no doubt wished to legitimise the survivors, his story perpetuated the stereotypes of the diaspora as feminine, passive and weak and the *Yishuv* as masculine, active and strong. The female survivor's inferiority vis-à-vis the male *sabras* is evident.

Zertal takes it a step further and argues that Sadeh's 'sermon', published at the height of the postwar illegal immigration, does not illustrate what Sadeh allegedly meant, that is the glorification of the Zionist absorption myth, according to which the survivors were received lovingly and unconditionally by the Erez Israelis. Instead it confirms the stigma of exile and the stigmatisation of the survivors themselves, and the very reasons for their survival. The text is presented as a series of binary oppositions between a group of male *Palmach* soldiers versus a single female stranger; a group of 'young and healthy' men versus a 'dirty, dishevelled' woman; male power in the plural versus female weakness in the singular. In short: the strong, rooted, brave Erez Israeli Zionism versus the defeated, desperate, death-wishing diaspora. 'Zionism as an organised discourse of masculinity and power built on the Jewish catastrophe' (Zertal, 1996a: 492).

By putting words into the young woman's mouth, Sadeh indicates Zionism's attitude to the survivors, despite expressions such as 'we love you' and 'before my sisters I kneel down'. The young woman is 'dirty, dishevelled', her body is tattooed, she has been made sterile. Sadeh makes her say: 'there is no place for me in the world. I don't deserve to live..'. implying that he, the Erez Israeli Sadeh, believes that the survivors as a totality, represented here by the lone young woman, not only do not deserve to live, they also do not deserve to have 'young and healthy' Erez Israeli men endanger their lives for them. Furthermore, Sadeh presents the young woman as tainted: 'the evil have tortured her and made her sterile'. But upon her arrival on the Erez Israeli beach, the refugee Jewish woman, who survived the Shoah, is (discursively) tainted once again:

> Sadeh's sub-text, in accordance with the popular Erez Israeli discourse of those days, implies that the woman remained alive, survived the Shoah ... because she did not maintain her purity, because her [Jewish] body was used by [Nazi] officers ... The woman who comes from the Shoah is condemned by Erez Israeli justice, and is tainted by Sadeh's masculine judgement ... [although] if she kept the purity of her feminine body, her Jewish body, she would have caused its death ... The deep layer of the text is Erez Israel's moral judgement which would become Israeli society's dominant discourse about the survivors ... The survivors committed a moral sin, through which they survived. But even those who did not survive are not exempt, since they went, as we all know, 'like lambs to the slaughter'. (Zertal, 1996a: 495–6)

Zertal uses Sadeh's text to argue that deep down, the Erez Israeli subjects were terrified of the defeated diaspora objects they were carrying (literally) on their shoulders from the ships to the Erez Israeli beaches. She uses Freud's 1919 article *Das Unheimlich* (Freud, 1958) in which he deals with the very brittle boundary between the *heimlich* (belonging or pertaining to home, familiar) and the *unheimlich* (strange, unfamiliar, dark, threatening, uncanny). If the meaning of the un-familiar is derived from its opposite, the familiar, the real threat

is in the familiar, but repressed, which, as it resurfaces from the unconscious, becomes potentially terrifying. Zertal argues that the
encounter between Erez Israel and the post-Shoah diaspora is indeed
'the return of the diaspora as Zionism's unconscious' (Zertal, 1996a:
499): stigma as reflecting upon both the normals and the stigmatised.

Zertal, however, does not tell us about Freud's intention when he
differentiates between the *unheimlich* and the *heimlich*: the process by
which what is familiar and becomes strange is situated as the male's
relation to the female body (Doane, 1987: 289):

> It often happens that male patients declare that they feel there is some-
> thing uncanny about the female genital organs. This *unheimlich* place,
> however, is the entrance to the former *heimat* [home] of all human
> beings, to the place where everyone dwelt once upon a time and in the
> beginning ... whenever a man dreams of a place or a country and says
> to himself, still in the dream, 'this place is familiar to me, I have been
> there before', we may interpret the place as being his mother's ... body.
> In this case too, the *unheimlich* is what was once *heimlich*, homelike,
> familiar; the prefix *un* is the token of repression. (Freud, 1958: 152–3)

The uncanny for Freud is the return of the repressed, and what is
repressed is a certain vision of the female body as the signifier of castra-
tion; but it can also be seen as a desire to return to the womb. Femininity, according to Felman's analysis of Freud's article, is uncanny in that
it is not the opposite of masculinity, but 'that which subverts the very
opposition of masculinity and femininity ... Femininity inhabits masculinity, inhabits it as otherness, as its own disruption' (Felman, 1993:
65). Sadeh's narrative, focusing on the tainting of the diaspora female
body returning to haunt the Erez Israeli men, who themselves had at
some recent past come from that very diaspora they were now negating,
can be read as a gendered tale of the male terror of the female unfamiliar, uncanny body, which, perhaps, is also a diaspora mother's familiar,
yet negated, womb: 'you shall be our sister, our bride, our mother'. Erez
Israeli masculinity is disrupted by the diasporic femininity; it finds itself
discursively castrated and emasculated by the murder and tainting of
the feminine diaspora, whose 'dirty, dishevelled' and sexually mutilated
daughter it is forced to carry to the safety of its shores, all the while constructing the myth of its unconditional love and acceptance for those
'tainted', haunting, shaming, passive stranger-survivors.

*

In November 1992 I interviewed three members of kibbutz *Lochamei
Hagetaot* who are children of survivors, two men, kibbutz secretary

Motti Re'ut and Hilik Bugamolsky, and one woman, librarian Dalia Gai. *Lochamei Hagetaot* lives in the shadow of its Shoah museum, a large square building towering over the kibbutz landscape. *Lochamei Hagetaot*, I argue, is a microcosm of the complex relationships between Israelis and the Shoah. Like the kibbutz, the state of Israel has lived with 'the Shoah museum' while continuing its daily existence. The interview with the three kibbutz members confirms the silence of Shoah families and the discrimination of the survivors upon their arrival in Israel. The gendered differences between the woman and the two men inadvertantly confirm the 'masculinisation' of Israel versus the 'feminisation' of the Shoah, and intimate memory versus national-ised messages. Dalia Gai, stressing the complexities of personal, inti-mate memory, believes the aim of the kibbutz museum is not to give a message or:

> to remember the Shoah with fireworks once a year ... but to remember it as a memory of people who lived, of a nation who was and is no longer ... accepting the people who experienced the Shoah, each one in his or her own way ... and each story is as heroic as any other story.

Bugamolsky and Re'ut, on the other hand, posit a more Israeli, heroic, masculine message, using nationalistic discourses, such as 'Massada will not fall again' and 'we shall never again go like lambs to the slaughter':

> The message, a short, sharp message which people remember for years ... begins with 'The *Stetl* Burns' [14] and ends with 'The Partisans Song ... ' This is why the museum is designed the way it is designed, like a fortress, with shooting apertures, the stairs going down to the [ghetto] bunker. And the stairs shaped like a swastika are not accidental ... Masada will not fall again, we will never again go like lambs to the slaughter, and we remember ... The message is that we must be strong ... (Bugamolsky)

> ... we have to guard our existence. The more we use the Shoah to educate the nation to guard itself, the more we avoid the danger to our existence ... We must never reach a situation of another Shoah. We must have more people here, and we must be strong because otherwise ... (Re'ut).

This chapter has drawn on Goffman's (1968) theory of stigma as a social grading mechanism, distinguishing the Israeli 'normals' from Shoah survivors, Israel's stigmatised ambivalent strangers (Bauman, 1991) and on Boyarin's (1997a; 1997b) theoretical links between Zionism and masculinity. Chapter 7 posits the centrality of counter-narratives, of which the narrators' works are prime examples, and of auto/biographical personal narratives in bridging the gap between experience and representation, and teases their performative possibilities in re-occupying the territories of silence surrounding the Zionist myths about the Shoah.

Notes

1. As the first kibbutz, Degania has a pride of place in Zionist history; Shchunat Borochov was a labour Zionism quarter outside Tel Aviv.

2. In 'The arrangement between the sexes' (Goffman, 1987), in which he integrated sexual division of social action into his particular form of symbolic interaction, Goffman views gender, which he sees as 'purely sociological', as a basis for inequality, therefore classification. His language, however, is often subject to the same discriminatory limitations he criticises (Wedel, 1978). The only example of gender reference in Bauman's rather Eurocentric *Modernity and Ambivalence* seems to be his inclusion of 'masculinity' together with 'guts' and 'stamina', when he describes the internalisation of German *Volkisch* values by German Jews at the height of their ultimately pointless efforts to assimilate (Bauman, 1991: 136).

3. Western feminist theories of 'woman' as a universally subordinated 'other' have been successfully challenged by Black and majority world feminists (e.g., Mohanty et al., 1991). In a sweeping attack on universalising models of liberalism, humanism and Marxism, many contemporary feminists opt for analyses of the local, rather than the global, the specific, rather than the general, seeking to 'destabilise' hierarchical binary oppositions (Barrett and Phillips, 1992).

4. A similar discourse can be found in Israeli descriptions of Palestinian Arabs as either 'fleeing refugees' or 'aggressive killers'. Rosenthal (1994: 55) views both images as serving Zionist myths. Almog (1998: 304–10) argues that Zionism constructed the Arab as a blood-thirsty and cruel enemy, and as 'barbaric' and 'hot-headed' in opposition to the construction of the Israeli Jew as morally and culturally superior.

5. In recent years several women have been accepted into hitherto male preserves such as élite airforce units, but only after lengthy legal battles and in 2000 a law ensuring women's participation in combat duties was introduced to the legislature and seen, by some Israeli feminists, as a major achievement.

6. Sharoni points to the multiple meaning of the Hebrew word *kibbush* (occupation) denoting the Israeli occupation of the West Bank and the Gaza Strip, and conquest either of a military target or of a woman's heart. 'This conflation of women and military targets is not merely linguistic ... During military training exercises, for example, the strategic targets are quite often named after significant women in the soldiers' lives: women, like military targets, must be protected so that they will not be conquered by the "enemy" while men must fight, occupy, and protect' (Sharoni, 1994: 126).

7. Ironically, Palestinians too name themselves 'sabras' – the Palestinian novelist Sahar Khalifa's *Al Subbar* (1978) tells the story of 'valiant' *sabra* Palestinian fighters.

8. *Stetl* (Yiddish) – small Jewish urban settlement in Russia and Poland in the nineteenth century.

9. Ben Amotz's life surfaces in the narratives, and in Orna Ben Dor's film *Newland* (1994), in the story of Uri, a Polish-born Israeli who re-invents himself as a *sabra* (see chapter 3).

10. By 1947, a quarter of the one million Jewish Shoah survivors were concentrated in displaced persons camps in Germany, Austria and Italy. In 1948, 118,993 Jews immigrated to Erez Israel: of them 102,498 were survivors. In 1949, there were 141,608 immigrants, of whom 95,165 were survivors; 80 per cent of all immi-

grants during the War of Independence, between December 1947 and July 1949, were survivors (Yablonka, 1994: 9 fn).

11. According to Yablonka, the small size of survivor families, 80 per cent of survivor families had no children or only one child, may be due to the high age of immigration by women survivors or to the reproductive experimentation carried out by the Nazis. It may also derive from the harsh economic conditions in the early years of the state, as attested by my narrators.

12. Interestingly, until 1950, more men than women survivors immigrated. Because of the war, the *Yishuv* institutions, selecting who could immigrate, preferred men between the ages of 18 and 40 who could be mobilised into the military. Yablonka (1994: 11) argues that this gender imbalance was a consequence of the genocide, although there are no definitive figures for the proportions of men and women survivors, or estimates of the dead by gender. Using deportation and survival figures, Ringelheim makes several tentative gender-specific assertions: more women were deported than men and women were murdered in greater numbers than men in the killing centres. In the displaced persons camps in 1946/1947 there were approximately four women to six men (Ringelheim, 1993: 393–4).

13. Initials for *Giyus Hutz La'aretz* – foreign mobilisation.

14. A Yiddish song about a *Stetl* burning under the attack of the antisemites.

CHAPTER 7

COUNTER-NARRATIVES:

RE-OCCUPYING THE TERRITORIES OF SILENCE

Researching and writing this volume was *necessary* for me in order to put myself inside the story that is Israel and the Shoah. Working on this book, and at the same time writing fiction which returns again and again to my relationship with Israel and the diaspora, began in early childhood, when Grandmother Charlotte and Grandfather Yossel's relatives, who began arriving from Transnistria in the early 1950s, congregated in Charlotte's glass panelled room and talked of 'there'. These relatives were everything we, the Israeli children, were 'not'. I knew I had to include this part of the story. Talking about Great-Grandmother Yetti, for instance, who, in her late seventies, looked much older, her thin white hair pulled back, her little face wrinkled and ravaged, her big haunted eyes staring, her toothless grin senseless. Yetti had lost her husband, a son and a granddaughter in the camp, and arrived, penniless, her health and sanity gone, to spend her final years on her daughter Charlotte's veranda, asking, every hour, on the hour, 'Is it already ten? Is it already eleven?' I knew I had to include this part of the story. I am not sure I have, but it casts a dark shadow on every word.

I knew that I had to include this part of the story, to envision the stigmatisation of my own relatives, whom I did not understand as a child, but whose stories I excavated in *Night Train to Mother* (Lentin, 1989). To re-visit the exclusion of my Romanian-born parents from the main narrative of East European early Zionism. To (en)gender, 'as a feminist', the binaries Israel versus the diaspora, Israel versus the Shoah, Shoah versus *gevurah*, personal narratives versus official discourses. These binaries are the story of my life and the lives of so many women of my generation, and to explore them, as I attempt to do in this volume, was 'to do sociology'. This book, a feminist auto/biographical process, is a sociological undertaking, which also aims to deconstruct the separating lines between 'doing sociology', 'doing personal narratives', and 'doing literature'. As a fiction writer, who is also a sociologist, who works with fiction and poetry writers and film-makers who are also expert commentators on Israeli society and its relationship with the Shoah, I have moved between the sociological, the literary and the personal, and between a literary prologue, auto/biographical personal chapters, 'sociology' chapters, and a literary epilogue.

I am all these voices.

*

To what extent has my methodology confirmed my theoretical assumption that by constructing a masculinised Zionist subjectivity, Zionism and Israeli society not only silenced, discriminated against and discursively stigmatised, but also feminised the survivors?

Starting from the premise of the masculinisation of Zionism's 'new Hebrews', I have deduced the parallel fem(m)inisation of the diaspora, the Shoah and Shoah survivors. The legacy of the Shoah in Israeli society and its effect on the 'second-generation' links the masculinisation of Israeli society and the ensuing feminisation of the survivors with the discursive subordination of the Jewish diaspora and the Shoah on the one hand, and the stigmatisation of Shoah survivors on the other.

One of my aims has been to add to breaking the silences, imposed by a society (and a world) ambivalent about coming to terms with the Shoah, and more specifically, the silence in Israeli society about the encounter with the survivors upon their return from the Nazi hell. One way of breaking these silences, in sociology, is to have made the study of the legacy of the Shoah in Israeli society part of a sociological inquiry. However, as an auto/biographical quest, this book seeks to answer not merely questions about processes of social formation, but also 'pressing problems in living' (Reinharz, 1983: 176). These 'pressing problems in living', to which the narrators and I have been seeking answers, resonate with some of the existential 'problems in living' which Israeli society has been grappling with since its establishment, in the wake of the Second World War.

These 'problems in living' were nurtured, understandably, by an age-old Jewish fear and the resulting determined centrality of armed struggle to establish an independent state in the Jewish historical homeland, disregarding that land's indigenous inhabitants. One consequence was the wish to divest the Israelis of their Jewishness, and, to quote Nava Semel, turn 'the Jew, the lamb to the slaughter, the diaspora type ... who accepts his fate resignedly' quickly into an Israeli hero. Another was the belief, internalised by many Israelis, that the new Israeli ethnic subjectivity was indeed the masculine antithesis of the feminised, weak, 'old' Jewish diaspora. These existential questions resulted in a series of accepted myths constructed by Israeli society. These myths included not only the inevitability of continuous war, but also the open-armed reception Israelis allegedly gave to the survivors upon their arrival.

I have argued that the construction of a new type of Jew was at the heart of the Zionist enterprise. It was probably a necessary construction, if Zionism was to conquer the hearts and minds of Europe's Jews and persuade them that immigration to the promise of Zion was a preferred alternative to their diaspora existence. However, necessary as it seemed to Zionism's founding fathers (and, it must be admitted, mothers), erasing the Jewish past took its toll. One consequence was hegemonic masculinity constructed as 'friend' versus the Arab 'enemy' and privileging military solutions to political problems. This silenced not only women's voices, but also the voices of non-hegemonic subordinated groups. This hegemony was engaged in a self-imposed war of attrition against its 'enemies'. In order to perpetuate itself, it had to silence Shoah survivors, its ambivalent 'strangers', who, by challenging that very hegemony, disrupted the Zionist order. Giving survivors space to speak of their suffering and of the suffering of the Jews who did not survive, might have destroyed Zionism's carefully constructed masculine hegemony.

One thing the narratives, and the analysis of Zionist discourses, put paid to, is the Israeli myth of not differentiating between Shoah victims and survivors and of casting both groups as passive, weak, and unheroic (Zertal, 1996a: 496). If victims are people who are acted upon, survivors are active subjects (Linden, 1993: 89). The narrators are daughters of survivors, who made a life for themselves and their children in Israeli society. These daughters, viewed by some less clement reviewers of their works, and sometimes by themselves, as requiring special understanding because of their parents' suffering, are in fact a living proof of the falsity of these myths. If anything, by being creative, vocal, published and successful, these daughters prove that their parents' survival had equipped them with special tenacity and strength. They were motivated by the legacy of their parents' suffering during the Shoah and their stigmatisation in Israeli society to become cultural producers who, through their works, broke the conspiracies of silence and affected the cultural climate of post-Shoah Israel.

One of the dilemmas of working with personal narratives of women whose experience as daughters of survivors resonates with my own, was finding the appropriate representational voice and a way of closing the gap between traumatic memories and the discourses available to represent them. Apart from allowing a multiplicity of their (often contradictory) voices to emerge in my presentation of the narratives, I have attempted to create what Barbara Myerhoff calls the 'third voice' of the 'ethno-person', born by virtue of the collusion between interlocutor and subject (Kaminsky, 1992: 5). By quoting lengthy extracts of the narrators' words, I attempted to find a compromise to the burning issue of how social scientists represent and edit narrators' words without assuming a researcher's power over them. This notion of the 'third voice' proposes a dialogic principle for editing narrators' utterances. This does not mean that I have consulted the narrators regarding my interpretation, but that the edited text adheres to the process of the interview, which is one reason why I decided to reproduce Nava Semel's narrative in its entirety. Semel's narrative is not only a 'key story' articulating the main issues of the relationship between Israel and Shoah survivors, as seen from the standpoint of a daughter of survivors. It is also, through our dialogue and my intervention, by incorporating divisions and sub-divisions, my additions and interpretations into the text, a representation of the process of producing the meaning of Semel's utterances. It is possible, Myerhoff argues, for an ethnographic text to tell a theoretically sophisticated tale in the voice of a 'native' storyteller. A text of this kind dialogises 'what the ethnographer knows and what the informant said' (Kaminsky, 1992: 8).

Turning now to the conclusions to be drawn, it seems clear that the narratives have adequately confirmed the stigmatisation not only of the narrators' survivor-parents, but also the legacy of that stigmatisation for the narrators themselves. My 'theory' of the 'feminisation' of the survivors found less direct confirmation in the narrators' testimonies and here a critical re-reading of some Zionist discourses was brought in. The 'findings' are auto/biographically relevant to me as researcher, but also as an 'experiencing, therefore knowing subject' (Stanley, 1993) and can be summarised under four main headings.

Firstly, the study has demonstrated that by telling our stories, we make our selves. As Myerhoff puts it:

> One of the most persistent but elusive ways that people make sense of themselves is to show themselves to themselves, through multiple forms: by telling themselves stories; by dramatising claims in rituals and other collective enactments; by rendering visible actual and desired truths about themselves and the significance of their existence in imaginative and performative productions. (Myerhoff, 1992: 257)

For me, the research process was a process of re-'making' my Israeli subjectivity. For my narrators the process began in the early 1980s, when they began making and publishing their works about their 'second-generation' experiences, 'dramatising [their] claims in ritual and other collective enactments'. I have published such a 'dramatised' investigation of my own 'split subjectivity' already in 1978. In the short story 'Like a Blindman' (Lentin, 1978) I examined my relationship with the Shoah, through the tale of a young Israeli woman who befriends a group of young Germans, in Israel to atone for Nazi crimes. I was living in Ireland at the time of publication, which may have made it easier for me to confront the issues involved, publishing in Israel and 'hiding behind my words' as Semel puts it. However, it took the process of academic research to enable me to re-name and re-make my self as a daughter of a family of survivors. The narrators, who grew up in 'silent homes', had first-hand experience of their parents' post-Shoah suffering and stigmatisation. It took them until the early 1980s to begin articulating it, first privately, by writing, then publicly, by publishing. The research process enabled me to place the narrators' personal experiences within my gendered reading of that suffering and stigmatisation.

Secondly, the study has enabled me to understand, 'as a woman', the relationship between Israelis and the Shoah. Zertal describes her reading of Sadeh's 'My Sister on the Beach' (Zertal, 1996a) as a 'feminine reading, that a man would not have been able to make' (Karpel, 1996: 30). I have read both the narrators' texts and Zionist discourses not only 'as a woman' but also 'as a feminist'. This led me to a feminist, post-colonial understanding of Israeli Jews as the descendants of dispersed, exiled world Jewry, identified as passive, incapable of self-government and weak and therefore seen, as are the 'natives' in a colonised territory, as everything the dominant majority is 'not'. One result of observing rigid gendered roles in order to assert the masculinity and right of power of the male after colonisation, is hegemonic masculinity. This hegemony, like 'imagined communities', implies a large measure of consent, in which the majority of men benefit from the subordination of women and in which men and women of the dominant group benefit from the subordination of stigmatised groups. The other result is the feminisation of the colonised, the Other, the 'ambivalent stranger'.

I also posit Zionism as a military-masculine hegemony, resulting from discourses of a 'no choice' ongoing military conflict with the Arab 'enemy' and from privileging discourses of 'national security'. This hegemony informs the specificity of Israeli masculine 'normality', which silenced its women and stigmatised its ambivalent 'others'. This translates into gendered relations between male occupiers and female 'occupied territories' on both the personal and the discursive level. I am one daughter of a generation of women who colluded, forcibly, with prevailing discourses of 'national security' and military conquest in our relations with the men-soldiers, always on the way to or from battle, and always sexually demanding (Lentin, 1996a). Hopefully, this, like other Israeli accepted 'truths', is in the process of being challenged by Israeli feminists, as argued, for instance by Rapoport and Elor, who posit 'growing feminism in an unfriendly environment', and a 'shift [of] the "female" point of view from the margins to the centre'. (Rapoport and El-Or, 1997: 573–380)

Thirdly the process has enabled me to make sense, 'as a woman', of the deeper existential relationship between 'Jewish' fear and Israeli responses and behaviours in the Israeli-Arab conflict. Some argue that Zionism has served its function – the creation of a Hebrew nationality/ethnicity in Erez Israel. It has had its day and must now make room for a 'post-Zionist' era, as Evron puts it:

> 'Post Zionism' is not a new political or historical school, nor is it really 'new' ... The perpetuation of Zionism, now that world Jewry is no longer in serious danger, is exploited in order to discriminate against Israel's non-Jewish citizens ... and negates the establishment of a state which belongs to its citizens and not to some nebulous 'Jewish nation' living in 'the diaspora'. (Evron, 1996: 20)

'Post-Zionism', however, is a debatable concept, having become a central 'critical moment' in the Israeli intellectual discourse along with the growing tendency to put central founding Zionist myths under the microscope. Being a 'post-Zionist' is a pejorative term hurled at 'new historians' and 'new sociologists' by their opponents. However, criticising Zionist colonialism or positing a relationship between Zionism and imperialism is not necessarily post-Zionist, but rather part of classic Zionism, according to Zimmermann (1999):

> Those who are called 'post-Zionists' are usually... critics of Zionism, while those who oppose 'post-Zionism' are themselves the true post-Zionists. The label 'neo-Zionists' given to them by Ram (1996; 1999) compliments them but misses the point... Real post-Zionism does not emanate from the 'self hating left,' but from the terrifying link between nationalist romanticism and religious fanaticism – a link which has become the heart of the Israeli consensus. (Zimmermann, 1999: 487)

The critical approach to the Zionist narrative includes posing questions about the causal link between Israel and the Shoah, which, Zimmermann argues, is untenable, since Zionism existed prior to the Shoah and its success did not depend on the Shoah.

Against 'post-Zionism', I define myself, like Boyarin (and others, friends who have been my political colleagues since the late 1960s) as 'anti-Zionist.' As an anti-Zionist, I not only, like Boyarin, posit anti-Zionism as the only way of being Jewish. I also make a political and ontological, not only a theoretical link, between the continuing occupation and the gendering of the relationship between Israel and the Shoah. Boyarin puts it thus:

> Now, having declared that the Jews' 'de-colonisation' was based on 'neo-colonialism', I have to admit that I am a partner to Herzl's discourse. I too am looking for a Jewish political subject who has a place in modernity. As a Jew... I see modernity as a dilemma... The very struggle against colonialism, homophobia and sex discrimination – a struggle which gave birth to my work – is identical to Herzl's struggle for 'manhood' and its signifiers: colonialism, homophobia and sexism. He lived in a colonial world. I live in a post-colonial world, but my people are involved in one of the last colonial enterprises. Although I am appalled by the apparently inevitable injustice performed in my name by the Jewish state, my reaction to this stage of Jewish praxis is the same revulsion which moved Herzl ... Whereas Herzl argued that only Zionists can be Jews – and his opinion was taken up by the majority –mine is the opposite, equally subversive, strategy; I argue that only anti-Zionists can be Jews.
>
> This, in order to re-open a space for an anti-Zionist Jewish polity, in Palestine and elsewhere. (Boyarin, 1997b: 140)

Ultimately, masculinity, according to Brod (1998: 512), was Zionism's Achilles Heel. Theorising Jewish males as 'giving re-birth' – as in the Genesis story of the sacrifice of Isaac, he argues that when Zionists came to Israel to give birth to the new state, the presence of prior inhabitants (and, I would add, their diasporic Jewish past) did not seem to have hindered their vision. Brod posits a 'feminist Zionism', not as egalitarian Zionism, but rather 'as a Zionism that would have at the centre of its vision a consciousness of the other people already on the land when modern Zionism began the work of giving birth to the state of Israel'.

By nationalising the memory of the Shoah, deemed necessary in the process of establishing the state of Israel, and by centring its commemoration machinery around the un-written principle of an Israeli 'victory over the Shoah', Israel erased the very memory of the Shoah itself. Zertal (1996a) invokes Freud to argue that the repressed 'uncanny' diaspora always returns to haunt the Israelis, causing deep terror, not because it represents something new and unfamiliar, but precisely because it is so intimately familiar. For me, the return of Israel's repressed diasporic self, that Jewish 'other' symbolised by the Shoah and epitomised by its survivors, also means being able to embrace a Jewish past and incorporate it into an Israeli present. An Israeli present which has become able, since around its fortieth anniversary in the mid-1980s, to begin to make space for a re-examination of the legacy of the Shoah, through, among other means, the narrators' stories and films, read and viewed by many Israelis. This, I would argue, signalled a turning point in the relationship between Israeli society and the Shoah.

Homi Bhabha (1994) posits counter-narratives emerging from the nation's margins, from cultural and national hybrids, which slot into the inter-national space of the stranger, between 'enemies' and 'friends'. Such counter-narratives, although often silenced in the process of nation building, disturb the 'ideological manoeuvres through which "imagined communities" are given essentialist identities' (Bhabha, 1994: 149). The performative possibilities of these either/or narratives disrupt the national narrative – in this case the Zionist inversion of the stereotypically passive 'Jewish' diaspora, and the re-invention of the 'new Jew' as masculine and heroic. They provide a 'liminal signifying space that is *internally* marked by the discourse of minorities, the heterogeneous histories of contending peoples', a double-writing, or 'dissemi-nation' which posits a cultural liminality *within the nation* (Bhabha, 1994: 148).

The narrators' stories, which construct anti-heroic antagonists to the heroic Zionist narration of nation (such as, for instance, the tormented children of survivors in Semel's stories, the war widows and bereaved mothers of soldiers in Aini's and Gur's novels, lonely survivors caught up in fantasies of sex and revenge in Keren's novels), are, I would argue, such counter-narratives. Despite the hurt, the stigmatisation and the silencing, daughter-writers speak of their deep need to write and deal, even subconsciously, with the presence of the Shoah in their lives. Writing about the legacy of silence, 'second-generation' daughters have been forging an 'ambivalent third' space, providing 'a place from which to speak both of, and as, the minority, the exilic, the marginal and the emergent' (Bhabha, 1994: 149).

Rigid binaries are in the process of shifting and blurring. In her introduction to the 1998 re-issue of Nava Semel's 'A Hat of Glass', Govrin links the change in the level of acceptance of intimate Shoah memories to the survivors' ageing and says that 'the collective accusation of the survivors as "lambs to the slaughter" has made room for better understandings of the complex, impossible, horrific situations people had to face "there"'. (Govrin, 1998: 3). According to Burg's somewhat optimistic account:

> Only in the last few years have the black flowers begun opening... parents talk, grandchildren listen, journeying [to Europe] in search of their roots. Slowly, thanks to the second-generation victims (yes, the Shoah did not end with the extinguishing of the crematoria but continued to

burn in the hearts of the survivors and in the tormented souls of their children, born to national independence outside and to the continuing terrors of the Shoah at home), Israel is becoming a listening and not merely an occupying society. (Burg, 1999: 6)

The process has also enabled me to understand the contradiction between Israeli myths of the Shoah and the 'reality' of the survivors and their children. Far from being weak, 'human dust', or 'psychologically disturbed', survivors, despite their suffering and stigmatisation, and the discrimination against them in the early years of the state, proved their strength and resilience. Far from being the 'feminised other' of the hegemonic Israeli masculinity, survivors and their children contributed greatly to all strata of Israeli society (as argued for instance by Yablonka, 1994). I have also been able to appreciate, 'as a woman', the real strengths of second-generation daughters, who are challenging conventional female roles to become producers of works of significant cultural worth. However, despite their artistic success, several narrators still feel despair in the face of an uncomprehending society. A society which refuses to hear their subversive 'collective story' and accept the challenge it offers to the mythical 'cultural story' of the Shoah as a memory which has to be repressed, or re-written, in order that Israelis can continue to engage in their armed struggles.

Fourthly, researching and writing enabled me to begin the reckoning process and to provide a forum to bridge the 'memory gap' between Jewish experiences of the Shoah and its Israeli representations. More specifically, the dilemma of bridging the split between genocide and gender in the memories of witnesses and the historical reconstruction of researchers (Ringelheim, 1995: 4), arises because our understanding of the Shoah as a break with the past conflicts with our knowledge of the continuities that are present in these events. That break, Ringelheim quotes Arendt as saying, has something to do with 'our inheritance [being] left to us by no testament' (Arendt, 1961: 3): no one to speak and no one to receive the message: 'a howl–unheard'. (Delbo, 1995: 33)

In order to work through the 'gap between past and future', some have constructed the Shoah as 'unique' and uncontextualised in history. Others work through that 'memory gap' via testimonies and personal narratives, the only way to bridge that gap. When responding to his Israeli-born son's request to take him to his native Vilna and show him 'the place', Abba Kovner argues that neither art nor history can 'tell' or remember the Shoah. All we have are 'stories', or personal narratives: 'There is no such *place* ... [stories] as opposed to historical research, do not have to answer the difficult questions: how did it happen and how could it happen, at the heart of Europe, at the centre of Western civilisation, in the twentieth century'. (Kovner, 1991: 14)

Experience is at the heart of feminist epistemological processes; it rejects

> the key foundationalist myth of the detached scientific observer/ researcher [and] instead positions an experiencing and comprehending subject at the heart of intellectual and research life, a subject whose onto-logically-based reasoning processes provide the grounds for knowledge-claims and thus for all epistemological endeavour. (Stanley, 1996: 47)

Beyond representations there exists a being, an experience, or 'trou-bling categories I can't think without' (Linden, 1996). The researcher's experience 'includes indirect as well as direct experience and knowl-edge gained second – and third – as well as first-hand' (Stanley, 1996: 46). Doing this work has enabled me to bridge the gap between the ontology of the narrators' silenced Israeli post-Shoah experiences and the representations of that ontology, via their personal narratives. In the process, and by putting my intellectual auto/biography at the cen-tre of the inquiry, the study transformed me, its author.

The narrators, working through their parents' Shoah and post-Shoah materials, and against the dominant Shoah-silencing Zionist discourse, created new narratives, which privileged intimate memory over nationalised memory. Narrators also negotiated a written gen-dered 'self', reflecting a gendered 'life', thus bridging the auto/bio/gra-phy gap between women's selves, lives and writing. These new narratives, some more explicit in depicting survivors' stigmatisation and the construction of new Israeli identities than others, were pro-duced one generation after the Shoah. Narrators argue that this was probably the right time for individual survivors, and for the Israeli col-lectivity, to begin grappling with the traumatic past. Just as narrators report that for them, writing was not a choice, so exposing and explor-ing the painful relationship between Israel and its Shoah stigmatised 'other' is a necessary stage in Israel's coming of age.

The strangerhood of Shoah survivors as Israeli normality's 'ambivalent third' is possibly permanent, even in the face of the changes in Israel's coming to terms with the Shoah. Strangerhood, Bauman (1991:15) argues, is the waste of nation-state building, and the efforts to dissolve the ambivalent category of strangers result in yet more ambivalence and prove to be counter-productive. Shoah sur-vivors, Zionism's ambivalent strangers, far from being the patholo-gised entities they were presented as, proved to be *us*, our own repressed 'uncanny' other. The Shoah is not only a traumatic reality Israel is trying to come to terms with. It is also a metaphor for uproot-edness, a collective Israeli experience as a society of immigrants. The narrators' popular works of fiction and cinema have been instrumental counter-narratives in shifting the binary oppositions of Israeli versus the diaspora, and Shoah versus *gevurah*, in that Israelis are beginning to be able to discuss and deconstruct those very oppositions.

Perhaps the Israelis' existential anxiety that 'it' – another exile, another *khurban*, another Shoah – may happen, to us *as Jews*, once again, may be the underlying reason for our ongoing military imperative, our occupation excesses and our apparent reluctance to let go and make peace. In attempting to reoccupy the territories of the silence regarding the relationship between Israelis and the Shoah, this volume is also an attempt to reassure ourselves that this deep terror is no longer realistic, despite its resurfacing, together with the 'Shoah code', every time there is an attack on Israeli targets.

More research is needed in order to break another silence, the silence about the sexual exploitation of women during the Shoah, which women survivors, who are now getting older, are beginning to signal they need to speak about, before it is too late. Ringelheim argues that scholars tend to think that sex during the Shoah is 'a function of media hype' and that interviewers often find it impossible to listen to survivors' accounts of rape and sexual exploitation during the Shoah (Ringelheim, 1995: 15). Because 'photo and film documentation does not exist for many of the situations that involve women, e.g., few photos of women in Auschwitz for instance', Ringelheim insists that 'words have to be used to portray gender' (Ringelheim, 1995: 18). This means that survivors' personal narratives must be told and listened to. Criticising the permanent exhibition at the United States Holocaust Memorial Museum for its lack of representation of what happened to women, Andrea Dworkin argues that 'what women cannot bear to remember, will die with them; what happened will die with them' (Dworkin, 1994: 58). Unless, that is, we begin to listen and offer a forum to tell.

However, if acknowledging Israel's repressed diasporic other has proved difficult, absorbing Israeli women survivors' sexual exploitation may prove even more threatening. Israeli masculinity was disrupted by a diasporic, tainted and sexually compromised femininity, and constructed it as a prostitute, whom it failed to embrace, despite declaring its 'love' for that femininity. If femininity is masculinity's otherness, its own disruption (Felman, 1993: 65), Israeli hegemonic masculinity will have to acknowledge that survivors' testimonies of the Shoah and of their post-Shoah experiences in Israel, as well as the abuse of its survivor mothers and sisters, no longer endanger Israel's very existence, or signal another Shoah.

David Lloyd (1999), speaking of the Irish famine, argues that commemoration of trauma does not mourn the dead, but rather those who lived on. Mourning and rage are an attempt to free ourselves from the legacy of the past – commemoration as therapy, reproduction as align-

ment with modernity. If Lloyd is right that mourning does not commemorate the dead, but rather condemns them, it is clear that official
Israeli coupling of Shoah and *gevurah* condemned, rather than
mourned the victims.

For me, the research and writing process paralleled the acts of reckoning and of asking forgiveness which Jews engage in on the Day of
Atonement. It enabled me to name myself as a daughter of a family of
survivors and ask forgiveness for my insensitivity towards survivor family members. It has also enabled me to name myself publicly, for the first
time, as an anti-Zionist, opposed, that is, to an exclusively Jewish state,
which discriminates against its Palestinian citizens. Conducting the
research as an auto/biographical project meant not only reoccupying
the territories of silence about the Shoah in sociology, and about the
link between Shoah and gender. It also enabled me, by privileging my
'split subjectivity', to begin grieving individual and collective losses and
reifying and recapturing the Shoah, beyond the textual. The research
process has been an attempt to close the gap between ontology and
epistemology, between memory and discourse, between reckoning and
mourning. Writing this book has been auto/biography as an act of
reckoning, and of re-casting the past, but also of envisioning an uncertain future in the light of that painful past.

JOURNEY'S END(S)

1

Where did the journey begin? Was there ever a time when you didn't journey, searching mother's hand, gasping for air, your asthmatic bronchials rasping to her reassuring voice? You were too thin, too ill, not eating enough, not sleeping enough, standing obstinately shaking your cot sides for nights on end, never secure in the knowledge.

You could have been a child from there, but they did all they could so you would be a child from here, a strong, earth-smelling *sabra*... Did they, secretly, think you wouldn't have survived had you been born there? (Lentin, 1989: 13).

Researching the gendered relations between Israel and the Shoah, what did I need to know?

Did I seek the reassurance Nava Semel still searches that I, she, we, are not 'the classical lamb to the slaughter'?

The fear that I would not have lasted, even one day, was always present. None of your 'survivors as indomitable spirits' discourse. Certainly no 'luck of the survivor' for me. I knew we were being lied to.

Me? An 'earth-smelling *sabra*'?

Far away from that evening light, new dia-sporas, new exiles, am I still afraid?

2

What did I need to know?

Scrutinising Israeli discourses of *gevurah*, and of 'new Hebrews', I, who was never a fighter, what did I need to know?

Was I trying to still the Jewish voice, crying salty tears in my head every night before going to sleep, the voice which said 'had you been there, you would not have been saved'? Am I still trying to still that voice?

Loving something so badly that all you can see is its faults – is this Israel for me? Did I need (research as *necessity*) to put the crystal ball that is Israel up to the light to detect all the air bubbles, all the defects, so as to justify leaving it? Leaving Father and Mother? Leaving that evening light?

3

Have I ever left? Or do I carry home on my back, snailing my way across the old-new continent of Europe, where our journeys began?

Split subjectivities – neither a daughter of survivors nor a 'new Hebrew'.

Or, in leaving home (the home I carry with me wherever I go), have I returned to the dia-spora of Mother's youth?

> Coming back to... Dorna is like coming home. It feels like you have never left Dorna, like (Mother) had never left it. Yet every waking moment you bless her for not having stayed behind... (Lentin, 1989: 23)

Home on my back. Triple exile – Bukovina as home, Jerusalem as home, Dublin as home. Is the journey coming to a bumpy, abrupt end? Is exile my bumpy, abrupt end?

Or are journey's ends new beginnings? Beginnings from which to speak in many voices, not only those of the sociologist and the 'mere woman', but those of Bukovina, of Mount Carmel, of Jerusalem, of Dublin.

Layers upon layers of exile.

Exilic Jew celebrating her Israeliness, 'new Hebrew' woman celebrating her (m)otherness in the exiles of her later life.

4

Where did the journey begin?

When was the first time you remember being told about there? Was it Grossonkel Adolf or Grosstante Helene who first spoke about there and when they saw you listening, stopped talking...?

> The word Dorna rang golden on their lips but other words, *Tate, Gross-mutter*, Transnistria, *Tod*, were only whispers. Lost and poor... they replayed a solitary board game in Oma's glass-panelled room, passing

the code words cautiously, hoping their Israeli-born grandchildren wouldn't pick up the clues. (Lentin, 1989: 12)

And what about the fear? Am I still trying to still the frightened child, the child who read every Shoah book she could lay her hands on? (My brothers never asked). Am I still afraid?

Tempting to bring this to a closure and speak of journey's end(s). But the Shoah is a story without a closure, a story without redemption. A very 'non-Christian' tale.

It is still 'a howl – unheard'.

Do I hear it at all? Has my 'new Hebrew' subjectivity silenced the 'shout in our direction without a sound reaching us'? (Delbo, 1995: 33)

Or has my daughterhood allowed me to see the tears rolling silently on the cheeks of those who were saved, and to wipe them lovingly?

And to cry my own salty tears for the *gevurah,* not of the Ghetto fighters, but of mothers, holding a child's hand on the way to the gas chambers, whispering hoarsely, 'Don't worry, little one, Mother is here with you'.

5

Journeys end wherever we are. Many endings.

I think I know now what I needed to know when I embarked on the journey which began in 1984 in Bukovina.

Or in 1944 in Haifa, at the end of that war, before all the other wars of my life.

Or in 1992, with the conversations with my Israeli sisters-daughters, about our beloved country, the home we carry on our backs, our imperfect crystal ball.

I needed to put words to the pain that was my beloved country, my beloved evening light. The light which darkened our past, seeking to reinvent it, erasing the hurt of the code words passed cautiously in Grandmother's glass-panelled room.

I needed to have my Jewish exilic past returned to me, my European maiden name returned to me.

And I needed to forgive my Israel for darkening the light.

And to be forgiven – for leaving the only home I have never left.

Even in exile.

If I forget thee oh Jerusalem, oh Dorna, oh Transnistria,
may I forget my past
my home
my exile
my pain, the depth of my sorrows.

BIBLIOGRAPHY*

Abdo, Nahla and Nira Yuval-Davis. 1995. 'Palestine, Israel and the Zionist settler project', in Daiva Stasiulis and Nira Yuval-Davis (eds.) *Unsettling Settler
Societies: Articulations of Gender, Race, Ethnicity and Class*. London: Sage.

Adler, Rachel. 1991. 'A question of boundaries: towards a Jewish feminist
theology of self and other'. *Tikkun*, vol. 6 / 3: 43–6.

Adorno, Theodor W. 1949. 'After Auschwitz', in Theodor W. Adorno, *Negative Dialectics*, New York: Continuum (1973).

——— 1962. 'Commitment', in A. Arato and E. Gebhardt (eds.) *The Essential
Frankfurt School Reader*, New York: Continuum (1982).

——— 1965. 'Engagement', in Theodor W. Adorno, *Noten zur Literatur III*,
Frankfurt am Main: Suhrkamp Verlag.

Ahmed, Leila. 1982. 'Western ethnocentrism and perceptions of the harem'.
Feminist Studies, vol. 8 / 3: 521–533.

Ahronson, Shlomo. 1994. 'Hahistorionim hachadashim ve'etgar haShoah
(The new historians and the Shoah challenge)'. *Ha'aretz Magazine*, 24
June: 52.

Aini, Lea. 1988. *Dyokan* (Portrait). Tel Aviv: Hakibbutz Hameuchad.

——— 1991. *Giborei Kayiz* (Sea-Horses' Race). Tel Aviv: Siman Kria, Hakibbutz Hameuchad.

——— 1991. *Keisarit Hapirion Hamedumé* (Empress of the Imagined Fertility). Tel Aviv: Siman Kria, Hakibbutz Hameuchad.

——— 1992. *Geut Hakhol* (Sand Tide). Tel Aviv: Siman Kria, Hakibbutz
Hameuchad.

——— 1995. *Mishehi Muchracha Lihiyot Kan* (Someone Must be Here). Tel
Aviv: Siman Kria, Hakibbutz Hameuchad.

* When citing Hebrew book titles, I transliterate the Hebrew title as phonetically as possible. I then cite in brackets the English version (which is not always a direct translation) as cited by the publisher in the copyright page. When there is no English version,
I translate the title myself. Citing Hebrew journal, magazine or newspaper articles, I
transliterate the titles and then translate them myself.

——— 1997. *Hardufim: Sipurim Mur'alim al Ahava* (Oleanders or Poisoned Stories about Love). Tel Aviv: Zmora-Bitan Publishers.

——— 1999. *Ashtoret.* Tel Aviv: Zmora-Bitan Publishers.

Ainsztein, Reuben. 1974. *Jewish Resistance in Nazi-Occupied Europe.* London: Elek.

Alcoff, Linda 1988. 'Cultural feminism versus post-structuralism: the identity crisis in feminist theory'. *Signs,* vol. 13 / 3: 405–436.

Aleksandrowicz, Dov. 1973. 'Children of concentration camp survivors'. *Yearbook of the International Association for Child Psychiatry and Allied Professions,* vol. 2: 385–394.

Almog, Oz. 1997. *Hatsabar: Dyokan* (The Sabra: A Profile). Tel Aviv: Am Oved.

Aloni, Shulamit. 1976. *Nashim Kivnei Adam* (Women as Human Beings). Jerusalem: Keter.

Anderson, Benedict. 1983. *Imagined Communities: Reflections on the Origin and Spread of Nationalism.* London: Verso.

Antisemitism World Report. 1995. London: The Institute of Jewish Affairs and the American Jewish Committee.

Appelfeld, Aharon. 1965. *Kfor al Haaretz* (Frost on the Ground). Tel Aviv: Masada.

——— 1999. *Sipur Haim* (The Story of a Life). Jerusalem: Keter.

Arad, Yitzhak. (ed.). 1978. Aba Kovner, in a pamphlet read at a meeting of the Pioneering Youth in Vilna, 1 January 1942. *Hashoah Bete'ud* (The Shoah in Docomentation). Jerusalem: Yad Vashem.

Arad, Yitzhak, Yisrael Gutman and Abraham Margolit. 1981. *Documents on the Holocaust: Selected Sources on the Destruction of the Jews of Germany and Austria, Poland and the Soviet Union.* Oxford: Pergamon Press.

Arendt, Hannah. 1956. *Eichmann in Jerusalem: A Report on the Banality of Evil.* New York: The Viking Press.

——— 1961. *Between Past and Future.* New York: The Viking Press.

Artzi, Yitzhak and Nava Semel. 1999. *Davka Zioni* (Glad to be a Zionist). Tel Aviv: Yediot Aharonot.

Ayalon, Ofra. 1981. *HaIsraelim* (The Israelis). Tel Aviv: Adam.

Bar El, Adina. 1992. *Hem Yaru Gam Ba'Orvim* (They Shot The Crows Too). Tel Aviv: Am Oved.

Bar On, Dan. 1994. *Bein Pachad Letikva: Sipurei Haim Shel Khamesh Mishpachot Nitsolei Shoah, Shlosha Dorot Bamishpacha* (Fear and Hope). Tel Aviv: Beit Lochamei Hagetaot, Hakibbutz Hameuchad.

Barkay, Tamar and Gal Levy. 1999. 'Kedma school', in Adi Ofir (ed.) *Fifty to Forty-Eight: Critical Moments in the History of the State of Israel.* Special issue of *Theory and Criticism,* vols. 12-13: 433–40.

Barocas, H. and Barocas, C. 1979. 'Wounds of the fathers: the next generation of Holocaust victims'. *International Review of Psychoanalysis,* vol. 6: 331–41.

Barrett, Michèle and Anne Phillips (eds.) 1992. *Destabilizing Theory: Contemporary Feminist Debates.* Cambridge: Polity Press.

Barth, Frederic. 1969. *Ethnic Groups and Boundaries.* London: Allen and Unwin.

Bauer, Yehudah (ed.). 1989b. *Remembering the Future: Working Papers and Addenda.* Oxford: Pergamon Press.

———— 1978. *The Holocaust in Historical Perspective*. London: Sheldon Press.

———— 1980. *The Jewish Emergence from Powerlessness*. London: MacMillan.

———— 1982. *A History of the Holocaust*. New York: Franklin Watts.

———— 1989. *Out of the Ashes: The Impact of American Jews on Post-Holocaust European Jewry*. Oxford: Pergamon Press.

———— 1993. 'Auschwitz haya be'43, lo be'93 (Auschwitz was in '43, not in '93)'. *Ha'aretz* , 30 April: B5.

———— 1994a. *Jews for Sale? Nazi-Jewish Negotiations*. New Haven, London: Yale University Press.

———— 1994b. 'Ani mamshikh lefakhed (I am still afraid)'. *Ha'aretz Magazine*, 22 July: 35–64.

———— 1994c. 'HaShoah adayin kan (The Shoah is still here)'. *Ha'aretz* , 22 April: 8.

Bauman, Zygmunt. 1989. *Modernity and the Holocaust*. Cambridge: Polity Press.

———— 1991. *Modernity and Ambivalence*. Cambridge: Polity Press.

Baumel, Judith Tydor. 1998. '"Lezikhron olam" – hanzakhat haShoah biyedey haprat vehakehila' ("For ever" – Individual and communal Shoah commemoration'), in Yoel Rappel (ed). *Zikaron Samui, Zikaron Galui: Toda'at HaShoah Bimdinat Israel* (Memory and Awareness of the Holocaust in Israel), Tel Yitzhak: Masu'a and the Ministry of Defence Publishing House.

———— 1999a. *Double Jeopardy: Gender and the Holocaust*. London: Valentine Mitchell.

———— 1999b. 'Women's agency and survival strategies during the Holocaust', *Women's Studies International Forum*, vol. 22 / 3: 329–347.

Ben Amotz, Dan. 1968. *Lizkor ve-lishkoach* (Remember and Forget). Tel Aviv: Amikam.

———— and Netiva Ben Yehuda. 1972, 1982. *Milon LeIvrit Meduberet, Aleph u'vet* (Dicionary of Colloquial Hebrew, Vol A and Vol B). Tel Aviv: Zmora-Bitan.

———— 1973. *Lo Sam Zayin* (Don't Give a Fuck). Tel Aviv: Bitan.

Ben Dor, Orna. 1984. *Sipura Shel Kol Isha* (Everywoman's Story). 25 min, 16 mm. Graduation film, Tel Aviv University Film and Television Studies.

———— 1986. *Mania Shochat: Yoman Massa* (Mania Shochat: Travel Log). 45 min, 16 mm. Produced for Israel Broadcasting Authority (IBA).

———— 1988. *Biglal Hamilchama Hahi* (*Because of That War*). Documentary film, 90 min, 16 mm.

———— and Daphna Kaplanski. 1988. *Shever Anan* (Cloud Burst). 60 min, 16 mm. Film directed by Orna Ben Dor and produced by Daphna Kaplanski for Israel Television, first shown in June 1989.

———— 1991. *Sarah*. 72 min, 16 mm. Produced for IBA.

———— 1992. *Buba Yemima* (The Puppet Yemima). 90 sec, 35 mm. Commercial for International Women's Day, 1992.

———— 1993. *Shoah Tova* (Good Shoah). Feature film, 25 min, 16 mm.

———— 1994. *Erez Hadasha* (*Newland*). Feature film, 107 min, 35 mm. Produced by Sharir Magicfilm.

Ben Eliezer, Uri. 1995. *Derech Hakavenet: Hivazruto shel Hamilitarism HaIsraeli 1936–1956* (Through the Rifle-Sight: the Construction of Israeli Militarism 1936–1956). Tel Aviv: Dvir.

Ben Gurion, David. 1949. *Labour Party Archives,* 22-23 July, 1949.

——— 1955. 'Tsav Tel Hai (The legacy of Tel Hai)'. Speech made at a youth conference on the grave of Trumpeldor and his colleagues, 1943.

Ben Natan, Naomi. 1986. *Mary Khas.* Film.

——— 1988a. *40 Jahre Israel* (40 Years to Israel). Film produced for ZDF.

——— 1988b. *The State of Israel vs. John Ivan Demjanjuk.* 50 min, Beta SP. Produced for NOS, Holland.

——— 1992. *Born in Berlin: Three Women.* 85 min, Beta SP. Produced for IBA.

——— 1995. *Hachakira* (The Investigation). Beta SP. Produced by Belfilms.

Ben Simon, Daniel. 1997. *Eretz Akheret – Nitzahon Hashulayim: Eich Karas Hasmol Veala Hayamin?* (Another Country – The Victory of the Margins: How did the Left Collapse and the Right Gain?) Tel Aviv: Arieh Nir Publishing.

Benvenisti, Meron. 1994. 'Kir haneyar (The paper wall)'. *Ha'aretz,* 23 September: 8.

——— 1997. 'Hamapa HaIvrit (The Hebrew map)', *Theory and Criticism,* vol. 11: 7-30.

Ben-Yehuda, Nachman. 1995. *The Masada Myth: Collective Memory and Mythmaking in Israel.* Madison: University of Wisconsin Press.

Ben Yehuda, Netiva. 1981. *1948 – Bein Hasphirot* (1948 – Between Calendars). Jerusalem: Keter.

Bergmann, Martin S. and Milton E. Jucovy. 1982. 'Prelude', in Bergmann, Martin S. and Milton E. Jucovy. (eds.) *Generations of the Holocaust.* New York: Columbia University Press.

Berkovich, Nitsa. 1993. 'Imahut kimesima le'umit (Motherhood as a national mission)'. *Noga,* no. 27: 24–7.

Bernstein, Deborah S. (ed.) 1992. *Pioneers and Homemakers.* Albany, New York: SUNY Press.

——— 1993. '"Bein haisha-ha'adam uvein eshet habayit": isha umishpacha betsibur hapoalim hayehudi haironi bitkufat hayishuv (Between "woman-as person" and "housewife": woman and family in the Jewish urban worker population during the Yishuv period)', in Uri Ram (ed.) *Hachevra HaIsraelit: Hebetim Bikorti'im* (Israeli Society: Critical Perspectives). Tel Aviv: Breirot Publishers.

Bet Zvi, Shabtai B. 1977. *HaZionut Hapost Ugandit Bemashber HaShoah* (Post-Ugandan Zionism and the Shoah Crisis). Tel Aviv: Bronfman.

Bhabha, Homi K. 1984. 'Of mimicry and men: the ambivalence of colonial discourse', *October,* no. 28: 125–133.

——— 1994. *The Location of Culture.* London: Routledge.

Bialik, Haim Nachman. 1960. 'Metei midbar (The dead of the desert)'. First published 1902. 'Ir hahareiga (The city of slaughter)'. First published in 1904. In Haim Nachman Bialik. *Kitvei H.N. Bialik* (Collected Writings of H.N.Bialik). Tel Aviv: Dvir.

Bienstock, B.E. 1988. 'Daughters and Granddaughters of Female Concentration Camp Survivors: Mother-Daughter Relationship'. Unpublished PhD Thesis, Florida Institute of Technology, School of Psychology.

Bijaoui-Fogel, Sylvie. 1992. 'From revolution to motherhood: the case of women in the kibbutz, 1910–1948', in Deborah S. Bernstein (ed.) *Pioneers and Homemakers.* Albany, New York: SUNY Press.

Bilski, Liora. 1999. 'The Kästner trial', in Adi Ofir (ed.) *Fifty to Forty-Eight: Critical Moments in the History of the State of Israel.* Special issue of *Theory and Criticism,* vols. 12-13: 125–35.

Bloom, Anne R. 1991. 'Women in the defence forces'. In Barbara Swirski and Marylin P. Safir (eds.) *Calling the Equality Bluff: Women in Israel.* New York: Pergamon Press.

Blovstein, Rachel (Rachel). 1950. 'El artzi (To my country)' (1921) and 'Ve'ulai (And perhaps)' (1922), in Rachel Blovsetin. *Shirat Rachel (Rahcel's Poetry).* Tel Aviv: Davar.

Bock, Gisela. 1993. 'Racism and sexism in Nazi Germany: motherhood, compulsory sterilisation and the state', in Carol Rittner and John K. Roth (eds.) *Different Voices: Women and the Holocaust.* New York: Paragon House.

Boldo, Bella. 1983. 'Dor Sheni Lashoah (The Second-generation to the Shoah)'. Unpublished MA dissertation, Department of Sociology and Anthropology, Haifa University.

Bondi, Ruth. 1975. 'Belev hamizrach (At the heart of the orient)', in Ruth Bondi. *Lefeta Belev Hamizrach* (Suddenly, at the Heart of the Orient). Tel Aviv.

——— 1997. *Shevarim Shlemim* (Whole Fractures). Tel Aviv: Gevanim.

Boyarin, Daniel. 1997a. *Unheroic Conduct: the Rise of Heterosexuality and the Invention of the Jewish Man.* Berkeley: University of California Press.

——— 1997b. 'Neshef hamaseikhot hacoloniali: Zionut, migdar, khikui (Colonial drag: Zionism, gender and mimicry)' *Theory and Criticism,* vol. 11: 123–44.

——— 1997c. 'Masada or Yavneh: gender and the arts of Jewish resistance', in Jonathan Boyarin and Daniel Boyarin (eds.) *Jews and Other Differences: The New Jewish Cultural Studies.* Minneapolis: University of Minnesota Press.

Brod, Harry. 1998. 'Of mice and supermen: images of Jewish masculinity', in Michael S. Kimmel and Michael A. Messner (eds.) *Men's Lives.* Boston: Allyn and Bacon.

Brog, Muly. 1996. 'Merosh Metsada ad lev haghetto: hamytos kehistoria (from the top of Masada to the heart of the ghetto: myth as history)', in David Ohana and Robert S. Wistrich (eds.) *Mytos veZikaron* (Myth and Memory: Transfigurations of Israeli Consciousness). Jerusalem: Van Leer Jerusalem Institute, Hakibbutz Hameuchad.

Bronowsky, Yoram. 1995. 'Eich nolda ha'alila? (how was the plot born?)'. *Ha'aretz,* 18 August: B8.

Bruner B. and Segev, Tom. 1995. *Hamillion Hashevi'i* (The Seventh Million). Two-part documentary for television, broadcast on Israel Television, August, 1995.

Burg, Avraham. 1994. 'Lama atem son'im tiulim? (Why do you hate hikes?)' *Haaretz Magazine,* 27 May: 61.

——— 1999. 'Everyone's frog', *Ha'aretz Book Magazine,* 17 February 1999: 6.

Celan, Paul. 1968. '*Ansprache*'. In Paul Celan, *Ausgewählte Gedichte.* Frankfurt am Main: Suhrkamp Verlag.

Chodorow, Nancy. 1978. *The Reproduction of Mothering.* Berkeley: University of California Press.

Cohen, Yaacov. 1903. 'Birionim (Hooligans)', in Yaacov Cohen, *Collected Writings*: 86–7. Bern.

Cohn, C. 1987. 'Sex and death in the rational world of defense intellectuals'. *Signs*, vol. 12: 687–718.

Connell, Robert W. 1987. *Gender and Power*. Cambridge: Polity Press.

――― 1994. 'The state, gender and sexual politics: theory and appraisal', in L.H. Radtke and H.J. Stam (eds.) *Power/Gender: Social Relations in Theory and Practice*. London: Sage Publications.

Danieli, Yael. 1980. 'Families of survivors of the Nazi Holocaust: some long and short term effects', in N. Milgram (ed.). *Psychological Stress and Adjustment in Time of War and Peace*. Washington, D.C.: Hemisphere Publications.

――― 1982. 'Countertransference in the treatment and study of Nazi Holocaust survivors and their children'. *Victimology: an International Journal*, vol. 5 / 3–4.

Dankner, Amnon. 1992. *Dan Ben Amotz*. Jerusalem: Keter.

Dasburg, Haim. 1987. 'Hachevra haIsraelit mul trauma meurgenet, o: hametapel mul hanitsol' (Israeli society confronting organised trauma: the therapist confronting the survivor)'. *Sichot*, vol. 1 / 2: 98–103.

Davidson, Shamai. 1972. 'The treatment of Holocaust survivors', in Shamai Davidson (ed.) *Spheres of Psychotherapeutic Activity*. Jerusalem: Medical Department, Kupat Cholim Centre.

――― 1980. 'Transgenerational transmission in the families of Holocaust survivors'. *International Journal of Family Psychiatry*, vol. 1 / 1: 95–112.

――― 1981. 'Nitsolei hashoah umishpachoteihem: nisayon clini psychotherapeuti (Clinical and psychotherapeutic experience with survivors and their families)'. *Rofe Hamishpacha*, vol. 6 / 2: 313–20.

――― 1985. 'Bereavement in Israel from war, Holocaust and terror'. *Cruse Academic Papers* no. 4. Richmond, England.

Dawidowicz, Lucy. 1975. *The War Against the Jews 1933–1945*. Harmondsworth: Penguin.

Dayan, Yael. 1961. *Envy the Frightened*. London: Weidenfeld and Nicolson.

――― 1967. *Sinai, Yuli 1967* (*Sinai, July 1967*). Tel Aviv: Am Oved.

De Beauvoir, Simone. 1949, 1993. *The Second Sex*. Harmondsworth: Penguin.

Delbo, Charlotte. 1995. *Auschwitz and After*. New Haven and London: Yale University Press.

Derrida, Jacques. 1978. *Writing and Difference*. London: Routledge.

Doane, Mary Anne. 1987. 'The "woman's film": possession and address', in Christine Gledhill (ed.) *Home is Where the Heart Is: Studies in Melodrama and the Woman's Film*. London: BFI Publishing.

Dror, Zvi. (ed.). 1984. *Dapei Edut* (*Testimonies of Survival: 96 Personal Interviews from Members of Kibbutz Lochamei Hagetaot*). Kibbutz Lochamei Hagetaot: Beit Lochamei Hagetaot, Hakibbutz Hameuchad.

――― 1992. *Hem Hayu Sham: Bimchitsat She'erit Hapleita* (They Were There: With the Remnant of the Deliverance). Tel Aviv: Hakibbutz Hameuchad.

Dubnow, Simon. 1956. *Divrei Yemei Am Olam* (A General History of the Jewish People). Tel Aviv: Dvir.

Duvdevani, Shmulik. 1994. 'Hapurim spiel haZioni' (The Zionist masquerade'). *Ma'ariv*.

Dvorzky, Mark. 1956. 'She'erit hapleita beIsrael (The remnant to the deliverance in Israel)'. *Gesher*, vol. 1: 83–115.

Dworkin, Andrea. 1994. 'The unremembered: searching for women at the Holocaust Memorial Museum'. *Ms Magazine,* November/December 1994.

Ehrlich, Avishai. 1993. 'Chevra bemilchama: hasichsuch hale'umi vehamivne hachevrati' (A society at war: the national conflict and the social structure)', in Uri Ram (ed.) *Hachevra HaIsraelit: Hebetim Bikorti'im (Israeli Society: Critical Perspectives).* Tel Aviv: Breirot Publishers.

Eldar, Akiva. 1994. 'Dor sheni laShoah? Ein davar kazeh. (Second-generation to the Shoah? There isn't such a thing)'. *Ha'aretz,* 7 October: B7.

Elkana, Yehudah. 1988. 'Bizechut hashichecha (In favour of forgetting)'. *Ha'aretz,* 2 March: 13.

Elon, Amos. 1971. *The Israelis: Founders and Sons.* New York: Bantam Books.

El-Or, Tamar. 1998. *Bepessach Haba* (Next Pessach: Literacy and Identity of Young Religious Zionist Women.) Tel Aviv: Am Oved.

Elshtain, Jean B. 1981. *Public Man, Private Woman.* Princeton, New Jersey: Princeton University Press.

Enloe, Cynthia. 1983. *Does Khaki Become You? The Militarisation of Women's Lives.* London: Pluto Press.

Epstein, Helen. 1979. *Children of the Holocaust: Conversations with Sons and Daughters of Survivors.* New York: Penguin Books.

Eshkoli, Hava. 1994. *Elem* (Muteness – Mapai and the Shoah 1939–1942). Jerusalem: Yad Yizhak Ben-Zvi.

Evron, Boaz. 1996. 'Medinah kehilchata (A proper state)'. *Iton 77,* 1996: 20–1.

Ezrahi, Sidra Dekoven. 1980. *By Words Alone: The Holocaust in Literature.* Chicago: Chicago University Press.

Falk, A. 1990. 'History, culture and psychoanalysis'. *Mind and Human Interaction,* vol. 1, 3: 5–6.

——— 1991. 'Biglal haevel shelo ubad: beirur musagim (Because of the unworked-through mourning: terminology)'. *Davar,* 19 March.

Farrago, Uri. 1982. 'Toda'at haShoah bekerev no'ar lomed beIsrael tav shin mem gimmel (Shoah awareness among Israeli school students, 1982)'. *Dapim Lecheker Tekufat Hashoah,* vol. 3: 159–78.

Fein, Helen. 1979. *Accounting for Genocide: National Response and Jewish Victimization during the Holocaust.* New York: Free Press.

——— 1987. 'Introduction', in Helen Fein (ed.) *The Persistent Question: Sociological Perspectives and Social Contexts of Modern Antisemitism.* Berlin and New York: Walter de Gruyter.

Feldman, Yael. 1990. 'Feminism under siege: the vicarious selves of Israeli women writers'. *Prooftexts,* vol. 10 / 3: 493–514.

——— 1992. 'Whose story is it, anyway? Ideology and psychology in the representation of the Shoah in Israeli literature', in Saul Friedländer (ed.) *Probing the Limits of Representation: Nazism and the 'Final Solution'.* Cambridge, Mass: Harvard University Press.

Felman, Shoshana and Dori Laub. 1992. *Testimony: Crises of Witnessing in Literature, Psychoanalysis and History.* New York and London: Routledge.

Felman, Shoshana. 1993. 'Textuality and the riddle of bisexuality', in Shoshana Felman, *What Does a Woman Want? Reading and Sexual Difference.* Baltimore and London: The Johns Hopkins University Press.

Fenelon, Fania. 1981. *Playing for Time.* New York: Athenaeum.

Fercek, Ronnie and Uri Klein. 1994. 'Yomanim Palestinai'im (Palestinian diaries)'. *Haaretz*, 13 April:B8–9.

Fogelman, E. and B. Savran. 1979. 'Therapeutic groups for children of Holocaust survivors'. *International Journal of Group Psychotherapy*, vol. 29: 211–36.

Foucault, Michel. 1967. *Madness and Civilization*. London: Tavistock.

——— 1973. *The Birth of the Clinic*. London: Tavistock.

——— 1977. *Discipline and Punish: the Birth of the Prison*. London: Tavistock.

Fox, Tamar. 1999. *Inherited Memories: Israeli Children of Holocaust Survivors*. London: Cassells.

Fox-Genovese, Elizabeth. 1994. 'Difference, diversity, and divisions in an agenda for the women's movement', in Gay Young and Bette J. Dickerson (eds.) *Color, Class and Country: Experiences of Gender*. London: Zed Books.

Fresco, Nadine. 1984. 'Remembering the Unknown'. *International Review of Psychoanalysis*, vol. 11.

Freud, Sigmund. 1925. 'Narration', in James Strachey (ed.) *The Standard Edition of the Complete Psychological Works of Sigmund Freud*. Vol. 19. London: Hogarth, 1953–73.

——— 1958. 'The uncanny', in Benjamin Nelson (ed.) *On Creativity and the Unconscious*. New York: Harper and Row.

Friedländer, Saul. 1978. *History and Psychoanalysis: An Inquiry into the Possibilities of Psychohistory*. New York: Holmes and Meier.

——— 1982. *Kitsch UMavet: Al Hishtakfut HaNazism* (Reflections of Nazism: An Essay on Kitsch and Death). Jerusalem: Keter.

——— 1988. 'Roundtable discussion', in Berel Lang (ed.) *Writing and the Holocaust*. New York: Holmes and Meier.

——— 1992. (ed.) *Probing the Limits of Representation: Nazism and the 'Final Solution'*. London and Cambridge: Harvard University Press.

——— 1997. *Nazi Germany and the Jews. Vol. I: The Years of Persecution, 1993–39*. London: Widenfeld and Nicolson.

Fuchs, A. 1995. *HaShoah Bimekorot Rabbani'im* (The Shoah in Rabbinical Sources). Tel Aviv: Hotsa'at Hamechaber.

Fuchs, Esther. 1986. *Israeli Mythogynies*. Albany: State University of New York Press.

——— 1999. *Women and the Holocaust: Narrative and Representation*. Lanhan: University Press of America.

Funkenstein, Amos. 1993. 'The incomprehensible catastrophe: memory and narrative', in Ruthellen Josselson and Amia Lieblich (eds.) *The Narrative Study of Lives*, Vol. 1. Newbury Park: Sage.

Gai, Karmit. 1992. *Masa Leyad Hannah* (Back to Yad Hannah). Tel Aviv: Am Oved.

——— 1995. *Hamalka Nas'a Baottobus: Rovina veHabimah* (Hanna Rovina). Tel Aviv: Am Oved.

Galili, Israel. 1943. *Work Diary*. Tel Aviv: Galili Archive.

Gampel, Yolanda. 1982. 'A metapsychological assessment based on an analysis of a survivor's child', in Martin S. Bergmann and Milton E Jucovy (eds.) *Generations of the Holocaust*. New York: Columbia University Press.

Gashmit, Sarah. 1988. 'Hanoar chunach al yachas shel zilzul klapei haShoah (The youth has been educated to despise the Shoah)'. *Zakhor*, 10: 159–63.

Gavish, Ofer. 1998. 'Shir al sapat hapsychiater: shirei Shoah shenichtevu ba'aretz (A song on the Psychiatrist's couch: Israeli Shoah songs)', in Yoel Rappel (ed.) *Zikaron Samui, Zikaron Galui: Toda'at HaShoah Bimdinat Israel* (Memory and Awareness of the Holocaust in Israel), Tel Yitzhak: Masu'a and the Ministry of Defence Publishing House.

Ghanem, As'ad, Nadim Rouhana and Oren Yiftachel. 1998. 'Questioning "ethnic demoncracy"', *Israel Studies*, vol. 3 / 2: 253–267.

Giddens, Anthony. 1984. *The Constitution of Society*. Cambridge: Polity Press.

Gil, B.A. 1957. *Settlement of New Immigrants in Israel 1948–1953*. Jerusalem.

Gilbert, Martin. 1985. *The Holocaust: A History of the Jews of Europe during the Second World War.* New York: Holt, Rinehart and Winston.

Gilead, Zerubavel (ed.). 1957. *Sefer Hapalmach* (The Palmach Book). Tel Aviv: Ma'arachot.

Gilligan, Carol. 1982, in *A Different Voice*. Cambridge, Mass: Harvard University Press.

Gluzman, Michael. 1997. 'Hakmiha leheterosexualiut: Zionut uminiut beAltneuland (Longing for heterosexuality: Zionism and sexuality in Altneuland)', *Theory and Criticism*, vol. 11: 145–162.

Goffman, Erving. 1968. *Stigma: Notes on the Management of Spoilt Identity*. Harmondsworth: Penguin Books.

——— 1987. 'The arrangement between the sexes', in Mary Jo Deegan and Michael Hill (eds.) *Women and Symbolic Interaction*. London: Allen and Unwin.

Goldenberg, Myrna. 1990. 'Different horrors, same hell: women remembering the Holocaust', in Roger S. Gottlieb (ed.) *Thinking the Unthinkable: Meanings of the Holocaust*. New York: Paulist Press.

Goldhagen, Daniel J. 1995. *Hitler's Willing Executioners: Ordinary Germans and the Holocaust*. New York: A. Knopf.

Golomb, Eliahu. 1953. Speech on 18 January 1944, Hakibbutz Hameuchad conference, in Eliahu Golomb, *Hevyon Az* (Fierce Hiding) *Vol 2*. Tel Aviv: Ayanot.

Gonen, Jay. 1976. *A Psycho-History of Zionism*. New York: Meridian.

Gonen, Nitza. 1994. *Dor Sheni* (Second-generation). Video. Produced by Erez Moledet Production, producer Ido Bahat, director Nitza Gonen. Broadcast on Israel Television second channel, Yom HaShoah, 1994.

Gover, Yerach. 1996. 'Hasiach hatarbuti keneged atsmo: ideologia vetarbut beIsrael (Cultural discourse against itself: ideology and culture in Israel)'. *Iton 77*, no. 196: 28–30.

Govrin, Nurit. 1998. 'Foreword', in Nava Semel, *Kova Zekhukhit* (A Hat of Glass). Tel Aviv: Sifriat Poalim.

Grodzinsky, Yosef. 1994a. 'Lehilachem baZionizatsia shel haShoah (Fighting the Zionisation of the Shoah)'. *Ha'aretz*, 27 May: B5.

——— 1994b. 'Historionim o to'amlanim? (Historians or propagandists?)' *Ha'aretz*, 27 May: B6.

——— 1998. *Khomer Enoshi Tov* (Good Human Material). Or Yehuda: Hed Artzi Publishing.

Grossman, David. 1986. *Ayen Erech: Ahava (See Under: Love)*. Tel Aviv/Jerusalem: Hakibbutz Hameuchad/Keter.

Grunfeld, Uriel. 1995. 'Holocaust, movies and remembrance: the pedagogical challenge'. Unpublished paper, Pennsylvania State University.

Gur, Batia. 1988. *Retsach Beshabat Baboker* (Death on Saturday Morning). Jerusalem: Keter.

——— 1989. *Mavet Bakhug Lesifrut* (Death in the Department of Literature). Jerusalem: Keter.

——— 1991. *Lina Meshutefet: Retsach Bakibbutz* (Cohabitation). Jerusalem: Keter.

——— 1994. *Lo Kach Tearti Li* (Afterbirth). Jerusalem: Keter.

——— 1996. *Hamerchak Hanachon: Retsach Musikali* (Orchestral Murder: a Musical Case). Jerusalem: Keter.

——— 1998. *Even Tachat Even* (Stone for Stone). Jerusalem: Keter.

Guri, Haim. 1963. *Mul Ta HaZkchkchit* (The Glass Cage: The Jerusalem Trial). Tel Aviv: Hakibbutz Hameukhad.

Gutman, Yehudah. (ed.) 1990. *Haencyclopaedia shel HaShoah* (The Shoah Encyclopaedia). Tel Aviv: Sifriat Poalim.

Habas, Bracha. (ed.) 1937. *Meoraot Tarzav* (The 'Events' of 1936). Tel Aviv.

Habibi, Emile. 1986. 'HaShoah shelachem, ha'ason shelanu (Your Shoah, our disaster)'. *Politica*, no. 8: 26–7.

Hacohen, Rina. 1994. *Olim biSe'ara* (Immigrants by Storm). Jerusalem: Yad Yitzhak Ben Zvi Press.

Hadar, Tania. 1975. *Ein Rachamim Acherim* (There is No Other Mercy). Tel Aviv: Hakibbutz Hameuchad.

——— 1991. *Beartsot Hachaim* (In the Lands of the Living). Tel Aviv: Hakibbutz Hameuchad.

Ha'ir, 1995. 'Bazbezani ad me'od (Too wasteful)'. *Ha'ir*, 6 January.

Hammermann, Ilana. 1995. 'Zichronot lo-kru'im (Uninvited memories)'. *Ha'aretz Books*, 30 August: 5.

Haraway, Donna. 1988. 'Situated knowledge: the science question in feminism and the privilege of partial perspective'. *Feminist Studies*, vol. 14: 575–99.

Harding, Sandra. 1987. 'Is there a feminist method?' in Sandra Harding (ed.) *Feminism and Methodology: Social Science Issues*. Bloomington, Indiana: Indiana University Press.

Hartsock, Nancy. 1990. 'Foucault on power; a theory for women?' in Linda Nicholson (ed.) *Feminism/Postmodernism*. London: Routledge.

Hass, Aharon. 1990. *In the Shadow of the Holocaust: The Second-Generation*. Ithaca: Cornell University Press.

Hazan, Yoram. 1987. '"Dor sheni laShoah": Musag besafek ("Second-generation to the Shoah": An arguable term)'. *Sichot*, vol. 1 / 2: 104–7.

Hazelton, Lesley. 1978. *Tsela Adam: Ha'isha Bachevra HaIsraelit* (Israeli Women: The Reality behind the Myths). Jerusalem: Idanim.

Heller, D. 1982. 'Themes of culture and ancestry'. *Psychiatry*, no. 45: 247–261.

Herzl, Theodor. 1896. *Der Judenstaat, Versuch einer modernen Lösung der Judenfrage* (The Jewish State: a Search for a Modern Solution to the Jewish Question). Leipzig, Vienna: M. Breitenstein. English translation by Sylvie d'Avigdor, published 1935. London: Central Office of the Zionist Organisation.

——— 1934. *Sifrei Hayamim – Mivchar Kitvei Herzl* (The Diary – A Selection of Herzl's Writing) *Vol B.* Entry on 29 February 1898. Tel Aviv: Mitzpe.

——— 1936. *Sifrei Hayamim – Mivchar Kitvei Herzl* (*The Diary – A Selection of Herzl's* Writing) *Vol A.* Entries in June 1895. Tel Aviv: Mitzpe.

Hever, Hanan. and Moshe Ron. 1983. *Ve'ein Tichla Lakeravot Velahereg* (Fighting and Killing without End: Political Poetry in the Lebanon War). Tel Aviv: Siman Kria, Hakibbutz Hameuchad.

Hilberg, Raul. 1980. 'Significance of the Holocaust', in Henry Friedlander and Sybil Milton (eds.) *The Holocaust: Ideology, Bureaucracy, and Genocide.* Milwood, New York: Kraus International Publications.

——— 1983. *The Destruction of European Jews.* New York: Holmes and Meier.

——— 1988. 'I was not there', in Berel Lang (ed.) *Writing and the Holocaust.* New York: Holmes and Meier.

——— 1992. *Perpetrators, Victims and Bystanders: The Jewish Catastrophe 1933–1945.* London: Lime Tree.

——— 1995. *Unerbetene Erinnerung Der Weg eine Holocaust-Forschers.* Frankfurt am Main: Fischer.

Horowitz, David. 1998. 'Netanyahu hails ultimate Jewish victory over Nazism', *The Irish Times,* 24 April: 10.

IDF (Israeli Defence Forces). 1976. *Yom Hazikaron laShoah velagevurah* (Remembrance Day to the Shoah and Gevurah). Chief Education Officer, IDF, April 1976.

Ilan, Shachar. 1995. 'Hashavua shekhidesh hofa'ato takhat shem akher (*Hashavua* republished under a different name'). *Ha'aretz,* 28 December: 3.

Iton Tel Aviv, 1991. 'Venish'elet hashe'ela: ha'im lehishaer? (The question is whether to stay?)'. *Yediot Acharonot, Iton Tel Aviv,* 1 February: 7.

Izraeli Dafna, N. 1981. 'The Zionist women's movement in Palestine, 1911–1927: a sociological analysis'. *Signs,* vol. 7 / 1: 87–114.

——— 1984. 'Tnuat hapoalot be'erez Israel mereishita ad 1927 (The Erez Israeli women workers movement from its inception until 1927)', *Katedra,* no. 32: 109–140.

——— 1989. 'Effect Golda Meir' (The Golda Meir effect). *Politica,* July 1988: 44–47.

———, Ariella Friedman and Ruth Shrift. 1982, 1992. *Nashim Bemilkud: Al Matsav Ha'isha BeIsrael* (The Double Bind: Women in Israel). Tel Aviv: Hakibbutz Hameuchad.

Kafri, Yehudit. 1983. *Haziat Gevul* (Border Crossing: Poems from the Lebanon War). Tel Aviv: Sifriat Poalim.

Kaminsky, Marc. 1992. 'Introduction', in Barbara Myerhoff, *Remembered Lives: The Work of Ritual, Storytelling, and Growing Older.* Ann Arbor: The University of Michigan Press.

Kaniuk, Yoram. 1969. *Adam Ben Kelev* (Adam Resurrected). Tel Aviv: Amikam.

Karpel, Dalia. 1995. 'Kach nolad hamilitarism haIsraeli (This was how Israeli militarism came about)'. *Ha'aretz Magazine,* 27 October: 33–38.

——— 1996. 'Al gabam shel hanitsolim (On the back of the survivors)'. *Ha'aretz Magazine,* 31 May: 29–32.

Karpf, Anne. 1996. *The War After.* London: Heinemann.

Katz, Ruth. 1991. 'Jewish and Druze war widows', in Barbara Swirski and Marylin P. Safir (eds.) *Calling the Equality Bluff: Women in Israel.* New York: Pergamon Press.

Katzetnik. 1953. *Beit Habubot* (*House of Dolls*). Tel Aviv: Dvir.

Kemp, Adriana and Hanna Herzog. 1999. 'A "sense of home" in the narratives of Ravensbrük Jewish women survivors', paper presented at the workshop on victims and survivors, 2-3 July 1999, Berlin, Frei Universität Berlin.

Keren, Nili. 1998. 'Masa le'itzuv hazikaron: siurei talmidim lePolin (A journey to the shape of memory: students' journeys to Polans'), in Yoel Rappel (ed). *Zikaron Samui, Zikaron Galui: Toda'at HaShoah Bimdinat Israel* (Memory and Awareness of the Holocaust in Israel), Tel Yitzhak: Masu'a and the Ministry of Defence Publishing House.

Keren, Rivka. 1973. *Kati* (Kati: a Young Girl's Diary). Tel Aviv: Am Oved.

––––– 1986. *Kayitz Atsuv, Kayitz Meushar* (Sad Summer, Happy Summer). Tel Aviv: Shocken.

––––– 1990. *Ta'am Hadevash* (A Taste of Honey). Tel Aviv: Am Oved.

––––– 1992. *Ahava Anusha* (Mortal Love). Tel Aviv: Am Oved.

––––– 1993. *Anatomia shel Nekama* (Anatomy of Revenge). Tel Aviv: Am Oved.

––––– 1995. *Tita Vehasatan* (Tita and the Devil). Tel Aviv: Siman Kria, Hakibbutz Hameuchad.

Khalifa, Sahar. 1978. *Hatsabar* (The Sabra). (Hebrew translation by Salman Maslaha). Jerusalem: Galileo.

Kimmerling, Baruch. 1983. *Zionism and Territory: The Socio-Territorial Dimensions of Zionist Politics.* Berkeley: Institute of International Studies, University of California Press.

––––– 1993a. 'Yachasei medina-chevra beIsrael (The relationship between state and society in Israel)', in Uri Ram (ed). *Hachevra HaIsraelit: Hebetim Bikorti'im* (*Israeli Society:* Critical Perspectives.) Tel Aviv: Breirot Publishers.

––––– 1993b. 'Militarism bahevra haIsraelit (Militarism in Israeli society)'. *Theory and Criticism*, vol. 4: 123–140.

––––– 1994. 'Socharei hacharadot (the anxiety merchants)'. *Ha'aretz Magazine*, 24 June:50–52.

Klein, Hillel. 1972. 'Holocaust survivors in kibbutzim: readaptation and reintegration'. *The Israel Annals of Psychiatry*, vol. 10 / 1: 78–91.

––––– 'Children of the Holocaust: mourning and bereavement', in Anthony, E. James and Cyrille Koupernik. (eds.). *The Child and His Family: The Impact of Disease and Death.* New York: John Wiley.

Klein, Uri. 1995. 'Idun eino shem hamis'chak (Subtlety is not the name of the game)'. *Ha'aretz*, 10 January.

Klepfisz, Irena. 1990a. 'Cherry Plains: I have become a keeper of accounts', and 'Solitary acts', in Irena Klepfisz. *A Few Words in the Mother Tongue: Poems Selected and New 1971–1990.* Portland, Oregon: The Eighth Mountain Press.

––––– 1990b. 'East Jerusalem, 1987', in Irena Klepfisz. *A Few Words in the Mother Tongue: Poems Selected and New 1971–1990.* Portland, Oregon: The Eighth Mountain Press.

––––– 1990c. 'Fradel Schtok', in Irena Klepfisz. *A Few Words in the Mother Tongue: Poems Selected and New 1971–1990.* Portland, Oregon: The Eighth Mountain Press.

Kovner, Aba. 1955. *Panim el Panim: She'at HaEfes* (Face to Face: the Eleventh Hour). Tel Aviv: Sifriat Poalim.

——— 1991. 'Midor ledor (From one generation to the next)'. *Yalkut Moreshet*, no. 50, April 1991: 13–16.

Kristeva, Julia. 1991. *Strangers to Ourselves*. Hemel Hempstead: Harvester Wheatsheaf.

Krystal, Henry. (ed.) 1968. *Massive Psychic Trauma*. New York: International Universities Press.

——— 1978. 'Trauma and affects', in Ruth, S. Eisler et al., (eds.). *Psychoanalytic Study of the Child*, no. 33: 81–116.

Labov, William. 1972. 'The transformation of experience in narrative syntax', in William Labov (ed.). *Language in the Inner City: Studies in the Black English Vernacular*. Philadelphia: University of Pennsylvania Press.

——— 1982. 'Speech action and reaction in personal narrative', in Deborah Tannen (ed.). *Analyzing Discourse: Text and Talk*. Washington, D.C.: Georgetown University Press.

Lagerwey, Mary D. 1998. *Reading Auschwitz*. Walnut Creek: AltaMira Press.

Lamdan, Yitzhak. 1927. *Masada*. Tel Aviv: Dvir.

Langer, Lawrence L. 1975. *The Holocaust and the Literary Imagination*. New Haven: Yale University Press.

——— 1991. *Holocaust Testimonies: The Ruins of Memory*. New Haven: Yale University Press.

Laor, Yitzhak. 1994. 'Halashon hakeru'a (the torn tongue)'. *Ha'aretz*, 19 September: B6–7.

——— 1995. 'Me'ein hakdama (A kind of introduction)', in Yitzhak Laor, *Anu Kotvim Otach Moledet* (Narratives with No Natives: Essays on Israeli Literature). Tel Aviv: Hakibbutz Hameuchad.

——— 1999. 'Akharei shehaShoah hafkha le"Shoah" (After the Shoah became the "Shoah")'. *Haaretz*, 26 June: B14.

Layoun, Mary. 1993. 'Telling spaces: Palestinian women and the engendering of national narratives', in Andrew Parker et al., (eds.) *Nationalisms and Sexualities*. London: Routledge.

Lehman, Arielle. 1993. '*Erez Zion shel neyar: nituach textim utopi'im Zioni'im* (A paper Zion: an analysis of utopian Zionist texts)'. Unpublished paper, Hebrew University, Jerusalem.

Lentin, Ronit. 1976. 'Even hatoim (Stone of claims)'. *Siman Kria*, vol. 6: 109–143.

——— 1978. 'Ani keiver (Like a blindman)'. *Siman Kria*, vol. 8: 275–287.

——— 1982. *Sichot im Nashim Palestiniot* (Conversations with Palestinian Women). Jerusalem: Mifras.

——— 1989. *Night Train to Mother*. Dublin: Attic Press.

——— 1990. *Night Train to Mother*. Pittsburgh: Cleis Press.

——— 1995. *Woman – the Peace Activist who Isn't There: Israeli and Palestinian Women Working for Peace*. Limerick: The Irish Peace Institute Research Centre, University of Limerick.

——— 1996a. 'A *Yiddishe mame* desperately seeking a *mame loshn*: the feminisation of stigma in the relations between Israelis and Holocaust survivors'. *Women's Studies International Forum*, vol. 19 / 1/2: 87–97.

—— 1996b. *Songs on the Death of Children*. Dublin: Poolbeg Press.

—— (ed.) 1997. *Gender and Catastrophe*. London: Zed Books.

—— 1998. 'Israeli and Palestinian women working for peace', in Lois A. Lorentzen and Jennifer Turpin (eds.) *The Women and War Reader*. New York: New York University Press.

—— 1999a. 'The rape of the nation: women narrativising genocide', *Sociological Research Online*, vol. 4 / 2

—— 1999b. 'Because she never let them in...: articulations of diaspora and antisemitic immigration controls in light of present-day immigration restrictions'. Paper presented at the International Sociological Association, Race and Ethnicity Interim Conference, July 1999, Tel Aviv and Jerusalem

Lerner, Motti. 1994. *Mishpat Kästner* (The Kästner Trial). Jerusalem: Or Vatsel, Rashut Hashidur.

Lev, Eleonora. 1989 (reissued 1999). *Sug Mesuyam Shel Yatmut: Edut al Masa* (A Certain Kind of Orphanhood: Report of a Journey). Tel Aviv: Am Oved.

—— 1993. 'Yehudi echad veNazi echad (One Jew and one Nazi)'. *Hadashot*, 3 November: 13.

Levin, Eyal. 1990.*Chromosomim shel Shoah: Rishumei Masa BePolin* (Shoah Chromosomes: Impressions of a Voyage to Poland). Bet El: Sifriat Bet El.

Lezekher Haverim. 1950. Hulata: Hachsharat Hamachanot HaOlim.

Liebman, I. Charles. 1981. 'The Shoah myth in the Israeli society'. *Tfutsot Israel*, vol. 19 / 5–6:101–114.

Liebrecht, Savyon. 1986.*Tapuchim Min Hamidbar* (Apples from the Desert). Jerusalem: Keter.

—— 1987. *Shem Nirdaf* ('Deadline'). Television play, written with Aliza Olmert, Israel Television.

—— 1988. *Susim Al Kvish Geha* (Horses on the Highway). Jerusalem: Keter.

—— 1992. *HaAsistent shel Elohim* ('A Touch of Magic'). Television play. Israel Television.

—— 1992. *Kidonim veOrchide'ot* ('Spears and Orchids'). Television play. Israel Television.

—— 1992. *Sinit Ani Medaberet Eleicha* ('Its Greek to Me', She Said to Him). Jerusalem: Keter.

—— 1995. *Tsarich Sof Lesipur Ahava* (A Love Story Needs an Ending). Jerusalem: Keter.

—— 1998a. *Ish veIsha veIsh* (A Man, A Woman and A Man). Jerusalem: Keter.

—— 1998b. *Sonia Mushkat*. Play, produced by Habimah National Theatre.

—— 2000. *Barvazim* ('Ducks'). Play, produced by Habimah National Theatre.

Lieder, Osnat. 1985. 'Tfisat av ketokpan ve/o kekorban etsel bnei nitsolei Shoah' ('The perception of the father as aggressor and/or victim by children of Shoah survivors'). Unpublished Masters dissertation, Bar Ilan University, Ramat Gan, Israel

Lifton, R.R. 1978. 'Advocacy and corruption in the healing profession', in C.R. Figley (ed). *Stress Disorder among Vietnam Veterans*. New York: Brunner Mazel.

Linden, R. Ruth. 1993. *Making Stories, Making Selves: Feminist Reflections on the Holocaust*. Columbus: Ohio State University Press.

———— 1996. 'Troubling categories I can't think without: reflections on
women in the Holocaust'. *Contemporary Jewry*, vol. 11: 18–33.

Lipstadt, Deborah E. 1993. *Denying the Holocaust: The Growing Assault on
Truth and Memory*. Harmondsworth: Pengiun Books.

———— 1998. 'Why is *The Wall Street Journal* now devaluing women's Holocaust experience?' *Lilith*, vol. 23 / 3: 10–13.

Lloyd, David. 1999. 'Colonial trauma/postcolonial recovery'. Paper presented at the 'Defining Colonies' conference, NUI Galway, June 1999.

Lomsky-Feder, Edna. 1997. 'Sipurei haim shel khayalim meshukhrarim (Life
stories of war veterans: the interplay between personal memory and the
collective memory of war)', *Theory and Criticism*, 11: 59–80.

Lorber, Judith. 1994. *Paradoxes of Gender*. New Haven and London: Yale University Press.

Maimon, Ada. 1972. *Le'orech Haderech: Mivhar Dvarim veIgrot (Along the
Way: a Selection of Writings and Letters)*. Tel Aviv: Am Oved.

Maor, Haim. 1998. 'Hatsabarim shelo halkhu basadot (The *sabras* who did not
walk in the fields)', in Yoel Rappel (ed). *Zikaron Samui, Zikaron Galui: Toda'at
HaShoah Bimdinat Israel* (Memory and Awareness of the Holocaust in
Israel), Tel Yitzhak: Masu'a and the Ministry of Defence Publishing House.

Marcus, Dina. 1986. 'Emotional Features in the Experiences of Motherhood
among Daughters of Holocaust Survivors.' Unpublished M.A. Thesis,
University of Haifa, Department of Psychology.

McVeigh, Robbie. 1992. 'The specificities of Irish racism', *Race and Class*, vol.
33, no. 4.

Meaney, Geraldine. 1991. *Sex and Nation: Women in Irish Culture and Politics*.
Dublin: Attic Press.

Megged, Aharon. 1958, 1989. *Hanna Senesh*. Tel Aviv: Or Am.

———— 1994a. 'Yetser hahit'abdut haIsraeli (The Israeli suicide impulse)'.
Ha'aretz Magazine, 10 June: 27/92.

———— 1994b. ''Erez hadasha: aval ayeh ota erez?' ('Newland, but where is
this land?') *Shishi*, 31 December.

Melman, Yossi. 1994. 'Ani hayiti nishbar (I would have broken down)'.
Ha'aretz, 9 December: B5.

Memmi, Albert. 1967. *The Coloniser and the Colonised* . Boston: Beacon Press.

Milner, Iris. 1994. 'Hatiul hashnati: semel haIsraeliut vehakesher hakadosh
la'adama (The annual hike: the symbol of Israeliness and of the holy link
to the soil)'. *Haaretz Magazine*, 7 May: 20–23.

Minow, Martha. 1990. *Making All the Difference: Inclusion, Exclusion and
American Law*. Ithaca: Cornell University Press.

Mintz, Alan. 1984. *Hurban: Responses to Catastrophe in Hebrew Literature*.
New York: Columbia University Press.

Miran, Reuven. 1993. 'Hanuskha bolelet midai (The formula is too obvious)'. *Haaretz Book Supplement*, 3 November: 6.

Mohanty, Chandra Talpade, Anne Russo and Lourdes Torres (eds.) 1991.
Third World Women and the Politics of Feminism. Bloomington, Indiana:
Indiana University Press.

Morris, Benny. 1987. *The Birth of the Palestinian Refugee Problem
1947–1949*. Cambridge, Mass: Cambridge University Press.

——— 1993. *Israel's Border Wars 1949–1956: Arab Infiltration, Israel's Retaliation and the Countdown to the Suez War*. Oxford: Clarendon Press.

——— 1994. 'Historia obyektivit (Objective history)'. *Ha'aretz Magazine*, 1 July: 40.

Moses, Raphael. 1977. Lecture at Colloquium of Trauma: Jerusalem (Manuscript).

Mosse, George L. 1985. *Nationalism and Sexuality*. New York: Howard Fertig.

——— 1992. 'The Jews and the civil religion of nationalism', in Jehuda Reinharz and George L. Mosse (eds.) *The Impact of Western Nationalisms, Essays dedicated to Walter Z. Laqueur on the Occasion of his 70th Birthday*. London: Sage.

——— 1996. *The Image of Man: The Creation of Modern Masculinity*. New York and Oxford: Oxford University Press.

Myerhoff, Barbara. 1980. 'Re-membered lives'. *Parabola*: vol. 5: 74–77.

——— 1992. '"Life not death in Venice": its second life', in Barbara Myerhoff, *Remembered Lives: The Work of Ritual, Storytelling, and Growing Older*. Ann Arbor: The University of Michigan Press.

Nandy, Ashis. 1983. *The Intimate Enemy: Loss and Recovery of Self under Colonialism*. Delhi, Oxford: Oxford University Press.

Natan, Tiqva. 1982. 'Dor sheni lenitsolei Shoah' (The second-generation in psycho-social studies'). *Dapim Lecheker Tkufat HaShoaha*. Haifa: University of Haifa and Lochamei Hagetaot.

Netanyahu, Binyamin (ed.). 1986. *Terrorism: How the West Can Win*. London: Weidenfeld and Nicolson.

——— 1993. *A Place among the Nations: Israel and the World*. London: Bantam Press.

Nevo, Amos. 1994. 'Achim chorgim (Step brothers)'. *Yediot Acharonot*, 15 April: 12-14, 62.

Niederland, William G. 1968. 'Clinical observations on the "Survivor syndrome": symposium on psychic traumatisation through social catastrophe'. *International Journal of Psychoanalysis*, vol. 49: 313–315.

Niv, Kobi. 1989. 'Le'at, le'at, aval batuach, hevanti (Slowly, slowly but surely, I understood)'. *Politica*, no. 27: 34–5.

Noga. 1993. 'In the Knesset'. *Noga*, no. 25: 3.

——— 1998. 'Kmo retzach al kvod hamishpacha (Like murder in the name of family honour)', *Noga*, no. 35: 32-5 & 38.

Noi, Bilha. 1990. 'Gishot shel yeladim klapei haShoah (Children's attitudes towards the Shoah)'. *Museon haLochamim vehaPartisanim*, no. 7, April 1990:5-19.

Nordau, Max. 1955. 'Muscular Jewry' (first published 1900), in Max Nordau. *Zionist Collection, Vol B*.

Ofer, Dalia. 1993. 'Mishpat Kästner vedimuya shel haShoah batoda'a haIsraelit (The Kästner trial and the Shoah image in the Israeli consciousness)'. *Katedra*, no. 69: 152-9.

——— 1998. 'Gender issues in diaries and testimonies of the ghetto: the case of Warsaw', in Dalia Ofer and Lenore J. Weitzman. *Women in the Holocaust*. New Haven: Yale University Press.

—— and Lenore J. Weitzman. 1998. *Women in the Holocaust*. New Haven: Yale University Press.

Ostrowitz, Rachel. 1996. 'Al hamatsav (The situation)'. *Noga*, no. 30: 9.

Oz, Amos. 1979. *Beor Hatchelet Ha'aza* (Under This Blazing Light). Tel Aviv: Sifriat Poalim.

—— 1983. 'Hitler kvar met, adoni rosh hamemshala (Hitler is dead, Mr Prime Minister)', in Yehudit Kafri (ed.), *Haziat Gevul* (Border Crossing: Poems from the Lebanon War). Tel Aviv: Sifriat Poalim.

Pappe, Ilan. 1994. 'Shiur behistoria chadasha (a lesson in new history)'. *Ha'aretz Magazine*, 24 June: 53–4.

Park, Robert. 1928. 'Human migration and the marginal man'. *American Journal of Sociology*, XXXIII, May 1928: 891–2.

Parker, Andrew, M. Russo, P. Sommer, and P. Yaeger. (eds.) *Nationalisms and Sexualities*. London: Routledge.

Passerini, Luisa. 1992. 'Introduction', in Luisa Passerini (ed.) *International Yearbook of Oral History and Life Stories, Vol. 1 – Memory and Fascism*. Oxford: Oxford University Press.

Personal Narratives Group. 1989. *Interpreting Women's Lives: Feminist Theory and Personal Narratives*. Bloomington, Indiana: Indiana University Press.

Pines, Dinora. 1993. 'The impact of the Holocaust on the second-generation', in Dinora Pines. *A Woman's Unconscious Use of her Body*. London: Virago.

Pinsker, Leon. 1882, 1935. *Auto-Emancipation*. First published in Berlin, 1882. 1935 edition: New York: Masada, Youth Zionist Organization of America.

Porat, Dina. 1986. *Hanhaga Bemilkud* (The Jewish Leadership in Palestine and the Holocaust 1939–1945). Tel Aviv: Am Oved.

Porian, Ronit. 1996. 'Vehigadeta levinkha (And you shalt tell your son)'. *Ha'aretz*: 28 September: B6.

Prat, E. 1993. 'Keshehakahal boche, hakuppa tsocheket (when the public cries, the cash register laughs)'. *Iton Yerushalaim*, 22 October: 36–38.

Rabinowicz, Yoske. 1947. Speech at Hakibbutz Hameuchad executive committee, Na'an, 10 May 1947 (cited in Yablonka, 1994: 58).

Rakoff, V. 1966. 'Long term effects of the concentration camp experience'. *Viewpoints*, no. 1: 17–21.

Ram, Uri (ed.) 1993. *Hachevra HaIsraelit: Hebetim Bikorti'im* (Israeli Society: Critical Perspectives). Tel Aviv: Breirot Publishers.

—— 1993b. 'Hachevra umada hachevra: sociologia mimsadit vesociologia bikortit beIsrael' (Society and social sciences: establishment sociology and critical sociology in Israel'), in Uri Ram (ed.) *Hachevra HaIsraelit: Hebetim Bikorti'im* (Israeli Society: Critical Perspectives). Tel Aviv: Breirot Publishers.

—— 1996. 'Zikaron vezehut: sociologia shel vikuach hahistorionim beIsrael (Memory and identity: a sociology of the historians' debate in Israel)', *Theory and Criticism*, vol. 8: 32-9.

—— 1999. 'Bizkhut hashichecha (The right to forget)', in Adi Ofir (ed) *Fifty to Forty-Eight: Critical Moments in the History of the State of Israel*. Special issue of *Theory and Criticism*, vols. 12-13: 349–357.

Rapoport, Tamar and Tamar El-Or. 1997. 'Cultures of womanhood in Israel: social agencies and gender production'. *Women's Studies International Forum*, vol. 20, 5/6: 573–80.

Rappel, Yoel. (ed.) 1998. *Zikaron Samui, Zikaron Galui: Toda'at HaShoah Bimdinat Israel (Memory and Awareness of the Holocaust in Israel)*, Tel Yitzhak: Masu'a and the Ministry of Defence Publishing House.

––––– (ed.) 1999. *Likrat Masa: Bimkhozot Hazikaron beMizrakh Europa (Landscapes of Memory: a Companion to a Voyage in Eastern Europe)*. Tel Yitzhak: Masu'a and the Ministry of Defence Publishing House.

Rattok, Lily. 1994. 'Afterword', in Lily Rattok (ed.) *Hakol Ha'acher: Sifrut Nashim Ivrit* (The Other Voice: Women's Fiction in Hebrew). Tel Aviv: Siman Kria.

Ravnitsky, Avi. 1986. 'Hama'avak al hazehut' (The struggle for identity)'. *Politica*, vol. 8: 47–48.

Reibenbach, Tsipi. 1993. *Bechira Vegoral* (Choice and Destiny). Documentary film, 16 mm, 118 minutes.

––––– 1998a. *Shalosh Akhayot* (Three Sisters). 16 mm. 68 minutes. Tsipi Productions.

––––– 1998b. *Shalosh Akhayot* (Three Sisters). Film notes.

Reinharz, Shulamit. 1983. 'Experiential analysis: a contribution to feminist research,' in Gloria Bowles and Renata Duelli Klein (eds.). *Theories of Women's Studies*. London: Routledge and Kegan Paul.

––––– 1992. *Feminist Methods in Social Research*. New York: Oxford University Press.

Renan, Ernest. 1990. 'What is a nation?' in Homi K. Bhabha (ed.) *Nation and Narration*. London: Routledge.

Rich, Adrienne. 1986. 'If not with others, how?' in Adrienne Rich, *Blood, Bread and Poetry: Selected Prose 1979–1985*. London: Virago.

Richardson, Laurel. 1990. *Writing Strategies: Reaching Diverse Audiences*. Newbury Park: Sage Publications.

Riessman, Catherine K. 1993. *Narrative Analysis*. Newbury Park: Sage Publications.

Ringelheim, Joan M. 1984. 'The unethical and the unspeakable: women and the Holocaust', in *Simon Wiesenthal Annual*, vol. 1:69–87. Chappaqua, New York: Rossel Books.

––––– 1985. 'Women and the Holocaust: a reconsideration of research'. *Signs*, vol. 10 / 4: 741–761.

––––– 1992. 'The Holocaust: taking women into account'. *Jewish Quarterly*, vol. 39 / 3: 19–23.

––––– 1995. 'Gender and genocide: a split memory'. Paper presented at a conference on 'Memory and the Second World War'. Washington, April 1995.

––––– 1997. 'Genocide and gender: a split memory', in Ronit Lentin (ed.) *Gender and Catastrophe*. London: Zed Books.

––––– 1993. 'Women and the Holocaust: a reconsideration of research,' in Caro, Rittner and John K. Roth (eds.) *Different Voices: Women and the Holocaust*. New York: Paragon House.

Rittner, Carol and John K. Roth (eds.) 1993. *Different Voices: Women and the Holocaust*. New York: Paragon House.

Rogers, Annie. 1994. *Exiled Voices: Dissociation and Repression in Women's Narratives of Trauma.* Paper presented as part of the 1993–4 Stone Centre Colloquium Series on Women's Psychological Development: Theory and Application, Wellsley College, MA.

Rokem, Freddie. 1999. 'Arbeit macht frei vom Toitland Europea', in Adi Ofir (ed.) *Fifty to Forty-Eight: Critical Moments in the History of the State of Israel.* Special issue of *Theory and Criticism,* vols. 12-13: 389–399.

Rosenthal, Gabriele. 1993. 'Reconstruction of life stories: principles of selection in generating stories for narrative biographical interviews', in Ruthellen Josselson and Amia Lieblich (eds.). *The Narrative Study of Lives,* Vol 1. Newbury Park: Sage.

Rosenthal, Ruvik. 1994. 'HaAravi haboreach vehaAravi hamitnapel (The fleeing Arab and the Assailing Arab)'. *Haaretz Magazine,* 25 March: 55.

Roskies, David. 1984. *Against the Apocalypse: Responses to Catastrophe in Modern Jewish Culture.* Cambridge, Mass: Harvard University Press.

Sadeh, Yitzhak. 1945. 'Achoti al hachof (My sister on the beach)', in Zerubavel Gilead (ed.) 1955. *Sefer Hapalmach (The Palmach Book).* Tel Aviv: Hakibbutz Hameuchad.

Saghiyeh, Hazem and Saleh Bashir. 2000. 'Universalizing the Holocaust'. *Ha'aretz,* 21 February 2000: B3.

Said, Edward. 1978. *Orientalism.* New York: Vintage Press.

Samet, Gideon. 1993. 'Semalim Ba'aron (Symbols in the closet)'. *Ha'aretz,* 23 April: B1

——— 1995. 'Nitskhon hapashtut' (The victory of simplicity)'. *Ha'aretz,* 17 January: B1.

Sassar, Moshe. 1995. 'Olam keminhago noheg (As ever)'. *Ha'aretz Books,* 17 January: 10.

Schatzker, Haim. 1998. 'Hora'at haShoah – retzef dilemmot' ('Shoah teaching – a series of dilemmas'), in Yoel Rappel (ed.). *Zikaron Samui, Zikaron Galui: Toda'at HaShoah Bimdinat Israel* (Memory and Awareness of the Holocaust in Israel), Tel Yitzhak: Masu'a and the Ministry of Defence Publishing House.

Schnall, David. 1979. *Radical Dissent in Contemporary Israeli Politics.* New York: Praeger.

Schnitzer, Meir. 1988. 'Helem (Shock)'. *Ha'ir.*

Schoenfeld, Gabriel. 1998a. 'Auschwitz and the professors', *Commentary,* June 1998 (cited in *Lilith,* vol. 23 / 3: 10.

——— 1998b. '... And from the far right', *Lilith,* vol. 23 / 4: 42-3.

Schweid, Eliezer. 1983. 'Mussar hagevurah hayehudit baZionut (Jewish heroic morality in Zionism)', in Eliezer Schweid, *Miyahadut leZionut: Massot* (From Judaism to Zionism: Essays). Jerusalem: The Zionist Library.

Scott, Sara. 1997. 'Giving birth to death: ritual abuse survivors accounts of reproductive abuse', *Auto/biography,* nos. 1, 2 & 3: 15–26.

Segev, Tom. 1991. *Hamillion Hashevi'i: HaIsraelim vehaShoah* (The Seventh Million: The Israelis and the Holocaust). Jerusalem: Keter.

——— 1995a. 'Evlam shel hayeladim' (The children's grief)'. *Ha'aretz,* 8 January: 8.

——— 1995b. 'Shalom bein korbanot' (Peace between victims)'. *Ha'aretz,* 3 October: B1.

Semel, Nava. 1985 (reissued 1998). *Kova Zechuchit* (A Hat of Glass). Tel Aviv: Sifriat Poalim.

———— 1986. 'Iguf bein-nishmati: lichtov al haShoah (Inter-soul outflanking: writing about the Shoah)'. *Politica*, no. 8: 44–45.

———— 1987. *Hayeled Meachorei Haeinayim* (*The Child Behind the Eyes*). One-woman play.

———— 1988. *Gershona Shona* (Becoming Gershona). Tel Aviv: Am Oved.

———— 1990. *Becoming Gershona*. New York: Viking Penguin.

———— 1991. *Maurice Havivel Melamed Lauf* (Flying Lessons). Tel Aviv: Am Oved.

———— 1993. *Rali Masa Matara* (Night Games). Tel Aviv: Am Oved.

———— 1995. *Flying Lessons*. New York: Simon and Schuster.

———— 1996. *Isha al Neyar* (Bride on Paper). Tel Aviv: Am Oved.

Shadmi, Erella. 1992. 'Women, Palestinians, Zionism: a personal view'. *News from Within*, vol. 8 / 10–11: 13–16.

Shafir, Gershon. 1989. *Land, Labour and the Origins of the Israeli-Palestinian Conflict, 1882-1914*. Cambridge: Cambridge University Press.

Shahak, Israel. 1994. 'Im yechupar lachem ha'avon haze ad temutun (If this sin be forgiven until your dying day)'. *Ha'aretz*, 5 August: B9.

Shamir, Moshe. 1947. *Hu Halach Basadot* (He Walked in the Fields). Tel Aviv: Am Oved.

———— 1951, 1990. *Bemo Yadav: Pirkei Elik* (With His Own Hands: Elik Chapters). Tel Aviv: Am Oved.

Shapira, Anita. 1992. *Herev Hayona: HaZionut Vehakoach 1881–1948* (Land and Power). Tel Aviv: Am Oved.

Sharoni, Simona. 1992. 'Every woman is an occupied territory: the politics of militarism and sexism and the Israeli-Palestinian conflict'. *Journal of Gender Studies*, vol. 4: 447–462.

———— 1994. 'Homefront as battlefield: gender, military occupation and violence against women', in Tamar Mayer (ed.) *Women and the Israeli Occupation: The Politics of Change*. London: Routledge.

Shiloh, M. 1980. '*Havat hapoalot bakinneret 1911–1917 kepitaron libeayat hapoelet ba'aliya hashnia*' (The women workers farm at Kinneret 1911–1917 as a solution to the problem of the woman worker in the second aliya)'. *Katedra*, no. 14: 81–113.

Shlonski, Avraham. 1971. '*Neder* (Vow)', in Avraham Shlonski, *Shirim* (Poems), Vol. D. Tel Aviv: Sifriat Poalim.

Shochat, Orit. 1996. 'Hayom shebo megarshim et hakhamsin (The day in which the desert wind is banished)'. *Ha'aretz*, 27 September: B8.

Shohat, Ella. 1991. 'Making the silences speak in Israeli cinema', in Barbara Swirski and Marilyn P. Safir (eds.) *Calling the Equality Bluff: Women in Israel*. New York: Pergamon Press.

Sigal, J. 1971. 'Second-generation effects on mass trauma'. *International Psychiatry Clinics*, vol. 8: 55–65.

———— 1973. 'Hypotheses and methodology in the study of families of Holocaust survivors', in E. James Anthony, and Cyrille Koupernik (eds.) *The Child and His Family: The Impact of Disease and Death*. New York: John Wiley.

Simionovics, Mark. 1999. *To Say Kaddish and Leave*. Documentary film, edited
and produced by Mark Simionovics, directed by Zoltan Terner. Israel Educational Television.

Simmel, George. 1971 (1908). 'The stranger', in Donald K. Levine (ed.)
George Simmel on Individuality and Social Norms. Chicago: University of
Chicago Press.

Sivan, Immanuel. 1991. *Dor Tashach: Mythos, Dyokan veZikaron* (The 1948
Generation: Myth, Profile and Memory). Tel Aviv: Ma'arachot.

Smith, Anthony D. 1986. *The Ethnic Origin of Nations*. Oxford: Blackwell.

Smith, Dorothy. 1990. *Texts, Facts and Femininity: Exploring the Relations of
Ruling*. London: Routledge.

Smooha, Sammy. 1998. 'Ethnic democracy: Israel as an archetype', *Israel
Studies*, vol. 2 / 2: 198–241.

Soker, Y. 1920. 'Leinyanei hasha'a (Current affairs)'. *Hapoel Hatsa'ir*,
27.2.1920.

Spivak, Gayatri Chakravorty. 1992. 'The politics of translation', in Michèle
Barrett and Anne Phillips (eds.). *Destabilizing Theory: Contemporary Feminist Debates*. Cambridge: Polity Press.

Stacey, Judith. 1991. 'Can there be a feminist ethnography?' in Sherna .B.
Gluck and Daphne Patai (eds.) *Women's Words: The Feminist Practice of
Oral History*. New York: Routledge.

Stanley, Liz (ed). 1990. *Feminist Praxis: Research, Theory and Epistemology in
Feminist Research*. London: Routledge.

——— 1992. *The Auto/Biographical I: Theory and Practice of Feminist
Auto/Biography*. Manchester: Manchester University Press.

——— 1993. 'The knowing, because experiencing subject: narratives, lives and
autobiography'. *Women's Studies International Forum*, vol. 16 / 3: 205–215.

——— 1996. 'The mother of invention: necessity, writing and representation'. *Feminism and Psychology*, 6 / 1: 45–51.

——— and Sue Wise. 1983. *Breaking Out: Feminist Consciousness and Feminist Research*. London: Routledge and Kegan Paul.

——— and ———. 1990. 'Method, methodology and epistemology in feminist research processes', in Liz Stanley (ed.) *Feminist Praxis: Research, Theory and Epistemology in Feminist Research*. London: Routledge.

——— and ———. 1993. *Breaking Out Again: Feminist Ontology and Epistemology*. London: Routledge.

Stav, Yehudah. 1988. 'Khova lir'ot (Must see)'. *Yediot Acharonot*.

Steiner, George. 1969. *Language and Silence*. Harmondsworth: Penguin
Books.

Steiner, George. 1984. *A Reader*. Harmondsworth: Penguin Books.

Sternhell, Ze'ev. 1994. 'Preida mikever ha'avot (Farewell to the tombs of the
fathers)'. *Haaretz*, 25 March: B4–5.

Swirski, Barbara and Marylin P. Safir. 1991. 'Living in a Jewish state:
national, ethnic and religious implications', in Barbara Swirski and Marilyn P. Safir (eds.) *Calling the Equality Bluff: Women in Israel*. New York:
Pergamon Press.

Tabenkin, Moshe. 1946. Hakibbutz Hameuchad 15th Annual Conference,
Yagur, 7–13 June 1946 (cited in Shapira, 1992: 441).

Tal, Avraham. 1995. 'Katav zar oyen' ('Hostile foreign correspondent'). *Ha'aretz*, 15 August: A3.

Tal, Yerach. 1993. 'Netanyahu in the Likud Conference', *Ha'aretz*, 18 May:1.

Talmon-Garber, Yonina. 1962. 'Social change and family structure'. *International Social Science Journal.*

Talmor, R. 1992. 'Likro vela'asot lehefech (To read and do the opposite)'. *Yediot Acharonot*, 27 November: 23.

Tchernichovsky, Shaul. 1958. 'Lenochach pesel Apollo (Looking at Apollo's Statue)'. (First published Odessa-Heidelberg, 1899), in Tchernichovsky, Shaul, *Shirim (Poems)*. Jerusalem and Tel Aviv: Schoken.

Tec, Nechama. 1986. *When Light Pierced the Darkness*. Oxford: Oxford University Press.

The Seventh Day. 1970. *Soldiers Talk about the Six-Day War*. London: Andre Deutsch.

Tlalim, Asher. 1993. *Al Tig'u Li Bashoah (Don't Touch my Shoah)*. Film produced and directed by Asher Tlalim.

Tong, Rosemary. 1993. *Feminist Thought*. London: Routledge.

Trossman, B. 1968. 'Adolescent children of concentration camp survivors'. *Canadian Psychiatric Association Journal*, vol. 12: 121–3.

Turner, Bryan. 1987. *Medical Power and Social Knowledge*. London: Sage Publications.

Tzahor, Ze'ev. 1988. 'Holocaust survivors as a political factor'. *Middle Eastern Studies*, vol. 24 / 4: 432–444.

Ushpiz, Ada. 1994. 'Mikre Ein Shemer vehachomer ha'enoshi (The case of Ein Shemer and the human material)'. *Haaretz*, 22 April: B5.

van Dijk, Teun. 1993. *Élite Discourse and Racism*. Newbury Park: Sage Publications.

Veiel, Andreas. 1993. *Balagan*. Producer Klaus Volkenborn, Journalfilm Berlin.

Waintrater, Regine. 1991. 'Living in a state of siege', in Barbara Swirski and Marilyn P. Safir (eds.) *Calling the Equality Bluff: Women in Israel*. New York: Pergamon Press.

Wardi, Dina. 1990. *Nos'ei Hachotam* (Memorial Candles). Jerusalem: Keter.

Wasserman, Henry. 1986. 'Hal'amat zikhron sheshet hamillionim (Nationalising the memory of the six millions)'. *Politica*, no. 8: 6–7.

Wedel, J. 1978. 'Ladies, we've been framed!' *Theory and Society*, vol. 5: 113–125.

Weiss, Meira. Forthcoming. *The Chosen Body: The Politics of the Body in Israeli Society*. Stanford: Stanford University Press.

Weitz, Yechi'am. 1993. 'Hashinui bidmuto shel Israel Kästner (The Change in the image of Israel Kästner)'. *Katedra*, no. 69: 134–51.

——— 1994. *Muda'ut Vechoser Onim* (Awareness and Helplessness – Mapai and the *Shoah* 1943–1945). Jerusalem: Yad Yitzhak Ben-Zvi.

Widdershoven, Guy. A.M. 1993. 'The story of life: hermeneutic perspectives on the relationship between narrative and life history', in Ruthellen Josselson and Amia Lieblich (eds.). *The Narrative Study of Lives*, Vol 1. Newbury Park: Sage.

Wiesel, Elie, 1960. *Night*. New York: Hill and Wang.

——— 1984. 'Bdiduto shel elohim (The loneliness of God)'. *Dvar Hashavua*.

Wieseltier, Meir. 1984. 'Milim (words)', in Meir Wieseltier, *Kitzur Shnot Hashishim (A Summary of the Sixties)*, Tel Aviv: Siman Kria / Hakibbutz Hameuchad.

Wigoder, Shimshon and Me'ir Wigoder. 1999. 'The Matzpen movement', in Adi Ofir (ed.). *Fifty to Forty-Eight: Critical Moments in the History of the State of Israel*. Special issue of *Theory and Criticism*, vols. 12–13: 199–203.

Winkler, Yehudit. 1996. '*Hayom-yom shel haShoah* (The everyday of the Shoah)'. *Ha'aretz*, 9 August: B7.

Witztum, Eliezer and Ruth Malkinson. 1993. 'Shchol vehantsacha: hapanim hakfulot shel hamythos hale'umi (Bereavement and commemoration in Israel: the dual face of the national myth)', in Ruth Malkinson, Shimshon S. Rubin, and Eliezer Witztum (eds.) *Ovdan Ushchol Bachevra HaIsraelit* (Loss and Bereavement in Jewish Society in Israel). Jerusalem: Ministry of Defence Publishing House.

Woolf, Virginia. 1978. *Moments of Being*. London: The Hogarth Press.

Ya'ari, Meir. 1947. 'Barosh verishona yadayim (First and foremost hands)'. From a letter to Hashomer conference, 1918, in Me'ir Ya'ari. *Bederech Aruka* (On a Long Way). Tel Aviv: Sifriat Poalim.

Yablonka, Hanna. 1994. *Akhim Zarim* (Foreign Brethren: Holocaust Survivors in the State of Israel 1948–1952). Jerusalem: Yad Yitzhak Ben Zvi Press and Ben Gurion University Press.

Yahav, Galia. 1999. 'Avi Pitchon', in Adi Ofir (ed) *Fifty to Forty-Eight: Critical Moments in the History of the State of Israel*. Special issue of *Theory and Criticism*, vols. 12–13: 379–387.

Yahil, Haim. 1980. 'The activities of the Erez Israeli delegation to the remaining to deliverance, 1945–9'. *Moreshet*. 30, November 1980: 7–40.

Yehoshua, A.B. 1984. *Bizechut Hanormaliut* (Between Right and Right). Tel Aviv: Schoken.

Yizhar, S. 1948. *Yemei Ziklag* (The Days of Ziklag). Tel Aviv: Am Oved.

Young, James E. 1990. *Writing and Re-Writing the Holocaust: Narrative and the Consequences of Interpretation*. Bloomington, Indiana: Indiana University Press.

——— 1993. *The Texture of Memory: Holocaust Memorials and Meanings*. New Haven: Yale University Press.

Yuchtman-Yaar, Efraim. and Gila Menachem. 1989. *From Generation to Generation: The Absorption of First and Second-Generation Survivors in Israel*. Discussion Paper no 10–89. Tel Aviv: The Pinchas Sapir Centre for Development, Tel Aviv University.

Yuval-Davis, Nira. 1982. *Israeli Women and Men: Division behind the Unity*. London: Change International Reports, Women and Society.

——— and Floya Anthias (eds.). 1989. *Woman – Nation – State*. London: MacMillan.

Zak, Moshe. 1991. 'Ha'am haYehudi vehaShoah bemishnato hamedinit shel Menachem Begin (The Jewish nation and the Shoah in Menachem Begin's political thought)'. *Gesher*, no. 125: 49–56.

Zertal, Idith. 1995. 'Agadat Rabin' ('The Rabin legend'). *Ha'aretz*, 10 November: B3.

———— 1996a. *Zehavam Shel Hayehudim: Hahagira Hayehudit Hamachtartit Bashanim 1945–1948* (From Catastrophe to Power: Jewish Illegal Immigration 1945–1948). Tel Aviv: Am Oved.

———— 1996b. 'Charoshet hazikaron (The memory industry)'. *Ha'aretz*, 12 April: B1.

———— 1999. 'Hannah Arendt in Jerusalem', in Adi Ofir (ed) *Fifty to Forty-Eight: Critical Moments in the History of the State of Israel*. Special issue of *Theory and Criticism*, vols. 12–13: 159–167.

Zerubavel, Yael. 1994. 'Mot hazikaron vezikhron hamavet: Metsada vehaShoah kemetaphorot historiot (The death of memory and the memory of death: Masada and the Shoah as historical metaphors)'. *Alpayim*, no. 10: 42–67.

Zimmermann, Moshe. 1999. '"Post-Zionism" and post Zionism', in Adi Ofir (ed) *Fifty to Forty-Eight: Critical Moments in the History of the State of Israel*. Special issue of *Theory and Criticism*, vols. 12–13: 487–495.

Zingal, Shoshana. 1985. *Massa el Toch Atsmenu: Bnei Nitsolim Medabrim* (A Voyage into Ourselves: Children of Survivors Speak). Tel Aviv: Elissar.

Ziv, Yehuda. 1998. '"Venatati lahem beveiti yad vashem": zikhron haShoah al mapat Israel ("And I gave them a memory and a name": the memory of the Shoah on the Israeli map)', in Yoel Rappel (ed). *Zikaron Samui, Zikaron Galui: Toda'at HaShoah Bimdinat Israel* (Memory and Awareness of the Holocaust in Israel), Tel Yitzhak: Masu'a and the Ministry of Defence Publishing House.

Zuckermann, Moshe. 1993. *Shoah Bacheder Ha'atum* (Shoah in the Sealed Room: The 'Holocaust' in Israeli Press during the Gulf War). Tel Aviv: Hotsa'at Hamechaber.

INDEX